TINKER BELLES AND EVIL QUEENS

Members of the Gay Male Chorus of Los Angeles celebrating Halloween in West Hollywood as various Disney villainesses.

SEAN GRIFFIN

TINKER BELLES AND
EVIL QUEENS

The Walt Disney Company from the Inside Out

New York Uni  *k and London*

NEW YORK UNIVERSITY PRESS
New York and London

© 2000 by New York University
All rights reserved

Library of Congress Cataloging-in-Publication Data
Griffin, Sean.
Tinker Belles and evil queens : the Walt Disney Company from the
inside out / Sean Griffin.
p.   cm.
Includes bibliographical references and index.
ISBN 0-8147-3122-8 (alk. paper) — ISBN 0-8147-3123-6 (pbk. : alk. paper)
1. Walt Disney Company. 2. Homosexuality and motion pictures.   I. Title.
PN1999.W27 G75 1999
384'.8'06579794—dc21   99-050550
                                                      CIP

New York University Press books are printed on acid-free paper,
and their binding materials are chosen for strength and durability.

Manufactured in the United States of America

10   9   8   7   6   5   4   3   2   1

Contents

All illustrations appear as a group following p. 104.

Acknowledgments

I would like to thank a number of people for helping me in my work on this project. First and foremost, my appreciation to the faculty, staff and student body of the Critical Studies Department at the University of Southern California. While almost everyone there has influenced the final shape of this work in some fashion, I would like to especially thank Marsha Kinder, Lynn Spigel and Sandra Ball-Rokeach for their encouragement, involvement and thoughtful criticism during my writing. Joseph A. Boone and Rick Jewell were also key contributors to rounding out the research and theoretical concepts necessary for tackling this project, and Lee Stork provided enormous support and guidance throughout. From New York University Press, I am extremely indebted to Eric Zinner for his enthusiasm and his support. I also thank Dana Polan and the anonymous reader for NYU Press for their comments and suggestions.

Research entailed numerous areas, and everyone was extremely forthcoming. I especially wish to thank Ned Comstock and the rest of the staff at USC's Cinema-Television Library and Archive. I also must thank the many former and present employees of The Walt Disney Company who took the time to speak with me, particularly those members of the LEsbian And Gay United Employees, who welcomed me into their meetings and social events warmly and without reservation. Although not all of those interviewed are specifically quoted in this work, their comments profoundly influence many of the analyses presented throughout this work. My thanks also go to the ONE Institute for helping me find back issues of gay periodicals not usually collected by major universities and libraries. Without their initial help, it is doubtful that this project would have ever seen the light of day. Others who have contributed to this project include Eric Smoodin, Eric Freedman, Maureen Furniss and *Animation Journal*, and all the members of the Society for Animation Studies.

I also deeply appreciate the support and influence of my family and friends, many of whom contributed to this volume in a myriad of fashions: Drew, Jim, Roger, Steve, Sue, Dana, Owen, Mary, James, Janice, Donna, Pam, Karen V., Clark, Robert and John, Eric, Rich, Michael, Karen Q., Martin, Kirk, Rick, Ed, Tammy, Cathie, Vicky, Lydia, Barb—and Dale, Steve, Rene and Scott. A special belated thanks needs to go to Ashraf Wassef and Robert Jahn, whom I hope somehow realize the affect their friendship had on my life. And lastly, I cannot express enough thanks to my partner Harry Benshoff for teaching me, counseling me and bringing me a love I didn't think possible.

Introduction

Whose Prince Is It, Anyway?

In the summer of 1988, I was hired by New Wave Productions as a courier, production assistant and general all-around "go-fer." New Wave Productions functioned in the film industry as a "trailer house"— a company producing theatrical trailers and TV and radio spots for feature films. New Wave worked exclusively on projects for the Walt Disney Company, making ads for all of its feature films, both under the Disney label and under its newer logos Touchstone Pictures and (beginning in 1990) Hollywood Pictures. Although New Wave wasn't the only trailer house working exclusively for Disney, and New Wave was not a subsidiary of the company, for all intents and purposes, I was working for Disney.

Disney had become a major force in the film industry by the summer of 1988. Over the preceding Christmas season, the studio, under the new management of Michael Eisner, Frank Wells and Jeffrey Katzenberg, had released its first film to bring in over $100 million domestically at the box office—*Three Men and a Baby*. Only a few weeks later, *Good Morning, Vietnam* was released, which also made over $100 million. That summer, Disney would surpass all of the other Hollywood studios in box-office share, with the Tom Cruise star-vehicle *Cocktail*, the re-release of *Bambi* (1942) and the top summer hit *Who Framed Roger Rabbit?* It was stunning to begin work for a studio that was riding on a crest of energy, ambition and measurable success.

As I continued my career at New Wave, I was gradually promoted up the ladder—first as an all-around assistant to a producer of spots, then, more specifically as the assistant producer overseeing the sound mix of the TV spots, and finally as a producer myself. The success of 1988's summer releases were followed by the next summer's *Dead Poets' Society* and *Honey, I Shrunk the Kids*, then the Christmas 1989 release of

The Little Mermaid and the early spring 1990 release of *Pretty Woman*. It was hard not to "catch" some of the giddy adrenaline that results from such steady success. Even in a lesser capacity, working on spots for the films instead of the films themselves, I could feel some sort of contribution to the success and notoriety of the studio. I could see my work readily on TV, and some of the ads themselves became the topic of journalistic reports. One TV spot for *Dick Tracy* (1990), cut to (and intercut with the video of) Madonna's song, "Vogue," even got mentioned in *TV Guide*.[1]

Yet, the economic success of the Disney studio (and my own) during my employment at New Wave wasn't the only reason for the elation I felt. As with most American men and women my age, Disney had been around me for most of my life. As a child, I had been surrounded by Disney in the form of films, TV shows, children's books, comic books, coloring books, games, toys, puzzles, records, ice shows and theme park visits. The earliest memory I have is that of holding my father's hand as we walked down the street to a movie theatre that was playing *The Jungle Book* (1967). My unbridled anticipation of the movie has helped to keep this memory alive in my consciousness. Working for a company that evoked such deep emotional memories helped carry me through the often late nights and weekend hours of work.

The other factors that helped me through the stress of deadlines and expectations of hyperperfectionism imposed by the studio were the immediate people that worked with me on the projects. A tight group that varied over time from between five to eight people, my co-workers often felt like a second family to me. I developed a father-son relationship with the producer I assisted that extended beyond the workplace. Many of us included each other in our social lives and helped each other through a number of personal crises. Amongst these crises was my gradual "coming out" process. Although I had already come to terms with my sexuality within myself, it took a long while for me to tell others. A number of events amongst my co-workers made me feel safe enough to make them the first group of people to talk to about my homosexuality. In late 1990, the producer that I assisted died of an AIDS-related disease. Although he welcomed me into his family, which included his male partner, and probably suspected that I was gay, I was never able to bring myself to tell him, and this weighed heavily on me after his death. That next spring, a female co-worker went through a traumatic breakup, ending a six-year relationship. Her admission to me of her pain, and that the other party was a woman, allowed me to admit my own orientation.

Looking back, I could see how Disney's films had at times created a space for me during adolescence to (secretly) express my budding sexual orientation. I remember quite clearly the first twinges of desire in the mid-1970s as I watched Kurt Russell as *The Strongest Man in the World* (1975) and Jan-Michael Vincent as *The World's Greatest Athlete* (1975). But it wasn't until late 1992, as I sat in a Hollywood picture palace to watch Disney's latest animated feature *Aladdin*, that I suddenly realized that the ties between Disney and homosexuality extended much farther than my own individual history. The film was preceded by a live stage show—a medley of various Disney songs, sung by men and women dressed up as the live-action versions of the studio's famous animated characters—Snow White and Cinderella (with their princes), Ariel the mermaid, and Beauty and her Beast. The huge audience roared with approval and laughter—an audience made up largely of adult males who seemed to enjoy the campy nature of the performances. At another screening in the same theatre, Joseph Boone remarked that the mostly gay male audience during the pre-show "shared recognition of the likely *non*-heterosexuality of several of the men performing as straight Prince Charmings on stage (some of whom were singled out by friends' exclamations—'look, it's XXX!!'—from the audience)."[2] The "queer appreciation" of the pre-show continued through both my and Boone's screening of the film, in which every "gay" joke uttered by Robin Williams as the Genie was loudly applauded by the respective audiences.

It became apparent to me during this screening just how important Disney figures in the lives of a number of lesbians and gay men (including myself). Beyond my co-workers at New Wave, I had met a number of men in gay bars and found out through conversation that they too worked for Disney—either at the studio or for the parks. When I later joined the Gay Men's Chorus of Los Angeles, a disproportionate number of members were presently or had been Disney employees. Furthermore, many of these people shared the same fascination with Disney that I did. The producer I assisted was a huge fan of *Peter Pan* (1953). Many gay men I knew owned shelves of Disney merchandise. Others seemed positively obsessed with Disneyland and went to the theme park in Anaheim repeatedly. In the 1990s, Disneyland and Disney World have held "Gay Nights" (and even "Gay Weekends"). Gay camp has appropriated many of the cartoon villains in Disney films. The AIDS quilt is covered with Disney imagery. Gus van Sant described his fantasy of

> a full-budget Disney animated feature with gay leads—for example, *The Prince and the Stable Boy* or *Peter Pan: Love in Never-Never Land* or *The Little Mermaid 2: Ariel and Samantha*. With love songs between the two and full promotions. Y'know, McDonald's Happy Meals with the characters. It would be great.[3]

If Disney figured so strongly in the gay community, then it might be possible to see how Disney was helping individuals to define their identity as part of the gay community and how various Disney texts worked as a factor in the understanding of their sexuality. Similar to my adolescent preoccupation with Kurt Russell, others have told me about the formative influence of the television serial "The Adventures of Spin and Marty" shown on the original *Mickey Mouse Club* (1955–59; rerun in syndication, 1977–78). Wayne Koestenbaum, in *The Queen's Throat: Opera, Homosexuality and the Mystery of Desire*, describes how his fascination with Adriana Casselotti's contralto as the voice of Snow White helped build the foundation of his identity as an "opera queen."[4]

The idea that lesbians and gay men could be watching Disney and using the texts (films, TV shows, theme parks, records, etc.) to further a definition of their sexuality is initially stunning and provocative. Of all the major Hollywood studios, only Disney has maintained a public awareness of a "house style" up to the present day. Whereas moviegoers in the 1930s might have been able to distinguish the look and feel of a Warner Bros. film from an MGM film or a Paramount film, today there is no brand differentiation amongst studios—except for Disney. The Walt Disney Company has established for itself since the 1930s an image of conservative American family values—values which uphold the heterosexual patriarchal family unit in a nostalgic remembrance of some bygone era of small-town Midwestern Protestant ideals. Obviously, this image is usually considered antithetical to conceptions of homosexuality—and even, to an extent, sexuality in general. Since the films, TV shows and theme parks are geared mainly towards children, or adults with children, there is often an elision of anything that could be construed as referring to sexuality, whether heterosexual or homosexual. In the cartoon shorts, for example, no one is ever the offspring of another character: Donald has an Uncle Scrooge, but no father—and three nephews, but no sons. In the early 1930s, the studio removed the udder from Clarabelle Cow because it was too suggestive of sexual organs. Only the constant replication of a middle-class heterosexual family indicates that "something" is going on off screen.

One of the main purposes of this work, then, is to explore what particularly there might be within the Disney image and its various manifestations that attracts lesbians and gay men. By viewing Disney's animation, live-action films, television series, theme parks and various other products created by the company through a "queer sensibility," one can come to understand the variety of motifs and characteristics of Disneyana that lend themselves readily to such a reading. Since the company has stood for so long as an upholder of heterosexual normativity, it is vital to recognize and discuss the long-standing (though basically hidden, denied and underexplored) relationship that has existed between the Walt Disney Company and the communities and cultures of homosexual men and women that emerged during the twentieth century. By acknowledging the presence of lesbians and gay men both within the studio and within the viewing audience, this work also attempts to bring greater awareness of the importance that Disney has had in twentieth-century homosexual culture.

Realizing the links between Disney and lesbian/gay culture was a bit of a surprise to me back in 1992 during the screening of *Aladdin*. Six years later, though, a number of individuals and organizations have recognized the relationship. In 1994, some fundamentalist Christians in Florida noticed that a "Lesbian/Gay Weekend" was being held at Walt Disney World and protested Disney's allowing it to take place (even though Disney itself was not involved in the organization of the event). Soon, others were jumping on the bandwagon of outrage at Disney. One anonymous writer on the Internet ominously asked,

> What should you think of the modern Disney? Are your children safe with the Disney mindset? Consider the people involved in making the recent Disney feature-length cartoons. Who are they? Renown [*sic*] singer, self-professed homosexual, and AIDS activist Elton John is in the employ of Disney. A not-so-well-known Disney employee died of AIDS shortly after completing a Disney cartoon. Look at the other credits in such films as "Beauty And The Beast" and "The Lion King" and "Pocahantos" [*sic*]. Are there more not-so-well-known sex

perverts and anti-family feminists in other decision-making positions at Disney—altering the direction of the plots, injecting "alternate life-styles tolerance" themes into the stories, and denigrating traditional family roles?[5]

A letter to the editors of the Lancaster, Pennsylvania, *Sunday News* complained that "According to Coral Ridge Ministries, Disney executives work with a homosexual advocacy group that strives to promote a homosexual agenda in the workplace, along with advertising in the homosexual magazine *Out.*"[6] By 1997, Southern Baptists (the largest Protestant denomination in the country) decided to "refrain from patronizing the Disney Co. and any of its related entities" in reaction to Disney's growing tolerance for homosexual employees and customers.[7]

Since the 1980s, a number of other entertainment-oriented companies have either equaled or surpassed Disney's acceptance of homosexual employees and customers. These include companies with divisions aimed directly at children and family audiences, such as Viacom/Paramount, which owns the Nickelodeon cable network. Yet, Southern Baptists and others have focused specifically on Disney, seemingly due to the aforementioned long-standing "brand-name" image of the company as "clean" and "safe." As Operation Rescue protestors would write on placards to protest the 1998 "Lesbian/Gay Weekend" at Disney World, "What would Walt think?"[8]

With this in mind, writing a book that goes into detail about the relationship between Disney and homosexuality might only add fuel to the fundamentalists' fire, giving them page after page of proof that there *is* some conspiracy afoot, that Disney has become part of a "gay agenda." The phrase "gay agenda" has been commonly bandied about by many right-wing groups to combat the growing public awareness and acceptance of homosexuality across American society. Cries of a gay agenda have been used in efforts to deny "special rights" to homosexuals (labeling nondiscrimination in the workplace, equal opportunity housing and parental custody rights as somehow "special rights"), in arguments against legalizing same-sex marriages, as well as in debates over allowing homosexuals to serve openly in the military. These conservative alarmists argue that the homosexual community schemes to concertedly undermine heterosexuality, "the foundation of American civilization."[9] Yet, while accusations of a gay agenda have been used in diverse controversies, most complaints point at the entertainment industry—claiming that a "gay Mafia" of homosexual executives is attempting to sway public opinion with films, TV shows, music acts, etc. biased in favor of homosexuality. Consequently, Disney's EEO policy (which covers sexual orientation) and its domestic-partner benefits program have been used by critics to prove the existence of a gay agenda within the company.

While this work aims to describe the importance of Disney to gay culture, and conversely the growing importance of gay culture to Disney, in no way does this discussion somehow prove the existence of a gay agenda within the corporation or anywhere else. This relationship *is* a longstanding one in terms of lesbian/gay culture's use of Disney, but the relationship has been ever shifting, and the company's attitudes towards homosexuality have to be analyzed carefully. Whereas the new Disney includes sexual orientation within its EEO statement, gay and lesbian employees during Walt's life by and large remained closeted for fear of harassment and being fired. Whereas the company now seems to be very aware of its gay and lesbian customers, it seems quite likely that Walt and most members of the studio during his reign had no idea of how lesbians and gay men were relating to their output. Also, the newer policies do not necessarily hail a radically pro-gay-rights attitude for the company. Rather, they are largely a reaction to changes in the entertainment industry at large and attempts by Disney to remain economically competitive. In order to analyze the distinct shifts in the relationship between Disney and lesbian/gay culture, I have divided my discussion into two sections, each discussing a separate period. The first section focuses on the history and texts of the Walt Disney Company during Walt's lifetime, when the studio and American society at large attempted to ignore and deny homosexuality's existence; the second section deals with the relationship between Disney and lesbian/gay culture since the 1960s, when gay rights activism grew stronger and louder in American society and when the company went into an economic and creative tailspin until Michael Eisner took charge in 1984.

A few more words are in order on the concept of a "gay agenda" as it relates to one of the structuring issues of this piece. In order to envision such an agenda, one needs to assume there is an easily defined idea of a "gay community." Successfully encircling such a community quickly proves impossible. Homosexuals have spent most of the twentieth century hiding from persecution. Hence, individuals often remained isolated from each other—making it hard to speak of a unified community outside of large urban areas that allow a relatively small space for gay and lesbian neighborhoods or ghettos to develop (such as West Hollywood, Greenwich Village and the Castro District). To speak of a "gay community" also begs the question: who is included in this community, and how can one talk about only "one" community? Many lesbians feel themselves separated from gay men (and vice versa) because of gender. Transgendered individuals don't easily fit the prescribed paradigm for either lesbians or gay men. There is wariness on the part of many homosexuals towards bisexuals. Homosexuals are also not above the biases and prejudices of the society in which they are raised, and issues of racism and class prejudice in homosexual communities have begun to come to the foreground recently. Similarly, so-called "fringe groups" such as the North American Man/Boy Love Association (NAMBLA) and the S&M subculture continually have to fight to be recognized within the homosexual community. One can see the fragmented nature of the homosexual community within the relationship of Disney to homosexual culture. While chapters 2 and 4 attempt to show how lesbians and gay men could find Disney texts to appreciate from their own perspectives, both chapters clearly show that, due to the prevalence of the patriarchal viewpoint in mainstream filmmaking, there is much more material to enjoy as a gay man than as a lesbian (the wealth of male characters, the "drag queen" nature of the cartoon villainesses, etc.). Hence, while this work attempts to discuss the wide range of "non-straight" sexual orientations, discussing Disney's relationship with "homosexual culture" perforce overemphasizes gay male response. It is precisely the problematic nature of describing an all-encompassing "homosexual culture" that complicates the seemingly more accepting attitude of Disney towards homosexuals over the past decade, a problem upon which the final three chapters directly focus.

With such fragmentation in mind, it becomes hard to envision a concerted, mutually agreed upon "gay agenda." On the other hand, it is much easier to recognize the existence of two other agendas at work when discussing the relationship between Disney and homosexual culture. The first is a "heterosexual agenda" that has tried to deny, repress and erase the existence of any and all sexualities that do not fit within its narrow framework. From the concerted elision of passages dealing with same-sex acts in modern European translations of Greek and Roman texts to specific bans of materials dis-

cussing such matters (including book burnings and arrests) to denying funding to research that supported the existence of "non-straight"
desires, modern Western society has worked ceaselessly to naturalize
heterosexuality and demonize or pathologize all other conceptions of
sexuality.[10] The history of Disney itself can be viewed as a specific example of a conscious heterosexual agenda. As chapter 1 attempts to
show, the success and power of the Walt Disney Company has been
primarily based upon upholding the discourse of heterosexual pri-
macy. While Walt and his various (if not necessarily all) employees
agreed with such a viewpoint by and large, historical evidence shows
that the Disney image was shaped by very specific outside forces im-
pacting upon the company. Early animation by Walt Disney and his
studio points out that there was not an inherent interest in "moral,
upstanding entertainment," but the company learned quickly that
power, wealth and critical regard lay in heeding messages from audiences, church groups, other Hollywood studios and even the federal
government about making shorts and feature films that preserved the
constructed heterosexual imperative. The accusations by conservative groups in the 1990s of a gay agenda can consequently be viewed
as another concerted attempt to squelch mainstream acknowledgement of the existence of the polymorphous workings of sexual
desire.

The second agenda analyzed throughout can be termed a "capitalist agenda," which works tirelessly to maximize profits, control market
share and expand revenue and control by continually diversifying
products and seeking out new customers. Some at first may not see how
such a capitalist agenda would affect a company's attitudes towards
sexuality, but economic considerations have strongly influenced Disney's discourse of sexuality throughout the twentieth century. Chapter
1 describes how profit margin and corporate finances most definitely
guided the studio's move towards a "family" image. Similarly, chapters
3 and 5 examine how that same capitalist discourse has been primarily
responsible for markedly shifting the company's regard towards homosexuality in recent years. Typical of all late capitalist conglomerates
(following the ideas of Ernest Mandel and Frederic Jameson), Disney
has had to find new markets to tap into in order to further expand its
power.[11] Remaining within the narrow confines of its former image endangered the future of the company in the early 1980s, with profit margins dwindling and hostile takeovers threatening. When Disney moved

to find new markets, it was probably inevitable that the studio would reach out to the untapped "gay community" for their dollars. In doing so, Disney was following the strategy of many other companies, both within and outside of the entertainment industry. While obviously delighting many lesbian and gay individuals in the process, such a shift is marked more by economic concerns than by gay political activism. Disney wants more money, and if that means giving a nod to potential homosexual customers, then so be it.

It is important to recognize that it is these economic pressures—this capitalist agenda—that have led Disney to recognize a "gay market" for its product, and *not* a "gay agenda." Yet, it is even more important to acknowledge how this capitalist agenda also impacts upon those who identify themselves as homosexuals, not just within the company's employee roster but within the audience. Non-straight consumers of Disney are just as affected by the capitalist system as is Disney itself (if not moreso). If Disney's attitude towards sexuality is affected by economic decisions, then these same economic decisions have the potential to control and limit the possible uses of Disney products by non-straight consumers. To address this issue, each section is divided into separate chapters that alternately focus on production and reception. Chapter 1 examines how the studio produced a discourse of sexuality during Walt's life; chapter 2 examines how homosexual individuals seemed to have used the "Disney discourse" during this time frame. Similarly, chapter 3 examines the changes within the Walt Disney Company towards sexuality since Walt's death, while chapter 4 examines how these changes seem to have affected how Disney was used by homosexual consumers. Chapter 5 acts as a synthesis, examining specifically how production strategies attempt to affect the use of Disneyana by homosexuals. Through this organization, Disney's relationship with gay culture is specifically analyzed as a manifestation of capitalist discourse attempting to define and regulate the modern conception of homosexuality.[12]

Numerous writers recently have focused on how various societal factors, or discourses, have affected concepts of sexual identity in Western society—medical, legal, religious, etc. Such "social constructionist" discussion seems opposed to the work of numerous researchers who have searched for a medical or genetic cause for sexual preference from the end of the nineteenth century to today.[13] This research eventually may show that gay men and lesbians do not simply "choose" to be homosexual. Such findings would bolster calls for civil-rights legislation—and certainly put to rest the notion that homosexuality can be somehow "unlearned."[14] Yet, even if a "gay gene" is eventually found, this in no way invalidates the importance of social conditioning on human behavior and thought processes. Even though most of Western society views heterosexuality as a natural drive, many would also acknowledge the differences between cultures or the changes over time in ideas of beauty and attractiveness—from the Rubenesque full female form to the thin waifish figure of Twiggy, for example. Similarly, a "gay gene" would not explain the diversity of expression which comes under the heading of "homosexuality." Would a "gay gene" work for a male-to-female transsexual who desires men? And would it work in the same way for a "conventionally" masculine gay man? Would a "gay gene" determine if a lesbian was butch or femme (or none of the above)? Tied to this work, would a "gay gene" *mean* all homosexuals would respond identically to Disney films or theme parks?

Historical research seems to indicate that the conception of the term "homosexuality" itself is not fixed and has shifted meaning throughout the twentieth century. During the first half of the century, it was common to define homosexual men as effeminate. Both "straight" hegemonic culture and the marginal homosexual culture accepted this definition. Those men who were attracted to other men, but played the "masculine" role, weren't as easily considered to be homosexual.[15] Similarly, lesbian culture in the middle of the 20th century often mandated identification with either a "butch" or "femme" persona, and frowned upon individuals who broke from this binary structure.[16] Such examples stress how social concepts affect identity and behavior and deconstruct the idea of sexuality as a natural, biological inevitability. Instead of some predetermined essence, sexuality is defined by a network of social discourses that surrounds the individual, such as the discourse of the medical profession or the law. These discourses attempt to "naturalize" their opinions, trying to convince the individual that the discourse is inevitable and taken for granted. In so doing, social constructionism describes a power relation between the individual and these social forces.

One of the most powerful discourses in modern Western society is the mass media. A steady output of movies, television, popular music and literature represent to individuals certain learned conceptions of how the world functions. People learn how to relate to others (and even more importantly to themselves) by identifying with characters or narratives presented in popular culture. Rather than overt oppression by police or the armed forces forcing people into behaving and thinking a certain way, "ideological state apparatuses" (as Louis Althusser named them) such as the church, the family structure or popular culture work more subtly and benignly to draw the individual into the thought patterns of the ruling culture. While societal pressures obviously try to inculcate the individual as heterosexual, social discourse also addresses (sometimes obliquely, sometimes violently) non-heterosexual identities. With the conception of heterosexuality, the conception of its opposite or "other" is also present—homosexuality. Constructionists argue that heterosexuality needs a conception of homosexuality to differentiate and define itself more clearly. This study of Disney's ties to gay culture provides one example of how popular culture affects the construction of one's self-identity as a homosexual, even as it primarily attempts to naturalize heterosexuality.

Michel Foucault's landmark study of the development of "sexuality" as a method of self-definition has had profound influence on those who analyze the social construction of sexualities. Many have found hope in Foucault's discussion of turning social discourse on sexuality back upon itself. In *The History of Sexuality*, Vol. 1, *An Introduction*, he writes

> Discourse can be both an instrument and an effect of power, but also a hindrance, a stumbling-block, a point of resistance and a starting point for an opposing strategy . . . homosexuality began to speak in its own behalf, to demand its legitimacy or "naturalness" be acknowledged, often in the same vocabulary, using the same categories by which it was medically disqualified.[17]

But, there are reservations with using such a position to celebrate freedom from homosexual oppression. Homosexuals may find their own voice—but they are using the system's words, rather than finding their own. In doing so, the system remains empowered. As Foucault says in the last sentence of the book, "The irony of this . . . is having us believe our 'liberation' is in the balance."[18]

By focusing on the power of economic discourse in the social construction of homosexuality, one can see readily the irony Foucault is describing. Foucault describes how conceptualizations of sexuality are "linked to the economy through numerous and subtle relays . . . proliferating, innovating, annexing, creating and penetrating bodies in an increasingly detailed way."[19] As I have mentioned, Disney's need to create newer consumer bases for its product has pushed the conglomerate (and many other corporations during this period) to annex, penetrate and create a concept of "the homosexual consumer." While many lesbians and gay men may find acknowledgement and recognition a major victory in the battle for "liberation," studying Disney's marketing towards "the homosexual consumer" in chapter 5 will exemplify exactly how limited the "liberation" can be. Disney's growing acceptance of a "lesbian" or "gay" audience, I will argue, has the ironic potential of decreasing an individual's ability to use the company's products through a wider "queer" sensibility.

I make an important distinction between the term "queer" and the terms "lesbian" and "gay" in the ensuing pages. The terms "lesbian" and "gay" occur frequently, particularly in reference to concrete individuals and their readings of Disney (and of themselves). Yet, these two terms are also used to demarcate a specific sexual identity—and to examine how these two specific identities have been shaped by social discourse. In contrast, "queer" is used here to acknowledge and discuss the wide range of expression of sexual desire, a range that includes *but goes beyond* "gay" or "lesbian." Activists such as Queer Nation began to use "queer" in the late 1980s to be more inclusive of gay men, lesbians, bisexuals, transsexuals—in short, the wide variety of sexualities (and, hopefully, the diverse racial/ethnic and class identities) which are created by the matrices of social discourse. Soon, academics began to use the term to discuss theories of sexuality, specifically the slippage or breakdown of attempts to categorize individuals according to a gender or sexuality. Alexander Doty describes this new use of "queer" as "an attitude . . . that begins in a place not concerned with, or limited by, notions of a binary opposition of male and female or the homo versus hetero paradigm."[20] This is not to say that a self-identified "queer" individual is somehow successfully outside of hegemonic discourse and thus somehow "freer" or "better" than a self-identified "lesbian" or "gay man." It is impossible to completely escape societal constraints in one's conception of the world and self-identity. Yet, this use of "queer" attempts to recognize "homosexuality's" place in the social structure, and to complicate the regulation of self-identity created by such terms as "lesbian" and "gay"—to problematize (like Foucault) the notion of "gay liberation."

Historical evidence indicates that lesbians and gay men have read Disney artifacts from a non-heterosexual viewpoint throughout the company's history. In the early years of the studio, when Disney executives by and large did not realize or acknowledge a "gay sensibility" towards their product, such readings perfectly encapsulated how marginalized communities encounter and use objects from mass culture for their own ends (as theorized by such authors as Michel de Certeau, John Fiske and Henry Jenkins).[21] Yet, the growing awareness of the gay community in recent years by the Walt Disney Company, and a purposeful marketing towards this community, complicates and, at times, challenges the celebratory nature of many reception studies. By acknowledging the use of modern marketing techniques and current trends in audience research, this study will employ Foucault's theories of power and discourse to analyze the dialectic between the Walt Disney Company and homosexual consumers of their products, specifically how modern capitalism and advertising have affected how lesbians and gay men have defined and expressed their sexuality. Sometimes looking a gift horse in the mouth reveals the prize to be of Trojan lineage.[22]

When I first thought of delving into the relationship between Disney and gay culture, I encountered resistance and worried looks from a number of people. Some felt that I could not prove that such a relationship existed—as if I had to find a "smoking gun" within the files of the Walt Disney Company, some sort of secret memo signed by Michael Eisner saying to proceed with its "gay agenda." Also, people seemed worried that my work would only entail a series of outings of various artists and executives that had worked for the company—again, emphasizing the need to prove that someone had meant for Disney's output to be read queerly. I had never felt the need to prove intent by the Walt Disney Company; as long as evidence showed that homosexual *audiences* were understanding Disney through a "gay sensibility," then a relationship existed whether Disney approved of it or not. As time has gone on, specific events have shown that Disney is cognizant of the presence of lesbians and gay men within their employee roster and within their potential customer base. Yet, this does not mean that I now have proof of Disney's "gay agenda." Rather, this analysis shows how business interests have worked to make Disney acknowledge that homosexuality simply exists.

Lastly, there was the indication from the worries about possible outings that such a study would create a retaliation against Disney, which would then scale back its acknowledgement of homosexuals. Years have passed, though, and (to put it mildly) this is now like asking to shut the barn door after the horse has escaped. Furthermore, such trepidation is predicated by the fact that lesbians and gay men "had a good thing going" with Disney, an assessment with which I do not wholeheartedly agree. Since this development is directly tied to corporate plans for more profit and power, homosexuals have as much to be guarded about as Christian conservatives who have decried Disney's shift. As this work hopes to show, the "homosexual community" may gain some concrete benefits from such explicit acknowledgement, but there is a trade-off for such acknowledgement, in which capitalism increasingly works to control how homosexuality is conceived and addressed. If nothing else, the reluctance that some expressed to me about tackling this topic brought to light how important it was to drag this relationship "out of the closet" in order to point out the advantages and disadvantages of reading Disney queerly.

PART I

WITH WALT

I

Mickey's Monastery

Sexuality and the "Disney Mystique"

TO ASSERT THAT there is a construction of sexuality in Disneyana might seem to be stating the obvious since sexuality pervades all areas of culture. But to many, the Walt Disney Company has long stood as a safe haven from the "rampant" sexuality that can be found in most popular culture. In 1995, a letter to the studio from a coalition of Florida lawmakers described how

> For more than 50 years Walt Disney Company has represented all that is good and pure and wholesome in our nation. Families flocked to Walt Disney World and Disneyland because they knew that Walt Disney respected and nurtured the traditional American family and its strong moral values. Disney could always be counted on to provide parents and children alike with family-friendly, good-natured entertainment.[1]

Like these politicians, many consumers both in the past and present continue to value the studio precisely because they feel that Disney films, TV shows, theme parks and merchandise do not display sexuality (or, by implication, other forms of decadence or corruption).

Consumers did not create this vision of the Walt Disney Company of their own volition. The company has historically fostered this image, representing itself as an upstanding moral organization, committed to providing children with characters and narratives that would not unduly expose them to sex or violence. This carefully crafted "mystique" of asexuality so pervades the popular conception of the Walt Disney Company that as early as the 1930s, some in Hollywood had nicknamed the studio "Mickey's Monastery," in honor of the studio's biggest "star." The few kisses that get shown on screen between consenting adults in Disney cartoons are always chaste and short, with closed dry mouths (and often with plenty of comic support around to divert attention). There is never any indication that romance could lead to anything else but riding off into the clouds with Prince Charming or waltzing endlessly in a palace ballroom. Since no one is ever seen actually having sex, many viewers would argue that reading sexual messages into Disney's films is itself nothing but a perverse act.[2]

Although many historians and biographers have consciously reinscribed the asexual mythology of the company, Disney *has* consistently posited and reinforced an image of sexuality in films, television series, comic books, theme parks and countless other Disney texts: specifically, an image of American middle-class heterosexual courtship. Furthermore, through careful and untiring public relations, Disney has made this vision of sexuality seem such a given fact of life that most consumers are incapable of consciously acknowledging its construction. Disney consequently posits heterosexual courtship as the only "true" (if not the "only") method by which individuals may conceive of sexuality. Foucault states plainly that "power is only tolerable on condition that it mask a substantial part of itself. Its success is proportional to its ability to hide its own mechanisms."[3] With this in mind, the refusal to read the discourse of sexuality contained within the oeuvre of the Walt Disney Company displays the enormous power that the "Disney mystique" has on individuals.

Tied into the discourse of sexuality is a larger discourse of "the body." Foucault points out that "[sexuality] has been linked from the outset with an intensification of the body—with its exploitation as an object of knowledge and an element in relations of power."[4] Hence, power over the discourse of sexuality depends upon "proliferating, innovating, annexing, creating, and penetrating bodies in an increasingly detailed way."[5] Judith Butler's work (on how gender and sexuality are culturally inscribed) points out that in using "the body" to control and regulate sexual discourse, "the body" itself is culturally constructed: "Any discourse that establishes the boundaries of the body serves the purpose of instating and naturalizing certain taboos regarding the appropriate limits, postures, and modes of exchange that define what it is that constitutes bodies."[6] By making certain conceptions of "the body" seem "only natural" (its boundaries, its optimal use, its gender), the construction of the discourse of sexuality grows more powerful. For example, discourse on "the body" regulates definitions of "male" and "female," of "masculine" and "feminine," which are essential to a concept of heterosexuality (and homosexuality). If representations of women's bodies consistently display how they are "designed" for motherhood, a discourse that promotes heterosexuality becomes "normalized." The Walt Disney Company's emphasis in animation constantly forces the studio to consciously fashion and control bodies—drawing characters that somehow represent images of "men" and "women." From Snow White and her Prince to Tarzan and his Jane, careful work has been done to make sure that the heroes and heroines of these animated features "measure up" to certain gender expectations. Without such stringent scrutiny, the studio's promotion of heterosexual courtship would be compromised.

This chapter explores and analyzes how Walt Disney and his studio promoted a heterosexual paradigm through specific strategies of representing sexuality and the body. The chapter does not specifically engage with issues of homosexuality, but it is vital to deconstruct the naturalization of Disney's produced image of "normal" heterosexuality in order to understand more fully how queer individuals at this time could read Disney "against the grain."[7] Disney's motion picture and television production function as a form of social discourse used to control and regulate sexuality and the body and, in the early years, the studio concentrated on the "naturalness" of heterosexuality. Yet, the company's discourse on heterosexuality during Walt's lifetime also impacted the parameters of discourse on homosexuality that lesbian and gay audiences could find in these texts.

Of course, Disney is not in some manner unique or solely responsible for championing a heterosexual imperative. Rather, the messages historically constructed in Disney texts mirror the concepts of sexuality espoused by the Western hegemony in which it operates. Disney is only one voice in a multitude of discourses that attempt to fix, regulate and naturalize a certain version of sexuality. In fact, research into the history of Walt Disney and his studio reveals how other voices worked to help fashion Disney's representation of sexuality and the body. (To distinguish between Disney the man and Disney the company, I shall henceforth designate the man as "Walt" and the company as "Disney.") The influence of other, larger forces in molding the "Disney mystique" is easy to discern because Walt and his animators presented very different conceptions of sexuality and the body during different periods.

Disney's wholesome image began to coalesce as a specific method to maintain economic power and control.

The history of the Walt Disney Company's representations of sexuality and the body during the tenure of Walt Disney himself can be roughly separated into four periods: 1924–30, from Disney's first animated films to the success of the early Mickey Mouse cartoons; 1931–41, often described as Disney's "Golden Period," when his studio dominated the animation market worldwide; 1942–50, as World War II and the immediate postwar years changed and expanded what types of films the studio produced; and 1950–66, when the studio consolidated its financial successes and its corporate image. The "Disney mystique" had so solidified by the end of this era that when Walt died in 1966, the company seemed to continue apace with its image unfaltering for the next decade. The changes that occur at the borders of these periods point out how Walt and his studio consciously refashioned their representations of sexuality and the body, due to the influence (and sometimes specific economic support) of consumers, the Hollywood film industry, corporate America and even the federal government.

EARLY DISNEY: THE CARNIVALESQUE (1924–1930)

Contrary to the "Disney mystique" described in the letter from the Florida representatives, the very early Disney product seems to revel in the possibilities of sexuality and the potentiality of the body in every frame of film. Sexuality is not isolated in these texts; rather, it is always ready to assert its presence. The body is not a sacred temple with a sturdy foundation; it is a polymorphous sight of pleasure and excess. Consequently, unlike the cartoons aired on television or released on video, the cartoon characters from Walt's earliest series display bawdy humor and sexual aggressiveness—even that paragon of virtue, Mickey Mouse.

In his examination of Walt Disney's silent films, Russell Merritt finds Walt's traditional image as a moral conscience sorely tested. Rather than teaching the importance of hard work and respect, "Disney's sympathies are generally with those who goof off or tear the community apart. Authority figures are invariably absurd. . . . He shows kids cutting school, shoplifting and playing hooky, hoboes flee[ing] from having to work, prisoners escaping prison or Alice simply running away to have adventures."[8] Alice, the live-action heroine of Disney's first nationally distributed cartoon series, often led her cartoon friends on adventures that included escaping the police or other authority figures. In *Alice Gets in Dutch* (1924), for example, Alice (Virginia Davis) is forced to wear the dunce cap after misbehaving in class. She then daydreams of doing battle against an old-maid schoolteacher and three anthropomorphized schoolbooks. In *Alice the Jail Bird* (1925), Alice (now played by Margie Gay) and her animated feline pal Julius steal a pie, are arrested and successfully start a prison riot during which they escape.

This rebellion against authority was often manifested in the shorts through behavior that emphasized the bawdy or sexually licentious. This can be seen in the recurrent trope of the "party," which Merritt describes as "the most common expression of irresponsibility . . . an unauthorized free-for-all or jamboree where underlings . . . overturn the conventional order."[9] Merritt's description of the running motif of the "party" invokes the spirit of the "carnivalesque" that media scholars have adapted from Mikhail Bakhtin's work on Rabelais. The medieval carnival stressed bodily pleasure and excessiveness (particularly in regard to bodily functions) in order to overturn the received notions of morality, discipline and social order that ruled society outside of carnival time.[10] Disney's early work celebrates the spirit of the carnivalesque, including the constant reveling in the function and physical assault of the body. *Alice Rattled by Rats* (1925), for example, perfectly displays the orgiastic nature of carnival. Alice leaves Julius in charge while she's away, but while chasing some mice, Julius inadvertently falls into a basement tub of moonshine (another recurrent joke in Disney's films during this period of Prohibition). With Julius stumbling about drunk downstairs, the mice have a field day destroying the house with their makeshift celebration. Mice begin shimmying madly to the wild music being played. One mouse shimmies with such abandon that s/he drops her/his pants.

In Disney's use of the carnivalesque during this early period, much of the "low" humor common to broad farce, vaudeville and burlesque found their way into the shorts. The aforementioned "losing one's drawers" was a popular gag amongst Disney and his animators, showing up not only in *Alice Rattled by Rats*, but in *Alice in the Jungle* (1925) and *Alice's Tin Pony* (1925) as well. Later, in Disney's second cartoon series about Oswald the Lucky Rabbit, panties humor appears again. The climax of one cartoon, *Tall Timber*, shows Oswald being chased into a cave by a bear and a terrific fight ensuing off screen. Oswald emerges with a bearskin coat and the bear in nothing but a bra and panties. "Outhouse humor" often rules the day in the Alice Comedies and the Oswald cartoons. In *Alice's Orphan* (1926), Julius finds a discarded waif who comes complete with what appears to be a soiled diaper. The animation in *Alice's Egg Plant* (1925) takes particular delight in the physical exertion required by hens to lay eggs. Another recurrent image, if not necessarily a specifically recurring character, was the cow, who usually provided a good udder joke. The similarity of cow udders to human erogenous zones (female breasts in function, male genitalia in body location) was capitalized upon often in these cartoons. As the cows often found themselves stuck in confined spaces or needing to be hoisted, some other character would get a good squirt of milk in the face as a result. Cows would appear so regularly in the Oswald series that Merritt tries to argue that "the cow" is a character and sidekick to Oswald.[11]

The prevalence for violence upon the posterior of characters is another common motif, one that would recur throughout Walt's tenure at the studio. Characters are constantly landing butt-first into cacti or getting a round of buckshot in the behind. (Even live-action five-year-old Margie Gay as Alice gets a bullet in the rear in *Alice the Jail Bird*.) Walt must have found such "butt humor" amusing, because it becomes obvious throughout the years that animators at the studio were always ready to throw in some child with the back flap of their Dr. Denton's down or a quick whack to someone's bottom, presumably knowing that it would gain Walt's approval. The most blatant image of this humor appeared in the final credit of each Oswald cartoon: "The End" plastered across Oswald's round distended backside.

Along with such an emphasis on the body, Disney's cartoons also had strongly libidinous characters. Oswald quickly evinced a strong inkling for the ladies, flirting with female characters every chance he could get—which was often. Merritt refers to Oswald as "an incorrigible ladies' rabbit, unable to resist an opportunity for romance—even when he knew in advance that such dalliances would put him in danger."[12] Although Oswald had a semi-permanent companion (named Fanny, in another bow to posterior humor), there were numerous others whom he sidled up to hoping to win their favors.

To some present-day viewers, these early shorts might be scandalous. Yet, by and large, none at the time thought these cartoons to be shocking. The carnivalesque atmosphere was not unique to Disney animation in the silent era. Rather, it was more the norm in American animation. Most audiences enjoyed this type of humor in silent animated cartoons and would have been disappointed to find it missing. Two of the most popular series, Max Fleischer's *Out of the Inkwell* and Otto Messmer's *Felix the Cat* cartoons, reveled in the type of randy but good-natured hijinks found in Disney's first efforts. Fleischer animator Shamus Culhane readily admits that the Fleischer style was "kind of earthy, certainly crude, but honest."[13] Felix chased the girls around just as much as Oswald ever did. Rudolf Ising, who worked for Disney during this period, attempts to separate the silent Disney product from other producers when he says, "We never did like the . . . film ideas [of others] . . . some of it was kind of distasteful."[14] Yet, in his landmark survey of silent animation, *Before Mickey*, Donald Crafton finds that "the aspect that most set Disney's series apart from his competitors' was the overtly libidinous (but presumably naive) content of the humor."[15] The answer lies probably somewhere in-between: Disney's low humor was not necessarily any better or worse than what was being done elsewhere. What might impart a slight difference is the atmosphere for such humor. While Messmer and Fleischer worked out of New York, Disney was one of the first to set up shop in Los Angeles. Although, as Culhane puts it, most of the Fleischer animators were "East Side Jewish kids or people like me" living and working in a sprawling urban metropolis, Walt and most of his crew had moved from the Midwest to a Los Angeles that was itself still a relatively small town. Consequently, the bawdy nature of Disney's humor often centers around rural whimsy—falling into the outhouse, a squirt from a cow's teet, getting poked in the behind by a goat—unlike the more urban burlesque of the New York animators.

In Disney's attempt to break into the animation industry, it was inevitable that he would adapt to the humor already found popular in other cartoon series. This can be seen simply in the subjects and characters Disney worked on during this period. The Alice Comedies are a blatant reversal of the technological tricks used in *Out of the Inkwell* cartoons—putting a live-action girl into animation rather than a cartoon clown into live-action footage. The increasing reliance on the feline character Julius in the Alice Comedies also betrays the influence of Felix the Cat. Walt did not originate the idea for the Oswald series; rather Universal (his distributor at the time) told him that they wanted a cartoon series starring a rabbit. Crafton points out that Oswald is "essentially Felix the Cat with floppy ears."[16]

The similarities in humor and character design to the Fleischer and Messmer shorts betrays Walt's need to keep higher authorities happy. As his superiors, distributors Margaret Winkler and her husband consistently sent memos complaining about the content of Disney's Alice Comedies, as well as when Disney fell behind in schedule. Disney's first attempt at Oswald, a short called *Poor Papa*, was initially rejected by Winkler and Universal, and Disney had to make a second with a completely refashioned Oswald before the studio approved.[17] In 1927, as Walt went to renegotiate his contract with Winkler, he learned that many of his animators had been secretly wooed to sign contracts with Winkler—not Walt—the idea being to keep Walt working for Winkler but more firmly under control. Walt balked, and suddenly the animators and the Oswald character were out of his hands. Vowing not to let such a thing happen again, Walt set to work creating a new character that would be solely his. Walt's overarching desire for independence and control would lead to the creation of Mickey Mouse. Eventually, and more provocatively, this ambition would lead to a change in how sexuality and the body were conceived in his studio's work.[18]

It is easy to notice the early similarities between Mickey and Oswald, for the characters are almost identical. Ollie Johnston and Frank Thomas, animators at Disney since the early days, assert that "Mickey was essentially Oswald with round ears, a bulbous nose and a long skinny tail."[19] Reusing many of the plots from the Oswalds for the early Mickeys, one finds that Mickey originally shares much of the sexual aggressiveness that Oswald exhibited.[20] *Plane Crazy* (1927), the first Mickey made (although released after *Steamboat Willie*), provides a good case in point. Inspired by Charles Lindbergh, Mickey decides to make a plane out of material from the barnyard. He then decides to impress Minnie by taking her on a ride in his new contraption. Once in the air, he uses their isolation to pressure her into kissing him, and, when she refuses (pushing him away and even having to slap him), Mickey rolls the plane and does loops to frighten her into complying. Instead she bails out, using her panties as a parachute. This aggressive sexual desire would continue in the second Mickey cartoon, *Gallopin' Gaucho*. Here, Mickey jauntily enters a pampas saloon, grabs senorita Minnie (wearing falsies that accentuate the existence of breasts) and energetically throws himself into a tango *à la* Valentino in *The Four Horsemen of the Apocalypse* (1924).

Mickey's aggressiveness in these early pictures was directed in a number of directions—expressing a constant potential for comic violence on the body. Children's author Maurice Sendak has commented that the early Mickeys are "all about body parts: kicking the ass, pulling the ears, tweaking noses, twisting necks . . . (a) kind of passionate investigation of the body."[21] Richard Schickel concurred: "[Mickey] was quick and cocky and cruel, at best a fresh and bratty kid, at worst a diminutive and sadistic monster, like most of the other inhabitants of that primitive theatre of cruelty that was the animated cartoon."[22] *Steamboat Willie* (1928), the first Mickey short to be released, and one of the first sound cartoons in American theatres, presents a character who angrily attacks a parrot for making wisecracks and swings a cat by the tail as part of an impromptu musical performance. Richard Schickel notes that "there is something a little shocking about the ferocity with which Mickey squeezes, bangs, twists and tweaks the anatomy of the assembled creatures in his mania for [creating] music."[23] Throughout the early Mickeys, cows with huge dangling udders are still around squirting people, outhouses and chamber pots are still in evidence and female characters are constantly having to pull their skirts down after flashing their panties. There are many characters with the back flaps of their pants undone, lots of spitting and lots of violent abuse of animals for fun and profit (kicking ostriches, pulling on cats' tails, etc.). In *The Chain Gang* (1930), Walt had no problem putting Mickey in jail and having a climactic prison riot and jail break before throwing Mickey back into "the hoosegow." No attempt is made to tell viewers that Mickey was unjustly imprisoned, and the cartoon ends with Mickey firmly replanted in a guarded cell singing joyfully "There's no place like home." Mickey was an incorrigible bounder, and audiences loved it.

"THE GOLDEN PERIOD": CREATING THE "DISNEY MYSTIQUE" (1931–1941)

A rodent running around like a sex-crazed Harpo Marx is not the Mickey Mouse that most parents and their children remember, and certainly not the Mickey that greets visitors at the theme parks. The appearance of a kinder, gentler Mickey signaled a new era for the studio.

The studio in this new era, commonly referred to as "The Golden Period," would gain even greater success as it began to reject the carnivalesque attitude towards sexuality and the body. Taking its place—in both the films and in a concentrated public relations effort by the studio—was the "wholesome" image that is today considered essential to the "Disney mystique."

The "new and improved" Mickey did not evolve until a little over two years after his initial debut. During that time, much had changed. The United States had been plunged into the Depression, and many citizens looked for a scapegoat on which to blame the woes of the nation. Many found fault with bankers and stock brokers. Many others found the Depression the obvious result of the lax morality and lawlessness of the "Roaring '20s." Consequently, a new sense of moral rectitude began to rear its head in America.

One of the earliest indicators of this change was the publication of Henry James Forman's *Our Movie-Made Children* in 1933. Research for the book, done between 1929 and 1931, blatantly equated the loss of morality with the economic downswing. "Virtue may have been at a premium once—but apparently it slumped along with the other leading stocks," the work bemoaned.[24] Detailing the results of how motion pictures affected children, the book not so subtly indicated that the rampant violence and sexuality displayed on American movie screens had dire potential for the younger generation. The study claimed scientific veracity, but the researchers themselves obviously had preconceived opinions on the subject, which translated into survey questions that reinforced their beliefs that films had a detrimental effect on children.[25] Although today the methods of observation and statistical compilation seem incredibly unscientific and biased, the work was quite popular at the time, creating a call for stricter methods of film censorship. The industry had heard these charges before, and, in the 1920s, responded by hiring former Postmaster General Will Hays to ensure that films were "safe" for family viewing. This new call, though, made the film industry worry about the possibilities of federal regulation of censorship. Attempting to forestall this potential calamity, the Motion Picture Producers and Directors of America commissioned Martin Quigley and others to write out a Production Code in 1930. Although the Code provided no means of enforcement (that would come in 1934 with the establishment of the Seal of Approval provision), the document stringently declared all manner of sexuality and "blue" humor as off limits. In coming to terms with the new technology of sound, the Code went so far as to list specific words and noises (the flatulence of Bronx cheers, e.g.) that would be prohibited.

At the same time that this was going on, Mickey Mouse had quickly become the biggest star in animation, rivaling most live-action stars in recognizability and popularity. Many theatre marquees placed the title of the latest Mickey cartoon above the title of the feature being shown. By 1930, a barrage of Mickey Mouse-related merchandise had invaded store shelves, and Mickey had successfully been introduced to a number of foreign countries. Although many animation scholars stress that cartoon shorts during this period were not aimed solely at children and, as shall be examined later, the popularity of Mickey extended to numerous adults, there was no questioning the importance of younger audiences in Mickey's fantastic popularity during the 1930s. The sheer number of toys and dolls bearing Mickey's likeness testifies to children's involvement with the character. As early as 1929, exhibitors began creating "Mickey Mouse Clubs" specifically aimed at enticing children to their theatres.

With such a juvenile following, then, it is not so surprising to see Mickey and the shorts he appeared in targeted by certain reform groups in the early 1930s. Suddenly, the outhouse humor and sexuality that had always been in Disney's shorts was looked at with horror by such groups. Terry Ramsaye in the February 28, 1931 issue of the *Motion Picture Herald* describes how:

> Mickey Mouse, the artistic offspring of Walt Disney, has fallen afoul of the censors in a big way, largely because of his amazing success. Papas and mamas, especially mamas, have spoken vigorously to censor boards and elsewhere about what a devilish, naughty little mouse Mickey turned out to be.[26]

Various state censors had begun to ban certain Mickeys, such as the Ohio board barring of *The Shindig* (1930), which showed a cow reading Elinor Glyn's provocative novel *Three Weeks*.[27] *Time* reported in February 16, 1931 that

> the Motion Picture Producers and Directors of America last week announced that because of complaints of many censor boards, the famed udder of the cow in the Mickey Mouse cartoons was now banned.

Cows in Mickey Mouse . . . pictures in the future will have small or invisible udders quite unlike the gargantuan organ whose antics of late have shocked some and convulsed others. . . . Already censors have dealt sternly with Mickey Mouse. He and his associates do not drink, smoke or caper suggestively.[28]

To put it succinctly, as did the *Motion Picture Herald*, "Mickey has been spanked."[29] Mickey's own popularity had worked against him, just as Walt and his studio were beginning to achieve financial success. If the studio wanted to remain on the crest of this success, if Walt wanted to hang onto his new-found independence and control, changes had to be made quickly. Consequently, from 1931–33, one can find an overhaul of attitudes towards sexuality and the representation of the body in Disney's product.

The change in the Mickeys is quick and obvious. First off—no more udders. The cow, eventually named Clarabelle, would now have a skirt or dress to conceal the lower half of her body. Secondly, Mickey's environment shifted from the rambunctious barnyard to the more sedate middle-class small town. Mickey himself became a parent's dream icon—"the small-town boy from Middle America who . . . use(d) his wits to survive no matter what the obstacles were before him."[30] Mickey would still pursue Minnie, but with flowers and candy rather than by threatening to toss her out of a plane if she didn't "come across." In *The Birthday Party* (1931) and *Mickey Steps Out* (1931), Mickey's demeanor and surroundings have changed significantly, as he and Minnie portray conventional sweethearts in a more respectable setting. Most of the Mickeys now showed our hero listening to his girl play the piano in her living room.[31]

While there was an attempt to keep Mickey calmer and more moral, the 1931–32 cartoons evince bawdy humor nonetheless. Mickey still throws parties during this period in which characters inevitably shimmy to ragtime music or imitate "cooch" dancing. In an attempt to retain the anarchic energy of the early Mickeys, subsidiary characters were introduced to stir up trouble, trouble which Mickey as new upholder of the status quo would attempt to quell. The most successful of these subsidiary characters was Pluto (who officially appeared in late 1930), always upending things in his search for food or antagonism towards a cat. In *Mickey Steps Out* (1931), for example, Pluto chases a cat under a bed and accidentally runs into the chamber pot. Little kittens were found useful for destroying the suburban calm of Mickey's new environment, as were the dozen or so baby mice that appeared on occasion. *Mickey's Nightmare* (1932) consists of Mickey dreaming of marriage to Minnie, resulting in numerous offspring. The carnage of the infants' exploits in Mickey's home—swinging in one of Minnie's bras, breaking the chamber pot, tarring the walls (and a Greek bust that turns blackfaced with huge white lips), torturing the pet parrot and cat, as well as Pluto—completely threatens the dream of marital bliss, and Mickey wakes up to hug his dog Pluto and smash a Cupid statue. Thus, the transition away from anarchy and low humor was not immediate.

Yet, the anarchic exploits of these characters did not have the bawdy edge that had been presented in previous cartoons, mainly because these figures did not seem to understand the licentiousness of their actions. Granted, already by 1932, Disney's animation specialized in portraying characters who seemed to react or think. The success of Pluto is partly due to this development in character animation. Unlike Mickey, though, who was always portrayed as a humanized mouse, Pluto and the kittens consistently represent "dumb" animals. The anarchy they generate is created by their instinctual behavior rather than some evil machination or out-of-control sexual desire. Pluto upends Minnie's bedroom only because he's looking for a cat, not because he wants to go through her underwear drawer. The same can be said for the baby mice. Even though they, like Mickey and Minnie, are humanized, they are infants and can still be read as innocent of the havoc they are creating. The chaos these characters engender then is represented as only "natural" to them.

Disney's non-Mickey series of animated shorts, labeled *Silly Symphonies*, also showed a marked shift in attitude. The *Sillies* began only a year after Mickey's premiere in *Steamboat Willie*. *The Skeleton Dance* (1929) and many of the early *Sillies* shared much of the barnyard humor and animal abuse. Following the torture of black cats in *The Skeleton Dance*, *Hell's Bells* (1930) used the Underworld as its setting, "whose inhabitants include a three-headed dog and a dragon cow that gives fiery milk (even Hades has its barnyard aspects)."[32] Another in the series, *King Neptune* (1932), managed to include a few topless mermaids in its burlesque of an undersea kingdom. Before Disney animation came under the censor's eye, the *Sillies* tended to present a fantastic or foreign environment and used it for a random series of gags accompanied and patterned after a piece of classical music. Although wedding classical music to animation might be read as an attempt by Disney to gain some cultural notice (i.e., respectability), there is a marked Rabelaisian atmosphere in most of these early *Sillies* that link them to the bawdy/body humor of Disney's silent cartoons.

The carnivalesque died much more quickly in the *Silly Symphonies* than it did in the Mickeys, as the series took on a decidedly moral tone in its subject matter. No more *Skeleton Dances* or *Hell's Bells.* By the end of 1932, the emphasis on classical music had waned and the importance of narrative began to take precedence over the random anarchy of gags. In 1933, Disney would enjoy its biggest success since the introduction of Mickey Mouse when one of these new *Sillies*—*The Three Little Pigs*—became a box-office phenomenon. The Radio City Music Hall actually brought back the cartoon twice during the next year, and the cartoon would eventually earn $125,000, an unheard of amount for a short subject. With this success, the *Sillies* were dominated by popular fables and fairy tales traditionally used in socializing children. *The Three Little Pigs* taught audiences about the importance of hard work. A number of "lesson" stories followed: *The Grasshopper and the Ants* (1934), *The Wise Little Hen* (1934), *The Tortoise and the Hare* (1935), *The Golden Touch* (about King Midas) (1935), *The Country Cousin* (1936), and *The Moth and the Flame* (1938). *Lullaby Land* (1933) came almost directly after *The Three Little Pigs* and, in an almost nightmarish fashion, portrays a baby's dreamland in which the poor infant is set upon by all those things (scissors, razors, matches, pins) that its parents had warned, "Baby mustn't touch." This phrase echoes ominously as giant bogeymen chase the poor child and its little stuffed dog across the quilted comfort landscape after they dared to enter the "Forbidden Garden."

A more telling example of the direction that Disney and his studio went with the *Sillies* in the late 1930s is *The Flying Mouse* (1934). A young mouse, ostracized by the rest of the children mice, wishes that he could fly. After rescuing a small fly from a spider web, the fly turns into a beautiful female fairy. With misgivings, she grants the mouse's wish and gives him wings. Unfortunately, when the mouse goes to show off his newfound wings, he scares the entire mouse community who take him for a bat about to scoop off their children. Then, when he tries to live with the bats, they send him away by singing the song "You're Nothing But a Nothing." Finally, as the little mouse cries all alone, the fairy returns and rescinds his wish, and he scurries back home to the loving arms of his mother, having learned the lesson "Be yourself."

While this initial description of the short imparts the message that seems intended by the short, it is quite easy to find another lesson. Harry Benshoff's appraisal of the message is "that it is better to be like everyone else, because being different causes ostracism and misery."[33] Most of the fables Disney adapted for its *Sillies* similarly advised audiences to do what they were told and to not upset the status quo. Whereas the early *Sillies* often presented carnivalesque free-for-alls that celebrated the exotic and partying for its own sake, the later *Sillies* stress conformity and the value of work over play. Robert Sklar describes the tone as "Don't be too imaginative, don't be too inquisitive, don't be too willful, or you'll get into trouble—though there's always time to learn your lesson and come out all right."[34] There was to be no cheerful overturning of the established order as had happened in the Alice Comedies, the Oswald shorts or the early Mickeys or *Sillies*.

Even those *Sillies* that still presented fantastic worlds, and weren't specifically aimed at teaching a moral, were affected by this change. Sklar states that in these later cartoons "there is one right way to imagine (as elsewhere there is one right way to behave). The borders to fantasy are closed now."[35] Whereas something like *Hell's Bells* randomly threw in gags about the Underworld, later cartoons such as *Flowers and Trees* (1932), *The China Shop* (1934), *Music Land* (1935), *The Cookie Carnival* (1936) and *Woodland Cafe* (1937) all center around a male-female courtship.[36] The courtship (whether between two trees, two porcelain figures, two musical instruments, two bugs, etc.) always played out as if the American middle-class ideal was the norm even in these realms of fantasy. There were no lascivious looks, no unbridled passion, no innuendo. Rather, it was all flowers and candy and sitting on the front porch swing. This tendency to paint all romance as innocent heterosexual courtship rituals grew quite similar to Mickey and Minnie's small-town world of spending the evening singing at the piano.

Since most of the humor in Disney's pre-1930 animation focused on the polymorphous perversity of characters' bodies, the studio began to alter not just its carnivalesque *subject matter*, but also its animation *style*. The elimination of the udder from the cow was only the beginning of a process that continued apace throughout the 1930s, exacting ever more control over animated bodies. As Pluto and the baby kittens ably showed, characters acting "naturally" quickly became a crusade at the Disney studio during this new period, and, in order to get the desired effect, Walt soon decreed that a new type of animation was needed. This was done primarily by rejecting many of the early tenets of animated film in order to make bodies cohere to the "laws of nature."

Before Disney's ascent, bodies of characters in animated cartoons were often plastic and polymorphous, continually emphasizing their "flatness" and that these were, after all, only drawings and hence capable of manipulating their bodies in any possible manner.[37] Characters were instances of graphic design rather than volume and weight. Felix was made up of a series of right angles that served for a few specific poses. Mickey and Minnie were drawn using a number of circles—for ears, face, eyes, nose, hands and feet—with a pear-shaped body. Barely resembling an actual mouse, the rounded shape of Mickey made him visually appealing. Just as his predecessors, "from 1928 to 1931, the graphic design of Mickey Mouse was a fixed formula of circular shapes that seldom suggested weight, solidity, or life forces."[38]

As such, characters could be poked, prodded, flattened, taken apart by the limbs without any apparent discomfort or lingering harm. Often, the characters would just go on in this newly acquired appearance, or the dismembered parts would move around with a mind of their own.[39] Felix would constantly remove his tail to use it as a baseball bat or a telescope, for example. Koko the Clown was specifically shown as only a drop of ink, and parts of his body were erased and redrawn within the shorts themselves. Mickey, too, in his early days would adopt this plasticity. In *Gallopin' Gaucho* (1928), for example, he pulls out yard after yard from his tail until he has enough "rope" to scale a wall and rescue Minnie. In *Steamboat Willie,* Pegleg Pete yanks Mickey by the midsection and Mickey's body gets stretched like a piece of taffy that the mouse has to stuff back into his pants. Such jokes tended to emphasize the body as a site for polymorphous pleasure.[40] Yet, it was precisely this "pleasure" that parents were finding disturbing as Mickey gained more and more notoriety.

The move away from this older conception of animation began through the studio's use of technological advances. Since Disney had risen to popularity by wedding sound to his cartoons, the studio logically looked to further technological developments to maintain stature and success. An exclusive contract with Technicolor's new and improved (and "more lifelike") three-strip process resulted in *Flowers and Trees* (1932), which would win Walt his first Academy Award.[41] In 1937, *The Old Mill* premiered Disney's latest technological advance—the Multiplane camera, a device that created an illusion of depth.[42] *The Old Mill* would win Walt yet another Academy Award.

Such use of technological developments pushed the studio towards a greater "realism" that gave characters more solidity and dimension than during the silent days.[43] For example, *Flowers and Trees* used color to add depth to its forest setting. The figures in the background were painted in light pastels, while the figures in the foreground used bolder primary colors.[44] The Multiplane camera furthered the illusion of dimensionality and perspective. Consequently, animation styles at the studio had to adapt to fit this greater realism. In November of 1932, Walt instituted art classes for the studio, run by Donald Graham from the Chouinard Art Institute of Los Angeles. Walt believed that this "could give his output a kind of *fluidity* and *realism* such as had never been achieved in animated cartoons before."[45] Giannalberto Bendazzi's epic history of animated cartoons states plainly that Disney's cartoons were "no longer pure graphics, . . . [but] had become a real world in caricature, which obeyed logical laws."[46] In 1935, as this process was beginning to reap praise from critics and audiences, Walt explained the philosophy behind this trend towards more realistic motion: "I definitely feel that we cannot do the fantastic things, based on the real, unless we first know the real."[47]

The most important experiments during this shift in styles dealt with drawing characters. As former Disney animators Frank Thomas and Ollie Johnston state, "Disney animation has become synonymous with character drawings that appear to think, make decisions, and act of their own volition."[48] The success of "character animation" in differentiating the motions and personalities of the almost identical Three Little Pigs in 1933 strengthened this push for "realistic" action. Now, characters not only appeared to think, they appeared to have a solid mass that would have to answer to the "natural" laws of gravity and physics. Characters were no longer able to take off their tails and use them as tools. No one walked around in a flattened state after being hit with a falling safe. The body in Disney animation was no longer polymorphous and potentially perverse. It was proper and "natural"—an "illusion of life," as the new style came to be called around the studio.

The shift to the "illusion of life" style had its effect on Disney's new moralism—an effect that was more powerful because it wasn't as manifest. While Disney artists purportedly strived to create a more realistic world, the new style of drawing was never necessarily any more real than the previous "primitive" style; it only gave the *illusion* that it was more real. Richard Schickel's analysis of the development of rendering animals at Disney furthers this idea and points out the ramifications:

> At first glance they were natural representations, but over the course of a long film it became clear that the true intention of the artists was easy adorability. . . . To some degree the style of the early animators . . . served to check this tendency toward the cuddlesome; those creatures were much more clearly—if crudely—cartoon conventions, bearing only superficial resemblance to real animals. . . . The animals of . . . Disney . . . , as they grew more real, paradoxically grew more subtly false.[49]

By being able to hide the manipulation of animation conventions behind an "illusion of life," the audience member is more likely to be drawn into the world of the cartoon and not be distanced enough from the text to objectively analyze the messages being imparted by the work. Leonard Maltin, while attempting to praise Disney's technique in *The Flying Mouse*, inadvertently points out how the "realist" technique in the piece furthers its moralistic aims:

> The emotional impact of this fairy tale is realized . . . by remarkable use of color. The story takes place from morning till night, and the *light changes* in each successive sequence. The film opens brightly, with soft pastel colors; the sky is not a deep blue as yet. The colors become more intense as the story progresses, and when the mouse heads for the cave the colors deepen around him. The cave itself is dark; when the bats sing their song to the frightened mouse, the entire frame is jet black except for the characters in center frame. Outside the cave, the sky is still rich with color, but darkening. As the mouse sees his reflection in a pond, the sun is going down; rays of yellow and gold still light the horizon, while a deeper blue settles in above. When the princess transforms our hero back into an ordinary mouse and he heads for home, he casts a long shadow along the ground; by the time he reaches the front gate it is dark outside and there are stars in the sky. His mother stands in the open doorway, bathed in a warm glow of light, awaiting her son's return.[50]

The short presents color and lighting as if they were natural, the normal rising and setting of the sun in one day. But, in doing so, it makes the manipulation of the emotion that accompanies the story also seem as if it's "only natural" that the mouse's transformation should throw the world into darkness. The emotions that the colors and lighting attempt to instill in the audience work to make the audience feel as if those emotions are "natural" and not a manipulation of technique.

The technical advancements in the *Sillies* also changed Mickey's environment. The backgrounds become more detailed, and an increased use of perspective and modeling (a technique that draws in the shadows on the bottoms of heads or stomachs or the like) becomes noticeable. With *The Band Concert* (1935), the Mickey cartoons also began to be filmed in Technicolor. But there were problems with adapting the new look to the Mickeys. After watching the attempts at greater realism in *The Flying Mouse*, seeing Mickey and Minnie cavorting in the same middle-class suburban environment quickly proves jarring. Mickey and Minnie had successfully been changed in personality to fit the requirements of this new period in Disney's history—but they still remained characters that were designed from a previous era, one less concerned with creating an "illusion of life." Yes, as the 1930s went on, Mickey grew "rounder, sleeker (and far more humanoid in design)," but it was still a mouse that had two balloons for ears, and stood taller than his pet dog Pluto.[51] Furthermore, it was becoming more and more apparent that there was little that could be done with Mickey in cartoons anymore. As Walt himself opined, "Mickey was on a pedestal—I would get letters if he did something wrong."[52] Being so straitjacketed by the ever watchful eye of parents and censors, Mickey grew boring—and soon he was being thrown into co-starring shorts with new characters Donald Duck and Goofy (both who could express more imagination and passion than Mickey and usually took up more screen time than Mickey in these threesomes).

At the same time as Disney's animation was being laundered of its more burlesque elements, Disney's public relations went into high gear, to make sure that everyone knew how wholesome Disney's films were. Popular magazines in the United States during the early 1930s seemed to be swamped with feature articles about (and sometimes "by") Walt and his studio, that lauded Disney product, the technology used at the studio and most definitely the "upstanding" and "moral" tone of both the films and the man who oversaw their creation. Stories appeared in such diverse fare as popular news magazines, art and literary journals, film fan magazines, "high-class" periodicals, business and political journals, and women's and family magazines.[53] Starting in 1933, *Good Housekeeping* had an illustrated "Disney page" in every issue, with color artwork and nursery-rhyme poetry that described a short that was soon to be released.[54] The breadth of readership of these periodicals stretched to just about every group in the country, but parents and their children seemed to be the prime targets of these pieces, with the same vital information used over and over again to present a specific image of the studio to these readers. Gregory Waller describes how it seems "as if a host of journalists were treated to the same interview, taken on the same tour of the Disney Studio, and handed the same press releases. . . . 'Facts' and format played like a broken record."[55]

It is in the journal articles of this period that the "Disney mystique" of wholesomeness comes into focus for the first time. *Overland Monthly*'s article, "The Cartoon's Contribution to Children," attributed to Walt Disney himself, flatly states that "if our gang ever put Mickey in a situation less wholesome than sunshine, Mickey would take Minnie by the hand and move to some other studio."[56] The article attempts to erase Mickey's original personality by asserting that Mickey is "never mean or ugly. He never lies nor cheats nor steals. . . . He never takes advantage of the weak." Oddly, the article goes on to assert that "sex is just another work [*sic*] to Mickey, and the story of the traveling salesman of no more interest than the ladies' lingerie department."[57] While it is quite possible to read all sorts of interesting things into this last comment, its context suggests an awkwardly worded attempt to announce that Mickey takes no pleasure in sex, and that he doesn't like randy jokes any more than a "normal" male heterosexual would like wearing ladies' underwear. These articles continually cite approval from child psychologists and parents' groups as proof of this saintly image. Accompanying the *Overland Monthly* article, an inset box alerts readers:

> Mr. Disney is particularly anxious to get the reactions from various groups throughout the country on his pictures. He speaks with great pride of the fact that The Better Films Conference of San Diego takes the trouble to report their ideas of his cartoons. He expresses the wish that every organized group, Parent-Teachers, Women's Federations, in fact, everyone working for the betterment of Childhood

would write to him and give him suggestions and criticisms on his present pictures.[58]

When *Parents' Magazine* awarded Disney with its "medal for distinguished service to children" in early 1934, the ensuing article also stressed that "among the guests [at a luncheon held at the Disney Studio for the award presentation] were a number of distinguished leaders in parental education and child welfare work."[59] In 1934, *Photoplay* ran an article with the scandalous title "Is Walt Disney a Menace to Our Children?"[60] Although the author halfheartedly fears that some of the images in Disney's cartoons could scare children, the article spends most of its time reporting how many authorities praise Disney's cartoons, including parents' associations, university professors, psychiatrists and an editor of children's books. The general consensus of the experts was that "Mickey Mouse is a civilizing influence."[61]

By constantly publicizing these awards and assessments, the Disney studio was quickly capable of putting their censorship problems behind them and completely obscuring the earlier, more randy Mickey Mouse. Although articles during the early 1930s would sometimes make reference to the "udder" issue, Mickey was now referred to as if he had always been the "good little boy" that was now being presented weekly on theatre screens. In describing his appeal, *Time* claimed in 1933 that Mickey "can break all natural laws ([but] he never breaks moral laws)."[62] Gilbert Seldes ventured that "Mickey Mouse is far removed from the usual Hollywood product, with its sex appeal."[63] As the *New York Times Magazine* would declare in an article about "Mickey Mouse the Economist," "The laughter is always harmless, and the world likes decency."[64]

At the same time that Mickey Mouse was being rehabilitated in the press, Walt himself was building a reputation through the journal articles, a reputation that began gaining mythic proportions and somehow reaffirmed the American Dream. As *Overland Monthly* succinctly put it, "If Mickey is good it is because Walt is good."[65] After rhapsodizing about the cartoons themselves, and describing the process of creating an animated short at the Disney studio, many of the articles moved to a biography of the man himself. Such articles often repeated many of the same phrases and anecdotes that aimed to prove that Walt was separated from the scandalous social environment of Hollywood high life. The *New Yorker* confided that "Disney . . . shares hardly at all in

Hollywood's life. . . . He goes to pictures, but rarely to flash openings; he neither gives nor attends great parties."[66] *Time* concurred that "Hollywood hotspots seldom see him."[67] Similarly, both the *New Yorker* and *Time* point out that although Walt's wife Lillian was "a Hollywood girl . . . [she] has never had anything to do with the cinema."[68]

Rather, Disney was "down-to-earth, middle class," a "conspicuously average American." "Disney lives in the house he built five years ago . . . a six-room bungalow, the commonest type of construction in Hollywood; the car he drives is a domestic one; his clothes are ordinary."[69] "He works until 7 o'clock every night . . . drives his Packard roadster home to dinner, plays with his baby daughters . . . and goes to bed."[70] By 1934, *Fortune* was able to bypass many of these anecdotes and simply state that "Enough has been written about Disney's life and hard times already to stamp the bald, Algeresque outlines of his career as familiarly on the minds of many Americans as the career of Henry Ford or Abraham Lincoln."[71] The articles made sure to mention Disney's childhood on the farm and in the small towns of middle America, painting a bucolic existence that supposedly helped explain why the shorts he produced upheld the American ideal so well.

Although it is perfectly understandable why the Disney studio would attempt to redress its public image after the complaints of 1930, it might not be as understandable why the popular press would so willingly participate in this public relations campaign. Mickey Mouse was still an incredibly popular character, but the depth of collaboration with the studio in creating the "wholesome" image goes beyond merely commenting on Mickey's popularity. Disney's growing fame must in part be attributed to the situation facing the American film industry as a whole in the early 1930s. The conversion to sound financially strapped almost all of the major studios, just as the Depression hit the country. Although the novelty of sound was able to keep attendance high for a while, by 1931, many studios were finding precipitous declines in their revenue. By 1932, almost every studio was in debt, and some had even entered into receivership. In the face of this, most of the studios flaunted the provisions in the newly written Production Code. Although Disney was called to task in 1930, and answered the call by completely shifting the style and substance of the studio's output, it seems to have been the only studio to do so. Since the Code had no method for enforcement, and knowing that sex and violence always pulled in an audience, American films were rampant with gangster stories, women sleeping their way to wealth and fame, scantily clad chorines and barely veiled innuendo. Even in cartoons, Fleischer's Betty Boop was swaying and singing about her "boop-oop-a-doop." By 1933, when Mae West's first starring feature (*She Done Him Wrong*) premiered, protest groups such as the Catholic Church's Legion of Decency coalesced and began calling for boycotts and federal intervention.

Disney was spreading its publicity in the midst of this upheaval, and it seemed to many as if Walt was one of the few working in the film industry who was not appealing to the "low" interests of audience members. For example, *Parents' Magazine*'s award to Walt Disney was reported when the magazine was putting out "Family Movie Guides" in every issue that warned "Don't run the risk of letting your sons and daughters see movies that are harmful. Many pictures are unfit for children and adolescents."[72] Other articles in future issues of the magazine would include "Helping Youth to Choose Better Movies," "How to Select Movies for Children" and "Will the Code Bring Better Movies?"[73] Although it is hard to substantiate, it is probable that the Hollywood film industry as a whole heartily approved of Disney's promotionalism. By presenting a figure that was contributing to the well-being of children throughout the world, the entire industry looked better. Highly influential columnists Louella Parsons and Hedda Hopper made sure to promote Disney's brand of family entertainment quite often through the 1930s. In 1937, the Los Angeles Junior Chamber of Commerce, led by a panel that included Will Hays, announced Walt as their "Outstanding Young Man" of the year (for individuals under 35). It is certain that, by the mid-1930s, a number of film celebrities were voicing their admiration of Mickey Mouse and his creator, such as Mary Pickford, Will Rogers and Charlie Chaplin. By 1935, the conversion was absolute, and Walt was considered America's mythmaker in residence.

The "family-oriented" atmosphere of the Disney studio was not simply a public relations gambit though, for day-to-day life at the studio quickly began to mirror the moral image that was being advertised in the popular press. According to a 1936 article in *Harpers' Bazaar*, the studio looked "like a small municipal kindergarten with green grass for the children to keep off of.... Law and order reign there, without seeming unattractive."[74] The employees were considered by Walt as a family, and they were expected to share that conception. Everyone at the studio called their boss "Walt," whether they felt comfortable with it or not. Although everyone had specific titles and positions, it was not uncommon for everyone to help out in a number of different ways—coming up with gag ideas, drawing inspirational sketches, etc. Lunch breaks at the studio usually included volleyball games on the lot.

There was also a great deal of social propriety within the studio confines as well. A dress code was instituted for all employees. Men were expected to arrive at work in coat and tie (which could be removed when sitting at a drawing table). Pants on female employees were strictly forbidden. The women, who worked almost exclusively in the "inking and painting" department (coloring the animation cels), were often segregated from the male employees. One female employee, Phyllis Craig, recalls that the Ink and Paint Department was nicknamed "The Nunnery," and that they were given their lunch break at a separate time from the men.[75] In fact, as Disney biographer Leonard Mosley narrates,

> It was sometimes known among cynical acting types as Mickey Mouse's Monastery, and . . . anything less than circumspect behavior while appearing on the lot would result in instant dismissal. You did not carouse, raise your voice off the set, look lecherously at a member of the opposite sex, or, in fact, indulge in any kind of hanky-panky at Disney.[76]

In all ways, it seemed that Disney and his studio had created a specific, carefully circumscribed concept of sexual decorum, one that upheld the American bourgeois heterosexual norm.

This is not to say that the attempt to construct this image amongst the employees at the studio always proceeded smoothly apace. In specifically mandating only one type of proper behavior for its employees, the studio was inadvertently highlighting those practices that were not to be condoned. And, in so doing, it was inevitable that various incidents would occur to challenge the image that the studio was publicly advertising. One of the earliest examples of a rebellion against this new era for the Disney studio among employees is also one of the best known. When Walt hired art school teacher Don Graham to teach animators (including some who had worked in the industry for decades) a new way to draw, many of them resented the changes and resisted. Possibly understanding that this new "illusion of life" concept was somehow tied to the crackdown on sexual humor in Disney's cartoons, some animators who grumbled at being forced to take these sketching classes used their new skills to anonymously protest. Biographer Bob Thomas describes that "Scornful cartoons appeared on the studio bulletin boards, depicting Mickey Mouse with an anatomically detailed pelvis."[77] Although these drawings were only momentary, they made explicit what was being changed at the studio with this new style of animation.

A more potentially disruptive event happened later in the 1930s:

> One of the animators who had thrown away his glasses as a result of a new therapy involving eye exercises began approaching girls around the studio who wore spectacles. . . . He enticed a number of the girls to do the eye exercises with him and explained that a prerequisite of the routine was that they must first relax by taking off their clothes. . . . One girl panicked . . . and rushed home to tell her parents; they demanded the immediate arrest [of the man]. . . . [The studio] compensated the girl for her embarrassment . . . [and] the animator . . . was summarily dismissed.[78]

This event gains importance when examining how Walt and the few other employees who knew about the incident handled it. "Walt told [studio lawyer Gunther] Lessing to keep it a secret, . . . [to keep quiet] that the Disney studio could be just like the rest of Hollywood."[79] Such a statement presupposes that Walt and his assistants were quite aware of what small-town America thought of "the rest of Hollywood" and had already actively attempted to distance themselves from this image.

One other incident from the 1930s amply displays the constructedness of propriety at the studio. *Snow White and the Seven Dwarfs* (1937), the studio's first feature-length animated cartoon, was a project that pushed every employee to the brink through long hours, impossible deadlines and a constant push for perfection. After the film's phenomenally successful release, Walt decided to show his thanks by inviting the entire studio employee roster (and their spouses) to join him and his wife in a weekend getaway at the Narconian Hotel resort at Lake Narco. The group of young men and women (most of the company's employees were 35 or younger, like Disney himself) quickly turned the vacation into precisely the carnivalesque free-for-all that had become taboo at the studio and in their films:

One of the animators who was there said, "By the end of the first evening, something snapped. All the animators and assistant animators and inkers, who had always been so staid and contained at the studio, suddenly let go. Nobody worried here whether your shorts fit or not, because everybody's were suddenly slipping. Playsuits flew out of the windows. There were naked swim parties in the pool. Inhibitions, respectability, and tensions vanished with each new bottle of champagne, and all those circumspect characters who had damped down their lecherous instincts around the studio for years were suddenly reaching out and grabbing someone. Everybody got drunk. It developed into what was practically an orgy, with animators reeling around tipsily and staggering off to sleep with whomsoever took their fancy, which was more likely to be that demure little inker from desk number 17 rather than the mother of their children. You'd be surprised who woke up with whom next morning."[80]

Walt and his wife quickly left the resort the next day, and the incident was not spoken of at the studio for a number of years. Yet, the explosion of rampant uninhibited sexuality exemplifies how much of a conscious construction Disney's "happy little family" was.

Of course, these events were never reported by the mainstream press—which was quite happy to help Walt and his brother Roy maintain the image of their studio as a happy leisurely family-oriented studio and even played down the extremely divisive strike that erupted at the studio in 1941.[81] This is not to say that behind the studio's calm facade was a cauldron seething with passion and scandal that rivaled the rest of Hollywood. The studio was probably no more open than any other studio in the ways male and female employees expressed their sexuality. What marked Disney as different from other studios was the constant publicity about the "family" atmosphere at the studio, the wholesomeness of the environment (complete with pictures of Walt standing on the studio lawn benevolently watching over employees picnicking their lunch) and how such a climate supposedly transferred into the films the studio was making.[82] After the enforcement of the Code's restrictions in 1934, other studios would also attempt at various points to portray themselves as big families led by benevolent fatherly figures (most notably MGM's Louis B. Mayer and his roster of young contractees, such as Freddie Bartholomew, Jackie Cooper, Mickey

Rooney and Judy Garland), but Walt had been there earlier and with greater frequency.

By the end of the 1930s, it seemed that Disney's successful climb to economic prosperity and artistic independence had been achieved. A new distribution contract with the RKO studio resulted in the studio receiving more revenue from box-office returns than ever. Walt and his animators took the lessons that they learned (technical and otherwise) in making the Mickeys and the *Sillies* and applied them to creating animated feature-length films. The combination of moral-driven narrative and "illusion of life" character-based animation was used in all of the features of Disney's "Golden Age": *Snow White and the Seven Dwarfs* (1937), *Pinocchio* (1940), *Fantasia* (1940), *Dumbo* (1941) and *Bambi* (1942).[83] The release of *Snow White and the Seven Dwarfs* was successful beyond almost everyone's expectations, becoming for a short time the most popular film in the history of American cinema.[84] The Disney studio seemed to have solidified its formula for success.

Bambi, possibly more than any of the features from this era, functions as the acme of the studio's changes in attitude towards sexuality and the body. Critics and film analysts often point to *Bambi* as the high point of Disney's push towards a "realistic" style in animation. Deer and other animals were brought to the studio for animators to study and sketch, and test footage was shot of various species in motion so that animators could isolate the body movements. As R. D. Feild, writing in 1942, described, "it was decided that the animals must be allowed to tell their own story as far as it was possible! The continuity must be based not upon what man has read into nature but upon what man can learn from nature."[85] The emphasis on rendering the illusion of animal figures in motion has consequently been criticized for negating the purposes of animation—to do what live-action film cannot. This is not entirely true, for the characters are not necessarily drawn realistically. The young Bambi is only vaguely related to what a true fawn looks like. Furthermore, the background paintings are often very impressionistic in their design, and certain sequences (Bambi's dream of love, his fight with the rival buck) approach a type of surrealism.

The criticism that *Bambi* is *too* realistic does not recognize that the animation creates an *illusion* of realism, thus allowing Disney and his animators to naturalize (possibly more than ever before) messages about sexuality and the body. Just as in *The Flying Mouse*, a cycle of time is used to make the lessons of the film's narrative seem logical and in-evitable. Bambi is born in the spring, reaches his lowest emotional and physical point during the barren winter months and emerges tri-umphant in the following spring. During this period, the film promotes a patriarchal order (Bambi is "the young Prince" who will eventually take over his father's position as "King of the Forest" and is forced to shed his dependence on his mother when she is killed halfway through the film) and asserts that all animal species engage in bourgeois hetero-sexual courtship that leads to a serene family life for all. Possibly more effectively than anything that the studio had previously done, *Bambi* used the "illusion of life" style to tell a moral-driven narrative that es-sentializes messages about sexuality and the body by animating a story told "in nature."

DISNEY AT WAR: FEDERALLY SPONSORED EDUCATION (1942–1949)

In the 1940s, the studio came into greater contact with the United States government and armed forces. These ties started for the studio another evolution in representing sexuality and the body, a change stressing more than ever before the pedagogical nature of these representations by trying to teach servicemen (and others) federal guidelines on hy-giene and body maintenance. While still working to provide entertain-ment, these films first and foremost were produced and screened as "educational" films, attempting to specifically regulate, prohibit and generate an approved discourse of proper sexual conduct and control of the body. Although initially speaking to the military services, Dis-ney's move into educational films soon spread to ordinary citizens, both in the United States and beyond.

The government was able to influence Disney's output so greatly because, as scholars agree, Disney's ties to the federal government during World War II saved the studio from bankruptcy.[86] It might seem surprising to find that, so quickly after the huge success of *Snow White*, the studio was on the brink of collapse. The studio poured the profits from its first feature into its next two, *Pinocchio* and *Fantasia*. Neither came close to matching *Snow White*'s box-office. With the books in the red, the studio was also crippled by animators striking for union representation. Due to the long and (at times) ugly strike, production at the studio on *Bambi* was delayed for months, and the studio was forced to shut down completely for a while. According to Douglas Gomery, "Through 1941 and 1942 the Disney company lost a total of one million dollars."[87]

In early 1941, Disney held a meeting with various representatives from industry and the United States and Canadian governments to discuss the possible use of animation in education and propaganda. Disney had already made a training film called *Four Methods of Flush Riveting* (1940) for Lockheed and presented this as an example of how films could help train engineers and military personnel. Canada, already at war, contracted Disney to make both instructional films and a series of four short trailers using various Disney characters (the Three Pigs, the Seven Dwarves, Donald Duck, etc.) to promote the sale of Canadian war bonds.[88]

The United States government was not far behind Canada in seeking out Disney's help. Even before the Japanese attacked Pearl Harbor, Disney was negotiating with the government to make educational films for the armed forces.[89] After December 7, 1941, the armed forces made their presence felt at the studio in a number of palpable ways. Beyond the dozens of military training films that the studio cranked out with amazing alacrity (and amazingly low budgets) over the next four years, armed forces personnel set up camp within the studio. Offices at the studio were vacated for use by Lockheed personnel. Because of the presence of Lockheed employees, anti-aircraft troops also moved into the studio and most were quartered within its confines. With the soldiers came three million rounds of ammunition that were stored in the studio's parking lot.

Beyond the training films, Disney worked on a series of animated shorts for a number of different governmental departments, such as *The New Spirit* (1942), made in coordination with the Treasury Department to help explain and promote the country's new tax laws. Most famously, Disney worked with the Office of the Coordinator of Inter-American Affairs (CIAA), which was created to strengthen the ties between the United States and Latin America, in order to keep South and Central America from becoming allied to Nazi Germany. In 1940, even before Disney began to work on training films, the CIAA had contacted Walt personally to make a goodwill tour of South America, with the possibility of gaining material for films that would promote what was soon being called the "Good Neighbor Policy." Walt complied, taking a crew of animators with him, and two feature films resulted—*Saludos Amigos* (1942) and *The Three Caballeros* (1945).

In continuing to make business for Disney, the federal government helped keep the studio afloat for the duration of the war. The government also cleared the path for the studio to obtain access to chemicals to make film stock—a valuable commodity since the same chemicals were essential for making weapons and were, hence, in very short supply.[90] According to many historians, the government also helped Walt through the drawn-out strike. Animator Jack Kinney points out that the State Department arranged for Walt's goodwill trip to occur at the height of the strike, thus removing him from the debate and countering the news reports with widespread, favorable counterpublicity.[91] Eric Smoodin goes even farther in his assessment of governmental support during the strike:

> Memos show that the government had an even more active role during the strike, supporting Disney financially or at least planning to support him. [John Hay] Whitney [producer and member of the Office of Inter-American Affairs] wrote that "we are proposing to execute the contract immediately on the understanding that he [Disney] cannot afford to continue his present outlay and risk and that he will have to abandon the project if we cannot support him temporarily."[92]

The implication in the memo points out just how close the working relationship between Disney and the federal government had become during this period.

The work that Disney did for the armed services during this period was posited as strictly educational: technical, scientific and objective. Through the use of "cutaway" or "x-ray" diagrams, drawings purported to show how the interior of guns or motors actually looked and worked. The use of the term "x-ray" by the studio to describe this animation technique emphasizes its scientific use. This conception, though, was often challenged by the fact that a significant amount of the films ended up presenting erroneous information. The series that Disney did to help identify war planes was entitled WEFT, standing for the four areas of the plane that could be examined for identification: Wings, Engine, Fuselage and Tail. Richard Shale reports that the Navy regularly rejected films in the series because of rampant errors. "The WEFT series . . . proved to be less successful than originally hoped and became jokingly referred to as Wrong Every Fucking Time."[93] The series was discontinued before the contract was completed.

The use of animation immediately compromises the veracity of the lessons being taught. The films do not display actual guns or warplanes, but only representations of them—drawn and then filmed. Yet, just as Disney's prewar theatrical output attempted to naturalize a specifically constructed image of sexuality, Disney's military films often used a "scientific" attitude to mask wartime propaganda. This seemed to be precisely what the United States government wanted from the studio. Disney's use of character-based "illusion of life" animation and moral-driven narrative to "educate" viewers proved to be ideal for the government's needs. With the war, the pedagogy became even more explicit and manifest. *Stop That Tank* (1941), one of Disney's shorts for the Canadian government, displays this ably. While ostensibly made to train personnel on the use of the Boys MK–1 Anti-Tank Rifle, the film includes a sequence of a caricatured Hitler in a tank being blown literally to hell by Canadian Anti-Tank Rifles being fired from "trees, haystacks, barnyards . . . , and even a latrine."[94] Disney's feature film *Victory Through Air Power* (1942), although released to domestic audiences, was basically a feature-length version of an instructional film that used maps, charts and scientific theory to explain how important air power was to Allied victory. Yet, it too included blatant propaganda in the midst of supposed objective argument. The film concludes with Japan animated as a giant octopus strangling the world, until a giant flying eagle, in a brutal and strongly visceral scene, attacks and vanquishes the beast. The victorious bird then turns into a gold eagle on top of a flag pole waving the Stars and Stripes as a patriotic refrain fills the soundtrack.

Amongst the topics covered in these instructional shorts were health issues. The armed services worked with Disney to describe methods for maintaining dental hygiene, caring for the mentally ill and the treatment and prevention of venereal disease.[95] As a result of the South American goodwill trip that Walt and his animators took, and the subsequent features, the Center for Inter-American Alliance also requested that Disney do a series of fifteen health and hygiene films for distribution in Latin American countries. Thus, certain of Disney's government-sponsored films dealt specifically with sexuality and regulating how the body should behave and be treated. In doing so, the government was backing Disney's naturalization of specific concepts of sexuality and the body. As one studio report put it, these films would purportedly teach "the fundamentals of social science free from religious or political influence."[96] The shorts presented this discourse as objective data, using the same "x-ray" techniques, but this time on human bodies instead of weapons and military transport.

Tuberculosis (1945) provides a good example of supposed scientific examinations of the body. The short at one point employs "x-ray" animation when a "cutaway" of a human body shows two lungs being infected by tubercular germs. Yet, the supposed objectivity of the shot is completely undercut when this "x-ray" dissolves to a shot of two lung-shaped leaves that are being eaten by insects. *Defense Against Invasion* (1943) is even more blatant in its use of metaphor while claiming to be scientific. The "x-ray" animation in this short portrays the human body as a city having to combat the evil enemy. The heart is portrayed as a central office building, and germs are represented by black spidery creatures. The narrator (a doctor in a live-action wrap-around story) intones, "This city, or man, died because he did not have arms and ammunition." Richard Shale points out in his description of this short that even the use of color is in variance with scientific facts. "Though it is the *white* blood cell that provides the body's resistance to disease, the Disney artists insisted on making the corpuscle soldiers red since red is a good fighting color and blood is usually thought of as red."[97]

Lisa Cartwright and Brian Goldfarb, in analyzing these films, point out that:

> the films fix intently on the private bodies and domestic lives of the subjects. . . . The most personal aspects of bodily care, from eating to coughing to defecating, become the subject of a repetitive and paternalistic discourse. The pedagogical strategy used in these films is to didactically associate illness and poverty with particular bodily "customs," and health and prosperity with Western scientific standards of hygiene.[98]

Cleanliness Brings Health (1945) works in just this way. A paternalistic narrator introduces two households, "the careless family and the clean family." Johnny, the child of the careless family, writhes in pain inside his family's dilapidated house. The narrator then describes how antiquated and unenlightened local custom causes Johnny's entire family to come down with dysentery. The already ailing Johnny goes to the cornfield to defecate. "The cornfield was where everybody went," explains the narrator. "It was the custom. But it was a very bad custom." The film then shows Johnny's father as he works with his hands in the contaminated soil, eats a meal without washing the soil from his hands and subsequently suffers from dysentery. The "clean" family, on the other hand, uses an outhouse, covers its food with mosquito netting and cooks on a fire that is raised above the ground to keep it away from contamination.

These films were distributed throughout Latin America with 16 mm prints taken from village to village and projected often from a flatbed truck and generator onto a temporarily hung sheet. Although made with government backing, American companies working in Latin America, such as United Fruit, quickly found the films useful as well. "Disney's public health and education films were, in part, attempts to provide models for domestic life for the local workers these companies hired, to be administered as 'teaching aids' by managers, many of whom could not speak Spanish or Portuguese well enough to communicate with their employees."[99] Implicit in the films is the notion that hard work is needed to combat illness, that laziness breeds disease. Hence, the shorts induce the local population to work for the American-owned companies presenting the films, conveniently avoiding the point that "U.S. development [itself] was primarily responsible for placing the health of communities in crisis."[100]

The success of such educational shorts, and the boom of 16 mm that resulted from government-sponsored war documentaries, caused the Disney studio to institute the Educational and Industrial Film Division—a sideline to its higher profile theatrical features. In 1945–1951, the studio produced a series of educational films backed by corporate sponsors to be rented to American schools. In addition to revising the South American hygiene shorts for use in the United States, these films also covered such topics as how to bathe an infant, how to prevent catching a cold and the dangers of driving too fast. Possibly the best remembered of these films is the one Disney made for International Cellucotton in 1946, *The Story of Menstruation*. The work by Janice Delaney and others on the cultural history of menstruation describes this short subject, which was shown in schools to pubescent girls well into the 1960s:

In the Disney world, the menstrual flow is not blood red but snow white. The vaginal drawings look more like a cross section of a kitchen sink than the inside and outside of a woman's body. There are no hymen, no clitoris, no labia; all focus is on the little nest and its potentially lush lining. Although Disney and Kimberly-Clark advise exercise during the period, the exercising cartoon girls (who look like Disney's Cinderella) are drawn without feet; bicycles magically propel themselves down the street without any muscular or mental direction from the cyclist. The film ends happily ever after, with a shot of a lipsticked bride followed immediately by a shot of a lipsticked mother and baby.[101]

Cloaked with the same declaration of objectivity and scientific knowledge, *The Story of Menstruation* represents white middle-class American heterosexual domesticity as the natural outcome of this biological change in the female body. Just as the South American shorts "used" science to help American industry get more labor from native workers, *The Story of Menstruation* uses a seminar on female bodily functions to encourage young women to consume the hygiene products manufactured by the film's sponsor, International Cellucotton.

The description of the short also points out an ironic change in animation style in this series of educational shorts. Vaginal drawings that look "like the cross section of a kitchen sink" and women bicycling without any feet exemplify the move towards a more "limited" animation. Due to the rushed schedules of wartime, and the small margin of anticipated profit from these films in postwar years, the studio quickly adapted a style antithetical to the "illusion of life" philosophy of its theatrical animation. This style used fewer drawings, and the drawings themselves often used less detail. Human figures became more like stick figures and their motions were often limited to the most effective poses necessary to get the desired point across. Ironically, the more overtly pedantic these shorts became, the more abstract the representations of the human body became. As can be seen in *The Story of Menstruation,* such abstraction actually "bleaches" the more "unsavory" parts of the lesson, such as making the menstrual flow white instead of red. By making menstruation abstract in the extreme, the use of limited animation eradicates details that might make young women question the benefits of International Cellucotton's goods, much less the benefits and normalcy of suburban motherhood.

Although production of these shorts would not officially continue past 1951, Disney's expansion in TV during the 1950s created a market for a number of similar educational programs, such as the *I'm No Fool* series starring Jiminy Cricket. Karl Cohen, in researching Walt Disney's FBI file, discovered a proposal for another educational short subject to be made in conjunction with the Bureau in the early 1960s:

> In the course of a conversation between Disney and an FBI agent, discussion drifted to a recent kidnap, rape and murder of a child. Disney was then told of the FBI's educational program to warn children about being approached by strangers. The memo observes that Disney stated he ". . . thought this was a very fine program, and then began to express himself along lines that he felt that a nonprofit film of a type made by Disney utilizing some of the animal characters which he had made famous could be very effective in the education of children of tender years against child molesters." He called in some of his staff and asked them to initiate research for the project and the possibility of their doing up to three films on the subject in order to reach various age groups. Disney made no commitment to the project and told the agent it would require funding from outside the studio. He did plan to meet again with the agent to discuss ideas his researchers developed.[102]

There does not seem to be any evidence that any of the three films were actually produced, but the conversation depicted in the memo displays the overt and conscious role that Walt and the studio took on after the 1940s as educators of America's children on social and sexual issues.

UNCLE WALT: CONSOLIDATING THE CORPORATE IMAGE (1950–1966)

Although the 1940s were a time of explicit pedagogy within much of the studio's work, the company soon discovered that such blatant representations of sexuality and the body would not be economically profitable outside of a wartime situation. In the first few years after the war, the studio attempted to move farther along the educational path that had helped keep it economically solvent. Yet, by 1950, Walt and the rest of the company had discovered that American postwar society preferred the "soft-sell" approach. Although the company would expand in a number of different directions during the 1950s (documentaries, live-action features, television, theme parks), all the product returned to messages that "naturalized" the middle-class patriarchal heterosexual paradigm instead of the overt discussions prevalent in the films made during the war. This development did not occur overnight. Each of the areas that had been affected by the war effort show a gradual adaptation to this aesthetic during the postwar 1940s, resulting in a new and phenomenally successful Walt Disney Company by the beginning of the 1950s.

Nowhere was the realignment more apparent than in the studio's theatrical animated features. During the 1940s, Disney's bread-and-butter product, its animation, declined in popularity and critical regard. The box-office disappointments of *Pinocchio* and *Fantasia*, and the ballooned budget of *Bambi*, necessitated scaling down the ambitions of future animated features and ended Disney's "Golden Period." For the next eight years, the studio's animated features consisted of collections of short subjects (some longer than the normal half-reel, some shorter) released as "package" films. Although the first of these packages, *Saludos Amigos*, was very well received, each successive feature (*The Three Caballeros, Make Mine Music* [1946], *Fun and Fancy Free* [1947], *Melody Time* [1948] and *The Adventures of Ichabod and Mr. Toad* [1949]) gained less and less favorable reaction.

Although most analyses of Disney's animated features during this period stress the lack of budget and vision on the part of the studio during these lean times, one can also find in the contemporary criticism of these films a distinct disfavor with the sexual nature of certain sections of these films. In fact, during the mid-1940s, there is a marked return to the carnivalesque atmosphere that suffused Disney animation in the early years—and reviewers didn't seem to take kindly to it. The critical reaction to *The Three Caballeros* quickly expressed the discomfort of seeing Donald Duck in a sexual frenzy as he runs pell-mell towards every live-action Latin American beauty that crosses his path, sometimes embracing his male cohorts in the midst of the chaos. *Time*'s review of the film stated baldly that Donald's "erotomaniacal regard for these full-blown young ladies is of strictly pathological interest."[103] *The Saturday Review* concurred, wondering "why Mr. Disney and his staff should ever have sent their caballeros on that magic serapi [sic] ride across a beach full of bathing beauties."[104] Smoodin's analysis of the reaction to

The *Three Caballeros* points out that the studio was not some innocent party while "perverted" critics lambasted the sexual ferocity of the film. He points out that

> In the same *Saturday Review* that discussed *The Three Caballeros*, an advertisement appeared for the film. It showed none of the animated characters but only a woman in a bathing suit, hand poised on hip in typical bathing suit fashion. The ad copy exclaimed "Yes! She's real! Alive and lovely in a Walt Disney Picture! It's amazing, wonderful and thrilling!"[105]

This was not only an isolated incident, as publicity photos of Walt sketching a lineup of bathing beauties on the Disney lot during this period point out.[106] Clearly, the studio's promotional strategy accentuated rather than diminished the sexuality in the film.

In "All the Cats Join In," one of the shorts that comprise *Make Mine Music,* a teenage girl's naked silhouette appears behind an opaque shower door, and possibly "too much" is revealed as she reaches out for a towel. The Production Code Administration thought it was too much at least and wrote to the studio that "These scenes should be eliminated" from "All the Cats Join In," one of the rare times in which Disney was admonished.[107] Yet, somehow the offending scenes were able to be retained and still get a Seal of Approval. Their inclusion resulted in *Time* describing the piece as "a jukebox setting of Benny Goodman's record, in which orgiastic hepcats and bobbysoxers, mad on chocolate malteds, tear all over the place."[108]

The appearance of such elements in Disney animation at this point needs to be seen in the larger context of social and industrial changes during the 1940s. The entire country had experienced during the war a huge upsurge in more explicit sexuality. An entire industry of "cheesecake" posters and glossy photos was created to keep overseas soldiers aware of "what they were fighting for." With the American population basically segregated by gender (whether in the armed forces or on the home front), the restrictions placed on sexual relations became more pronounced. Of course, being segregated by gender, many homosexual men and women who had never come in contact with others who felt the way they did were suddenly thrust into close quarters with each other. Men and women in the service were also lectured to specifically about sexual matters in order to prevent the spread of venereal disease and to warn against homosexual tendencies. Film was used as part of this education, and, as the overview of Disney's relationship with the government shows, animation figured strongly. Hence, with such blatant reference to sexuality occurring in American culture, it is not unreasonable to find Disney participating in it.

Such considerations take on further merit when looking at the status of Disney animation itself during this period. During the 1930s, Walt Disney and his studio stood so far ahead of other animation departments at other studios that it often seemed as if Disney was the only studio making cartoons. Yet, by the 1940s, the other animation factories had shortened the lead that Disney held and created a distinctly different philosophy and style than Disney. The work of William Hanna and Joseph Barbera at MGM (with Tom and Jerry), and numerous artists at Warner Bros. (with their menagerie of cartoon characters led by Bugs Bunny) challenged the preeminence of Disney animation. Their work adopted much of the "full animation" style that Disney's studio developed in the 1930s, but was not as concerned with the "illusion of life," and furthermore stressed the violent, burlesque and risqué humor that was rarely found in Disney animation.

The most blatant example of using Disney's "full animation" to ends other than those of the moral-driven narratives of the Disney studio was the work of Tex Avery (at both Warner Bros. and MGM). In one of the most popular cartoon shorts of the war, *Red Hot Riding Hood* (1943), the wolf goes after not a sweet young girl but a voluptuous leggy redhead performing at a nightclub in various stages of undress. The wolf's reactions visualize quite strongly his raging hormones in a variety of hilarious and physically impossible ways. The liberties taken with the wolf's body (eyes popping out larger than his body, tongue rolling out for miles, etc.) as well as the "illusion of life" fetishism of Red's body on stage (animated by Preston Blair) was antithetical to the Disney philosophy. Yet, the short often garnered such a strong reaction from audiences (particularly soldiers) that some theatres reported having to stop the feature film and run the short again to appease the crowd.[109]

Disney animators in the 1940s tried to answer the challenge that Avery and the other animation factories had created by inserting more violence and more sexuality into their work. The influence of these other studios can be seen in the slapstick and violent humor of the 1940s series of Goofy cartoons comically demonstrating different sports (*The

Art of Skiing [1941], *How to Play Football* [1944], *Hockey Homicide* [1945]). Mickey Mouse's sweet persona appeared less and less on screen in favor of the angry antics of Donald Duck, who seemed to more suit the challenge posed by Bugs Bunny and Daffy Duck. It is also more understandable why Disney would have Donald chasing Latin lovelies around in feature films when Avery's wolf was hooting at Red's bumps and grinds.

Unfortunately, Disney and his studio's public relations department had already staked out an image for itself as wholesome and family oriented, and such displays of sexual aggressiveness (although no more suggestive than Mickey in his early period) were not appreciated. Disney could speak overtly of the female body in manifestly pedagogical texts such as *The Story of Menstruation*, but audiences did not approve of such things in the studio's theatrical product. The studio eventually learned this lesson, and 1950 saw a full-scale return to the fairy-tale format that audiences wanted from Disney. *Cinderella* was the biggest animated success the studio had had since *Dumbo* and gained a sizable profit due to the cutbacks and "cheats" that kept the cost of the production low. (Disney animators admit to using more rotoscoping, or tracing live-action figures, on this film than in any other.)[110] Sexual imagery was again submerged into images of patriarchal heterosexual romance—dancing, walking in the moonlight and a chaste kiss in the wedding carriage.[111] Throughout the rest of the decade, the studio would continue animating famous children's tales (*Alice in Wonderland* [1951], *Peter Pan* [1953], *Sleeping Beauty* [1959]). In adapting the familiar stories, contemporary concepts of gender and sexuality are conveyed more benignly than in the educational shorts of the 1940s. For example, Alice is made less willful and independent than in the original texts. On the other hand, Disney's Peter Pan is one of the most masculine versions of the character, a definite attempt to downplay the gender bending that traditionally occurs when actresses play the title role on stage. Donald Crafton's analysis of the film points out how the text attempts to teach young children the roles of masculinity and femininity as conceived in postwar America, even linking the pedagogical methods of *The Story of Menstruation* to *Peter Pan*.[112] Whether or not the studio consciously used its research for *The Story of Menstruation* in preparation for *Peter Pan*, the studio definitely found more financial success by presenting its messages about motherhood under the guise of Barrie's classic tale than in the more explicit lecturing on "the change of life."

The move into 16 mm educational films turned out to be more minor than the studio seemed to anticipate, and, after 1951, official production seems to have stopped.[113] The profit margin for these films was slim, since schools or libraries would buy one print of the film and then own it outright, often lending out the prints to other schools or institutions. As Carl Nater, head of the Educational Division for twenty years, explained, "Frankly, there was just not enough money to even get the cost [of production] back."[114] Yet, an outgrowth of Disney's educational productions during the war did result in a lucrative new direction for the studio in the late 1940s. A production made for the CIAA entitled *The Amazon Awakens* (1944) put the studio in contact with documentary filmmakers. By the end of the 1940s, the studio was producing a series of documentary shorts (and, by the 1950s, features) under the titles "True-Life Adventures" and (in the 1950s) "People and Places." Unlike the Educational Division, these productions were made for exhibition in major film theatres, and, when *Seal Island* (1949) turned a sizable profit and won the Academy Award for Best Documentary Short, the studio quickly turned out more. Just as the studio found that a return to the moral fairy-tale narrative that had begun the studio's feature film production was more successful than the rampant sexuality in the package films had been, the entertainment-oriented animal documentaries proved more economically viable and popular than the more specifically educational productions.

The "True-Life Adventures" became immensely popular and were converted to 16 mm for classroom exhibition and edited for episodes of Disney's television series. Focusing mainly on animal life, audiences warmed to vivid displays of what seemed to be creatures functioning in their normal habitat. Yet, as time went on, many began to notice the liberties the studio was taking with the footage shot by the documentarians. Many of the people working on the films had originally worked in animation. James Algar, who had been a sequence director on animated features, went on to direct many of the feature-length films in the True-Life Series. Ben Sharpsteen, who had worked on animated shorts and features during the 1930s and '40s, served as associate producer and later producer of the True-Life series. Consequently, the True-Life shorts and features often took on the look and feel of Disney animation, particularly *Bambi*.

Music was used blatantly to provide commentary on footage, making various animal activities seem like high comedy. One of the most notorious of these sequences is the "scorpion dance" from the feature film *The Living Desert* (1954). As the scorpions circle each other, the soundtrack blares a square dance, complete with a humorous dance caller. The studio also effectively used slow motion and reverse motion to get desired effects from the animals, such as ducks slowly slipping on ice and crashing into each other in *The Vanishing Prairie* (1955). Lastly, although always purporting to be examining animals in the wild, environments were often recreated within the studio's confines to better control the filming conditions. For example, in *The Vanishing Prairie*, a large section of the film is devoted to the life of prairie dogs. This is often done by presenting glass walled cutouts of prairie dog burrows—the better to see them scamper about underground—without regard to how such conditions might change how the animals act and react.

Much as the "illusion of life" helps naturalize discourse in Disney animation, labeling these films as documentaries essentializes their representations of sexuality and gender. Through clever editing, manipulative musical cues and especially paternal narration written and voiced by Winston Hibler, the True Life series consistently uses the spectacular footage shot by filmmakers to reinforce hegemonic norms, representing such norms as having their equivalent in "nature." As Derek Bouse points out in his analysis of Disney's animal films,

> Nature . . . emerges as a profoundly *moral* place, a seat of the kind of "values" which are the foundation of families and communities. In nature there are virtuous, brave and resourceful heroes, damsels for them to rescue or to win by their deeds, and villains who always pay the price of their transgressions. There is good and evil, right and wrong, punishment and forgiveness.[115]

Bouse concludes his argument quite succinctly: "Culture is 'naturalized' in the purest sense: by locating its source in nature."[116]

The Vanishing Prairie, the second full-length feature in this series, offers a perfect example of such naturalization of the hegemonic order. The narration professes in the opening that the film will represent the American prairie of "an earlier time. A time without record or remembrance, when nature alone held dominion over the prairie realm." In eliminating human society from the depiction of the prairie, the film attempts to place itself "outside of history as we know it. . . . Ultimately, the True-Life Adventures were not concerned with exploring real places or documenting real events, but with creating mythic places that conformed to the Disney style."[117] Yet, even as the narrator supposedly absents man from the environment, his voice-over continually posits animal behavior in distinctly human terms. For example, as various water fowl converge on a pond during the spring migration, Winston Hibler intones that they "all join in a lighthearted hubbub of gossip and chatter."

It does not take long for the birds to begin exhibiting (according to the film) desires for domesticity. A montage of bird couples scooting across the water is accompanied by an explanation that the viewer is witnessing a humorous mating ritual. Even though it seems in some of the shots that the birds are actually hunting for fish, the musical score emphasizes the courtship angle by playing Wagner's opening to Act III of *Lohengrin,* conventionally played during wedding recessionals. After this sequence comes "homemaking," as the male and female build their nest and care for their young. Hibler points out how the chores are split: "While mother sits on the nest, father takes care of the food supply." When he is forced to admit that sometimes the male sits on the nest, the film goes out of its way to laugh at the absurdity of such an occurrence: "Like most males, he's careless about domestic chores."

A running motif in the film associates the female with the raising of the young, usually with the male never even acknowledged. A mountain lion teaches her kittens, a mother coyote searches for food for her pups, and, in a stunning scene, the film shows the birth of a buffalo calf. (It is interesting to note that although the Production Code Administration never showed the slightest aversion to the rampant violence in this series—various predators stalking and running down deer and zebra— the PCA *did* monitor quite carefully how the public reacted to the birth of the calf, probably wondering if they should have been stricter in their job.)[118] The film repeatedly emphasizes the "natural" role of the female as nurturer. As the buffalo calf struggles to stand up, Hibler turns all the other buffalo into females as he describes that "all the mothers in the neighborhood seem eager to help the baby."

The prairie also often takes on the characteristics of an American suburb of the 1950s. This is nowhere more apparent than in the lengthy section that comprises most of the second half of the film on prairie dogs. The dogs are shown living in a little community, each with their own split-level burrows, with additions and repair work constantly going on. They are shown taking their children out on "picnics," arguing with their rowdy neighbors (owl and buffalo) and even harmonizing to the musical score as it plays "Home on the Range!" The box-office for these films shows that postwar America paid repeatedly to see animals recreate the hegemonic family ideal (no matter what tricks of music, narration, editing or artificial staging were required), and the studio would continue to turn out these documentary shorts and features throughout the 1950s.

The return to a fairy-tale format in animation and the expansion into documentary filmmaking in the 1950s helped solidify the company's success. Walt continued his expansion into new areas by being one of the first studio heads in Hollywood to embrace rather than fear the prospect of television. The studio also began to produce a number of live-action features, such as *Treasure Island* (1950), *20,000 Leagues Under the Sea* (1954) and *The Shaggy Dog* (1959). The most important event in the company's expansion occurred when the theme park Disneyland opened in the summer of 1955, providing a regular source of income for the company no matter what the annual success rate of feature film production might be.

Walt himself figured in the coalescing of the kindly paternal image of the studio and its products since, during the 1950s and 1960s, Walt would become one of the most familiar faces in popular culture. With the studio's expansion into television, Walt acted as emcee for the weekly anthology program initially called *Disneyland* (1955–57), then significantly *Walt Disney Presents* (1958–61). Known informally as "Uncle Walt," Disney presented the image of a soft-spoken, friendly older man who explained in a simple, entertaining fashion how animation was created, why man was destined to go into outer space or how animals lived their lives. In 1955, coinciding with the phenomenal popularity of the "Davy Crockett" episodes that appeared on his anthology series, Walt was honored at the Hollywood Bowl as a leader "who has blazed a new trail in American folklore."[119] The project of making Walt into a father-figure that had begun during the 1930s press barrage was completed with his appearances on television. In Walt's role as host for the series, viewers grew to associate him more intimately with a kindly paternal image that both parents and children could trust to provide both entertainment and education. Walt Disney was no longer a savvy businessman to most people in the United States—he was a member of the family. No one questioned his or the studio's integrity for the next three decades.

The creation of Disneyland opened up an entire "world" for Disney to make actual and physical the lessons that he and the studio were promoting on television and in films—a space that was highly controlled but gave visitors the illusion of freely roaming and exploring. Frontierland preserved a specific vision of the American West, Tomorrowland promoted "better living through chemistry," often with pavilions sponsored by various corporations, and Main Street created an ideal image of an America that never truly existed. Millions came out to the park, thrilling at and generally accepting everything that Disney put before them. By 1964, Disney's reputation as an educator of the American public had become so great that a number of various corporate sponsors employed the studio to create pavilions for the New York World's Fair. Amongst these attractions was the ultimate in control of the human body—"Great Moments with Mr. Lincoln." The development of an "audio-animatronic" robot that responded in movement to the soundwaves of a prerecorded speech was a perfect extension of the "illusion of life" philosophy. "Mr. Lincoln" would perform in exactly the same fashion every single show, amazing patrons as the sixteenth president stood and spoke a speech edited together from fragments of Lincoln's writings.[120] Somehow, this was "living history." By 1965, Dr. Max Rafferty would be able to declare in a *Los Angeles Times* article that Walt Disney was "The Greatest Pedagogue of All."[121]

Although the Disney studio was securely in the black from this point on, Walt and his company rarely veered from where they had evolved by 1950. There were no more experiments with how to represent sexuality and the body. On occasion, an errant live-action feature, such as *Bon Voyage* (1961), would alarm some parents with mildly risqué situations. In 1961, *101 Dalmatians* introduced a less realistic animation style (while maintaining the "naturalness" of the suburban heterosexual family through the corollary of a dog family who liked to sit at home and watch Disney cartoons on TV!). Still, the image of wholesome entertainment produced by a company dedicated to the cultural uplift of children would be maintained consistently for the next thirty years. Disney's reputation was so carved in stone within American culture that, at least once, the studio was able to transgress the Production Code during this period without anyone in the PCA, the Legion of Decency or any media watch group blinking an eye: the studio's version of *Pollyanna* (1960) opens with a shot of a young boy's rear end as he swings naked into a swimming hole. While such an image in, say, *Sud-*

denly Last Summer (1959) would have aroused ire from any number of groups, Disney's reputation signaled to audiences that this scene was only wholesome nostalgia for small-town American life.

By the time of Walt's death in 1966, he and the studio had perfected what they had learned about fashioning a "wholesome" image.[122] The company had quite consciously taken on the mantle of upholding traditional American values and was encouraged to find popularity and profit (from other studio executives, from consumers and from the United States government) through teaching these values to others. Even after the death of Walt Disney, the "Disney mystique" continued apace. For the next twenty years, the company maintained roughly the same critical and popular regard as before. Although Walt Disney was certainly not the only person in Hollywood to have espoused a white middle-class patriarchal heterosexual paradigm, for doing so he was often heralded in a manner that went beyond the accolades given to any other studio mogul at the time.

2

"Mickey Mouse—Always Gay!"

Reading Disney Queerly during Walt's Reign

IN THE MIDST of *The Celluloid Closet*, Vito Russo's groundbreaking work on representations of homosexuals in American film, there appears a poster advertising Mickey Mouse cartoons. As a joyous Mickey plucks out a tune on a harp, the poster proclaims, "Always Gay!" Underneath this picture, Russo writes the caption "When the word 'gay' meant happy and nothing else."[1] Although Russo separates Mickey's personality from the modern connotations of the word "gay," linking the word "gay" with "homosexual" had begun in various homosexual communities during the 1930s.[2] The word "gay" was used in these circles as a method of code to let others know that someone was "a member of the community" without declaring it to those who would physically or legally threaten them. Furthermore, although Walt and most (if not all) of his employees probably would not have known this new meaning to the word when they created the aforementioned poster in the 1930s, it seems that certain audience members were watching and enjoying Mickey's "gaiety" in all its connotations.

This dynamic becomes more apparent when certain historical evidence suggests that the phrase "Mickey Mouse" itself was bandied about by some homosexuals as a code phrase. Gay and lesbian historian Allan Berube found a photograph of a gay bar in Berlin during the 1930s called "Mickey Mouse."[3] A lesbian hobo of the 1930s who went by the name Box-Car Bertha related to Dr. Ben L. Reitman in 1937 that a group of wealthy Chicago lesbians threw soirees called "Mickey Mouse's party." Bertha maintained contact with these women in order to borrow money, introducing herself by saying "I met you at Mickey Mouse's party."[4]

With this evidence of the use of "Mickey Mouse" as a code phrase for homosexuality, seemingly benign uses of the name by homosexual figure take on heightened meaning. When openly gay songwriter Cole Porter wrote the lyrics for "You're the Top" in the early 1930s, he included the line "You're Mickey Mouse."[5] In *The Gay Divorcee* (1934), Betty Grable approaches Edward Everett Horton, who made a career out of playing the bumbling sissy in Hollywood films during the '30s, and sings to him "You make me feel so Mickey Mousey." Although what Grable's character means by this is left open to interpretation, in context she seems to mean that Horton stirs some emotion within her. Yet, "Mickey Mousey" might have had a sly double meaning—especially when a flustered Horton responds to Grable's assertion, "Well, no wonder!"[6]

Disney's animated shorts, feature films, documentaries and television series promoted a specific version of gender, sexuality and the body—"naturalizing" the heterosexual patriarchal family structure and replacing sex with romance. Yet, it stands to reason that not every viewer at all times accepted and endorsed Disney's representations of the conventional norms. The above examples open the possibility that gay and lesbian subjects watched and enjoyed Disney product from a completely different standpoint than was usually discussed in popular journals and newspaper reviews. By delving into these alternative reading strategies, one can begin to understand what seems to be a contradiction: how a company heavily promoting the heterosexual family ideal can have homosexual fans.

Such divergent readings by certain homosexual viewers epitomize the complexity of discussing how texts are received, understood and appreciated. Michel de Certeau proposes that readers do not always follow the prescribed path laid out in the text. Rather, they choose their own way, enjoy certain parts more than others and sometimes enjoy these parts in diverse fashion. "Readers are travelers; they move across lands belonging to someone else, like nomads poaching their way across fields they did not write, despoiling the wealth of Egypt to enjoy it themselves."[7] Similarly, Stuart Hall analyzes the ability of individual subjects to negotiate or resist the "preferred" position prescribed by the text.[8] Taking from both de Certeau and Hall, Henry Jenkins' work on media fan culture asserts that "Fans construct their cultural and social identity through borrowing and inflecting mass culture images, articulating concerns which often go unvoiced within the dominant media."[9]

The growth of reception studies in academic circles has much bearing on discussion of "gay spectatorship." Often denied the ability to openly produce texts dealing with homosexuality (through both the law and lack of economic means), the emergent gay and lesbian culture often relied on its ability to appropriate texts from the dominant heterosexual hegemony. Hence, a sense of homosexual community and identity can be traced in part to a strong emphasis on reading—specifically on "poaching" straight texts. From Bette Davis movies to *art nouveau* to Chet Baker, from James Dean to Wonder Woman, gay male and lesbian communities often coalesced around *re*-reading certain parts of popular culture. As de Certeau points out, these reading strategies do not supplant the dominant ideal subject position structured within the texts. Rather, they function as a series of "advances and retreats, tactics and games played with the text," a cultural bricolage. With this in mind, this chapter in no way suggests that the following "gay" readings of Disney are what is "really" going on. Rather, they analyze a different viewpoint, having no more—but importantly, *no less*—authority than other methods of reading. The possibilities opened by concrete individuals doing non-straight readings of Disneyana suggest there is no single definitive reading, challenging the privilege usually given to the "more obvious" heterosexual subject position. As Alexander Doty notes in *Making Things Perfectly Queer*, "I've got news for straight culture: your readings of texts are usually 'alternative' ones for me, and they often seem like desperate attempts to deny the queerness that is so clearly a part of mass culture."[10]

Oftentimes, a reader's "play" with the text means dissociating certain elements from the whole of the text, thus making it easier to rework. Due to the relative lack of texts explicitly dealing with homosexuality, enjoying a text from a lesbian or gay viewpoint often requires selecting out the scene, image or section from the text that suits the individual's needs and discarding the rest (i.e., ignoring the portion of the text that won't "fit" a "lesbian/gay reading"). In the documentary film based on *The Celluloid Closet* (1995), author Susie Bright describes sitting through entire movies just to see "that one moment"—such as Joan Crawford descending a staircase in pants and a man's black shirt in *Johnny Guitar* (1954). I would argue that many homosexuals enjoy (and have enjoyed) the output from the Walt Disney Company in much the same manner, taking portions and appreciating how certain narrative motifs, character types or stylistic choices somehow "speak to" their experience. As Jenkins puts it, media fans "fragment texts and reassemble the broken shards according to their own blueprints, salvaging bits and pieces of the found material in making sense of their own social experience."[11]

In theorizing readership, de Certeau makes a distinction between those who actually produce texts and those who receive them: "Writing accumulates, stocks up, resists time by the establishment of a place and multiplies its production through the expansionism of reproduction. Reading takes no measures against the erosion of time (one forgets oneself *and* also forgets), it does not keep what it acquires, or it does so poorly."[12] Yet, de Certeau bases his claim upon a notion that readers are isolated, and the play is usually for the individual's own minor enjoyment. Jenkins disagrees with this when he writes: "Fan reading . . . is a social process through which individual interpretations are shaped and reinforced through ongoing discussions with other readers."[13] This approach is especially true for gay culture, which has often been forged through sharing a unique appreciation of, for example, Judy Garland or classical opera. Through learning how to read "as a homosexual," individuals gain access to a community that is often hard to find and maintain.

Consequently, such "textual poaching" has often helped define an individual's sexual identity.[14] Many writers have described this as a "gay sensibility," which Jack Babuscio defines as

> a creative energy reflecting a consciousness that is different from the mainstream; a heightened awareness of certain human complications of feeling that spring from the fact of social oppression; in short, a perception of the world which is colored, shaped, directed and defined by the fact of one's gayness.[15]

Such a reading strategy is honed and sharpened (if not learned *en toto*) through interaction with other self-identified homosexuals. As mentioned at the beginning of this chapter, the association of "gay" with homosexuality was itself developed and passed on to others. Learning a "gay sensibility" further constructs an internalized notion of what it means to be "lesbian" or "gay." Reading through a "gay sensibility" may resist the hegemonic heterosexual imperative that dominates Western popular culture, but such reading stays within certain boundaries, limited by certain conceptions of what it means to be "homosexual."

Terms such as "homosexual," "lesbian" and "gay" are not stable and, over time, have meant different things to different individuals. Historical research suggests that men and women now recognized as homosexual understood their sexuality differently in their own time. In fact, defining one's self according to sexual orientation was not yet totally commonplace by the time Walt Disney began producing cartoons. Many still considered "acts of sodomy" simply as sinful actions and not indications of a personality type. The term "homosexuality" itself was only beginning to make its way out of the medical texts and into the larger public consciousness. Historian George Chauncey points out that in urban America at the beginning of the twentieth century, men who had sex with other men did not consider themselves all part of one category.[16] One group self-identified as "fairies," effeminate men who tended to take the "submissive" role in sex (although not always). On the other hand, many men self-identified as "queers," more conventionally masculine men who nonetheless did not consider themselves "normal" because of their sexual object choice (showing that this term has also changed meaning over time). There was even a third category—the "normal" men, or "trade," who engaged in sex with other men but did not self-identify as somehow outside the hegemonic norm because they maintained the dominant penetrative role in sex. They felt this way because social conventions at that time only associated "homosexuality" with those who "played the woman's part"; as long as an individual remained in the conventionally masculine role, he was still "normal." Similarly, "lesbianism" was mainly associated with inverting the gender roles—i.e., manly or "butch" women. Conventionally feminine women at this point were not pictured as "lesbian," even if they had relationships with other women. As Lillian Faderman has pointed out, many "proper" women lived together, formed primary bonds and shared living quarters with other women at the beginning of the century without being considered lesbian or, even more importantly, *considering themselves lesbian.*[17] Further, while certain urban areas had thriving homosexual subcultures, many living in small towns or rural areas had no idea that there were others "like them" and thus had to negotiate their own definitions of their sexual desires.

Such historiographic details must be taken into account when discussing "gay" or "lesbian" spectators from past decades. The terms used to describe same-sex relations during the early twentieth century were in various stages of contestation and coalescence. Individuals who appreciated Disney outside of the hegemonic norm probably differed both in how they understood their sexuality and in their conception of what made Disney's films so interesting to them. Consequently, it might be more accurate to consider such early readings under the more encompassing concept of "queer" (in the '90s sense) rather than explicitly "homosexual."

Armed with historical research on reading strategies by homosexual (or nascent homosexual) men and women, this chapter will explore possible methods of their enjoying Disneyana. Through close textual analyses of certain films and TV series, the chapter will discuss a variety of recurrent narrative patterns, characters and visual iconography in the Disney canon that might explain how Disney might have attracted (and might still attract) gay men and lesbians. As the chapter moves through the years, the analyses slide gradually from an amorphous "queer" viewpoint to a more definite "lesbian" or "gay" reading strategy, reflecting the growth of more agreed-upon definitions of these terms both from medical, legal and political discourses as well as from the emergent homosexual communities themselves.

"MICKEY-MOUSE" THEORY: FORSTER AND EISENSTEIN ON DISNEY

From the beginnings of Walt Disney's career, there was ample evidence that various audience members were watching and enjoying his films in very different ways. Before the age of television, animation was considered entertainment for adults as well as for children. Yet, even then there was a perception that cartoon shorts held a special attraction for young audiences. The Disney organization fostered this relationship with children through the merchandising of Mickey Mouse dolls, games, children's books, etc. Also, in the early 1930s, long before the premiere of the television series of the same name, the studio sanctioned the formation of various local "Mickey Mouse Clubs." The clubs were run by local exhibitors who would hold "meetings" at Saturday matinees that, of course, centered around the screening of the latest Mickey Mouse cartoon.[18]

Yet, at the same time that children were enjoying Mickey's adventures, a sizable contingent of the artistic elite took to Disney's films as well. Various art journals devoted space to analyzing the style of

Disney's animators.[19] In 1933, *Time* reported in its "Art" section that Manhattan's Kennedy Galleries were showing an exhibition of Mickey Mouse sketches and cels. In 1938, the Walt Disney studio signed a contract with Courvoisier Galleries, an exclusive San Francisco fine arts gallery, to sell original Disney art. By 1940, the studio's production of *Fantasia* virtually demanded a "high culture" reading strategy. In many of the major newspapers, the film was reviewed both in the film section and the music section. One *New York Times* article considered *Fantasia* not a radical departure for the studio but only the next logical step in Disney's artistic evolution, pointing out that *Steamboat Willie* had been "preserved for posterity in the archives of the Film Library of the Museum of Modern Art."[20]

The presence of these two widely different groups exemplifies the diverse reception of Disney texts. Yet, the gallery owners and cultural critics who admired Disney also provide an entrance into discussing how various homosexual individuals during the time might have appreciated Disney. Amongst the artistic elite that praised Disney were homosexuals. For the London *Spectator* in 1934, author E. M. Forster analyzed why Mickey Mouse was worshipped by the British Film Society.[21] Soviet filmmaker Sergei Eisenstein, also a huge fan of the Disney studio, made certain to visit Walt and his operation when he toured America in the early 1930s.[22] Neither Eisenstein nor Forster was writing from an explicitly homosexual standpoint (neither was totally "open" about his same-sex desires). As previously noted, it is not certain that their conception of their sexual identity would match current definitions of homosexuality, or even each other's. Yet, both took time to analyze the appeal of Disney's work, and both refer to the libidinous or the sensuous in their writings. Consequently, examining their comments with an awareness of their homosexuality can help shed light on how lesbians and gay men could have come to appreciate and enjoy Disney's films during the '30s and '40s.

Forster's attempt to discuss the appeal of Mickey favors the early, pre-1931 persona: "[Mickey] is never sentimental, indeed there is a scandalous element in him which I find most restful."[23] Although "scandalous" could mean a number of possibilities (defiance of authority, a violent nature, etc.), the ties between "scandal" and sexuality were made more explicit in an even earlier discussion from 1928, in which Forster compared Mickey to the Egyptian god Bes, a playful part-lion demon, worshipped for his excessive indulgences in music, sex and childbirth.[24] It seems that Forster enjoyed the pervasive sensuality of the early Mickeys. Forster's interest in the anarchic impulses of fantasy are clearly expressed in an entire chapter devoted to fantasy in his *Aspects of the Novel*. He describes the power of fantasy as "the stuff of daily life . . . tugged and strained in various directions, the earth . . . given little tilts mischievous or pensive."[25] Forster also compares fantasy to the free-for-all of a carnival sideshow: "Some readers pay with delight, it is only for the sideshows that they entered the exhibition, and it is only to them I can now speak."[26]

Forster's linking Mickey Mouse to free-floating meaning and the carnivalesque might explain how some communities of gay men and lesbians read and used Mickey Mouse. As the examples from the opening of this chapter indicate, the name of Disney's first cartoon star had become some sort of slang or code term in at least some circles of the homosexual subculture. Yet, what did it mean exactly, and how did the use of the phrase "Mickey Mouse" in '30s gay culture reflect a gay reading of the character Mickey Mouse?

The use of "Mickey Mouse" as a descriptive phrase is not unique to '30s gay culture. Over the years, the term has become common in American vernacular. *Webster's New Collegiate* Dictionary defines the term as "lacking importance; insignificant, petty."[27] *The Facts on File Dictionary of 20th-Century Allusions* says that "Mickey Mouse has come to mean somebody or something silly or inconsequential."[28] In Peter Blake's architectural analysis of the two United States Disney theme parks, he refers to "Mickey Mouse" as a term usually describing tacky or crass taste.[29] This would be in keeping with the general low regard that American animated cartoons have been held in relation to other art forms, including American live-action feature films. Yet, "Mickey Mouse" connotes a more complex notion than just "bad taste." There is also an aura of oddness or "askewness." In relation to its pejorative use, this aspect is read as unauthentic, hence cheap.

This aspect of the term most readily converts into usage by the homosexual subculture that was emerging in urban centers throughout the United States and Europe. Individuals in this culture were also being defined by the larger society as "off" or "askew," so why not use "Mickey Mouse" as a description, especially since it referred back specifically to a character who was a star across the world? In its own way, lesbian/gay use of "Mickey Mouse" might have been analogous to the '90s use of "queer," reappropriating and highlighting the positive aspects of the term. This would be especially true for lesbians, reworking the slang term "mouse," which referred to female genitalia, and celebrating the "oddness" of their sexuality. This use of mass media as a type of code was common during this period in homosexual culture and involved reshaping iconography from the hegemonic culture in a humorous, slightly parodic fashion in order to facilitate communication within gay communities under the ever-present eye of the heterosexual hegemony.

But, if Mickey Mouse's name was being used as a code term by various homosexuals, how does this reflect on the character? Mickey might have been an upstart and a troublemaker before the enforcement of the Production Code turned him into the iconic mouse-next-door that remains to this day, but what was there in him that could be appreciated as "queer"? The answer might be found in Soviet film director Sergei Eisenstein's attempts to analyze why he enjoyed the "oddness" and "absurdity" that occurred within Disney's films.

Eisenstein began writing on Disney as part of a larger (and never completed work) meant to examine how "the affectiveness of a work of art is built upon the fact that there takes place in it a dual process: an impetuous progressive rise along the lines of the highest conceptual steps of consciousness and a simultaneous enetration [sic] by means of the structure of the form into the layers of profoundest sensuous thinking."[30] Eisenstein planned to examine how the collisional dialectic between the conceptual and the sensuous worked in practice by analyzing the work of Griffith, Chaplin—and Disney. In notes and preliminary drafts, Eisenstein continually focused attention on the metamorphoses and juxtapositions that occurred in Disney's animation. In the Silly Symphony *Merbabies* (1938), he describes how "a striped fish in a cage is transformed into a tiger and roars with the voice of a lion or panther. Octopuses turn into elephants. A fish—into a donkey. A departure from one's self from once and forever prescribed norms of nomenclature, form and behavior. Here it's overt. In the open. And, of course, in comic form."[31] Although differing from Forster's specific focus on Mickey's rambunctiousness, Eisenstein's delight in watching objects transmogrifying in shape and substance and then used for purposes other than intended is extremely complementary to Forster's appreciation of Disney. While Eisenstein is more interested in the dialectical collision created by such odd juxtapositions than Forster is, both delight in the "askewness" or "queerness" that homosexuals often found somehow kindred to their lives.[32] Eisenstein writes, "here we have a being of definite form, a being which has attained a definite appearance and which *behaves* like the primal protoplasm, not yet possessing a 'stable' form, but capable of assuming any form and which, skipping along the rungs of the evolutionary ladder, attached itself to any and all forms of animal existence.—Why is this so attractive?"[33] He goes on to posit that Americans (and all individuals suffering under capitalism) are soothed and reinvigorated by witnessing in Disney's films a liberty and freedom from use-value pigeonholing. Of course, this neglects to explain Eisenstein's *own* attraction to these films, or what other absolutes or prescribed norms of behavior made *him* so value the freedom unleashed by such metamorphoses.

Metamorphosis was not some new technique that the Disney studio had invented or discovered. Far from it, metamorphosis had been one of the founding conceptions of animation, beginning with early French animator Emile Cohl.[34] Shape shifting and the like, for either fantastic or comic effect, is common in animating figures. Such transmogrification is one of the advantages of working in animation rather than in live action; not being grounded in the actual physicality of a live being, animated figures are capable of transforming at the whim of the animator.

Disney's unique mark on the tradition of metamorphosis in animation is tied directly into his development of character animation. While animators like Emile Cohl turned any object into any other object at their discretion, Disney's early silent films show their most promise when inanimate objects become humanized. Rather than specifically becoming human, the objects retain their same properties but begin to move and react as if they were human. Church steeples duck to avoid low flying planes, steam shovels seem to eagerly "eat up" gravel, etc. Through clever movements and body stances, viewers could intuit emotions from these objects—the early stages of character animation. (One of the studio's early exercises in drawing character was for animators to draw a half-full flour sack in a variety of moods—happy, sad, angry, scared—to practice poses.) Eisenstein describes examples from early Mickey Mouse cartoons: "There's the steamboat that folds logs like pastries; hot dogs whose skins are pulled down and are spanked; there are piano keys which bite the pianist like teeth, and much, much more."[35]

The example of hot dogs being spanked highlights the introduction of the erotic that occurred with such anthropomorphizing. As inanimate objects began to move like human beings, they also seemed to have erogenous zones. *The Whoopee Party* (1930) was a Mickey Mouse cartoon made during the shift in Mickey's character towards respectability. Yet, the animation of household props reintroduces the sexual energy that had been quelled within Mickey. As the party gets increasingly frenetic, the furniture begins to sway to the music. First, the piano stool under Minnie begins to move under her rear end, much to her initial shock. Soon, lamps and chairs are dancing in time. One lamp uses its shade as a skirt, constantly lifting it up in its own version of the "can-can" to show its "butt." A hat rack and a chair dance together, and each is gendered by the animation: the hat rack with its man's bowler and cane, the chair with its hourglass back and "bustle" seat. Finally, the bed gets up and starts to shimmy—and, depending on where one identifies the "head" of the now humanized object, the bed's pillows act as either a pair of breasts or its behind.

While the tradition of metamorphosis "queers" all objects in animation, Disney's anthropomorphizing of inanimate objects more specifically sexualizes everything. By equating specific props with specific body parts and often gendering the objects, it becomes simple to fetishize previously inconsequential objects. In the conclusion of the Silly Symphony *The Cookie Carnival* (1935), a jello mold woman starts shimmying out of control, turning a gelatinous dish into a "cooch show." For individuals who were attracted to "nonprescribed" objects of desire, such a reveling in polymorphous perversity would have an appeal.

The Disney studio's philosophy of the "illusion of life" emerged out of the tradition of metamorphosis as a consequence of this anthropomorphizing but eventually seemed to be at odds with the earlier concept. Rather than figures that changed shape at the slightest provocation, the "illusion of life" style attempted to keep bodies and objects under control. Yet, even during the height of Disney's "illusion of life," the "metamorphosis" tradition was never completely supplanted. Various characters such as "Johnnie Fedora and Alice Blue Bonnet" in *Make Mine Music* (1946), "Little Toot" in *Melody Time* (1948), *The Little House* (1952) and *Susie, the Little Blue Coupe* (1952) carried on the motif of humanizing inanimate objects. The short subject *Noah's Ark* (1959) literally took common household items (pipe cleaners, thread spools, etc.) and turned them into a menagerie of animals through stop motion animation.

As one might expect from the prevalence of anal humor found in Disney's films, many of the anthropomorphized objects in these films inevitably display some sort of buttocks. How to analyze why Walt enjoyed shots of baby derrieres or a character being paddled so much that even chairs, cars and tugboats were given rears to be spanked, prodded or wiggled goes beyond the capability of this research. Some have tried to tie this obsession with the anus to the anality of Walt's personality (his obsessive need for control and order).[36] While an interesting idea, this theory pushes at the realm of possible analysis. What is important to note, though, is that the constant display of behinds—and the fetishization of certain objects that seemed to "have" rear ends—would also appeal to a number of gay men and fits in with Forster's and Eisenstein's seeming appreciation of the "inappropriateness" in Disney's work.

Oftentimes human buttocks and inanimate "rears" shared screen or narrative space in these films. Many of the Silly Symphonies contain shots of toys that poke each other from behind, while the rosy dimpled butt cheeks of the children playing with the toys are exposed because the backs of their Dr. Denton's pajamas have come undone. (The children's butt shots reached their apex in the Pastoral Symphony section of *Fantasia,* ending with the behinds of two Cupids morphing into a Valentine's Day heart.)

Pinocchio serves as an exemplary text for using both animate and inanimate objects as a source of anal humor. In fact, in the opening fifteen minutes of the feature, this type of humor dominates the narrative. After the opening credits, Jiminy Cricket describes how he came to Geppetto's workshop to get out of the cold. Hopping to the fire, he turns his backside to a hot ember, while narrating, "As I warmed my . . . myself—." Geppetto enters the workshop to finish making his boy puppet, and Jiminy hides himself among the figurines that line the shelves. As he watches Geppetto and his puppet with interest, he unconsciously leans on the bustle of a female figurine and blushes in embarrassment upon realizing what he has done. Having finished the marionette, Geppetto introduces Pinocchio to his animal pets, and the puppet inadvertently kicks Figaro the cat in the behind. In the midst of this impromptu party, a variety of cuckoo clocks announce the hour for bedtime. One of these elaborate clocks shows a mother with a young boy over her knee with his pants down as she spanks him (his cries serve as the cuckoo chime). The dependence on anal humor lessens after this initial onslaught but never completely dissipates. The evil puppet show impresario Stromboli prominently wiggles his fanny as he announces his travel itinerary (particularly when enunciating "Con-stan-tin-opoly"). When Pinocchio and his friend Lampwick turn into "asses" on Pleasure Island, each gets his own butt shot, so that the audience can witness a donkey's tail suddenly protrude through the pants.

The Three Caballeros (1945) displays all these issues in seventy incredible minutes of comedy, chaos and color. As mentioned in chapter 1, the film marks a return to the carnivalesque mood that the Disney studio basically eschewed from its work after 1931. As Donald Duck receives a number of elaborate gifts from his friends in Latin America, the screen veritably explodes with music and design with hardly any concern with narrative coherence. Although the film starts out as yet another "package film" of various short subjects, the film gets increasingly audacious. Things start to come unraveled when Donald watches a film on native birds of South America. A wacky bird called the Araquan leaps off the screen and walks on the light beam of the projector to shake Donald's hand. Later, he moves so erratically he accidentally seems to run right off the film strip itself and has to pull the film back onto the screen.

When Donald opens his second gift, he remeets José Carioca (introduced in Saludos Amigos). From here on in, the film regularly turns quite surreal. On a trip to the town of Baia, the infectious rhythm of the Latin American music sets the entire town—not just the population, but chairs, tables, lampposts, cottages, buildings, and the mountains—to swaying. Animated roosters in cockfight blend into live-action male dancers. José is capable of shrinking, multiplying or transforming himself at whim, and he pulls Donald into such metamorphoses along with him. While watching a colorfully surreal abstract representation of the optical soundtrack to some Latin music, Donald's body gets sucked in and becomes part of the graphic manipulation. At another point, when Donald tries to unshrink himself, his body gets completely contorted like a twisted balloon.

The manipulation of the body is often associated with gender and sexuality. Both José and Donald also transform themselves at points into women. (José actually multiplies himself into four Carmen Mirandas!) Although throughout the film Donald is chasing after various Latin American women with unbridled ferocity, Donald often seems to forget or get confused. During a frenzied game of "blind-man's-bluff" with some bathing beauties, Donald ends up eagerly embracing José. Although Donald reacts with shock when this happens, he seems to quite enjoy it earlier in the film when José and the Mexican rooster Panchito are shown kissing up Donald's arms while singing "And pals though we may be . . ." This line comes from the title song, which begins, "We're three caballeros, three gay caballeros/They say we are birds of a feather."

In the final major section of the film, sexual desire is specifically tied to the wealth of metamorphosis and surrealism, as Donald goes off into a reverie inspired by the kiss of another live-action woman. In a very Freudian manner, Donald dreams of being a bee hovering over the woman's face, now transformed into the center of an exotic flower. Sexual object choice gets very confused, though, for every time Donald approaches her face to consummate the relationship, his two male buddies erupt out of the flower singing "we're three gay caballeros." At one point during this section, the three male cartoon characters' heads are matched up with the dancing legs of three live-action chorus girls.

The finale to this section shows Donald with the buddies again, repeatedly being struck from behind in a climactic frenzy of action. Donald Duck's behind gains special mention here. Throughout his career, the usual retribution for Donald's childish pranks or quick temper was a good thwack to his feathered posterior. Many of the Duck's cartoons also delight in watching him from the back, the better to see how his butt waddles. Still, the end of *The Three Caballeros* pushes to the limits the amount of abuse that could be sustained on the poor bird's backside, creating a sustained metaphoric representation of anal intercourse. Dressed as a bull in a fight with Panchito, José attaches a string of firecrackers to the bull's tail. As Donald shoots across the screen while the firecrackers explode, he is further accosted by two bottle rockets in the behind that function as daggers in the bullfight. Shooting out of the bull costume he was wearing, the bull takes on a life of its own—the better to gore Donald in the rear. Finally, as fireworks burst all over the place, Donald gets treated to a whirling circle of a fireworks that buzzes up his butt before reuniting with his two friends in one last hug of friendship.

In its use of anarchy, metamorphosis, sexual aggressiveness and "butt" humor, *The Three Caballeros* stands out as an example for everything that Forster and Eisenstein found fascinating in Disney. Forster's invocation of the trickster god Bes' gender ambiguity and playful anarchy is embodied by Donald's sexual frenzy being directed everywhere at once (and Donald's potential as both penetrator and penetrated). Eisenstein's fascination with how metamorphosis undermines the solidity and security of identities is embodied by the consistent manipulation of the characters' bodies. While it would be difficult to state that the film is squarely and unequivocally "homosexual," the chaos and carnivalesque nature of the film also makes it equally difficult to state that it is resolutely "heterosexual." In keeping with Forster's and Eisenstein's appreciation of Disney, what is valuable about *The Three Caballeros* is exactly its *queerness*.

FAIRY TALES: HOMOSEXUAL CULTURE AND FANTASY

The Disney *oeuvre* rationalized its retention of metamorphosis and anthropomorphization in its animation through a recurrent invocation of the world of fantasy. While almost every animator at some point has turned towards the world of make-believe, Disney consciously cornered the market on producing animated versions of fairy tales—so much so that literary critics at times have complained that Disney's version of certain fairy tales have completely supplanted the literary texts from which the films were derived.[37] Bruno Bettelheim, in *The Uses of Enchantment*, his famous study of the meaning of fairy tales, complains that "most children now meet fairy tales only in prettified and simplified versions which subdue their meaning and rob them of all deeper significance."[38] Yet, I would argue that, to use Bettelheim's own words, even Disneyfied fairy tales are "a major agent of socialization" and "intimate that a rewarding, good life is within one's reach despite adversity—but only if one does not shy away from the hazardous struggles without which one can never achieve true identity."[39]

Homosexual culture (particularly gay male culture) has long held a fascination with fantasy. The close association of gay men to the world of fantasy has contributed to some of the most common epithets for homosexuals in Western culture: "fairy," "queen" and "princess." Michael

Bronski, elaborating on what constitutes a "gay sensibility," stresses the importance of imagination to this sensibility: "Imagination is especially threatening to a culture that repressively and rigidly defines gender roles . . . because it can provide an alternative vision to the 'real' world."[40] Hence, fantasy contains a possibile critique of dominant society, as well as a picturing of an alternative. With self-identified lesbians and gay men living every day as an alternative to dominant culture, ties to fantasy seem logical.

Although not necessarily evoking a world of polymorphous perversity, fantasy is often described as a method of escape from the trials and tribulations of everyday reality. Living in a society that has outlawed homosexual desire, categorized it as a medical disease, labeled it as a sin against God and allowed (and often encouraged) violent retribution against homosexuals, homosexual culture has unsurprisingly embraced the potential for escape that fantasy and fairy tales provide. Heroes or heroines rise above their station—rewarded for all their hardship and vilification by finding Prince Charming and/or being crowned as royalty. Others leave their drab and shabby existence and find a fascinating other world in which anything is possible. This second scenario is the basis for one of the key texts in homosexual culture, the film version of Frank L. Baum's *The Wizard of Oz* (1939). In the narrative, an underappreciated adolescent girl in the barren Midwest is whisked away to a fabulous land filled with color and spectacle where she finds friends who value her more than her biological family seem to do. Although Dorothy, the main character, consistently declares her desire to "go home," almost every viewer (gay or otherwise) enjoys the film not for the sepia-toned representation of Kansas but for its breathtaking creation of a three-strip Technicolored Oz.

Disney's films often evoke this narrative of fantastic worlds. Walt himself was a large fan of Lewis Carroll's *Alice's Adventures in Wonderland* and *Alice Through the Looking Glass*, which Baum's works on Oz often resemble. Walt's first series were the "Alice Comedies"; a Mickey cartoon has the mouse go *Through the Mirror* (1936); an animated feature based on the stories was in planning during the 1930s and was finally made in 1951. After completing the film, the studio's next animated feature went from Carroll's Wonderland to homosexual author J. M. Barrie's Neverland in *Peter Pan* (1953). Yet, even without explicitly invoking Carroll's or Barrie's texts, Disney's animation often creates an environment similar to Wonderland or Neverland. The Silly Symphonies are filled with examples of plants' coming to life (*Flowers and Trees* [1932]), musical instruments' ruling kingdoms (*Music Land* [1936]), china shop figurines' throwing parties (*The China Shop* [1934]), and an insect Harlem nightclub where they "jitterbug" for hours (*Woodland Cafe* [1937]). Although all of these cartoons contain a narrative of heterosexual courtship (as mentioned in chapter 1), it is quite possible to ignore or skip over the hoary clichés of the romance and focus on the inventiveness and originality of the imagined world. Much as gay subjects often ignore Dorothy's reaffirmation of home life on the farm in favor of Oz's Technicolor dazzle, they can ignore the predictable "straight" romance in favor of an environment that seems to hold out a promise of radical possibilities.

Another narrative strand in Disney's films that would have a great appeal to homosexual subjects is the tale of the "outsider." Throughout the studio's history, Disney has consistently returned to stories about characters who don't "fit in" to society. Unlike the heroines of Carroll and Baum, these characters do not find another world to escape to and must confront their ostracization. Rebuffed by the upholders of what is normal and decent, these "rejects" eventually find acceptance and happiness by finding a use for those aspects of themselves that were originally thought to be deficient or "abnormal." Hans Christian Andersen, now recognized as homosexual himself, provided what is probably the archetypal version of the story, "The Ugly Duckling," which was filmed by Disney twice—in 1930 and again in 1939. Other versions of this type of story can be found in *Morris, the Midget Moose* (1950), *Lambert, the Sheepish Lion* (1952), *Goliath II* (1960), and the very popular feature film *Dumbo* (1941).

There are two Disney texts about outsiders, though, that are more easily read as specifically "gay" texts and delightfully affirming of "otherness." The first of these is the Oscar-winning short *Ferdinand the Bull* (1937). With backgrounds depicting a constantly sunny Spain, the cartoon tells the story of a young bull who is content to spend his life "just sitting quietly and smelling the flowers" rather than pursuing other more conventionally masculine pursuits. While Ferdinand is never shown having sexual interest in another bull, the character's quiet affection for flowers associates him with images of homosexuals then current in American culture. In the 1920s and '30s, gay men were frequently referred to as "pansies" or "buttercups," and certain flowers, such as green carnations, had been secret symbols of one's sexual interests since the days of Oscar Wilde.

Interestingly, the short never seems to suggest that Ferdinand is somehow depraved or deserving of contempt for his desires. Although his mother wants to know why he doesn't want to run and leap and butt heads like all the other young bulls, she accepts her son's "lifestyle" without much second thought. Ferdinand is never shown racked with guilt over his implied homosexuality or worried about what others may think of him. On the contrary, the cartoon continually shows close-ups of him batting his long eyelashes and sighing slowly and contentedly. Neither the narrator nor the visual design of the cartoon ever judge Ferdinand as somehow wrong in his choice. Rather, there is a bemused acceptance and delight in Ferdinand's attitude.

The film becomes even more intriguing when Ferdinand is taken to the Madrid bullring in the mistaken belief that he is a ferocious warrior. In yet another example of butt humor, Ferdinand's manic reaction to sitting on top of a bee creates this impression on the talent scouts. The toreadors are all caricatures of Disney animators, and the matador is a winking parody of Walt himself. "Walt the matador" has an angry fit when Ferdinand would rather smell the bouquet that some senorita threw into the ring than fight a "manly" fight. Finally, even "Walt's" masculinity is challenged by the bull when in frustration he tears his shirt open, revealing a flower tattoo on his chest which Ferdinand excitedly licks. As Walt, the toreadors and the entire crowd curse, boo and howl, Ferdinand is carted back from whence he came. The cartoon ends with a long shot of Ferdinand back under his tree on his sunny hill, smelling the flowers. He turns and offers us one last drowsy smile, showing that none of this has affected his self-worth in the slightest . . . and the film irises out to black.

This delight and acceptance of an effeminate male reoccurs in *The Reluctant Dragon* (1941). If anything, the effeminacy of the Reluctant Dragon in the title segment of the anthology film is even more pronounced than Ferdinand's. Like the bull, the dragon sports long emotive eyelashes and contains not an aggressive bone in his body, with the dragon prancing and pirouetting throughout the story. Yet, unlike the bull, the dragon has a voice—a high-pitched masculine voice with the accent of an English dandy. In fact, the dragon's long black fluffy ears often droop around the sides of his face in an approximation of *the* English dandy Oscar Wilde. Rather than fight battles with knights, this dragon wants to play music, hold high tea and write poetry. At one point, the dragon is specifically referred to as a "punk poet," at a time when the common slang definition for "punk" was "homosexual male." (This phrase is repeated about five times in one fifteen second period of the film.) One of his poems, "Ode to an Upside-Down Cake," is fraught with double entendre about sexual reversal:

> Sweet little upside down cake, cares and woes—you got 'em
> Poor little upside-down cake, your top is on your bottom.
> Alas, little upside-down cake, your troubles never stop.
> Because, little upside-down cake, your bottom's on your top!

A young lad who fancies himself an expert on knights and dragons warns the dragon that a knight has been hired by the town, thinking that the dragon is as ferocious as the legends tell, but both the lad and the dragon are surprised to find that the knight, Sir Giles, is as much a tea lover and poetry writer as the dragon is. The cartoon introduces both figures similarly—caught taking baths by the lad, and their figures contrasting sharply with the manly heroic illustrations contained in the lad's book.

Sir Giles and the dragon agree to stage a mock battle in order to please the town. The battle consists of hiding in caves or in smoke and dust—where the two hold tea and, at one point, waltz with each other, while yelping and howling for the benefit of the audience. Although the town has ostensibly hired the knight to kill the dragon, the townspeople watching the battle root for both sides as if it were a sporting event. When the dragon pretends to be killed, it seems that the town is in on the ruse. The story ends with the narrator intoning, "Having reformed the dragon, the satisfied villagers welcomed him into society," as the film shows the dragon being toasted to by the town.

There is no mistaking how the film makes fun of the dragon's mincing manner and prissy pretensions. Yet, the film also makes it quite clear that the dragon does not believe in fighting, and the film doesn't specifically make fun of him for that. Made just before the Japanese attacked Pearl Harbor, many in the United States were also trying to keep from fighting and, consequently, would not quickly dismiss the dragon's strongly held beliefs. Just as in Ferdinand the Bull, The Reluctant Dragon presents an easily read gay character under the guise of fantasy and shows characters accepting him as he is.

PRINCESS OR EVIL QUEEN? CAMPING
GENDER IDENTITY IN DISNEY

Although fantasy has held a place in gay culture for some time, the emphasis on the use of fantasy poses some potential problems. Medical texts of the twentieth century, particularly psychiatric texts patterned after Freud's writings on the subject, often defined homosexuality as a "phase" in normal human development that mentally healthy individuals would grow out of after a certain period in childhood.[41] According to these texts, those that remained exclusively homosexual showed "evidence of immature sexuality and either arrested psychological development or regression."[42] As early as the late nineteenth century, Italian criminologist Cesar Lombroso argued that homosexuals were at a lower stage of human development than heterosexuals.[43] Even in the 1970s, psychiatrist Charles Socarides theorized that homosexuality resulted from "massive childhood fears."[44] Although most psychiatrists now reject this notion (the American Psychiatric Association removed homosexuality from its official list of mental diseases in 1973), the recurrent use of fairy tales or fantasy—kids' stuff—in homosexual culture might reinforce for some this conception of homosexuals as "undeveloped" or "regressive."

Yet, this equation of fantasy with childhood interest oversimplifies the relationship that gay culture has with fantasy. Just as Mickey Mouse cartoons were enjoyed on different levels by children and by the artistic elite, so, too, is it possible to differentiate how children engage with fantasy and how adult homosexuals use fantasy. Although Bruno Bettelheim spends most of *The Uses of Enchantment* "explaining" what various stories "really" mean, Bettelheim acknowledges in his introduction that

> as with all great art, the fairy tale's deepest meaning will be different for each person, and different for the same person at various moments in his [sic] life. The child will extract different meaning from the same fairy tale, depending on his interests and needs of the moment. When given the chance, he will return to the same tale when he is ready to enlarge on old meanings, or replace them with new ones.[45]

This is not to say that adult homosexuals share nothing in common with how children enjoy fantasy. *Most* adults return to fantasy or fairy tales at some point "to master . . . psychological problems . . . overcoming narcissistic disappointments . . . becoming able to relinquish childhood dependencies; gaining a feeling of selfhood and of self-worth."[46] Society has conditioned homosexuals to conceive of themselves as "bad objects." Consequently, many homosexual individuals battle feelings of self-hatred and insecurity. The turn to fantasies that bolster one's self-image as a defense against this situation makes good sense and is not an indication of further proof of "arrested development."

But lesbians and gay men also come to fantasy with a knowledge that children, for the most part, have not acquired. At the same time that gay individuals revel in the affirmations and opened possibilities that fantasy creates, there is also an awareness and acceptance of the impossibility of fantasy—as well as the absurdity of it all. Cassandra Amesley's concept of "double reading," although written in regard to media fandom in general, also applies to a lesbian or gay subject position. Amesley writes that a reader can "maintain and understand two divergent points of view at once, and use them to inform each other. In this way identification and distanciation may occur simultaneously."[47] In regards to lesbian/gay use of fantasy, an irony exists—a simultaneous indulgence in and distancing from the work being engaged—which is far more developed than the normal child's response. A lesbian/gay individual can sit through *Snow White* and dream of being taken away from a drab life to a castle on a hill, but s/he can also enjoy the absurdity of Snow White's grotesquely warbling contralto. Michael Bronski sees such a double reading in Barrie's *Peter Pan*. While conventionally thought of as a children's story, Bronski describes it as "a deeply disturbing meditation on the impossible desire for flight . . . not so much a fantasy of escape as it is a clear-eyed exposure of escape's impossibility."[48] The original 1904 play ends with Peter alone, and Barrie adds in the stage directions, "It has something to do with the riddle of his being. If he could get the hang of the thing his cry might become 'To live would be an awfully big adventure!' but he can never quite get the hang of it, and so no one is as gay as he."[49]

Fantasy often walks hand in hand with camp, one of the cornerstones of gay culture. Susan Sontag declared in her influential article "Notes on 'Camp'" that camp was "a way of looking at things . . . a quality discoverable in objects and the behavior of persons."[50] Most importantly for this discussion, Sontag observes that "camp sees everything in quotation marks . . . to perceive Camp in objects and persons is to understand Being-as-Playing-a-Role."[51] Taking from this, but expressly tying "camp" to the homosexual subculture (which Sontag downplays in her analysis), Jack Babuscio asserts that "camp, by focusing on the outward appearances of role, implies that roles, and in particular, sex roles, are superficial—a matter of style."[52] Babuscio and others describe how camp was used as a communication device within homosexual culture, as well as a weapon to deconstruct the heterosexual essentialism of the dominant culture.

Gay camp appreciation of Disney usually centers specifically on "Being-as-Playing-a-Role," since animation renders drawings that impersonate gender and sexuality. Recent scholarly work on animation has begun to discuss how animation creates its "illusion of life" through the illusion of movement. Characters reveal their personality through the rhythm of their walk or the way they manipulate their facial expression. "Animation thus poses the very questions of life itself, movement itself and their relation . . . suggesting that the two . . . can only be thought through each other."[53] In this exploration of the importance of motion in the creation of identity, recent animation theory ties directly into current social constructionist arguments about sexual identity, that all genders and sexualities (not just homosexuality) are learned and performed. Eve Sedgwick's "universalizing" view of sexuality defines it "as an issue of continuing, determinative importance in the lives of people across the spectrum of sexualities."[54] Sedgwick argues from a "universalizing" standpoint, which forces not only homosexuality to come to terms with its construction but heterosexuality as well. If so, all renditions of heterosexuality in animated films are just as performative as any rendition of homosexuality. Mickey and Minnie's repeated courtship rituals are carefully enacted performances of heterosexuality as much as the Reluctant Dragon's sissified flouncings are portrayals of homosexuality.

With the tradition of metamorphosis in mind, the surface quality of Mickey Mouse's gender suggests a deeper reason why certain gay and lesbian communities invoked his name as a code word. His masculine identity was accepted mainly because of his name. But, if one decided to think about it, a viewer could easily problematize Mickey's gender. First, Mickey's voice was not a deep "manly" baritone but a high-pitched falsetto (and his voice for the first eighteen years would be supplied by Walt Disney himself!). If this wasn't enough, it didn't take much to see that there weren't very many differences between Mickey and his girlfriend Minnie. The beauty of Mickey's design was its simplicity, all circles and tubes. But Minnie was the *same* design. All animators did was put Mickey in pumps with a polka-dot skirt and three long eyelashes on each eye, and presto!—he was now a she. The obvious similarities between the two expose gender considerations as an issue of costume, revealing "masculinity" and "femininity" as somehow "Mickey Mouse." Furthermore, these animals are never drawn with sexual organs. Many never wear clothing, and those that do tend to wear only tops (such as Donald Duck and his nephews). Yet, the sexual organs of the animals are not visible. Granted, such practices were instituted to keep parents and censors happy, but without these signifiers, the performativity of gender in animation is made even more acute. These cartoons must rely on voices and attire to assign gender.

Moving even farther, Mickey and most of his friends (excepting Pluto) are "in drag" as human beings. Although much early animation featured human characters such as Mutt and Jeff, Bobby Bumps or the Katzenjammer Kids, by the early 1920s, many of the stars of various cartoon series were anthropomorphized animals. (Even Betty Boop began her career as a humanized dog, complete with long floppy ears.) From Felix the Cat to Mickey Mouse and his friends to the menagerie of characters created at Warner Bros., these animals only rarely referred to the characteristics of their supposed species, acting instead as human. A mouse as large as Mickey or Minnie (standing taller than their dog Pluto) would belong in the Guiness Book of Records. Mickey and Minnie also walk upright rather than on all fours. Consequently, to see Mickey is to see a *drawing* of a *gender-neutral mouse* acting like a *human male*. The levels of impersonation reach the sublime, to the point where boundaries seem impossible to nail down. This breakdown of categories is precisely what Sedgwick and others have attempted to promote through the reinvestment in the term "queer."

Judith Butler's deconstruction of the categories of identity in *Gender Trouble* proposes as an answer to the material oppression of sexuality not some imagined overthrow of the system or impossible "return" to a pre-history that is itself a construction.[55] Rather, Butler sees how the multiple discourses occurring within culture (which attempt to regulate, prohibit and generate certain hegemonic conceptions) often overlap, complicate and contradict each other. Hence, possibilities for resistance occur when the complications of these multiple discourses are revealed. The material discourses of power that define identity are subverted by playing them out in such a manner that the various levels reach absurd and parodic extremes, exposing the constructedness of gender and sexuality. I would argue that a perfect instance of multiple discourses swirling within one text, exposing the constructedness of gender and sexuality through parodic redeployment is the animated cartoon. Animation has conventionally been used for creating comic narratives, holding anything and everything up to the light of surreal ridicule, including gender and sexuality. Consequently, animation is usually ripe for camp reading.

Unlike the anarchic humor and celebration of metamorphosis that reigned at other studios, the Disney studio tried to present "believable" humans and animals making "natural" movements. The "illusion of life" style would seem to solidify character identity, quell the animation tradition of identity as simply a role or costume and restrict the possibilities of a camp reading. The move toward an "illusion of life" focused specifically on drawing the human body—often the female body. In an attempt at greater realism, rotoscoping or tracing of actual human figures was employed in the drawing of Snow White and all of her successors—the Blue Fairy, Cinderella, Alice, Wendy, the Princess Aurora, Ariel, Belle, Jasmine.

Yet, rotoscoping was always "improved" upon to give the character more "appeal," a term Disney animators Frank Thomas and Ollie Johnston list as one of the "principles of animation" that the studio developed to create the "illusion of life."[56] They contend that "your eye is drawn to the figure that has appeal, and, once there, it is held while you appreciate what you are seeing."[57] With this definition in mind, the concept of "appeal" emphasizes (à la Laura Mulvey) the process of fetishization at work in many instances when the female form is animated in Disney films.[58] Grim Natwick's rendition of Betty Boop for the Flieschers, and later his work at Disney drawing Snow White, emphasize heads larger than the scale of the rest of the bodies and smaller than normal torsos. As Natwick himself admitted, "Snow White was really only about five heads high. (A realistic human form is usually six). . . . She was not actually that real."[59] The concern with fetishistic "appeal" at the studio becomes more apparent when one remembers the anecdote in which Walt Disney felt more confident with the decision to make *Snow White* after the success of the character of Jenny Wren in the short *Who Killed Cock Robin?* (1935), a caricature of Mae West.

With its mixture of "appeal" and "realism," Disney's tradition of animated human forms consistently creates performances of gender.[60]

Consequently, a camp reading of these animated texts strongly empha-sizes the "illusion" side of the equation—reveling in the constructed-ness of "life." If anything, the attempt by studio animators to stress the "lifelikeness" of their animation style makes camp readings of Disney all the more enjoyable, because the reading is so contradictory to the supposed intent of the text.[61] These are not men or women but draw-ings configured and filmed to construct an enactment of a man or woman. The fabulously false femininity of Walt Disney's fairy-tale heroines almost screams out for a camp reading, especially when live performers at the theme parks are stuffed into real-life versions of the characters' dresses and outfitted with wigs that have been shellacked into duplicating the hair styles in the cartoons. Frank Browning, in *The Culture of Desire: Paradox and Perversity in Gay Lives Today,* describes Ggreg Taylor, a member of the activist group Boys with Arms Akimbo, visiting Disneyland:

> Resplendent in his white quilted leisure suit and blue mirror plat-forms—an up-to-date parody of the now-thrift-shop-available seven-ties—Ggreg walks up to Alice. The shameless Orange County sun bounces off her soft golden tresses, illuminates her pleated, puff-shouldered blouse. Beside her stands Cinderella, whose golden hair is arranged in a tight bun, not a single strand dangling loose.
>
> "Are you from Wonderland?" Alice asks Ggreg. . . .
>
> "N-o-o-h," Ggreg answers with a verbal dip. "I'm from San Fran-cisco. Can't you tell?"
>
> "Well, we simply must talk later," Alice answers, floating off across the asphalt with Cinderella. . . .
>
> "Sometimes it's hard to tell who's really queer," Ggreg observes, adjusting his leather biker's cap.[62]

A female employee trying to glide her arms and legs smoothly and gracefully overemphasizes the masquerade of gender identity. For all intents and purposes, these are women in female drag.

Usually, the most obvious impersonations of gender in Disney's an-imated features are the villains—and gay culture seems to have a spe-cial fondness for Disney villainy. In fact, a whole subculture of Disney fandom has grown up over Disney's villains and villainesses. In the 1990s, stores opened within the Disney theme parks devoted exclu-sively to "villain merchandise." Although the fandom is too amorphous and unorganized to gain data about percentages, the number of gay men who dress in drag as Disney villains for costume parties or for Halloween testifies to the attraction that these characters have in gay culture.

Tied into camp, much of recent gay and lesbian studies has focused on drag culture. Subjects enact female or leather (or whatever) personae, becoming subject and object simultaneously, consciously "performing" subjectivity. Consequently, drag embodies Mary Ann Doane's theory of "masquerade" in which subjects "put on" different personae rather than having one stable subject position.[63] Drag is thus easily equated with the notion of simultaneous identification and distanciation posited by Amesley's definition of "double reading." Judith Butler describes the gay culture of drag as that which "constitutes the mundane way in which genders are appropriated, theatricalized, worn and done: it implies that all gendering is a kind of impersonation and approximation . . . gender is a performance that produces the illusion of an inner sex or essence or psychic gender core."[64]

The fascination that many gay men have with Disney villains is precisely over how they theatrically perform their gender roles, to the point where the "naturalness" of their gender can be called into question. Although the vengeful Queen in *Snow White* and the evil sorceress Maleficent in *Sleeping Beauty* (1959) are ostensibly gendered female, they both wear clothing that completely covers almost every inch of their bodies, including cowls or hoods that cover their heads. Only the hands and face are exposed, leaving the rest of the body cloaked. Their faces both have highly defined features (etched cheekbones, thin sharp noses, strongly set jaws) in contrast to the softer designs of the heroines, and they also seem to have access to makeup, especially mascara and eye shadow. Although Cruella de Vil in *101 Dalmatians* (1961) is not clothed like these two characters, her facial design fits perfectly into this description. In other words, these villainesses look like drag queens. Jon Adams, in his reading of Disney villains as queer figures, writes:

> Never does the storyline lead the viewer to believe that Cruella is actually a man in drag. However, her masculine attributes could not be more exaggerated, as Leonard Maltin notes in his book *The Disney Films*. Maltin states that Cruella "revels in the stylistic exaggeration of reality" with a "bony and angular" face. He calls her design a "caricature." But a caricature of what? A stylistic exaggeration of what real-

ity? Certainly not the ideal of femininity. Perfectly flat-chested, Cruella struts around in two-tone hair, drives a mile long convertible like a bat out of hell. Her voice, wonderfully performed by Betty Lou Gerson, is one of booming tones and terrific accent as she rolls through "Anita Dahlings" and "Mahvelous, Mahvelous'" that put Billy Crystal's to shame.[65]

Traditionally, Disney's animated villains move and speak with enormous style and panache—so much so that they often "steal" the scenes from the supposed leading characters in the stories. In this way, they more overtly "overperform" their gender roles and readily become the targets of camp readings. Like the evil Queen in *Snow White* and the wicked stepmother in *Cinderella* before her, Maleficent moves with grand sweeps of her cape and long-flowing gown, and strikes magnificent "diva"-like poses. It should also be mentioned that all her movements and poses are timed to the highly emotive melodies and rhythms of Tchaikowsky's version of *Sleeping Beauty*—a homosexual composer of the "romantic" school. She also gets a number of well-placed pithy lines of dialogue. She makes a stunning entrance into the celebration of Aurora's birth, then regards the royal pageant as if it were a soiree at the Hotel Algonquin in New York City. "Well, quite a glittering assemblage, King Stephan," she observes coldly. "Royalty, nobility, the gentry, and . . . ," she says, pausing to notice the three "good" fairies before adding with a low throaty chuckle, "Oh, how quaint—even the rabble."

Cruella de Vil similarly sweeps into every scene like a grand dame making a stage entrance for an enthusiastic crowd. Constantly carrying an absurdly long cigarette holder, she uses it repeatedly to further overemphasize every gesture and inflection. No movement or line of dialogue is subtle or underplayed. Instead, her every moment is "played to the cheap seats." Whether trying to write out a check for the Dalmatian puppies or driving her roadster down a mountain road, Cruella overdoes everything. All these inflections seem to be attempts by the character to show her astounding chic and cultured femininity. Yet, in her attempts to be the epitome of feminine glamour (which is why she wants the Dalmatian coat that spurs the narrative), she consistently and quite hilariously points out the concept of gender-as-role-playing.

As described in chapter 1, Disney's films increasingly emphasized heterosexual courtship as the studio moved more heavily into narrative and character animation. Fairy tales like "Snow White," "Cinderella" and "Sleeping Beauty" lent themselves quite easily to this celebration and promotion of heterosexuality. Consequently, on a more basic level, gay culture's appreciation of Disney villains is a humorous cheering on of those forces within the narrative that disrupt and frustrate heterosexuality's dominance. *Sleeping Beauty's* Maleficent actively works to spoil two generations of heterosexual coupling. The film begins with the convention of a book opening to announce "Once upon a time. . . ." During this overtly narrated introduction, strong emphasis is placed on procreation, particularly on the king and queen's difficulties in having a child. The story proper begins with the countrywide celebration of the birth of the princess Aurora. When Maleficent arrives, she is informed quite bluntly that she is "not wanted." Maleficent retaliates by placing a death sentence on the child to be fulfilled on her sixteenth birthday. In this way, she attempts to take away the procreative success of the king and queen and kill the princess just at the moment when she herself would be about to explore heterosexual courtship.

Of course, villains regularly disrupt and frustrate heterosexual courtship in conventional Hollywood narrative. But usually, the villain attempts to break up the hero and heroine because he desires the girl for himself (or, conversely, the villainess wants the hero for herself). This rarely occurs with Disney's villains. In fact, there are often a number of signifiers that make it easier for homosexual viewers to read the villains not only as "anti-couple" but specifically as "queer" figures. Their attempts to break up the couple is never based upon a desire to "steal" a partner. The evil Queen is jealous of Snow White's beauty, not because the Queen loves Prince Charming herself. Maleficent causes chaos throughout the land seemingly because of her ostracization from Aurora's birth celebration. As one of the "good" fairies describes Maleficent, she "doesn't know anything about love or kindness or helping others. Sometimes I think she's not really happy." Cruella de Vil kidnaps puppies not through some desire to be a mother but because she wants a coat![66]

Although Disney's animated features lean heavily towards female villains, this is not to say that the few male villains do not fit into this paradigm of "queerness." On the contrary, the foppishness of Honest John the fox and Figaro the cat in *Pinocchio* makes them easily read as a gay couple, as Vito Russo did in *The Celluloid Closet*.[67] Another possible gay couple would be Smee and Captain Hook in *Peter Pan*. As with Honest John, Hook attempts to hide his deviant villainy behind the refined airs commonly associated with the English dandy. Voiced by Hans Conreid, Hook speaks and moves floridly, as if every action was high melodrama. He also dresses the part of a dandy: introduced holding two cigars in a long gold cigarette holder, he wears a lavender blouse with ruffles. Later, as he prepares for battle, his companion Smee helps him don a purplish plumed hat and a deep red velvet coat and provides Hook with a lavender handkerchief to stuff in his shirt sleeve. Though cutthroat, the pirates under Hook's command are not above singing about the pleasures of being a pirate while doing minuets and then waving tiny pirate flags while they wiggle their hips in precision like chorus girls.[68]

Smee is constantly at Hook's side, and, although Hook is the gruff maniacal master in the relationship, Smee is obviously the steady emotional rock that keeps Hook balanced. Whenever Hook encounters the crocodile that took his hand, he wails like a banshee for Smee. While Hook battles with Peter, Smee loads up the lifeboat in anticipation of defeat. In a most revelatory scene, Smee advises Hook to hoist anchor and head to sea, because there's "women trouble on the island" and he doesn't want to have anything to do with it.

Both Honest John and Captain Hook are represented as using their cultured dandyism to hide their evil designs, and both are focused on a young boy. Similarly, the tiger Shere Khan in *The Jungle Book* (1967) also moves and speaks in an "overcivilized" manner, yet again with the intention of luring a young boy from "safety."[69] Voiced with exceptional archness by English actor George Sanders, Shere Khan is introduced stalking a young deer, and, when he is interrupted, he merely mutters "Beastly luck." His prospects brighten, though, when he overhears of a "young man cub" who is wandering alone in the jungle. He whispers to himself, "How delightful," and vows to arrange "a rendezvous" with the boy. As he searches through the jungle, he plays the total gentleman—although Kaa the snake bitterly points out, "Who does he think he's fooling?"

Unlike Honest John and Hook, though, Shere Khan does exude serious menace. He is not an underling for a more threatening villain (as Honest John is). Although witty, he is never portrayed as a buffoon (as Hook invariably is). Rather, even the most whimsical of the tiger's lines contains an underlying threat. By 1967, when the film was released, Walt had already had his discussion with the FBI about the possibilities of making educational films to warn children about homosexual pedophiles. While it is impossible to draw direct correlation between this meeting and the villainy of Shere Khan, the character's threat might have some connection to the changes that were beginning to occur in American society—changes that seemed to be drawing the younger generation away from traditional values and morals. When Mowgli tries to escape from having to be brought to civilization, he encounters a beach bum bear, a quartet of Liverpudlian vultures and an African-American orangutan (who resides in an ancient city that plainly needs some urban assistance).[70] Mirroring the breakdown of societal conventions that was occurring during the late 1960s, it is unsurprising, then, to find a predatory male with a clipped British accent more frightening than he had been years before.

SPIN AND MARTY AND JET AND JODIE: GROWING UP GAY WITH DISNEY

Although adult homosexuals are capable of reading Disney texts (and much of "straight" popular culture) through the eyes of "camp" or other doubled positions, this is not to claim that only lesbian and gay male adults appreciate and understand the "queerness" of Disney's work. It is impossible to determine just when an individual begins to self-identify with the term "homosexual." Some claim that they "always" knew, others say they knew they had "those feelings" at an early age, others don't "realize" until fairly late in their adolescence, or even far into adulthood. Whether one subscribes to a strictly biological determinism or a more socially learned causality for sexual identity, an individual's exposure to culture in some fashion shapes how sexuality is conceived and expressed. Young people come into contact with mediated images almost from the moment they are born and use those images to help make sense of the world. Henry Jenkins, in his study of children watching Pee-Wee Herman, describes how "children draw upon . . . characters and situations of popular culture . . . reworking them to satisfy their own needs and desires."[71] Children, in other words, "poach" from culture just like any other group that is marginalized from power.

This is not to say that children rebel against the reading strategy that is expected of them. Jenkins points out that "[children's] play may and often does reinforce parental values."[72] Boys and girls who follow the example of conventionally gendered behavior and hetero-sexual courtship implicitly abide by the norms expressed in most mass media—watching how people kiss each other, how men are por-trayed as aggressively active and how women are portrayed as pa-tient and nurturing. But, as Jenkins goes on to point out, children's play "also contains a countersocial potential; it may be used to ex-press the child's feelings of outrage over the expectations imposed upon him or her by the social formation."[73] Arguably, when proto-queer youth—whether tomboys, sissies or just young boys or girls with crushes on members of the same gender—read mass media to understand these budding feelings, they perfectly embody Jenkins's "countersocial potential."

American children have been regularly exposed to Disney films and television since the early 1930s. Promoted as "family-oriented," parents often emphasize Disney product over most other texts. Chapter 1 described how Disney's output foregrounds the formation of a mid-dle-class heterosexual family as "natural" and "inevitable." Most young viewers would more or less accept this representation of life. Yet, just as adult homosexuals often read Disney texts differently than was expected, it is not surprising to find that proto-queer individuals would do the same—especially as Disney dominated their viewing habits right at the moment when they were attempting to come to grips with recognizing in themselves a "difference" which they might not even have had an ability to name.

Two quick examples should suffice. Renowned underground comic artist R. Crumb and his dysfunctional family are the subject of the hailed documentary *Crumb* (1995). In the film, R. Crumb acknowledges that he began drawing as a child when he collaborated with his brother. His brother loved creating comic books about the adventures of Long John Silver and young Jim from the Disney version of Robert Louis Stevenson's *Treasure Island* (1949), which they had seen as kids. Exam-ples of these early comics constantly emphasize the figure of Jim. To-wards the end of the film, it is revealed that R. Crumb's brother was gay, and that these early comics were an attempt to voice the brother's boy-hood crush/obsession with child actor Bobby Driscoll, who had played Jim in the film.

Another anecdote entails quite specific research into how one of Disney's films affected children's role models. One gay man has re-counted to me how, as a grade-school student, his class was shown

Sleeping Beauty and then questioned on who they identified with. He seems to have known that the researchers were expecting most boys to identify with Prince Philip and most girls to identify with Princess Aurora (Sleeping Beauty), although they figured that some boys would identify with the Princess and some girls would identify with the Prince. Yet, when he responded that he identified with the good (but stubborn and opinionated) fairy Meriwether, the researchers were stunned—so stunned, in fact, that his parents were called in to meet with the researchers to discuss the "oddity" of this child's choice. Even though memory might have enlarged the scope of what this individual could possibly have known or understood as a child, if his parents met with the researchers to discuss his identification with Meriwether, then the researchers themselves were acknowledging the "queer" reading position that this child had.

As this second anecdote points out, it is important to recognize how memory affects and alters experiences. Most evidence of proto-queer adolescents reading Disney through a "lesbian/gay sensibility" comes from self-identified homosexual adults viewing their memories as "evidence" of their future adult lives. Hence, childhood experiences are shaped to fit future results. Still, such shaping should not necessarily discount claims that some young men and women used Disney films and TV shows to explore their budding sexual desires.

When Michael Nava and Robert Dawidoff, the authors of *Created Equal: Why Gay Rights Matter to America,* spoke to a group of employees at the Walt Disney Company in 1994, they chuckled aloud about the importance of "Spin and Marty" in their lives. This comment elicited knowing chuckles from a number of people in the room. Similarly, at one point in Armistead Maupin's *Tales of the City* books, the main gay character Michael (nicknamed Mouse, at least in part because his family is from Orlando, Florida, home of Walt Disney World) commiserates with his lover Jon Fielding about "Spin and Marty":

> "'The Mickey Mouse Club' turned you queer?"
> "Well . . . You either got off on Annette's tits or you didn't. If you did, you were straight. If you didn't, you had only one alternative . . . *Spin and Marty.* God, I used to agonize over that show!"
> "I'd almost forgotten about that."
> "That's because you identified with Spin. Those of us who identified with Marty will never, ever, forget it."[74]

"The Adventures of Spin and Marty" was a continuing serial that was broadcast as part of *The Mickey Mouse Club* television show in 1955. Based on the novel *Martin Markham,* the serial told the story of city-bred Martin Markham's summer at a dude ranch. As the summer progresses, he learns to drop the chip from his shoulder and become "a regular guy"—Marty instead of Martin. The serial increased the role of Spin, another boy at the ranch who most of the kids acknowledge as the most "regular" guy at the Triple R Ranch. The relationship between Spin and Marty develops from guarded antagonism on Marty's part to minor jealousy on Spin's part as Marty learns the ropes (somewhat outshining Spin) to eventual close friendship.

The increased role of Spin makes sense when looking at Marty's persona in the early stages of the narrative. Before Marty even arrives at the Triple R Ranch, the ranch hands discuss him. Logan, the head of the ranch, tells his assistant, Bill Burnette, "I wanted a chance to talk to you about him—but I really don't know myself . . . yet. . . ." When Bill asks what it is that Logan "doesn't know," Logan responds, "Well, he's a little different from the rest of 'em. Might be some sort of a problem for you." It is just at this point that Marty is driven up by his English valet, Perkins. Marty steps out in suit and bow tie with a fedora on his head. When Bill greets him with "Hi, Marty," the boy responds in very precise diction, "Excuse me, sir—but my name is Martin."

Possibly worried that young male viewers would have a hard time identifying with someone so clipped and cultured, Spin was provided as a "butch" alternate figure. A natural athlete and a minor star at the ranch, Spin represents the ideal boy that Martin needs to become. The main narrative focuses on "masculinizing" Marty. In fact, Burnette declares as his mission, "I'll *straighten* that boy out if it takes all summer!" Throughout the early episodes of the serial, veiled references to Marty's "sissy" persona constantly crop up. It is revealed that he is afraid of horses, that (to quote Marty himself) "I don't know much about stuff like Spin there—sports, I mean," and that he has been raised by a stern grandmother with the implication that this is the source of his "problem." (In the 1950s, controlling mother figures were commonly blamed for turning their sons into homosexuals.)

Just like Maupin's character Michael, many adult gay men who were kids during the 1950s *did* strongly identify with Martin's persona and predicament. Since the serial eventually aims to makeover Martin into Marty, the early episodes work to make the viewer feel for Martin, even as the viewer dislikes the airs he puts on. In one dinner sequence, Martin is asked to stand up and introduce himself. As the other boys whisper somewhat audibly words like "drip" and mutter nasty jokes, Martin tries to gain some respect by claiming to play polo. This gambit only works somewhat. One boy comments, "He looks like the kind of guy who plays polo." Spin responds, "Yeah, maybe that's what's wrong with him." And, when Bill confronts Martin privately about the boast, the boy stresses the reason for such a lie: "I just didn't want the guys to think . . ." The rest of the sentence is too overwhelming to be spoken, and the pain and psychological motivation for this sequence probably resonated in the minds of a number of young proto-queer boys.

Amusingly, the attempt to "butch" up the story and shift the focus slightly away from the manners of Martin during the early stages of the narrative causes its own problems—or delights, depending on who's doing the reading. For, with the emphasis on the relationship between Spin and Marty, proto-queer boys were capable of reading a prepubescent romance between the two. The feelings that each character calls up in the other certainly make the relationship more intense than most boy-boy relationships represented in children's media. Throughout the narrative, the two are constantly watching each other. First, Martin envies Spin's natural athleticism and popularity. Although obviously thinking Martin a little odd, Spin unaccountably starts to defend him to the other guys—but always outside of earshot of Martin. When Marty starts to gain confidence on his horse, and win over some of the kids at the ranch, Spin watches with admiration but also a little fear that his position as "star" of the ranch is in jeopardy. At a certain point in the later half of the serial, places are somewhat switched, as Marty rescues a little boy on a runaway horse and Spin injures a horse accidentally while trying to play hero. When Spin falls from his pedastal a bit, Marty feels safe enough to make friendly contact with him at last. After watching Spin in secret for a bit, Marty approaches him saying, "I never thought a guy could make a mess of things like I always do." Marty actually is willing to sacrifice winning a prize at the rodeo just so Spin can win—but Spin calls Marty on his sacrifice and makes him do his best. Both end up winning prizes, and the two are shown at the end of the series lovingly brushing down their horses in adjoining stalls and smiling at each other—obviously having become "fast friends." The intensity of the friendship was made even more explicit in the sequel to the serial. The popularity of "The Adventures of Spin and Marty" necessitated

"The New Adventures of Spin and Marty"—and, this time, the slightly older boys would meet girls from the all-girl dude ranch across the lake. Marty enjoyed the girls' company, and Spin's desire to leave the girls could easily be read as jealousy over the potential competition for Marty's attention.

The focus on male relationships increased in Disney's output during the 1950s, due mainly to an increase in live-action production that tended to emphasize action and adventure rather than fairy-tale fantasy. The success of such live-action productions as *Treasure Island* (1949) and *Old Yeller* (1957), as well as the "Davy Crockett" episodes of the *Disneyland* TV series, spurred further "Boys' Life" stories, stories that often had the potential to fodder the imaginations of proto-queer young men as much as "Spin and Marty" did. Certainly, R. Crumb's brother's fascination with Bobby Driscoll in *Treasure Island* helps support this contention. Films such as *20,000 Leagues Under the Sea* (1954), *Tonka* (1958), *Almost Angels* (1962) and *Savage Sam* (1963) and TV series such as "The Hardy Boys" serial on *The Mickey Mouse Club* and *Zorro* (1957–59) had barely any women at all in the cast. Consequently, the deepest emotional bonds were forged amongst the male characters, often with some startling implications for those who chose to find them. In *Swiss Family Robinson,* for example, Tommy Kirk and James MacArthur play brothers who come upon a young woman disguised as a boy. Both find the boy strangely appealing and have trouble coming to terms with their hormonal reactions until the ruse is revealed.

An even longer sustained reading can be applied to the little-known *The Light in the Forest* (1958) starring James MacArthur as a white boy raised by Indians who is recaptured and must readjust to his new environment. Throughout the film, MacArthur's character rebels by peeling off his confining clothes and running off to wrestle and swim with his male Indian friend. It is only with the stern but loving hand of the Army camp commander (Fess Parker) that the young man begins to revise his attitude. It is an uphill battle, though, as a remarkable sequence in which the commander forces the boy to take a bath is supposed to demonstrate. In the scene, MacArthur sits in a small iron washtub with his knees sticking out, and Parker actually reaches between the boys' legs to get the soap and lather up his chest! Later, as MacArthur's character begins to look up to the commander, the camp holds a dance and one of the activities involves fighting for a prize, which the winner will give to the one he cares for most. MacArthur, of course, wins and immediately hands it to Parker. The rest of the crowd laughs and explains that it is meant for a *girl,* assuming that MacArthur just didn't understand. Such a moment makes it all the more plausible to read the feelings the boy has for the commander as an adolescent proto-queer crush.[75]

This is not to say that Disney had no place for girls in the 1950s. On the contrary, one of the girls in the "Spin and Marty" sequel was played by the biggest star to come out of *The Mickey Mouse Club*—Annette Funicello. Funicello would eventually star in her own serial within the show, called simply "Annette." Just as "Spin and Marty" was supposed to appeal to boys' love of outdoors and playing cowboy, "Annette" followed a number of narrative conventions of the women's film genre— pretty but lower-class female wins over the town and the most popular boy in school by her natural charm and lack of pretension. An emphasis on good manners and looking pretty made for perfect young girl entertainment in mainstream opinion. Yet, just as "Spin and Marty" provided proto-queer boys with a boy-boy romance, it was quite possible for proto-queer girls to read a girl-girl relationship into "Annette."

The character Annette moves to a new town from the country, and her first friend in the new school is a tomboy named Jet. Jet constantly provides the voice of common sense throughout the rest of the serial, giving Annette good advice, helping her fight her battles and sometimes literally getting into fistfights to defend Annette's good name. The chivalry and the downright "butchness" of Jet make it quite easy to read her as a proto-lesbian figure.[76] Jet herself becomes a problem for Annette. The other high school kids, and even Annette's aunt and uncle (with whom she is living), disapprove of Annette's friendship with Jet and tell Annette that she should be with a "better" sort of people. While part of this disapproval is based on class bias (Jet is obviously from a working-class environment), the leap to other conclusions is not so broad. Of course, Annette's uncle admits that he himself was friends with Jet's father "as a youth." This implies that such an attachment is only "a phase" that Annette will outgrow. Yet, when the uncle is played by gay actor Richard Deacon (best known as Mel on TV's *The Dick Van Dyke Show*), the viewer is left to wonder just much of a passing phase this friendship was!

"Annette," working within the conventions of the "women's film" genre, focuses more intently on heterosexual courtship than "Spin and Marty" ever does. This makes it slightly harder to reconcile a lesbian reading into the serial. Annette is matched with high school heartthrob Steve quite early on. Yet, the constant presence of Jet throughout the narrative always complicates and destabilizes things. The hit song from the "Annette" serial wasn't meant to add fuel to this subcultural reading, but when Annette sings the musical lament "How Will I Know My Love?," some proto-queer girls might have had Jet in mind as the answer.

Even though Disney moved increasingly into live-action films and television as the years went on, the studio's output still stressed the fantastic. In the live-action comedies of the late 1950s and early 1960s, this fantastic often focused on the human body—people flying, bouncing, transforming, shrinking, growing, etc. For pubescent viewers, watching various teenaged actors go through fantastic transformations could've been used as a method for dealing with the changes going on in their own bodies. Certainly, Tommy Kirk's metamorphosizing into *The Shaggy Dog* (1959)—one of Disney's most successful films from this period—can be understood as a portrayal of puberty gone amok. In a different manner, Hayley Mills' discovery of another Hayley Mills in *The Parent Trap* (1961) seems to have embodied a number of both gay and lesbian teen desires to be able to be two different people, one butch and one feminine, and shows how people can act out both parts.

This tradition continued into the 1970s, after Walt's death, when the studio focused almost exclusively on light comedies and mild adventure aimed at the preteen set. *Escape from Witch Mountain* (1975) told the story of two twelve year olds discovering that the strangeness they feel in the world is because they are actually aliens from another world. The rest of the film shows them using their paranormal powers in an effort to return to the community where they feel they belong. In an internet conversation about the film, one gay man remembered:

> For months after watching *Escape to Witch Mountain* I emulated [female lead] Kim Richards in a way which should have sent off huge warning bells for my parents. Remember the scene where [the characters] Tony & Tia were carrying their jackets? . . . Tony had his hand wrapped around the top of his jacket, all bunched together—the way you'd carry a bouquet of flowers. Tia, on the other hand, had her hand overtop of the top of her jacket—very limp wrist, hand dangling as though about to plunge into Palmolive for soaking, and fingers just

barely gripping the jacket. I thought it was so elegant, I carried my jackets that way all over town.[77]

In response to this, another gay man wrote, "OHMIGOD. Are you inside my head or something? . . . I made my parents take me to see this movie something like seven times."[78]

Just as proto-queer boys had Spin and Marty to fantasize over in the 1950s, their 1970s counterparts could watch the dimples and blue eyes of Kurt Russell in various Disney films that transformed his body. Playing Dexter Riley in a series of three films about Medfield University, Kurt was fused with a computer in *The Computer Wore Tennis Shoes* (1970), became invisible in *Now You See Him, Now You Don't* (1972) and then turned into *The Strongest Man in the World* (1975). In all the films, Dexter was comically antagonized by prissy Dean Higgins (Joe Flynn). He was also pursued by petty gangster Arno (Cesar Romero) and his sidekick, Cookie, the live-action equivalent of Honest John and Figaro. They are always together; they even share the same apartment. In one scene of *The Strongest Man in the World*, Cookie discusses plans with Arno while Arno stands in a tank T-shirt and shaves.

The final film in the series climaxes with a weight-lifting competition. The Medfield team is made up mostly of gangly weaklings who look over in awe at the tall, tanned and buffed State team, who are all also sporting the feathered hairstyle and thick moustaches that became commonly known in '70s gay male culture as "the clone look." Luckily, after Dexter disposes of Arno and Cookie, the Medfield team gets a handsome male of their own and defeats State.

Two years before *The Strongest Man in the World* was released, the studio produced *The World's Greatest Athlete*, starring Jan-Michael Vincent as Nanu the jungle boy. Nanu is introduced when Coach Archer (John Amos) eyes him running across the African veldt. The delight in Archer's eyes at watching Nanu's loinclothed body sprinting past was matched by many audience members, for Vincent was one of the main "pinups" in gay male culture during the 1970s. Throughout the film, Vincent's body is constantly on display, usually for the pleasure of other men. Besides Archer, Nanu is watched by Milo, the coach's assistant (Tim Conway); Gazenga, Nanu's godfather and the tribal witch doctor (Roscoe Lee Browne); Dean Maxwell (Billy de Wolfe, who commonly portrayed sissy comic roles in the 1940s) and his prissy son Leopold; and a trio of sportscasters, including Howard Cosell! The privilege of watching Nanu is almost exclusively given to these men. For example, the landlady of the rooming house where Archer places Nanu after enrolling him in Merrivale University is practically blind (played by Nancy Walker).

Only one other woman is ever introduced as a character (comically named Jane). Her presence may somewhat diffuse the rampant homoeroticism of the film, since she also objectifies Nanu's body. Working as his tutor, Jane introduces the subject of biology as "the study of muscles" and proceeds to touch various parts of his body to explain what the trapezius, deltoids and biceps are. Yet, the romance is consistently deflected, usually by introducing a male rival for Nanu's attention. Namely, Nanu often seems to prefer the physical affection of his tiger Harry to Jane. In one sequence, as Jane and Nanu run towards each other in slow motion across an open field, Nanu runs right past Jane to wrestle fondly with the tiger. At another point, Harry attempts to follow Nanu into the shower, and Nanu himself asks the tiger, "Is Harry jealous of Jane?" before assuring him that "Nanu love only you." Jane herself accidentally seems to push Nanu in this direction. Every time she starts to feel that their tutoring sessions are getting a little too personal, she suggests that they "move onto ancient Greece."

While there is no explicitly comparable film for proto-queer girls in the 1970s to match *The Strongest Man in the World* and *The World's Greatest Athlete,* there was Jodie Foster in *Freaky Friday* (1977). Another transformation comedy, this time a teenaged girl and her mother switch bodies. While not explicitly dealing with female-female desires, that the girl is quite the tomboy furthers the comedy when she finds herself inhabiting her quite-feminine mother's body, and vice versa. We are introduced to Annabelle (Foster) waking up in a mess of a room wearing a baseball jersey. As she readies for school, she threatens her little brother with bodily harm and swaggers through the house. As she narrates the type of life she leads, the film shows us clips of her as an aggressive star player for the school's field hockey team.

On the other side, her mother Ellen (Barbara Harris) is petite, wears makeup and plays the conventional housewife. Both are on each other's nerves, mostly because Ellen wants Annabelle to be more conventionally feminine. She complains to her husband, "Have you seen how she dresses lately?" Later, a boy across the street tells Ellen in an understanding tone, "You shouldn't blame yourself for the way Annabelle is." When the boy sees Annabelle's trashed room, Annabelle (in her mother's body) tries to claim that it is her brother's.

Neither the mother nor the daughter is particularly happy with her life. Annabelle wants to get through puberty quickly and Ellen is obviously very put upon by her insensitive husband, so they get to switch personalities, just as the two Hayleys did in *The Parent Trap*. Now the femme is in a butch body, and the butch is femme. The comic aspects of the switch show these two personalities trying to play the role correctly—the butch trying to put on false eyelashes and do the laundry, the femme trying to play field hockey (after a teammate pats her on the butt before the game). Although the structure of the film tries to keep things even amongst the two characters, Annabelle's narration invites the viewer to identify with Foster's butch teenager. Helping the film along are a number of tough cookie veteran character actresses who seem to almost work as adult models for those identifying with Annabelle. Patsy Kelly (as the housekeeper), Marie Wilson (as a schoolteacher) and especially Ruth Buzzi and Kaye Ballard as "go-out-and-kill-em" field hockey coaches constantly show women who are not following feminine ideals. It must be said that this film is a product of a feminist age (Annabelle comes to realize that her father is a "male chauvinist pig") and the film was written by Mary Rodgers, based on her novel. Yet, such affirmation of non-feminine roles for women was unusual for the conservative Disney. The film tries to show that both sides learn lessons—but mainly, Annabelle learns that her father really expects a lot from her mother, while the mother realizes that Annabelle is fine the way she is. Even though the film was not a financial success, for the few young girls in the audience who were trying to come to terms with their bodies and their desires, such a message must have been quite welcome.

CONCLUSION: THE CHANGING LOOK OF NANNIES

Author Chris Cuomo labels the last section of her article, "Spinsters in Sensible Shoes: *Mary Poppins* and *Bedknobs and Broomsticks*," "Lesbian Subtexts: The Opaque Spinster."[79] She suggests that "there are ways in which the characterizations of both Mary Poppins and Eglantine Price [the magical nanny/spinster of *Bedknobs and Broomsticks*] resonate with both homophobic and friendly representations of ghostly and witchy lesbians in the history of Western literature and film."[80] The conflation of middle-aged lesbian stereotypes with the clichéd images of the spinster makes such a statement feasible. Both Poppins and Price are essentially humorless in demeanor, direct in their actions and speech, and, although both care for children, neither seems to display a single maternal instinct.

Yet, Cuomo goes on to point out the more "easy-to-recognize" nature of Price's character. "Price has a classic lesbian look and no feminine fluff, and is tailored. . . . Villagers are wondering whether she'll ever have a (male) romantic interest. . . . Even her diet, which includes cabbage buds, rose hips, glyssop seed, elm bark, and stewed nettles and bran porridge, fits the contemporary and historical constructions of the puritanical, health-obsessed or vegetarian lesbian-feminist."[81] While Poppins seems unconcerned with what people say or think of her and her magic, Price is at pains throughout to keep her magical powers secret. After an introduction emphasizing her lack of male companionship, such secretiveness takes on extra meaning. When one of the children under her care announces, "Game's up, Miss Price. We know what you are," the possibilities loom even larger.

Unlike Poppins, who never seems to be quite of this world, Price is quite rooted in the real world, trying to make a comfortable life for herself in a small English coastal town instead of floating off into the clouds. Cuomo theorizes that this more realistic context makes Price seem more "truly" lesbian than Poppins, but it also makes it more necessary for Price's character to eventually be romantically matched with a man. Unlike Poppins, who opens her umbrella and disappears into the horizon at the end of her story, Price's humanity must be in the end heterosexualized, and a man whom she originally saw no use for becomes her romantic partner.

Mary Poppins was released in 1964 and was one of the last motion pictures that Walt Disney himself personally oversaw. *Bedknobs and Broomsticks* came out in 1971, four years after Walt's death. Although the later film owes a great deal to (and hoped to recapture the popularity of) the earlier film, Cuomo's reading points out that times had changed. As mentioned earlier, the more aggressive, threatening nature of the overcultured Shere Khan in *The Jungle Book* displays a shift in conception. Homosexuality in the late 1960s and into the 1970s was a much different way of life than it had been in the 1930s. As more and more lesbians and gay men came out of the shadows and closets, making their presence known, the subject of homosexuality became more common in American culture. Thus, it would be easier for anyone, not just a small group of homosexuals "in the know" to see "pansy" or "butch female" images as representations of homosexuality. Whereas Jet in the "Annette" series *might* be lesbian, depending on who was watching, it would be easier for anyone to think that the female field hockey coaches in *Freaky Friday* were lesbian. This increasing public awareness of homosexuality in America since the late 1960s, and the increasing activism amongst homosexuals that brought this awareness, would affect not only what Disney texts chose to portray but also eventually *how* they were made by the company.

PART II

SINCE WALT

3

Finding a Place in the Kingdom

Homosexuality at Disney during the Eisner Era

IN AUGUST OF 1992, a number of employees convened at the commissary of the Walt Disney studio in Burbank. Many who attended that first meeting remembered later the pervasive nervousness and uncertainty. A number of them knew others that had decided not to attend because they felt that it was some sort of a trap and that all those who attended would be put on a list and eventually fired. Some attendees said that they showed up mainly to "see what would happen," because they were so surprised to see a meeting like this occurring at Disney. The meeting was the first held for and, most importantly, *by* homosexual employees of the Walt Disney Company. The result of the discussions at that first gathering was a new employee group named LEsbian And Gay United Employees, or LEAGUE for short.

LEAGUE was the first lesbian/gay/bisexual employees group to form at any major Hollywood studio, a landmark achievement considering the "wholesome" and "family-oriented" image of the company almost since its inception. Obviously, the work force and the day-to-day atmosphere of the company had changed immensely from the days when the studio was referred to as "Mickey's Monastery." Many of those changes occurred not just within the Walt Disney Company but within the entire social framework of the United States. Yet, specific economic and business events within the history of the company after Walt's death also helped spur such changes.

This chapter will analyze how LEAGUE conceives of itself and how it works within the corporation, as well as how these conceptions affect the group's ability to materially change the lives of its members and other lesbians and gay men.

In order to fully comprehend the issues raised by LEAGUE's existence, one must examine two linked historical developments. Firstly, measurable shifts in the discourse about homosexuality occurred between Walt's death and the formation of LEAGUE. During the same time period, the Walt Disney Company itself went through a tremendous upheaval. Both of these developments created a specific environment and outlook that affected how LEAGUE could negotiate a place for itself, what form it would take within the corporate structure, as well as how sexualities would be conceived and addressed.

STONEWALL AND BEYOND: HOMOSEXUALITY SINCE THE 1960S

Without doubt, LEAGUE would never have come about had not the gay rights movement gained momentum in the late 1960s. Having previously tried methods of appeasement and "working within the rules," now gay rights activists took their cues from the radical protests of groups like the Black Panthers and the National Organization of Women. Instead of marching peaceably in a circle while wearing "respectable" clothes, these groups had organized confrontational demonstrations aimed at jolting the complacency of those who would deny them their rights. The Black Panthers began training their members how to handle weapons; women burned bras in Atlantic City just before the 1968 Miss America pageant. Most historians point to the riots that occurred in Greenwich Village in June 1969 outside the Stonewall Inn as the impetus for a new radical gay rights movement. Instead of allowing themselves to be arrested in yet another bar raid by the New York police, patrons of this Mafia-controlled gay bar fought back, instituting demonstrations that lasted for three nights. Allen Ginsberg would say, upon viewing the area during the riots, "They've lost that wounded look that fags all had ten years ago."[1] Word of this local incident rapidly spread to homosexual communities throughout the country, even though mainstream newspapers barely reported on the incident. Soon, a number of groups, like the Gay Liberation Front and the Gay Activists Alliance, coalesced (mainly on college campuses such as the University of California at Berkeley and Harvard) to organize political demonstrations for gay rights.

Foremost, they saw "coming out" as the most basic and important political action an individual could make. By overtly announcing one's self-identification as a homosexual, the rest of society would begin to see 1) how many homosexuals are actually within the community and 2) that homosexuality encompasses a diverse realm of individuals and not only the stereotypical versions of feminine men and masculine women. (Ironically, this attempt to shift preconceptions of what "being homosexual" meant often worked to favor certain images and disparage others—an issue to be discussed in detail further on in this chapter.) One of the most popular methods of gaining attention was an anniversary celebration of the Stonewall riots. By the end of the 1970s, the end of June had become "Gay Pride Week," and most large cities witnessed annual "pride parades" attended by thousands of lesbians and gay men.

Gay activists also organized highly visible confrontations to make their presence known to the larger society. "Kiss-ins" were held at restaurants that refused to serve gay customers; lesbian and gay couples made sure the media were present when they attempted to apply for marriage licenses; a protester broke onto the set of CBS News during one of Walter Cronkite's live broadcasts. "Zapping," as it was labeled by gay activists, became quite prevalent during the early and mid-1970s, as lesbians crashed the National Organization of Women (who were attempting to distance themselves from lesbianism) and gay men and women shouted down "experts on homosexuality" at conventions of the American Psychiatric Association (which had labeled homosexuality as a mental disorder until the protests helped overturn that decision in 1973).[2] The goal of these actions was to destigmatize sexualities that fell outside the dominant hetero paradigm and celebrate the wealth of sexual possibilities.

Unfortunately, the coalitions engendered by the initial euphoria of the post-Stonewall moment—drag queens, middle-class gay men, lesbian-feminists and bisexuals (to name a few) all working together—did not last. While the term "gay" had earlier encompassed both men and women, the overemphasis in much of the movement on men's issues resulted in lesbian culture disassociating itself from "gay." By the end of the 1970s, "gay" meant predominantly "homosexual male." In fact, "lesbian separatism" became widespread as lesbians detached from gay male society and (as much as possible) the patriarchal system itself. The drag queens and racial/ethnic minorities that had initiated most of the fighting at the Stonewall Inn in 1969 soon found themselves both shunted aside in various activist organizations in favor of white and conventionally masculine homosexual men and denounced by many lesbian-feminists for "parodying womanhood."[3] Just as the free-wheeling sexual experimentation of the '60s counterculture and the "sexual revolution" began to ebb, the now "liberated" gay community's diversity seemed to wane rather than prosper. For example, most urban gay areas were soon overrun by mustached, cowboy-booted, masculine men, a style aptly labeled "the clone look." One gay man remembered, "I got back from India in 1974, having been gone a couple of years. . . . I was twenty-one, and I had long hair and a full beard, and I couldn't get laid. People told me I was cute but that I'd better shave and get a haircut. Everyone looked like the Marlboro Man."[4] Abetted by advertisers marketing to a newly perceived "gay market" (a topic to be analyzed more fully in chapter 5), "the clone look" encapsulated how definitions of being "gay" ironically narrowed instead of expanded in the age of "gay liberation."

The discovery of the AIDS virus during the 1980s signaled an end to the "sexual revolution" of the '60s and '70s and forced (for a while at least) a reevaluation of these developments. The hypermasculine image of the "clone" disappeared as gay men saw how many "clones" had become early casualties to the crisis. The refusal of the government under President Ronald Reagan to even acknowledge AIDS (much less pave the way to fund research and treatment) brought individuals together in a shared cause. Lesbians joined with gay men in the fight against AIDS. "Safe-sex" organizations attempted to reach out beyond the largely middle-class white populations of gay men in the "gay ghettos" to the African-American, Latino and Asian-American communities. Radical gay rights activist groups such as ACT UP and Queer Nation gathered members from a number of diverse communities and demanded attention by breaking into press conferences, government offices and medical labs. Making sure that the media was present for these actions, the activists gained much publicity.

While ACT UP worked specifically to countermand negligent attention to AIDS, Queer Nation was founded to confront the dominant heterosexual society's attitudes towards non-straight sexualities. To accomplish this, Queer Nation organized protests, sit-ins and actions in which chanting, banner-waving groups descended on "straight bastions" such as suburban malls. Both groups, though, also attempted to "wake up" homosexuals as well, encouraging them to take action instead of remaining complacent. While not at the forefront of their concerns, most ACT UP and Queer Nation members also began fashioning new images of homosexuality that angrily rejected "normal" gender conventions. Participants (both men and women) sported hair that was bleached or dyed in unique colors, and some shaved their heads; men pierced their ears, and soon both men and women were piercing other body parts as well; fashions ranged from punk to drag to leather and everywhere in-between. Queer Nation focused directly on welcoming the panoply of individuals who did not identify as heterosexual. As Frank Browning described one Queer Nation meeting he attended in 1991, "Women have become steadily more vocal, and real effort is made to reserve time for Asisans, blacks, and Latinos to speak. . . . [This] is part of the Queer Nation commitment to creating a collective 'safe space,' a queer town meeting where the whole array of queer people will feel 'empowered' to speak."[5] Similar to the immediate post-Stonewall radical activism, Queer Nation and ACT UP worked to broaden instead of close down the possibilities for sexual identity.

In attempting to challenge dominant society's attitudes towards non-heterosexuals, it was probably inevitable that queer activists would eventually focus on Hollywood. Unlike the golden era of the '30s and '40s, Hollywood films since "gay liberation" provided a semiregular stream of identifiable lesbian and gay characters. As Vito Russo and a number of other critics were quick to point out, though, the predominant image of a homosexual in movies made after the "sexual revolution" was that of a deranged psychopath. From *The Detective* (1968) to *Freebie and the Bean* (1973) to *Looking for Mr. Goodbar* (1978) to *Cruising* (1979) to *Windows* (1980), homosexuals were twisted maniacs who usually met grisly ends as punishment for their demented deeds. When *Silence of the Lambs* (1991) revealed that a gruesome serial killer was a transvestite and when *Basic Instinct* (1992) told a tale of a murderous lesbian, gay rights groups took to the streets in protest. As a sign of Hollywood's understanding of sexuality, various industry statements argued that neither of these films had homosexual villains: a transvestite was different from a gay man, and the female killer in *Basic Instinct* was bisexual. These statements attempted to place the maniacal tendencies on even further marginalized sexual identities, rather than recognizing the oppressions shared by all non-straight sexualities.

Queer activists by and large didn't buy the arguments and planned a "full court press" on Hollywood. Although most of the protests by such groups as Queer Nation and GLAAD (Gay and Lesbian Alliance Against Defamation) dealt with how gay men and lesbians (and others) were portrayed in films and television, activists also focused on discrimination within the workplace. For example, actor Brad Davis, who died of complications due to AIDS, left an angry letter to be published posthumously that condemned the way the industry dealt with actors who had the virus. The proven ability of these organizations to get noticed by the news media made the entertainment industry quite nervous. When rumors went around Hollywood that gay activists would storm the Academy Awards in 1991, a *Daily Variety* headline announced "Academy Asks Gay Orgs for Restraint."[6]

In response to the increased and ongoing pressure from the publicity generated by these actions, studio heads attempted to control the damage being done. In 1991, Barry Diller, then head of 20th Century-Fox, and Sid Sheinberg, CEO at Universal, announced the formation of Hollywood Supports, an organization devoted to dealing with both AIDS discrimination and homophobia within the entertainment industry. Soon, other powerful figures in the industry, such as producer Steve Tisch and superagent Michael Ovitz, were also involved in Hollywood Supports. Amongst its primary short term goals was to encourage the inclusion of sexual orientation in studio nondiscrimination employment policies and to promote domestic-partner benefits for homosexual couples unable to legally marry. Richard Jennings, executive director of the organization, told *Out* magazine in 1994, "We've held over 800 AIDS in the Workplace seminars. . . . We've helped fund proper legal [recourse] for discrimination. And what I'm most proud of is that we've had nine companies—with more on the way—adopt domestic-partnership benefit programs."[7] In August of that year, openly gay Hollywood attorneys organized a benefit for the National Gay and Lesbian Task Force. Amongst those on the host committee for the benefit were Sheinberg, Warner Bros. chairman Bob Daly, ABC president Robert Igor, superagent Michael Ovitz—and Disney executive Jeffrey Katzenberg. A year later, the event was repeated, this time underwritten by such corporations as Sony, Fox, Warner Bros. and, to quote gay columnist Michelangelo Signorile, "amazingly, the Walt Disney Company."[8]

A KINGDOM REBORN: DISNEY, THE SEXUAL
REVOLUTION AND THE EISNER/WELLS ERA

Although surprising to some, by the early 1990s the Walt Disney Company was in some ways a few steps ahead of other studios in its attitudes about homosexuality. While protesters outside the 1991 Academy Awards pointed out the homophobia of *The Silence of the Lambs,* which would win Best Picture, that same night Disney had been nominated for Best Picture for their animated version of *Beauty and the Beast.* The studio had used the release of the film to honor the talent of lyricist Howard Ashman, an openly gay man who had helped resurrect Disney's animated features and who had recently died as a result of AIDS. At the Academy Awards, when Ashman posthumously won an Oscar with Alan Menken for Best Song, Ashman's partner Bill Lauch came to the podium to accept the award.

Ashman's award in March of 1992 and that August's formation of LEAGUE finally acknowledged what had probably been true from almost the beginnings of the Walt Disney Company—that amongst its employees there existed individuals who self-identified as homosexuals. While such a statement may be specifically hard to document, it is almost as hard to believe that there weren't any lesbians or gay men working at the studio during Walt's life. Working in an industry that has traditionally attracted a large number of homosexuals, it only stands to reason that some percentage of the work force was lesbian or gay during Walt's reign. Yet, society at large made most of these individuals hide their sexual orientation from others. Things were no less secretive during the first half of the century on the Disney lot than anywhere else, and with just cause. An anecdote related to the production of *Fantasia* (1940) describes the general attitude towards homosexuality during this time. Animator Art Babbitt recalled, "I started taking piano lessons. After the film opened, Walt heard about it, and in the presence of maybe fifty people at a story meeting, he said, 'I understand you're studying the piano.' I said, 'Yeah, that's true.' He said, 'Well, what the hell's the matter with you; are you some kind of faggot?'"[9]

A number of actors and actresses who were closeted homosexuals worked on Disney films throughout the years—Richard Deacon, Cesar Romero, Sal Mineo, Nancy Kulp, Patsy Kelly. Yet, it was precisely their secretiveness that kept them employed both at Disney and in Hollywood at large. For example, it is rumored that actor Carlton Carpenter was originally considered for the role of Davy Crockett's companion but was eventually passed over because executives had heard that he might be homosexual.[10]

The most notorious example to serve as a warning to gay and lesbian employees of Disney was the case of Tommy Kirk. Tommy Kirk

began as a juvenile actor in some of Disney's TV shows and films—
playing one of "The Hardy Boys" on *The Mickey Mouse Club* and then
starring in *Old Yeller* (1957) and *The Shaggy Dog* (1959). The inordinate
success of both films made Kirk a hot commodity at the studio. Kirk
himself remembers Walt Disney's introducing the youngster to Hedda
Hopper as his "good luck kid."[11] When the 1960s started, Kirk had become the most promising male actor under contract to the studio and
was often paired with the studio's reigning female star, Annette Funicello. (Of course, many might choose to remember more fondly his
brotherly friendship with James MacArthur in *Swiss Family Robinson*
[1960].)

Kirk's promising future ended quickly, though. "I was 18 [in 1961],"
Kirk recalled to an interviewer in the 1990s. "My body was still growing." It was around this time that Kirk seems to recall self-identifying as
a homosexual. Yet, for a young and easily recognized actor during the
early 1960s, there were very few avenues to explore this part of his personality without adverse attention. "I was young, and I had money,"
Kirk recounted, "I started fooling around and I got involved with a boy.
We saw each other about three times . . . once at a public pool in Burbank. The boy's mother found out and went to see Walt at the studio."[12]

Kirk was summoned to the studio to speak directly with Walt.
While Kirk tried to stammer out an explanation, he was informed that
his contract had been terminated. No criminal charges were placed on
Kirk, and the firing (much less the reasons for the firing) was never discussed in the press. Such a lack of reaction seems to suggest that the studio "dealt" with both the parents of the other boy as well as the press to
keep the story "under wraps."[13] Ironically, right after Kirk was let go,
Disney brought him back to film *The Monkey's Uncle* (1964), a sequel to
The Misadventures of Merlin Jones (1963). During the six weeks of filming,
Kirk became painfully aware that many of the people he was working
with had heard the rumors. "It was a terrible feeling. I was very uncomfortable, knowing that they were watching me closely."[14] Although
Kirk was subsequently able to land work in a few American-International "beach party" musical comedies (again partnered with Annette
Funicello), by the mid-1960s Kirk's career as an actor was over. A slide
into drug dependency and recovery followed until, in 1975, he began a
carpet and upholstery cleaning business. When Kirk returned in 1984 to
the Walt Disney studio as part of a *Mickey Mouse Club* reunion, he discovered that his reputation still preceded him. According to Kirk, an

employee from Disney's publicity department told him, "If I had my way, all you people would be buried in the same grave."[15]

It seems startling then to consider that, only eight years after Kirk's encounter with this openly homophobic employee, LEAGUE established itself at the Walt Disney Company. But only a few years after Kirk's contract was originally terminated at the studio, racial minorities, women and the younger generation in the nation began challenging the norms and conventions in American culture. Amongst these challenges was a questioning of sexual morals, eventually termed the "sexual revolution." Nineteen sixty-seven's "summer of love," couples "living together" rather than getting married, the popularity of the birth control pill and the Supreme Court decision affirming a woman's right to an abortion all contributed to an enormous upheaval in social conceptions of sex and sexuality. While helping open the door for gay rights activism to flourish, in an almost obverse trajectory, this "sexual revolution" adversely affected the status of the Walt Disney Company. As the gay community grew more visible and organized in American society, Disney grew weaker and less important in the film industry.

The rise of the counterculture was a direct defiance of any and all authority. Anything that represented power—from the federal government and the military to corporate institutions and the mass media—was considered the enemy. Faced with such a huge wave of disenchantment, the entire Hollywood film industry suffered one its worst recessions in 1969–70. During the previous three years, while the counterculture grew by leaps and bounds, studio executives blindly threw millions of dollars at large, empty-headed mainstream confections like *Doctor Dolittle* (1967) and *Paint Your Wagon* (1969), which invariably sank like stones at the box office. The Disney studio was no different. Trying to recapture the magic and success of 1964's *Mary Poppins*, the studio released another big-budget musical with an over two-hour running time. *The Happiest Millionaire* (1967) dealt with an irascible and eccentric millionaire who imposes his opinions and attitudes on his children's lives, yet the audience is supposed to find him charming and lovable. Expectedly for this "generation gap" era, the film was spectacularly unsuccessful.

The Happiest Millionaire was the last film that Walt Disney personally supervised before his death in 1967. This last film of his indicates that Walt himself was probably unprepared to deal with the seemingly rapid changes occurring in American culture. Yet, Walt had always been a man with a strong vision, and his death left the company without such a leader to guide them through the tumultuous years of Vietnam and Watergate. After Walt's death, brother and constant partner Roy took over the company. Yet, Roy had always been the bookkeeper, the accountant—*not* the seer or artisan. Luckily, Walt had laid out plans for a new theme park in Florida before his death, and Roy devoted the next four years to realizing this final vision of his brother's. Three months after Walt Disney World opened in 1971, Roy himself was dead. Neither Walt nor Roy had left behind a clear line of succession. Walt never seemed to consider the possibility of his two daughters, Sharon and Diane, inheriting the chairmanship of the company. Rather, two men seemed equally poised and anxious to take over: Walt's son-in-law Ron Miller and Roy's son (Walt's nephew) Roy, Jr. By the 1970s, both were members of the executive board, fighting against each other for control of the company.

Meanwhile, the daily decisions regarding film and television production, theme parks, merchandising and every other ancillary market were made by people trying desperately to keep Walt's vision alive. Almost every account of the company's history during this period comments that the phrase "What would Walt have done?" dominated executive meetings.[16] While it is impossible to know for certain what Walt would have done, his history as a risktaker and experimenter was definitely not what company executives took from the man's memory. Instead, the Walt Disney Company retreated into a shell—churning out almost identical family comedies, letting the animation department run on its own inertia and fretting over the most minute changes to any of the two theme parks.

Remarkably, and unfortunately in retrospect for the studio, one of the biggest box-office successes of 1969 was Disney's *The Love Bug*. Tapping into at least the look of the era by giving a soul and mind to a Volkswagen Beetle (whose quirky design had caught public fascination), Disney seemed to find a project that was "mod" in style, but conventional in narrative, as the heterosexual couple comes together and defeats the comic villain. As Joe Flower observes, the film's success "froze the bland, cornball Disney formula in the minds of the Disney executives for another decade, long after it had run its course in the marketplace."[17] Also, the company's public image as "family oriented" severely limited the projects that could be made without raising the hackles of shareholders. While other Hollywood studios were able to capitalize upon the loosened censorship restrictions of the late 1960s, Disney was obligated to refrain from embracing the sexual revolution. In 1968, after the unveiling of the new ratings system for motion pictures, Disney stayed strictly within the "G" rating (for all audiences). In the 1970s, other studios learned that most children over the age of ten were loathe to attend a "G"-rated film, viewing such fare as "baby stuff." Consequently, while Disney dwelt exclusively in "G"-rated material, the rest of the industry aimed for "PG" (parental guidance suggested) ratings. By the 1970s, Disney's public image had inadvertently ghettoized its films mainly to kiddie matinees.

On occasion, some signs of the times would emerge inadvertently. In the production number "Portobello Road" in *Bedknobs and Broomsticks* (1971), some of the dancers are actually non-white. Jodie Foster as Annabelle in *Freaky Friday* contemptuously calls her father a "male chauvinist pig." Kurt Russell's hair is slightly longish as Dexter Riley. Still, it was hard to find many similarities between Dexter Riley's Medvale University and just about any other contemporary college campus in the nation. While Disney continued to show teenagers and college students involved in wacky hijinks that usually climaxed with the school's big football game, California's Governor Ronald Reagan was authorizing the use of tear gas on UC Berkeley students. Soon, hardly any attempts were being made at reaching an adult audience, as the studio had done all through Walt's life. Films like *The Barefoot Executive* (1971), *The $1,000,000 Duck* (1971), *Gus* (1976) and *The Cat from Outer Space* (1978) appealed only to children and to those parents who didn't want their offspring seeing something like *Carnal Knowledge* (1971) or *The Exorcist* (1973).

The studio's reputation suffered another major blow towards the end of the 1970s, as critics and audiences began noticing that other studios were producing fantasy and family films that were more popular than Disney's output. While *Freaky Friday, One of Our Dinosaurs Is Missing* (1975) and *Unidentified Flying Oddball* (1979) drifted off into box-office obscurity, George Lucas' *Star Wars* trilogy (beginning in 1977) and Steven Spielberg's *E.T.: The Extra-Terrestrial* (1982) were becoming some of the most profitable films in cinema history. Trying to rectify this situation, the studio produced *The Black Hole* (1979), a *Star Wars*-inspired science-fiction epic with a huge budget. Its failure signaled to many in the industry that Disney had "lost its touch." The studio's income steadily decreased, from a $34.6 billion profit in 1981, to $19.6 million in

1982, then to a $33.3 million loss in 1983.[18] By 1983, the studio would only release three films.

Things were only marginally better with the theme parks. While consistently making money for the company, profits remained stable rather than increased. Attempting to rejuvenate the profit margin, the company sunk an enormous amount of money into the building of EPCOT (Experimental Prototype Community Of Tomorrow) at Walt Disney World. Opening to enormous fanfare, the increase in admissions was negligible and disappointing. As a result, when Japanese investors (under the name of the Oriental Land Company) proposed opening a Disney theme park outside of Tokyo, the company was risk-shy. While still demanding to oversee the construction of the park, the company was unwilling to devote much monetarily and allowed investors to basically license the Disney name. Consequently, the investors—not the company—would reap most of the huge profits after Tokyo Disneyland opened in 1983.[19] In the years immediately after designing EPCOT and Tokyo Disneyland, the "Imagineering" work force (as the Walt Disney Company designates those who help create the attractions for the parks) was reduced from 2,000 to 450.[20]

In March of 1983, Ron Miller was elected chief executive officer of the Walt Disney Company over the objections of rival and fellow board member Roy Disney, Jr. One of Miller's first moves was to form a new subsidiary to Walt Disney Pictures. The newly christened Touchstone Pictures would deal with more mature themes than those pictures under the Disney logo and would aim at attracting specifically teenagers and adults, possibly even with a "PG" rating. Yet, even with a branch of the company specifically created to reach beyond the stifling family image that the Disney name meant to most customers, the first picture to carry the Touchstone symbol engendered enormous controversy within the company.

Splash (1983) told the story of a mermaid who becomes human for a short while in her pursuit of the human male she loves. At any other studio during the 1980s, such a comedic premise would be occasion for lots of sexual innuendo and female "jiggle." The original script called for some brief nudity scenes, occurring before the mermaid learns that humans wear clothing. This had veteran Disney executives aghast. Even Miller was quoted as saying, "The day Disney makes an R-rated film is the day I leave the company."[21] The project was only given the go-ahead when these scenes were reworked. In the final film, Darryl

Soviet director Sergei Eisenstein (at right) during the filming of *Ivan the Terrible, Part Two*. Regarded today as homosexual, Eisenstein was fascinated with Disney animation, even visiting the Disney studio during the early 1930s.

Tommy Kirk (center) with Annette Funicello and Elsa Lanchester in American-International's *Pajama Party,* made just after Disney canceled the actor's contract. According to Kirk, Disney dropped him over rumors about his homosexuality.

Left: Bette Midler, who began her career singing in gay male bathhouses, became a regular fixture in Touchstone Pictures of the 1980s—usually in wild campy comedies. *Right:* Ellen DeGeneres became the first openly lesbian actress to play an openly lesbian lead character in an American TV series in *Ellen,* produced by Touchstone Television.

MATT STERLING PRESENTS
A GAY NIGHT

AT (Walt Disney) PICTURES

Aladdin

Plus a Live
on stage Pre-Show

Wednesday, December 23rd
7:45 p.m.
El Capitan Theatre
6838 Hollywood Blvd.
Easy Parking Directly Behind Theatre
Tickets at Sporting Club, Prime Cuts, The Abbey
For further information call 213-654-9909
All proceeds donated to PROJECT ANGEL FOOD
Suggested Donation $15

A flyer for a special screening of *Aladdin,* to benefit the AIDS charity Project Angel Food. The event was organized by Matt Sterling, better known for producing a number of gay male adult videos.

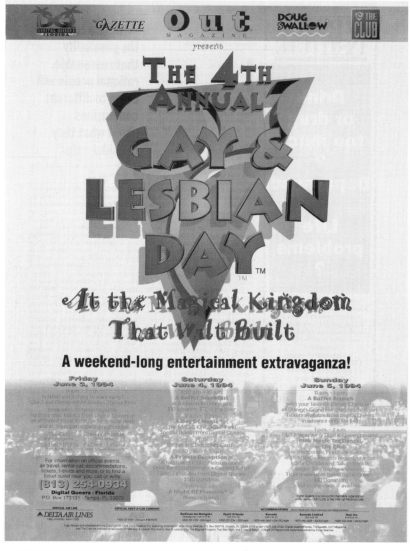

A full-page advertisement in the June 1994 issue of *Out* for "Gay and Lesbian Day" at Walt Disney World—but not sponsored by the Walt Disney Company. Although the ad points out this is the fourth of these events, it wasn't until 1994 that some fundamental Christian organizations noticed the events and began to object.

Hannah (who plays the mermaid) had her hair strategically taped to cover her breasts during scenes where the character was supposed to be topless. Many stockholders, though, were still dissatisfied that the company had "succumbed" to the pressures within the industry to loosen its morals. Although *Splash* was a sizable hit for the company (making $69 million in its original domestic release), the day that the film premiered Roy Disney, Jr. submitted his letter of resignation and began strategizing a hostile takeover bid for the corporation.

A few alert stock traders took the resignation to mean that Roy was distancing himself from the executive board in order to either start a proxy fight or attempt to buy out the entire company. While Roy worked with lawyer and confidant Stanley Gold to consolidate his plans, others began buying every piece of Disney stock that they could get their hands on. The first prominent threat to the studio was not Roy Disney but renowned financier Saul Steinberg, who had helped pioneer the wave of "leveraged buyouts," "junk bond schemes" and "greenmail techniques" that dominated 1980s corporate America. By April of that year, Roy owned just less than 5 percent of the company's stock, but Steinberg had bought up more than 8 percent and in May announced his intention to buy up to 49.9 percent.[22]

The company was able to keep Steinberg at bay eventually after paying him over $300 million to buy back his stock. Steinberg's attempt was only the beginning, and it alerted other big players in the market to Disney's precariousness. Soon, rumors were ripe that a number of sharks were circling the company, including such high-powered corporate raiders as Rupert Murdoch, Kirk Kervorkian and Irwin Jacobs. Roy Disney and Stanley Gold realized that they could not beat such competition in a head-to-head buyout, but they still retained enough power to force the company to place both of them on the executive board. As members of the board, they argued that a decisive management shakeup was needed to convince stockholders not to sell their holdings and to strengthen the company's image. It was not too long after this that Ron Miller was forced to resign, and hired to replace him were Roy's groomed choices: Michael Eisner and Frank Wells.

Frank Wells had already had an illustrious career at Warner Bros., and Michael Eisner had established himself at Paramount. Yet, both felt they had gone as far as they could go at their respective studios. Wells had retired for a few years in the early 1980s and returned to a basically ceremonial position at Warners; Eisner, after working his way up to president of Paramount Pictures, realized that political forces within the studio's parent company, Gulf & Western, were going to keep him from rising any higher. Together, they formed the new leadership of the Walt Disney Company. Eisner's creativity would be harnessed as the chairman and CEO of Walt Disney Productions, while Wells' attention to the details of business management would serve in his function as president of the Walt Disney Company. Together with Jeffrey Katzenberg, Eisner's right-hand man while at Paramount who accompanied him to Disney as Vice-President in Charge of Production, their reign over the studio almost completely and immediately revamped the philosophy and the day-to-day experience of life in the company.

The driving motive within the company now was no longer "What would Walt have done?" but "What will make a profit for the company?" Now, money was money, and any way to squeeze it out was considered. All aspects of the corporation were evaluated for their profit potential: the admission price for the theme parks was raised; films considered "too sacred" to release on home video were now going on video store shelves; marketing of the theme parks and film releases was substantially increased and reconceived. Although many executives and stockholders were sometimes aghast at the decisions implemented by this new team of executives, no one could argue their success rate. While in the early '80s, Walt Disney Productions held the lowest box-office market share of any major studio, by 1988, it held the top box-office share of any studio—a status it held by and large throughout the 1990s. In 1991, Disney became the first entertainment-based corporation to be placed within the Dow Jones average, signaling the economic community's conviction of the company's strength and longevity.

During these years, Eisner, Wells and Katzenberg did whatever they felt they could to pump up the strength of the company, even if it seemingly flew in the face of the Disney image and reputation. First and foremost in the minds of the new executives was Touchstone Pictures. They felt it vital to announce that the studio could and would make films aimed at adult audiences, with no intention of attracting children. In order to underline that point, Eisner and Katzenberg were determined that *Down and Out in Beverly Hills* (1986), the first Touchstone picture made under their tenure, would get an "R" rating. When Eisner screened the film for the executive board, he cut short any attempts to rework the material as had been done with *Splash* in 1983. According to *New York Magazine,* Eisner told the board, "This company has the reputation of being a censor." If the film were sanitized, this would imply that for all the hype about a new era for the company, nothing had really changed, and such talk might inhibit people from choosing to make films there.[23]

Down and Out in Beverly Hills was the first film to be released by the Walt Disney Company with an "R" rating, mainly for its sexual content than for any violence. Actress Bette Midler swears throughout the film and screams so loudly during a sexual orgasm that everyone in the entire household hears. Also included are scenes of Midler's husband (played by Richard Dreyfuss) and their houseguest (Nick Nolte) having sex with the Latina maid of the house, and there are intimations that the son in the family is gay. Older Disney executives gritted their teeth, and the film went on to make $62 million in domestic grosses. Following in this film's footsteps, *Ruthless People* was another flashy raunchy comedy with Bette Midler and an ensemble cast that went on to take in $71.6 million at the box office.[24]

By 1991, Team Disney, as the new executive team christened themselves, had swept out many previous employees and brought in their own people. Unlike many of the older employees who had been insulated from the rest of the film industry while at Disney, many of these new employees had worked with Eisner, Wells or Katzenberg at Paramount or Warner Bros., had numerous contacts with the rest of the film industry in Hollywood and "knew how the game was played." They were used to hustling, dealing and working long hours and on weekends to get projects moving. These employees also came from studios that were not as overtly concerned about a moral image as Disney had always been. In fact, many of these new employees were openly gay and lesbian, and they were not going back into the closet simply because they now worked for Disney.[25] In 1991, the entire company (not just the studio) formally instituted a nondiscrimination policy based on sexual orientation.

This development also tied into the concerted attempt by the studio to be taken seriously by those working within the industry and to attract talent that had never previously considered making a film for the company. In this new atmosphere, no one seemed to care what you did in your private life, as long as you helped bring in revenue to the company. Many of the high-profile artists who began to work predominantly at the Disney Studio were openly gay, such as song-writers Howard Ashman and Elton John and director Emile Ardolino. Jeffrey Katzenberg was so impressed by Ashman's talent and his ability to resurrect the popularity of Disney's animated features that Katzenberg and Ashman became extremely close friends. Ashman's death as result of AIDS seems to have had a profound effect on Katzenberg and, consequently, on those gay and lesbian employees working under Katzenberg.

Thomas Pasatieri, an openly gay composer and orchestrater who arranged scores for some of Disney's films over the past decade, described the music department as so gay-friendly that when one straight artist was let go from a project, he threatened to sue the studio for sexual discrimination against heterosexuals![26] An anecdote amongst Disney's homosexual employees, and reported in at least one industry periodical, demonstrates that even Disney's top-ranking executives often agreed that an inordinate number of homosexuals were now working for the company.[27] As homosexual Disney employees began calling for the company to grant domestic partners of homosexual employees the benefits that were given to the spouses of married heterosexual employees, an Apple computer executive met Michael Eisner at a charity function. When this executive cornered Eisner in order to discuss domestic partner benefits (Apple, like most of the computer industry, had already begun these benefits), Eisner reportedly stated that he feared a huge loss of money because he figured that about 40 percent of Disney's work force was gay or lesbian.

By November 1994, when the gay periodical *Out* released a special "Out in Hollywood" issue, a large number of those profiled were working for Disney or one of its subsidiaries—Touchstone or Hollywood Pictures.[28] Amongst these were: Lauren Lloyd, senior vice-president for Hollywood Pictures; Andreas Deja, a supervisor in the Animation Division; Tammy Balik, casting director for Touchstone Television's series *Ellen*; and Garrett Hicks, an administrative assistant in the Animation Division and then co-chair of Disney's employee group LEAGUE. It was this more accepting environment for openly lesbian and gay employees at the Walt Disney Company that helped the founding of LEAGUE. Yet, LEAGUE's founding and its first few years of existence were accompanied by trepidations, often over "queer" politics entering the workplace—worries shared not only by studio executives but also by a number of lesbian and gay employees.

A LEAGUE OF THEIR OWN: THE LESBIAN AND
GAY EMPLOYEES OF TEAM DISNEY

The startup of Hollywood Supports had a specific effect on the foundation of LEAGUE. According to Garrett Hicks, he and Sass Nielsen, who worked in the film information services department at Disney, met at a Hollywood Supports meeting. Together, they discussed the value of Hollywood Supports and brainstormed the notion of organizing a homosexual employees group at Disney. No other studio had such a group for Hicks or Nielsen to use as a model. In fact, Hicks and Nielsen never formally organized a plan together, and the two did not meet up again to discuss this idea.

Rather, Nielsen on her own initiative began getting things moving. Nielsen was aware of the number of various employee groups (ranging from a bowling group to the Mac Club, a computer users network). Such groups were sponsored by the company and advertised in the studio's employee newsletter, the *Newsreel*. Jeff Kurti, an employee in the corporate synergy department, recalled an "unwritten" policy that nurtured new clubs by running announcements of new organizations in the *Newsreel* and providing about $200 in start-up funds.[29] With this in mind, Nielsen asked Disney University, the division that publishes the newsletter, to print an announcement of a meeting of lesbian and gay employees.

The University responded that they did not run announcements for employee self-help groups. Nielsen pointed out that the *Newsreel* ran announcements for an employee Weight Watchers group, which could be easily labeled a self-help group. Next, the University argued that they did not print notices that were of a "sexual nature." The implication of this argument was that the company viewed this new employee group as a "sex club," with club members putting down plastic tarp in meeting rooms for events and then cleaning up afterwards! After these repeated attempts and failures, Nielsen wrote a letter directly to Michael Eisner about the situation and asked for permission to form the group and run an announcement in the *Newsreel*. According to Nielsen, "Within twenty-four hours of writing my letter, Eisner told Sandy Litvak [then vice-president of the law and human resources department] to run the announcement in the *Newsreel*."[30]

After the group first met in August of 1992, LEAGUE quickly decided that its primary goal was to win domestic-partner benefits. In

1992, Universal was the only studio to offer such benefits. LEAGUE members heard a number of reasons why Disney was reticent to move in this area. There were worries about the extra cost to the company, about the studio's legal standing in acknowledging domestic partnerships, about employees falsely claiming to have partners just to get friends health insurance and mostly worries about the bad publicity that granting such benefits would spark amongst conservative "family values" media groups. LEAGUE responded to these reservations by putting together "The ABCs of Domestic Partner Benefits," a report that attempted to answer all questions, both the perceptive and the asinine, in a manner that would put the studio at ease. Copies of this report were sent to Michael Eisner, Sandy Litvak and anyone else who could sway opinion within the company. LEAGUE members seemed to always assume that it was just a matter of time before these benefits would be granted. Jeffrey Katzenberg's involvement with AIDS charities as well as Hollywood Supports (partly as a result of his friendship with Howard Ashman) furthered a relative wealth of assistance and understanding from the studio towards employees suffering from AIDS, including extended sick leave and insurance coverage. With this in mind, the outlook for partner benefits seemed encouraging.

This is not to say that after finally getting approval to exist LEAGUE never encountered further friction from the company. After LEAGUE was formed, the company declared a formal policy on employee groups, ending the $200 start-up fund and restricting use by these groups of the Disney name or logo. Although the company insisted that the formation of a lesbian/gay employee group had no bearing on this new policy, its timing somewhat undercut this assertion. Nielsen stated, "I felt Disney was saying: 'O.K., if this is going to happen, we want to say how and [we want it to happen] as quietly as possible."[31] Nielsen's assertion, as well as Litvak's continuous supervision of LEAGUE in the ensuing year, exemplifies institutional attempts to control and regulate discourse on sexuality. Another example of such regulation occurred when thirty members of LEAGUE traveled to the District of Columbia in April 1993 to participate in the March on Washington, arguably the largest gay rights event ever held in the United States. Traveling with them was a parade banner announcing themselves as "part of the family at the Walt Disney Company." The studio's legal department immediately told LEAGUE that this violated the restrictions on use of the Disney name and insisted that the name be taken off an already printed banner. The group solved the problem by covering up the words "Walt Disney" with computer paper that had the word "THAT" printed on it. The banner, which now read "part of the family at THAT company," was carried in the march by LEAGUE members wearing mouse-ear beanies and carrying Mickey Mouse balloons. This same altered banner would march in a number of gay pride parades over the next year.

Slowly, though, tensions eased, and the studio seemed to relax some of its militant watch over the group. The company discovered that various religious or conservative groups, such as the American Family Association (AFA), did not seem to initially notice or care about the creation of this employees group. By 1994, LEAGUE was allowed to use the banner in parades without the word "that" plastered over the name "Walt Disney." Journal articles in both the gay and mainstream press about LEAGUE were published, although the studio did not allow any photos that included Disney iconography (citing that it might somehow imply the company's endorsement of homosexuality).

The relative ease with which the Disney studio became accustomed to having a lesbian and gay employees group was reached mainly by the personality of the employees group. When Sass Nielsen first broached the subject of such a group, many LEAGUE members felt that the studio pictured the organization as radical and politically insurgent. Jeff Kurti described Nielsen's approach as "too political or militant."[32] According to Garrett Hicks, Nielsen's letter to Eisner included veiled threats of litigation against the studio, which alerted the ever vigilant legal department of the company.[33] In an age when queer activists threatened to interrupt the Oscar ceremony and attempted to interfere with the filming of *Basic Instinct* on location in San Francisco, it is quite possible that many regarded the new group as an invasion of ACT UP or Queer Nation from within.

To prevent that possibility, the company guidelines on employee clubs were slightly altered in 1993, adding a phrase stating that clubs were social groups and explicitly *not* political in nature. For a short while, LEAGUE (as well as ALLIANCE, the gay/lesbian employees group at Disney World, which for some reason had been notified of this change before LEAGUE was) worried about the implications of this change. Garrett Hicks described the concern thusly: "What's considered political? You know, by our very nature, we are political because we are a gay and lesbian employee group and our issues and our concerns are a socially political issue. So does that mean we can't exist anymore?"[34] LEAGUE was quickly assured of their right to exist, but informed that the group could not specifically endorse a political platform or certain candidates in an attempt to squelch any possible moves by LEAGUE (or other groups) to protest or call for boycotts.

The studio's legal department and public relations team were not the only ones worried about the possible ties that LEAGUE could have to radical queer activism. Almost from the beginning, LEAGUE had to confront this issue inside its own ranks. Nielsen had been involved with radical rights groups, and this worried some lesbian and gay employees who did not desire to picket or boycott Disney's treatment or representation of homosexuals. A few who attended the first meeting found Nielsen's aggressive stance to be the opposite of what they were looking for. Instead of a social group that would help lesbians and gay men meet each other in order to support each other as employees, they found that Nielsen pictured the group as political, one that would work to make issues of sexuality a larger concern to the studio and the company at large. These employees didn't want to rock the boat and preferred to uphold a "respectable" image of homosexuality. When carrying the LEAGUE banner in parades, members tended to wear T-shirts and jeans or shorts instead of dressing in drag or leather or topless (realizing this might have had a hand in the company's eventual decision to let the banner use the Disney name). When the Disney-owned local television station KCAL began airing conservative funnyman Rush Limbaugh's syndicated show, many LEAGUE members were bothered when co-president Hicks voiced a protest in an interview to the *Los Angeles Times*. Those bothered by the interview seemed to feel that Hicks had gone outside of the prescribed company policy for registering complaints (i.e., writing an internal company letter to those in charge).

LEAGUE members themselves worried that even forming a group was perceived as too "in your face" by some employees—and not just heterosexuals. It is quite possible that many potential members of LEAGUE never attended a meeting precisely because they perceived the group as "too out." Those who became actively involved with LEAGUE quickly hypothesized that a large number of the lesbian and gay employees at Disney were still "closeted" about their sexuality and hence worried about the repercussions of even attending a LEAGUE meeting. To quell these worries, LEAGUE immediately agreed to keep their mailing list confidential, with only the officers expected to acknowledge their relationship to the group. The idea, as Jeff Kurti stated, was to create "a 'safe zone' for networking. . . . We knew there was a higher gay and lesbian work force, but we had to open the lines of communication to find a mission and purpose."[35]

Even being an openly lesbian or gay employee didn't necessarily mean you agreed with an activist agenda. Tina Shafer, who worked for Disney's corporate environmental policy department and became an eventual co-chair of LEAGUE, acknowledged, "I was afraid to go for a while because I worried it would jeopardize my relationship with my managers who had never appeared to have a problem with my sexuality."[36] There was just cause for this concern. Nielsen recounted that her career at the studio suffered after the formation of LEAGUE, due largely (in her opinion) to her efforts, and she was laid off about a year and a half later.

When Nielsen stepped down as chair after six months, LEAGUE quickly lost some of its radical edge—much to the pleasure of the company as well as many homosexual employees. Although the group's main goal was to win domestic-partner benefits for its employees, an "assimilationist" (rather than a "confrontational") philosophy became dominant. While the Workplace Issues Committee went through the channels that the company dictated it should go through, LEAGUE meetings became lunches with guest speakers—a chance for employees to meet lesbian and gay authors, filmmakers and politicians who couldn't believe they had been asked to speak at Disney about their sexuality. Social gatherings were held throughout the year, culminating in each year's march in the Los Angeles Gay Pride Parade. Reflective of the present philosophy of the group, Robert L. Williams, one of 1997's co-chairs of LEAGUE, told *Out* magazine that he considered "An employee support group's ultimate goal . . . is not to exist. We had problems of visibility and equality. Those were rectified. Now it's a process of normalization and maintenance."[37]

In attempting to quell company anxieties, the group often has ended up helping reinforce conventions of sexual identity rather than breaking them down. In fact, such accomodations often seem to affect how the organization as a whole conceives of sexuality in general. While LEAGUE is notable for acknowledging the existence of lesbian and gay employees within Disney's ranks, the group often helps reinforce boundaries of sexuality rather than helping dismantle them. For example, in the push for domestic-partner benefits, there was constant discussion as to whether benefits would only be available to homosexual couples (who are legally barred from marriage) or could extend to heterosexual couples who live together outside of marriage. Instead of seeing a shared cause with non-married long-term heterosexual couples, LEAGUE decided to conceptualize domestic partners as lesbians and gay men who *would marry* but were unable to by law.[38] Rather than challenging the importance of the institution of marriage (as many antagonists to domestic partner benefits argue will result from such programs), such a definition implicitly reaffirms the sanctity and desirability of marriage.

Also, LEAGUE's active membership weighs heavily towards white, middle-class men. Attendance at LEAGUE's meetings emphasized this fact, with women and non-Anglo employees always in the minority (and sometimes not present at all). This is not to say that the officers of the group were unaware of this condition, or unconcerned. When Hicks was co-chair, he maintained that the group was trying to make the organization seem more diverse and welcoming, appealing quite forthrightly in their monthly newsletter to those employees who were not represented at the meetings. Yet, active female members of LEAGUE often expressed privately the opinion that the group sometimes felt like a "boys' club." Although supposedly a large number of women attended the first meeting, within three months Women of LEAGUE was established. While not breaking off from LEAGUE, this "sub-group" would hold luncheon or dinner gatherings on a regular basis to create a space that was more comfortable for lesbian employees.

In dividing LEAGUE into male and female counterparts, the organization seemed to implicitly agree to hegemonic definitions of gender. This was made abundantly clear when a male-to-female transgendered employee decided to start coming to meetings. This employee, whom I will call "Bobbie," came to the group because of harassment she had received. Although the Walt Disney Company officially does not permit discrimination according to sexual orientation, Bobbie's superiors seemingly felt justified in harassing her because of her "indeterminate" state while she was pre-op. They refused to let Bobbie use the women's restroom and insisted that co-workers refer to Bobbie by her male name. While Bobbie came to LEAGUE looking for advice and support, the group often mirrored much of the confusion that Bobbie's superiors had expressed. Members of Women of LEAGUE felt uncomfortable having a "man" come to their meetings. Members sympathized with Bobbie's plight, but since LEAGUE is a studio-sanctioned employees group, they did not feel it was their position to put Bobbie in contact with a lawyer to possibly sue the studio for harassment. Bobbie was later laid off, along with a number of others who angrily let Bobbie know that they felt they had been let go only to hide the fact that the company wanted to get rid of her.

As unfortunate as this incident is, disparagement of LEAGUE for its capitulation to the studio's attempts to control and regulate the categories of sexual identity must be tempered by certain important factors. Expecting LEAGUE members to practice an idealistic "queer" experience privileges an academic and often abstract concept of sexual identity in the workplace over the actual lived experience of these individuals.[39] LEAGUE's members (and potential members) are *de facto* employees and thus imbricated and deeply involved in the economics of the company. While certain employees consider their work "only a job" and not somehow part of their identity, many often look at their employment as "a career" and are deeply invested in the work they do. From Walt's founding of the company to the present day, Disney has worked to foster in its employees a sense that they are "members of the family," drawing them into equating self-worth with the company's overall performance. Consequently, lesbian and gay employees often have to balance their self-identity as homosexuals with their self-identity as Disney employees. It would be unsurprising to find that individuals often attempt to reconcile the two by acquiescing to the officially sanctioned boundaries of sexual expression (or separating their personal life from their work in order to "play by the rules" at the office).[40] In the corporate world, lesbians and homosexuals of racial or ethnic minorities are often more consumed with trying to overcome the barriers placed upon them by their gender or race than with their sexual identity, which is not as easily perceived by superiors.[41] Because of these already-placed hurdles, many of these people remain closeted as a way to keep from dealing with multiple "glass ceilings."[42] To substantially challenge company policies would potentially endanger any non-straight employee's inclusion as "part of the family at the Walt Disney Company." This stands in contrast to non-straight *consumers* of Disney who have no direct self-investment in Disney and thus have more leeway to accept or resist the messages presented by the company's products. (Exactly how much leeway these consumers have is a matter discussed in chapter 5.)

Even with these barriers, LEAGUE has already had a lasting impact. The stability and strength of the group over the past few years has helped many Disney employees to start the process of "coming out," providing confidence and support. Hicks knew of a number of people who made their first movement out of the closet by attending a LEAGUE meeting. One such person, he remembered, was marching with LEAGUE in a gay pride parade a year after his first tentative attendance.[43] The impact of LEAGUE extends beyond the Walt Disney Company, for its success has inspired similar lesbian/gay/bisexual employee groups to form at almost every other major motion picture studio—and these various employee groups have been able to argue for and win domestic-partner benefits.[44] The report that LEAGUE wrote on domestic-partner benefits has been used by a number of different organizations including the Los Angeles Metropolitan Water District and Nestle's Gay and Lesbian Employee Association. Although LEAGUE works from within, and consequently often capitulates to the rules and regulations established by corporate society, it has unquestioningly helped better the lives of many lesbians and gay men.

MAIN STREET, U.S.A.: HOMOSEXUALITY AT THE THEME PARKS

LEAGUE's strength and resilience has helped it to stand as a model not only for the lesbian and gay employees at other studios, but for lesbian and gay employee groups within other branches of the Walt Disney Company. Although LEAGUE is open to all employees within the corporation—from Hollywood Records to the Disney Stores—most of its members are from within the motion picture and television divisions. Soon after the founding of LEAGUE, lesbian and gay employee groups announced their formation at Disneyland and Walt Disney World. The presence of LEAGUE announcements in the *Newsreel* alerted lesbian and gay employees in Florida, who gathered together to form ALLIANCE about five months after LEAGUE held its first meeting. Walt Disney World's ALLIANCE has always remained completely independent of the studio's employee group, but LEAGUE was quite involved in helping the employees at Disneyland get LEAGUE/Anaheim started.[45] Although a number of park employees were eager for such a group, no one seemed to have enough time, energy or courage to get the ball rolling. For example, some of the LEAGUE contingent that joined the March on Washington ran into some Disneyland employees, who were extremely enthusiastic, but nothing ever resulted.

Eventually, in August of 1993, LEAGUE put in a call to Disneyland's version of the studio's University, Cast Activities, and looked into setting up and announcing a meeting. Since LEAGUE already legitimized the right for such a group to exist, there wasn't a repeat of the travails Sass Nielsen endured. In fact, Garrett Hicks, then co-chair of LEAGUE, was frankly surprised at the level of assistance he received in planning this first meeting from Cast Activities. Hicks worked through an extremely enthusiastic female employee of Cast Activities, who told him, "'I have so many people that are asking about this, I'm so glad you guys are finally doing this!' She made sure the announcement ran two times in the *Newsreel*, she got this meeting room for me, she showed up at the first meeting."[46] Although still in communication with LEAGUE, LEAGUE/Anaheim now functions on its own, dealing with issues and concerns that are unique to the employee base of the park. Yet, since both function within the same corporate system (and since the studio's group has helped foster Disneyland's group), how sexuality is conceived of, monitored and regulated within ALLIANCE and LEAGUE/Anaheim is often quite similar to how it is managed within LEAGUE.

Day-to-day life for lesbian and gay employees of the two theme parks is quite different and distant from the workplace atmosphere of the motion picture and television divisions. First and foremost, Disneyland and Walt Disney World are physically separated from the Walt Disney Studios. While the studio is in the heart of Burbank, just over the hill from Hollywood and downtown Los Angeles (conventionally thought of as more liberal areas of the United States), Disneyland is situated in the middle of Orange County, one of the most conservative communities in the state of California. Walt Disney World, in Orlando, Florida, is located in the middle of the "Bible Belt." The letter signed by fifteen Florida lawmakers in late 1995 referred to at the beginning of chapter 1 adequately sums up the dominant social atmosphere of the state. Written specifically in response to the announcement that the Walt Disney Company had finally decided to extend domestic-partner benefits, the letter states, "We strongly disapprove of your inclusion and endorsement of a lifestyle that is unhealthy, unnatural and unworthy of special treatment. Those who practice homosexuality are engaging in a lifestyle that should not be given the same status as heterosexual marriages."[47] Most employees of the parks live in the immediate surrounding areas and hence often carry with them these prevailing attitudes towards homosexuality, even though officially the Walt Disney Company does not discriminate against homosexuality in its hiring or promotion policies.

The strength of "traditional" or conservative attitudes towards homosexuality within the parks may also come directly from the upper management team at Disneyland and Walt Disney World. Even as Team Disney was vitally rehauling the studio's employee base (firing over 400 people by early 1985), Eisner and Wells did not feel the need to make such a major sweep through the parks. Even in the darkest times of the company, both Disneyland and Walt Disney World maintained a steady (if, at times, unspectacular) profit. Often, the success of the parks had helped erase the red ink spilled on the film production end. As company board member Sid Bass claimed, "The executives at the park remembered how Walt had done it."[48] Symbolic of the "old school," Eisner and Wells kept Richard Nunis on as head of the entire theme park operation; Nunis had been involved with Disneyland before construction was even completed in 1955 and had risen to take over the division by 1971.

Nunis was not the only theme park executive to stay on as Team Disney formed. Consequently, the division's upper management still retained an almost exclusive white male heterosexual profile. Having been around prior to the opening up of the company to lesbian and gay employees, these executives have been conceivably resistant to this change. For example, Joe Flower reports that park managers at Disneyland were resistant to the idea of the *Captain EO* 3-D film attraction that debuted in 1986, complaining that the film's star Michael Jackson was "a wimp, he's a fag, he's gay."[49] Just before the entire company included sexuality in the EEO policy, one fired park manager successfully sued to be reinstated, claiming discrimination for being homosexual. According to the employees of the parks that I interviewed, there still remains an unspoken glass ceiling that keeps women, homosexuals and people of color from advancing to higher positions at the parks. In their opinion, an openly homosexual employee is unlikely, if ever, to be promoted to a supervisory position, much less an executive position. In an extreme example of some homosexual employees acquiescing to the unspoken regulation of sexuality, one former employee of Disneyland claimed to know of two gay men who married women in order to protect their future in upper management at the park. Most of the homosexual work force at the theme parks have not gone this far, and some have found a space to be both open about their sexuality and stay employed. Yet, most of this latter group are part of the day labor force.

Some gay men who started their work at Disneyland at hourly wage found a better chance for advancement by diverting into Imagineering, the division that devises the various attractions for the theme parks. Although directly tied to the parks, Imagineering is separate from the executives managing the parks, and, in trying to foster a creative and unrestrictive environment for its designers, Imagineering is somewhat less concerned with the sexual orientation of its employees. Yet, issues of sexuality are still monitored and managed in this division using the same economic incentives (raises and promotions, or the obverse, demotions or layoffs). Kent, an Imagineer who had begun by portraying Peter Pan in parades, found this out when the division asked him to relocate to France to help design EuroDisneyland in the early 1990s.[50] Although Kent had a partner, he had not officially come out to anyone in the company. The company had a policy of financing the move for a relocated employee's spouse, or paying for quarterly visits—a policy which Kent questioned, since he wasn't "legally married," as he told his superiors (avoiding an overt confrontation over his homosexuality). According to Kent, his superiors were livid when he turned down the assignment after they refused to alter the policy, informing him that looking for his replacement took "considerable cost and inconvenience" and that if he didn't accept the assignment, "we're not sure we'll have another assignment for you." Possibly as a result of this fracas, flying spouses back and forth is no longer offered to relocated employees.

In another incident, a slide presentation at an Imagineering holiday party inadvertently made a joke using a sketch of the seating arrangement on slave ships bound for the American colonies. *Eyeopeners*, the Imagineering division's newsletter, apologized for the affront and upheld a commitment to not discriminate against race, creed or gender. Livid at the exclusion of sexuality on this list, Kent went directly to Marty Sklar, the head of Imagineering, and in no uncertain terms came out while protesting. To his credit, Sklar agreed with Kent and, from that point on, consulted with Kent regularly. When a local troop of Boy Scouts planned a trip to the Imagineering offices and workshops, Kent informed Sklar of the Boy Scouts' discriminatory policy towards homosexuals. Sklar canceled the visit.

Garth Steever, a manager working within Disneyland, also came out to his superiors in a dramatic way. One of the female ticket sellers working under his supervision was let go, and she accused him of sexual harassment. In order to defend himself against this accusation, Steever met with the Disney lawyers and told them of his sexual orientation.[51] Although obviously not the most comfortable method of coming out on the job, Steever was able to use the situation to his advantage. Although many of the people Steever worked with might have had ideas about his homosexuality, the situation was similar to the Armed Forces' "Don't Ask, Don't Tell" policy. Much as Judith Butler describes social discourses creating overlaps and contradictions in speaking about sexuality, the park's economic interests (worries about being sued) ended up creating not only a space for Steever to be openly gay but created a *need* for him to be gay. Forced by circumstances to declare himself openly, Steever (like Kent) felt obliged to speak for other homosexual employees who didn't feel secure enough in the workplace to come out.

Still, even before coming out officially, Steever related the hardship in moving up the corporate ladder at Disneyland when superiors silently assumed he was gay. The discrimination was never outspoken, but executives could claim that because Steever hadn't at that point formally announced he was gay, they couldn't have discriminated against him. Still, Steever lists many indications of attempts to discourage his advancement. After passing through the supervisor training courses held at the Disney University, he was assigned to the Main Street, U.S.A. section of the park—notoriously one of the toughest areas to manage. (Since the entrance to the park is Main Street, this area is responsible for admissions and also handles most customer complaints.) After succeeding, Steever was told by *his* supervisor that he was expected to fail at this position (as had a previous openly gay management hopeful that Steever knew). Becoming a full manager, Steever has made his way into the upper division but feels that the process was inordinately stressful, that he still has to fight for "merit" pay hikes given on a regular basis to other managers at his level, and has been told surreptitiously that his evaluator "doesn't like his lifestyle."[52]

David Koenig's recounting of various lawsuits levied against Disneyland in his book *Mouse Tales: A Behind-the-Ears Look at Disneyland*, includes the case of a man who had worked his way up to the position of stage manager in 1985 but had been denied advancement, training or pay or benefit increases after the park learned that he had been diagnosed with AIDS. By 1989, he had been let go.[53] One employee remembered being told by a woman in personnel that anyone they perceived as gay during the interview process of hiring calls should be rejected.[54] (Luckily, this woman was gay-friendly and circumvented this dictate.) Under such circumstances, it is understandable that some employees at the parks choose to remain closeted. This trend seems even more pronounced at the Florida park than at Anaheim, possibly because at least the employees of Disneyland are somewhat close physically to the more open atmosphere of the studio in Burbank than those isolated in Orlando.

The strength of the conservative "traditional" discourse of the parks can be witnessed, furthermore, just by experiencing the parks as a customer. It is almost impossible to miss the repeated construction of the typical visitors as a heterosexual family of two. From the original House of Tomorrow (which assured visitors that the future would be designed with the two-child patriarchal heterosexual family in mind), to the seating diagrams for the Matterhorn rollercoaster (showing the international symbols for girl-boy-woman-man getting into cars in that order), to the photos of happy heterosexual families in the park brochure given to everyone who enters, to the decades-old jokes about mothers-in-law recited by the operators of the Jungle Cruise boat ride, to the Pirates of the Caribbean chasing lustily after female prey, the assumption and reinforcement of heterosexuality can be found wherever one turns.[55]

The restrictions extend even to the dress code mandated of park employees, who are referred to within the parks as "Cast Members," thus emphasizing the role-playing Disneyland mandates of its workers. Each employee, when hired, is given a brochure on "the Disney Look." The brochure's argument for enforcing these fashion guidelines is specifically tied to the heterosexual family: "Most amusement parks had bad reputations and were not considered suitable for the entire family. . . . Disneyland wasn't an 'amusement park,' it was a Theme Park where families could have fun together. . . . For this reason, anything that could be considered offensive, distracting or not in the best interest of our Disney Show . . . will not be permitted."[56] Most of the things considered "offensive" in the rules deal with fashions and looks that stress individuality. Men are not allowed to have long hair or shaved heads, facial hair of any kind, "unnatural" hair coloring or earrings. Most of these "looks" can be associated with the urban gay culture created in the wake of '80s gay activism. Similarly, women are not to have spiked hair or shaved heads, or "unnatural" hair coloring, and can only wear one small stud earring per ear. Another rule is accidentally ironic in its demand that female Cast Members only wear makeup that will "create a fresh natural appearance"![57]

Of course, the brochure provides ample evidence of the performative nature of heterosexual "normality." For, as hard as the theme parks attempt to control, regulate and limit the extent of the imagination of both employees and customers, Disneyland, Walt Disney World, Tokyo Disneyland and EuroDisneyland are actual physical locations where the carnivalesque potential of Disney's film and television texts can be played out 365 days a year. No matter how many restrictions are imposed upon individuals within the confines of the park, there are endless invitations to let the imagination run wild and free. A participant of the 1998 Lesbian/Gay Weekend at Walt Disney World describes the alternate reading strategies available to non-straight individuals in the park:

> When you put 100,000 gay people within [the park], . . . even familiar rides take on whole new connotations. The dark solitude of the "cars" at the Haunted Mansion, for example, weren't so much an attraction as an opportunity. Gives the term "thrill ride" a whole new meaning. . . . At what other time of year could I have gotten applause in The Hall of Presidents for booing a certain jelly bean loving individual? And the fabulous EPCOT attraction, Ellen's Energy Adventure . . . became like a gathering of disciples come to worship. As an additional bonus, waiting on lines . . . becomes a lot more fun when you can spend the time cruising.[58]

Lesbian/Gay Weekends or "Gay Nights" provide unique opportunities for reading, obviously, but the exhiliration and "magic" many customers (straight or gay) feel whenever they visit the parks seems to have special resonance for certain queer individuals.

Customers may have more potential to experience this sense of opened possibilities than employees, but many of the lesbians and gay men who work at the parks are there in part for the greater freedom they feel there—however limited that freedom actually is. The ability to "live," even for a short moment, in the fantasy world represented in Disney's motion pictures and TV shows, seems to have a strong appeal to many lesbians and gay men. For, even with all of the subtle discrimination and controls placed on them, a large percentage of Disneyland and Walt Disney World's employee base *is and has been* homosexual. If anything, the percentage is by all accounts higher at the theme parks than in the motion picture and television divisions. In her research into Walt Disney World employees, Jane Keunz reported that

> Casual estimates made to me of the park's gay and lesbian population ranged from 25 to 75 percent, depending on the department. On what basis people were making these determinations was unclear; certainly every person I spoke with believed there was a strong queer, particularly gay male, presence. "You're guilty until proven innocent," laughs one after telling me the same joke I'd already heard three times that week. Q: How many Disney straights does it take to screw in a light bulb on Main Street? A: Both of them.[59]

Although it is probably impossible to determine exactly when and how word spread, by the 1980s Disneyland was known throughout homosexual circles in Southern California as a place crawling with lesbian and gay employees. As this reputation grew, the pronouncements took on a self-fulfilling role. As more lesbians and gay men heard that other homosexuals were working at the theme park, more applied for jobs there. Sue Schiebler, a former Disneyland employee, also hypothesized,

> In terms of Orange County, there aren't that many places to be gay and lesbian when you're young. . . . [Here at Disneyland] we party and we're out and we're having a grand time and it's like a free-for-all. . . . It's a safe alternative, . . . especially if you're too young to do the bars and you can't drive to West Hollywood or Long Beach. I mean, where do you go when you're in Orange County? Or Laguna Beach? And if you're afraid of being gay-bashed or whatever?[60]

The location of Walt Disney World in the similarly conservative Orlando area of central Florida might also work to attract lesbians and gay men to employment there.

As employees, gay men and women can find a precious and rare space to express themselves without feeling oppressed. A young man flouncing down a major thoroughfare anywhere else in America would probably attract unfavorable attention—but (ironically) flouncing down Disneyland's Main Street, U.S.A. dressed as Peter Pan, or any Disney character, he gets greeted with love and affection by everyone who sees him. According to one of the Cast Members Jane Keunz interviewed, employees dressed as characters have special opportunities as well.

> "If you were watching the characters," says one . . . employee, "and there was a guy in there [the character's costume], you could see him looking at the men. Not too much, but you would know. But . . . in the park, everything would be tasteful. Nothing would be done so that anybody could say 'Oh my god, there's a queen in this costume.'"[61]

The scope and depth of the parks' homosexual employees is embodied in the appropriation of the term "the Disney Family"—commonly recognized in the Orlando area as Disney slang for the park's gay and lesbian contingent. When Keunz was interviewing a homosexual employee, she was asked with a wink if she was "Family." Walt Disney World's more adult section, Pleasure Island, is commonly host to unofficial lesbian and gay employee parties, known as "Family Nights."[62] This use of "Family" is not the only code word developed by the parks' lesbian and gay employees. Another popular expression was developed at Walt Disney World—"thu." A lisped abbreviation of the word "through," the term could also be signified by putting one's middle and index fingers to one's cheekbone wearily. As one employee defined it: "If someone were really annoying you, if you were annoyed, if you were tired, if you were exhausted from working a lot of overtime, you were thu. . . . It wouldn't necessarily mean, I'm in trouble, but I'm really over this."[63] Using this coded phrase or hand gesture, a lesbian or gay employee could communicate to other homosexual employees exasperation towards the predominantly heterosexual families one had to deal with.

The sense of solidarity and celebration implied by the term "thu" and the use of "Family" has had profound effects on a number of homosexual Cast Members. Given the barriers to serious advancement within the parks, almost all of the lesbian and gay work force are hourly

wage or temp labor. Yet, possibly because of the absence of strong identification as "part of Disney," the lack of career ties to the company
seems to foster more openness and support amongst the "Family" (i.e.,
less rigid control over sexual discourse). Certainly, working on the various attractions allows for banter and jocularity amongst co-workers
and sometimes some subtle performances for the benefit of "those in
the know." Garth Steever, the openly gay manager, recalls fondly his
days working the rides at Fantasyland while studying at the University
of California at Los Angeles. In fact, the gay-friendly atmosphere
amongst the day labor helped him to come out, and he met another gay
man working as a Main Street musician who is now his partner.[64] Sue
Schiebler also acknowledged that the closeness and comfort amongst
her co-workers helped her come out of the closet, saying "I've had
many friends that have come out through working there."[65]

Yet, while the park has a vibrant homosexual employee base, sexual discourse is self-regulated even amongst the part-timers. "It's
very open," one employee admitted, "but it's . . . underground. You
have to curtail it. It's prevalent to us, the people down there, but if
anybody sees that, of course, they'll start trouble for you. That makes
headlines and Disney doesn't like headlines."[66] Although lesbians
and gay men might be out to each other, in other words, they must remain guarded about how out they are to their superiors and to the
customers. "Thu" works as an indication of a homosexual attitude,
but it is also a coded reference intended to be read only by those "in
the know." While corporate discourse holds less sway over part-
timers, other social discourses often seem to work to keep their expressions of homosexuality muted or coded. Just as most of the work
force for the two parks reside in the surrounding largely conservative
areas, so too do most homosexual employees. The religious, political
and legal attitudes in such closed-minded communities would logically effect how homosexual individuals living and working in these
areas go about their lives and even how they self-identify as homosexuals. First and foremost, most of the parks' homosexual employees are not "politicized" or "activists." Even moreso than within
LEAGUE, lesbian and gay Cast Members rarely identify or agree with
the aims and philosophies of such groups as ACT UP and Queer Nation. As Sue Schiebler describes it, "A lot of the gays who work at Disneyland are already somewhat assimilationist, not militant anyway.
Because, if they were, they probably wouldn't fit in. . . . They would

get in trouble . . . with the whole rules structure. So you're already somewhat willing to give up a voice just to work there."[67]

Such attitudes have manifested themselves when gay activists turn their attention towards the parks. In 1980, Disneyland hosted an annual Date Night at the park at the end of the summer. Amongst the couples who visited the park that night were two gay male teenagers, Shawn Elliott and Andrew Exler. When the two went out onto the dance floor of the Tomorrowland Terrace, security guards came up to them and "suggested that the men find female partners."[68] When Exler asked why, they were told it was park policy. The couple refused and continued dancing. Guards then tried to break them up by cutting in on them, but the young men simply danced around them. Finally, two guards physically escorted Exler off the floor and instructed Elliott to follow them. At the security office, the officers took down the two teenagers' names, addresses and ages and then escorted them from the park. A week later, the two filed suit against the park, seeking damages and an injunction to prevent the park from prohibiting same-sex dancing. It took four years for the case to come to trial, with the jury ruling in favor of the couple.

This incident was not a random occurrence: Exler had phoned the park ahead of time to find out the policy about same-sex dancing and set out consciously to break the rules in an attempt to have the policy changed. While it is probable that a number of homosexual employees also felt this policy was wrong, the response from the "Family" to this incident was not too supportive. Rather, many homosexual Cast Members felt upset with Exler and Elliott. Acknowledging a dynamic where employees feel that *they* have the right to criticize Disney, but outsiders cannot, one employee remembers most of her homosexual co-workers feeling, "They shouldn't have been doing that, this is a family place. You shouldn't do that. Go to a club. They were just trying to cause trouble anyway."[69]

Two years earlier a similar event occurred at Disneyland on an even larger scale. For years, the management had allowed private parties to rent out the park after normal working hours during the off season (vaguely October through January). In 1978, an organization calling itself the Los Angeles Bar and Restaurant Association reserved the park for such a party. Just before the night of the party, Disneyland realized that the Association consisted of *gay male* restaurants and bars which had been selling tickets to the event to all of its customers. Unable to bar the event completely at such short notice, Disneyland made preparations for the worst. All live music was canceled to keep from encouraging same-sex couples to dance. Security was beefed up, and park supervisors "said that, for a night, courtesy was optional."[70] In a classic case of gay activist "zapping," 15,000 mainly gay male guests aggressively took over Disneyland. Some of the guests were heterosexual families who had no idea that they had bought tickets for a gay "zap" and were shocked to find very open displays of affection between men. Yet, the majority were homosexuals running rampant through the park, occasionally having it out with homophobic employees and joyfully engaging in what has been described by many of the people who worked at the park that night as a free-form orgy. Various stages of sexual coupling occurred in bathrooms, on park benches and even on the Submarine Voyage.[71] The response from the "Family" seems to have been equivalent to their stance on Exler and Elliott's dancing: disapproval. One homosexual employee who worked that night declared, "Oh my goodness! There were men cruising men all over, . . . and they were obnoxious. . . . Even the gay people like myself were a little appalled. Because we thought, 'Well, this is a little—pushing things too far.' I mean, it's one thing to come and have fun, but they were really in your face."[72]

Similar to the parks' gay community's apparent antipathy towards radical queer activism, the community often seems to reject the blurring of sexual boundaries espoused under the term "queer." Instead, categories based on older ideas about sexuality and gender identification are reinforced: that gay men are defined by their femininity and lesbians by their masculinity. For example, a number of lesbians favor working at Frontierland or the motorized cars of Tomorrowland's Autopia (as well as maintenance and janitorial work). Similarly, many young gay men tend to drift towards the fanciful nature of Fantasyland, or, even more likely, towards performing in the parades down Main Street. It is possible that, for these individuals, this is the only way they know how to "be gay," affecting (if not reinforcing ideas still common in conservative communities) how they identify as homosexual. Sue Schiebler relates, "We used to say Fantasyland were the gay boys and Tomorrowland were the lesbians. . . . It really is funny how all of it feeds stereotypes, but yet it does."[73] Such strict definitions might have an adverse affect upon some individuals. For example, women reported at both parks the importance of park softball teams within the lesbian work force. At least one formerly closeted lesbian said she thought, "I must not be a lesbian, you're supposed to like softball! What am I?"[74]

Such a strong division between effeminate gay men and "butch" lesbians often separates homosexual employees from each other, instead of uniting them under the "Family" umbrella—much as discussed above in regard to LEAGUE's members. Lesbian maintenance workers do not associate with young gay male parade dancers, for example. Granted, the constraints of the job descriptions often keep such disparate groups from interacting on any regular basis. Yet, within the social structure of the parks' homosexual community, cliques often form, and certain groups disparage the attitude and appearance of other groups. By all accounts, for example, "parade boys" are commonly looked down upon by many other groups as being flighty and unintelligent.

Announcement of the first LEAGUE meeting seems to have exacerbated the differences amongst homosexual employees rather than bringing them together. Most of the early meetings were attended by men only. A number of both lesbians and gay men decided not to attend under the assumption that only "parade boys" would be there. Garth Steever, for example, felt no need at first to get involved in LEAGUE/ Anaheim, because he was already out in the workplace and was in a managerial position. Others who wanted to talk about support for AIDS feared that the "parade boys" would come in and turn it into a dating club. This type of attitude has made the history of LEAGUE/ Anaheim less stable than LEAGUE's history. After setting up the first two meetings, LEAGUE relinquished any control or responsibility for LEAGUE/Anaheim to the park employees. Consequently, the organization and success of the group has ebbed and flowed. Slowly, some who were previously indifferent or antagonistic to the idea have gotten more involved. Steever decided to act as a role model and to help lead LEAGUE/Anaheim. Slowly, more women became involved with LEAGUE/Anaheim as well.

Yet, trying to organize any type of employees' group at the parks (not just for homosexual employees) is fraught with problems, predominantly because of the work schedules of the Cast Members. Unlike at the studio, where most employees take lunch around the same time, and work mainly "9-to-5" hours, park employees have staggered hours and alternate shifts. In order to deal with this problem, the very first

LEAGUE/Anaheim meeting was held twice on the same day (in the morning and again in the afternoon) to reach two different shifts. The prevalence of part-time labor at the parks not only creates problems in getting individuals together at the same time in one location, but it also significantly affects the issues that LEAGUE/Anaheim focuses on.

One such area is the attempt to advise and help those part-time Cast Members who wish to move into the Intern Program and move potentially toward a managerial position. Steever's growing involvement in the group has helped others make these career moves. An even larger area of concern for many employees—not just lesbian and gay—are benefits. While members of LEAGUE at the studio were working towards *extending* their benefits to cover their same-sex partners, members of LEAGUE/Anaheim have been faced with struggling to get benefits for *themselves*. The importance mentioned earlier that some gay and lesbian employees placed on AIDS support points out how most of the theme park's employees do not have the generous benefits extended to employees dealing with AIDS within the rest of the company. (This is true for all the theme parks, not just Disneyland.)

This had not always been the case. Until the mid-1980s, Disneyland had a benefits program for its large part-time work force that was possibly unmatched in the country: for working twenty hours a week, employees got full medical, dental and optical coverage, as well as paid vacation time and sick pay. As a consequence, a number of part-time employees stayed for years at the park. In the early 1980s, for example, mothers who had worked part-time since the day Disneyland opened in 1955 were still loyally punching in. Under this structure, HIV-positive part-timers would have been granted much if not all of the coverage that was eventually offered to the company's salaried staff in the late 1980s.

But, this structure did not weather the momentous events that the Walt Disney Company endured in 1984. Just as the company was staving off various hostile takeover bids, and desperately trying to scrounge money to buy back stock, the contracts for the five major unions that Disneyland works with in hiring its part-time employees came up for renegotiation. Disney opened the contract negotiations by stating the need for an up to sixteen percent pay cut over three years. It is almost certain that the executives knew this offer would be flatly turned down. In ensuing bids, the company presented a seemingly less drastic strategy—a hiring freeze, a lengthening of the pay increase schedule and, most importantly, a denial of benefits to new hires until they reached full-time status. While the adjustments to pay scales and hiring freezes obviously bothered employees, the rescinding of the benefits seems to have been the largest complaint. George Herold, an employee working at that time, noted, "What bothered me was them wanting to take away things that they had always given us, the benefits."[75]

Ultimately reaching a stalemate, Disneyland witnessed one of the most rancorous strikes in its history, in which protesters staged actions in front of the ticket booths, employees breaking the strike hid in the trunks of supervisors to get through the picket lines and one frustrated strike-breaker almost hit a pregnant striker with his car.[76] Lasting only twenty-two days, the park was successful in breaking the will of the strikers who ultimately feared losing their jobs when Disney advertised for new hires during the strike and got over a thousand applicants. In the end, benefits were only retained for those part-timers who had been hired before the new contract. These "statused" part-time employees discovered quickly a subtle strategy to drive them out by forcing them to work the worst hours or hardest jobs. Dennis Brent, a "statused" employee, recalled, "They took me out of a cushy job, 9-to-5 Saturdays and Sundays at the Circle-Vision theatre, and all of a sudden I found myself working private parties on the Jungle Cruise and Grad Nites, which I hadn't worked in ten years. It didn't violate the terms of the contract, but they obviously were trying to get rid of us."[77]

This loss of benefits has helped the more conservative theme park branch of the company keep from dealing with the issues LEAGUE raises. Not offering benefits to its part-timers, there's no need for discussion of domestic-partner benefits. Not offering health coverage to its part-timers, the parks feel no need to deal with treatment and support for the HIV-positive. In fact, a large amount of energy within LEAGUE/Anaheim has been spent specifically trying to get recognition from the park that HIV-positive employees even exist. Sue Schiebler noted that "Disney has been very hush-hush on the fact that we have HIV-positive people and people with AIDS working there at the park. Even among the employees themselves."[78] However limited by both corporate and self-regulation in attitudes towards sexuality, LEAGUE/Anaheim has worked to create as much a space for these employees to find support and assistance—and to voice their concerns and needs—as the conditions would allow.

CONCLUSION: OPENING DISNEY'S CLOSET

The formation of LEAGUE, LEAGUE/Anaheim and ALLIANCE all point to a strengthened presence of the lesbian and gay work force at the Walt Disney Company. Their existence has succeeded in helping more employees at Disney feel secure and safe enough to come out at the workplace. They have stood as models for employees at other studios and in other industries. And they have helped win benefits for homosexual employees that might not have been granted otherwise. For, more than three years after Sass Nielsen announced the first meeting of LEAGUE, the Walt Disney Company announced in October of 1995 that it would offer domestic-partner benefits to its employees beginning in 1996.

As this chapter shows, the growing solidarity of Disney's lesbian and gay employees does not necessarily guarantee a unanimity in conceptions of sexuality or even a blanket-agreement on workplace issues for "queer" employees. Various divisions of this conglomerate face different situations that create different conceptions of identity and experience, and thus require different strategies and answers by both the employee groups and the corporate structure. The dialogue between executive decision makers and these lesbian/gay/bisexual groups is an ongoing balance of power, as is the dialogue between the groups and within the groups themselves. Dealing with issues of health coverage, employment opportunity and job security is murky and complex, and varies with each situation.

Even though these relations are never smooth nor stabilized, one must recognize that such relations actually exist within the Walt Disney Company. In the past decade, attitudes towards homosexual employees within the company have radically altered. While not denying the presence of homosexual employees prior to the Eisner and Wells regime, the relatively open acceptance of these employees marks a new era in the company's history. In turning around the economic status of the company, this new executive board has also turned around the company's outlook towards the sexuality of its employees.

Yet, as this chapter has argued, the company's revamped attitude towards sexuality in the workplace is not an unleashing of a free-moving concept of sexuality. Instead, the existence of these employee groups often works to *contain* these issues and manage them to the economic interest of the corporation. Further, company *zeitgeist* attempts to draw its gay and lesbian employees into identifying as "Disney Family," hopefully causing them to internalize corporate attitudes and self-regulate their expressions of (and possibly even their conceptions of) sexuality. As a number of activists in the late '60s and in the '80s and '90s discovered, liberation is ever and always an elusive goal.

4

"Part of Your World"

Reading Disney Queerly in the Eisner Era

THE INCREASED VISIBILITY of gay men and lesbians as Disney employees reflects their increased visibility as a cultural and political force in society as a whole. Queer activism during the late 1980s, centralized in groups such as ACT UP, Queer Nation and GLAAD, helped pressure Hollywood studios like Disney to come to terms with their homosexual employees. At the same time, these groups became equally concerned with actively monitoring how the film and television industry represented homosexuals. The attempt to interrupt the filming of *Basic Instinct* (1992) stands as possibly the most notorious instance of activism against the industry's images of homosexuals. Various activist organizations continue to consistently alert the lesbian/gay community to what they consider to be "positive" or "negative" portrayals, to organize letter-writing campaigns, to initiate boycotts or (conversely) to announce awards for "positive" representations of homosexuality in order to make the community's attitude known to those in charge of film and TV production.

LEAGUE has not had a specific hand in making suggestions or organizing protests regarding Disney's production decisions and has been granted existence in part upon the specific provision that it *not* engage in such activism. Yet, the employee group has tried to do what little it can. Although some members disagreed with co-chair Hicks' granting an interview to the *Los Angeles Times* about the Disney-owned Los Angeles television station KCAL's airing of Rush Limbaugh's syndicated series, the members *did* agree to register their displeasure in an interoffice letter. LEAGUE also met with filmmaker Elaine Hollimann as a sign of support when the studio optioned the rights to turn *Chicks in White Satin* (1992), her Oscar-nominated documentary on a lesbian wedding, into a feature film. Furthermore, open homosexuals working for the studio have at times expressed the importance of their sexuality in the work they do, indicating that they have expressed outlooks and opinions about sexuality in their work for Disney.[1]

Greater visibility of homosexuality in American culture, and overt announcements and awards that attempt to draw attention to how lesbians and gay men appreciate films and television, has brought the hidden "coded-ness" of lesbian/gay culture more and more into the light. "Camp," to use one example, is no longer exclusively understood by a secret homosexual subculture. Now audiences from numerous backgrounds appreciate "camp."[2] Consequently, reading Disney texts from a "gay sensibility" has gotten "easier" and less "subaltern" since the mid-1980s.

In fact, one doesn't now necessarily need to identify as homosexual in order to find a subtext. CBS anchorman Dan Rather, in a special column for the *Los Angeles Times* in early 1992, noticed an AIDS allegory going on within Disney's film version of the fairy tale *Beauty and the Beast* (1991):

> Think of the spell [the Beast is under] as AIDS, with the same arbitrary and harshly abbreviated limitations on time, and you feel the Beast's loneliness and desperation a little more deeply. He's just a guy trying as hard as he can to find a little meaning—a little love, a little *beauty*—while he's still got a little life left.[3]

Cynthia Erb, writing for a more academic audience, agrees with Rather's interpretation of the film:

> The visual contrast made between the deteriorated form of the Beast and the painting of him as a beautiful young man possibly sets up a stereotypical opposition between ugliness and beauty reminiscent of Oscar Wilde's *The Picture of Dorian Gray*, but in this context the ugliness/beauty dyad also supports a tension, crucial to the film's AIDS allegory, between the issue of having health or not having it.[4]

Certainly, the lyrics written for "The Mob Song," in which the villagers set out to attack the Beast, add to this method of interpretation. In the song, the villagers state, "We don't like what we don't understand, in fact it scares us," and thus they must save their families and their lives by killing the Beast. The quotation reverberates strongly as a parallel to

AIDS panic that many individuals, as well as religious and political groups, expressed during the spread of the disease. As Harry Benshoff notes, many "recent critical essays on the mass media have demonstrated how the representational codes and narrative tropes of the monster movie . . . have been grafted onto much television and newspaper coverage of AIDS."[5] "The Mob Song" taps into this demonization of persons with AIDS (PWAs) but its placement in the film definitely sides with the demonized rather than the lynchers speaking.

The Beast is given the life span of a magical rose to find a cure to his curse (someone to love that will love him in return), and although missing the deadline means only that he'll remain a Beast permanently, the narrative contrives to have him on the brink of death just as the last petal falls from the flower. Also, the Beast goes through many of the "five stages" of emotional reaction to impending death: anger, denial, bargaining, depression and acceptance. The Beast is definitely an angry creature, and his initial attempts to woo Belle are blatant bargaining, done simply to remove the curse without necessarily feeling any actual love towards her. When he allows Belle to leave his domain, he enters a state of depression that makes him unwilling to defend himself against the mob that arrives to string him up. Most touchingly, the Beast reaches acceptance just at the moment of his seeming death. As a soft rain falls around them, Belle caresses the dying Beast, and the Beast ventures that "Maybe it's better this way." Belle protests, but the Beast looks up at her with love, touches her face as he says "At least I got to see you one last time" and then lapses into unconsciousness. (Of course, the tale resurrects the Beast and cures the spell when she says "I love you" just as he seems to expire.)

PWAs "poached" from Disney texts long before *Beauty and the Beast.* Lesbian and gay employees of the theme parks remark on how many of their AIDS-infected friends desire to visit Disneyland and Walt Disney World, specifically seeing their trips as a way of dealing with their status. Also, many AIDS quilt panels include Disney imagery—mouse ears, Disney song lyrics and the like. Some panels commemorate Disney employees, but some pay tribute to a fan's devotion to the studio's products. While wrong to conceive that every Disney-influenced panel *must* refer to a homosexual (thus implying that AIDS is only a homosexual disease), certain panels make the sexual orientation of the remembered person quite clear. For example, one particularly colorful panel commemorating an adult male depicts an underwater scene and contains a number of lines from songs written for *The Little Mermaid* (1989), the animated musical Disney made just before *Beauty and the Beast*. Amongst these are such quotes as "The men up there don't like a lot of blather," and "Don't forget the importance of body language." The attention paid by television and print news to the displays of the AIDS Quilt might have made some, like Rather, more aware of the importance of Disney in these people's lives, thus making it easier to understand the 1991 film as an AIDS allegory.

While not every audience member saw the feature and automatically thought, "Oh, this is all about AIDS," Rather's interpretation of the film was not looked on as a scandalous perversion of a cherished Disney film meant for family viewing. Instead of fearing accusations of having a "warped" mind or "reading too much into things," Rather aptly wrote, "The AIDS metaphor is just one way, a valid way, of looking at *Beauty and the Beast*."[6] Just as it is mistaken to assume that all the panels on the AIDS quilt commemorate homosexuals, reading the film as an AIDS allegory does *not* automatically signal homosexuality. Yet, the acceptance of the AIDS allegory can be linked quite directly to homosexuality. Beyond a wealth of "gay-tinged" jokes that will be analyzed in this chapter, the main reason for a lack of hue and cry against Rather's interpretation of the film was that most moviegoers knew that Howard Ashman, the film's lyricist and producer, was gay and had recently died as a result of the AIDS virus. The quilt panel described above is one of two dedicated to Ashman. The other features stenciled images of the Little Mermaid, Ariel, and her father, Triton, with the caption, "Oh that he had one more song to sing, one more song." Although Rather reports that those he talked with at the studio asserted that the project was already in the works before Ashman's condition was known, mention of Ashman's battle with the disease lends credence to reading the film in this manner.[7]

At this time, many film critics in the popular press were beginning to acknowledge more and more the "gay sensibility" of Disney's product. A number of factors contributed to this higher mainstream awareness of reading Disney from a gay or lesbian standpoint. As stated before, many filmgoers had a greater awareness of lesbian/gay culture and reading strategies such as camp. Secondly, the societal and industrial changes mentioned in the previous chapter led (albeit slowly) to more manifest representations of homosexuality in films, television and other areas of popular culture. The output from the Walt Disney Company in the Eisner era reflects the growth of homosexual representation throughout the entertainment industry and American society. Lastly, the openness of many artists regarding their sexual orientation (such as Howard Ashman) gave additional weight to reading "gay subtext" into certain cultural products.

This chapter will examine exactly what might have been present in various Disney films and television series since the mid-1980s that could be read through a "lesbian/gay sensibility" by numerous individuals—not just self-identified homosexuals. One of the main methods of doing this lies in analyzing exactly how the mainstream press expressed itself as it began to read homosexual subtexts into Disney. While media critics cannot be held up as typical audience members, their reactions often indicate larger patterns of interpretation. Some reviews comment on the reactions of the audience that viewed the film with the critic; some reviews comment on what is considered the "intended audience" of a certain film; and some reviews specifically refer to the publicity surrounding a film, indicating a certain prevalence for many audience members to watch a film through a certain mindframe. (Of course, critics' reviews in the mainstream press are part of the barrage that affects how audiences are pre-situated to view a film—an issue to be more deeply analyzed in the final chapter.)

This chapter will also focus on how these "more obvious" readings differ from the reworked understandings of Disney analyzed in chapter 2. Individuals who appreciated Disney from a non-straight perspective from the '30s to the '70s were subversively "reading against the grain" of what the studio had intended. In contrast, some characters in Disney-produced films and television were overtly homosexual, and mainstream newspapers were pointing out the openly homosexual artists who were working on other Disney films and television. Reading Disney from a "lesbian/gay sensibility" cannot be considered "radical" or all that subversive if the majority of the audience is also reading it that way.

The increasingly manifest nature of lesbian/gay characters or subjectivities in Disney texts is a major change from Walt's era. Yet, just as the discussion of LEAGUE points out how a "more open" workplace still works to manage and control expressions of sexuality, these "more obvious" readings limit conceptions and representations of sexuality. In chapter 2, I pointed out that definitions of sexuality were still in contestation in the early part of the twentieth century, and certain reading strategies were consequently considered more "queer" than specifically "lesbian" or "gay." In contrast, the "openness" of these later texts often supplants a free-floating "queer" response with a more precisely "lesbian" or "gay" subject position. Earlier, the unique position of LEAGUE members as part of the process of production was placed in contrast to potential non-straight consumers of Disney in terms of the company's ability to regulate and control discourse about sexuality. As this chapter will begin to outline, the increased openness of Disney to homosexuality potentially affects these consumers as well.

THE WORK OF FAIRIES: NOTES ON SEXUALITY AND *AUTEUR* ANALYSIS

As Rather's analysis of *Beauty and the Beast* demonstrates, knowledge of an open homosexual working on a film seems to make a homosexual reading position acceptable—in effect "authorizing" it. Many critics, commentators and average moviegoers implicitly assume that a homosexual filmmaker will in some way input issues of sexuality into the work s/he is involved in making. The general acceptance of an AIDS analogy in *Beauty and the Beast* was therefore legitimated by proposing that Howard Ashman was the film's *auteur*. As originally described by François Truffaut in the mid-1950s in his landmark essay "A Certain Tendency of the French Cinema," *la politique des auteurs* conceives (and promotes) the idea of an individual voice controlling and creating the filmic work.[8] In this way, viewers can find stylistic and thematic motifs that recur and develop across an individual's career much as an art critic can follow Pablo Picasso or Vincent Van Gogh through their different stages and periods. Truffaut (and Andrew Sarris, who popularized the theory in the United States with his book *The American Cinema: Directors and Directions, 1929–1968)* posited the director as the *auteur* of a motion picture, especially one who "authored" as much as possible of his or her films (writing as well as directing).[9] Yet, *auteur* critics also came to champion certain directors of the American studio system that seemed to "rise above" the constraints placed upon them by studio bosses, placing some sort of personal stamp on their work.

Since the 1960s, *auteur* theory has been pushed farther and farther to the sidelines in the academic study of film. By 1976, Bill Nichols was able to write, in his introduction to the "*Auteur* Criticism" section of

Movies and Methods, that "many argue that the debate about *auteur* criticism is passé."[10] The *auteur* theory in film studies has, by and large, been generally dismissed as a relic expressing romantic notions of individual achievement, ignoring both the collaborative structure of filmmaking and the sociohistorical circumstances that encode texts without necessarily the conscious design of the filmmakers. Furthermore, as reception studies gained greater importance in the academy, auteur analysis seemed to deny the power of the reader in favor of trying to understand what the filmmaker "really meant."[11]

Many of the "social constructionist" theories of identity seem to discredit the very core of the *auteur* concept—that "identity" is created through a social situation rather than through an essential inevitability. Feminist writers as well as those concerned with issues of race and sexuality have used this concept to challenge the dominance of the white heterosexual patriarchal system—destabilizing the essentialist ideas of this order by asserting that gender, racial and sexual identities are "a kind of impersonation and approximation . . . a performance that produces the *illusion* of an inner . . . essence or psychic . . . core."[12] Such concepts have been used to deconstruct the importance of the established pantheon of mainly straight white male *auteurs.*[13]

Interestingly, while some cinema studies programs have begun to devalue courses on individual *auteurs,* the importance of the individual experience of filmmakers has risen again through studies of race, gender and sexuality in media. Work in this area considers it vital to know that a filmmaker is African-American or female or homosexual (to take only a few examples) in order to fully appreciate the work being examined. The analysis of such critically conceived movements of the 1990s in American cinema as the rise of African-American directors or "New Queer Cinema" are fundamentally based on *auteur* concepts—but this time studying Spike Lee or Gregg Araki instead of white heterosexual men. While this development may seem to be a willful ignoring of the problems inherent in assigning agency or "authorship" to an individual, Richard Dyer points out that "not believing in sole and all-determining authorship does not mean that one must not attach any importance whatsoever to those who make films and believing that being lesbian/gay is a culturally and historically specific phenomenon does not mean that sexual identity is of no cultural and historical significance."[14]

While not denying the sociohistorical determinants that have factored into a particular filmmaker's self-identity, *auteur* studies can bring to light an individual's material social position in relation to ideological and cultural discourse, which will impact upon the texts s/he creates. How an individual self-identifies (by gender, race or sexual orientation) would tend to affect that individual's outlook on society and his or her place in it. The various discourses analyzed by Foucault and others attempt to categorize each individual. With the individual internalizing these conceptions, it becomes difficult (if not impossible) for him or her to conceive or articulate a sense of self outside of the matrices laid out by hegemonic discourse. For the purposes of this work, then, it is important to realize that as an artist self-identifies as "homosexual," that artist agrees to certain definitions of sexual identity (instead of a more free-floating conception of sexual desire) and that this identification may impact his or her work. In this way, social constructionist theories can help *inform*, rather than *deconstruct*, an *auteur* analysis.

Just as one can analyze the social performativity of gender, race and sexuality, one can examine "authorship" as a performance of identity. "All authorship and all sexual identities are performances done with greater or less facility, always problematic in relation to any self separable from the realization of self in the discursive modes available."[15] Conceptualizing "authorship" as a performance gains strength from historical evidence of publicity campaigns meant to encourage regular filmgoing audiences to think of certain films as expressions of a certain filmmaker's temperament long before Truffaut ever noticed that "certain tendency." Certain directors such as Alfred Hitchcock, Orson Welles and Cecil B. DeMille were just as famous to customers as the stars who appeared in their films. Their fame was encouraged through poster art, press junket interviews, and even trailers for upcoming films in which they performed their role as "author." The preview for Welles' *Citizen Kane* is narrated by himself specifically presenting the viewer with his work in progress. DeMille often made short films ostensibly showing the behind-the-scenes operations of a major film production, but actually working as publicity for his latest picture and making certain that everyone knew who was responsible for it all. Hitchcock's weekly performance as host to a television series cemented his image in the popular consciousness as a unique and recognizable filmmaker.

By recognizing the importance of the audience in conceptualizing an individual as an *auteur*, *auteur* studies can also be informed by rather than threatened by the emphasis on reception in media studies. A reader must acknowledge an author had an important hand in the work being read in order for the author to have an importance in the making of meaning. If an audience member does not know who "Howard Hawks" or "Frank Capra" are, then s/he can't ascribe intentionality or personal signature to the work. On the other side, if a viewer *is* aware of a supposed author, s/he can ascribe a personal signature that might not even have been put there intentionally. Obviously, if an audience is made aware of an author who is homosexual, that will encourage them to interpret his or her work through a homosexual framework regardless of whether or not all the facets discovered were purposefully placed by the "author" to comment on issues of sexuality.

The importance of reception in *auteur* analysis also challenges traditional critical precepts. Audience members can decide to assign "authorship" to someone other than directors or director/screenwriters. The study of star personae and their affect on film meaning acknowledges who audiences often consider the largest makers of meaning. Similarly, various critics have at points made *auteur* cases for writers, cameramen and producers. (Certainly, producer Walt Disney so successfully performed authorship of his studio's output during his lifetime that many customers thought Walt drew all the cartoons himself.) The collaborative nature of film brings a number of talents to bear on a final product, and each has some small effect on the film that would have been different without their involvement. A spectator can choose to focus on the contributions of any of these artists—the production design, the music score, the special effects technology, etc.

Consequently, it might be quite possible to do a homosexual-based *auteur* analysis of the work of orchestrater Thomas Pasatieri (who worked on the scores for *The Little Mermaid* and *Dick Tracy* [1990]), or producer Lauren Lloyd (who Disney recruited to become Vice-President of Production for Hollywood Pictures), or casting director Tammy Balik (who worked on Touchstone Television's *Ellen*). An analysis of lead animator Andreas Deja serves as a case in point. Openly gay, Deja has announced in various interviews that his sexual orientation has had its effect on the characters he draws. In drawing the villainous Jafar for *Aladdin* (1992), Deja admits to conceiving of the character as a gay man "to give him his theatrical quality, his elegance."[16] Although Deja has worked on a number of different types of characters, he has been most assigned to two types of roles: male villains and hypermuscular men. In the first category, Deja has worked as lead animator for Jafar, and for Scar in *The Lion King* (1994). Both are overly refined, fey and seething with frustration for feeling that their talents and abilities have been overlooked. One can read Deja's "sensibility" contributing to the history of campy "gay-tinged" villainy in Disney (as analyzed in chapter 2) by watching how Jafar arches his eyebrows in disdain, or in the sneer that curls Scar's mouth as he endures the heterosexual patriarchy in which he finds himself.[17]

In the second category, Deja has led the animation of Ariel's broad-chested father, Triton, in *The Little Mermaid*, the lead character in *Hercules* (1997) and, combining both of Deja's recurrent motifs, the boorish Gaston in *Beauty and the Beast*. All these characters present an exaggerated ideal of the masculine body, with massive shoulders, chest and arms, tight waists and rugged facial features. Although each character is slightly different in design, all three spectacularize the male body in a way rarely seen in Disney animation prior to *The Little Mermaid*.[18] In describing his conceptualization of Gaston, Deja looked to "these ridiculously vain guys you see in the gym today, always checking themselves in the mirror."[19] This quote describes how Deja's work simultaneously revels in and yet humorously deflates the "body fascism" that became a noticeable aspect of urban gay male culture by the 1980s. Deja gives the design of these characters "appeal," but also makes their muscularity so outlandish that it verges on the laughable. If there is one moment in all of Deja's films that encapsulates this tendency, it is the "Gaston" number in *Beauty and the Beast*. A narcissistic tribute to the character's manliness, Cynthia Erb suggests that the number is a "queer homage . . . to the male chorus number from the musical tradition . . . little more than an elaborate fetishization of the powerful male body."[20] At the same time, though, Deja's depiction of Gaston baring his hairy chest, flexing his muscles and stomping around in boots takes on a level of absurdity, ridiculing the hyper-masculinity that Gaston represents.[21] Deja's acknowledgement of the effect his sexual orientation has on his work marks a new era in reading subtext into Disney. His comments give legitimacy to reading these characters through a "gay sensibility" because they have been "authored" by an openly gay man, regardless if the "homosexual author" is the formal overseer of the entire project. Yet, as the influence of "muscle queens" on some of Deja's work indicates, the "authorial" position allows a specific reading influenced by a specific sociocultural identity—*not* a free-floating "queer" reading.

GIVING A BEAST HIS SOUL: THE IMPORTANCE
OF HOWARD ASHMAN

One might consider the work of openly gay or lesbian directors working within the Walt Disney Company (such as Emile Ardolino, who directed *Three Men and a Little Lady* [1991]) the strongest texts for discussing lesbian/gay authorship during the Eisner era. As the above discussion shows though, a number of film personnel can be considered *auteurs* in differing circumstances. Film's collaborative process is especially apparent at a studio like Disney, where a "corporate" style often seems to take precedence over any individual artist's viewpoint, and one cannot deny the importance that multiple artists bring to animated features like *The Little Mermaid* (1989), *Beauty and the Beast* (1991) and *Aladdin* (1992). Andreas Deja's contributions have already been recognized, but other talents also figure strongly. Linda Woolverton's script for *Beauty and the Beast* attempts to put forth a more progressive attitude toward women than had been expressed in *The Little Mermaid*.[22] Directors Ron Clemente and John Musker signaled the revival of the studio's animation in their first project, *The Great Mouse Detective* (1986), before moving onto directing the more financially successful *The Little Mermaid* and *Aladdin*.[23] Jeffrey Katzenberg, as Vice-President in Charge of Production, also had final say over all of these films and became increasingly fascinated and involved in the animated projects—even helping rewrite the final scenes of *Beauty and the Beast.*

Even with all these contributors, though, certainly the most prominently discussed authorial presence in these films has been lyricist Howard Ashman. Most critics signaled out Ashman's work in the fashioning of these films, and general audiences seemed to regard Ashman's first project with the studio, *The Little Mermaid,* as the start of a new "Golden Period" for Disney animation. This regard was strengthened when *The Rescuers Down Under* (1990), the animated feature released between *The Little Mermaid* and *Beauty and the Beast,* and without Ashman and his writing partner Alan Menken's involvement, performed poorly at the box office. Furthermore, Ashman worked not only as a lyricist for both *The Little Mermaid* and *Beauty and the Beast,* but as a producer as well. There are also reports that he functioned as a story consultant for *Beauty and the Beast,* overhauling certain plot points and helping conceive of some key characters. Dan Rather's analysis of *Beauty and the Beast* places special emphasis on

Ashman's contributions, as do a number of reviews of the various animated features on which Ashman worked.[24] Cynthia Erb states plainly that her theoretical dissection of *Beauty and the Beast* "is predicated upon the assumption of at least partial gay authorship, apparently traceable to creative input from producer/lyricist Howard Ashman."[25] This recognition was furthered within the studio as well. Around the time of *Aladdin*'s release, Katzenberg was quoted as saying, "We have two guardian angels. One is Walt Disney, who continues to touch every frame of our movies. The other is Howard Ashman, who continues to touch every note of our movies."[26] At the end of the credits to *Beauty and the Beast*, the studio added a tribute to Ashman, honoring him as the man "who gave a mermaid her voice and a Beast his soul." With such a salute to Ashman's talents included within the film itself, it would be hard to *not* consider Ashman as the *auteur* of this trio of animated musicals.

Although Ashman was the not the arbiter or final decision-maker on what projects the studio would produce as animated features, the three projects Ashman was involved with are all adaptions of popular children's tales that already had a history of importance in gay culture. *The Little Mermaid* was based on Hans Christian Andersen's tale. Many today regard Andersen as having been homosexual, thus giving the story of a sad and isolated mermaid who cannot have the human male she loves added importance to gay male readers. This frame of reading was further emphasized when the renowned homosexual Oscar Wilde revised the tale in "The Fisherman and His Soul." Wilde's version reverses the story, depicting a human male who desires a mermaid and must pay dearly for this love.[27] Cynthia Erb points out that Wilde uses his take on the fairy tale to critique "Catholicism's constraints on expressions of love."[28]

After *The Little Mermaid*, Ashman involved himself in *Beauty and the Beast*, which had already been the subject of a famous French film adaption by Jean Cocteau, a version that emphasizes the homoerotics of the story by drawing parallels between the Beast and Belle's human suitor. Both parts are played in the Cocteau version by actor Jean Marais, and the film is so concerned with the beauty or ugliness of the two male characters that "the title *La Belle et la Bete* now appeared to describe the relationship between the two male characters at least as much as the love story between Belle and the Beast."[29] Many of Ashman's changes to Woolverton's original script involve inserting aspects of Cocteau's film version into the tale. Ashman helped fashion the ego-driven character of Gaston to function much in the same manner as the male suitor in Cocteau's film. Ashman also "solved" the problem of the Disney film's second half by introducing the humanized household objects in the Beast's castle to act as comic supporting characters.[30] Although these objects fit precisely into the typical Disney scheme of having dwarves or mice or birds acting as companions to the lead characters, Ashman's solution is a Disneyfied version of the living candelabras and chairs that decorate the Beast's castle in Cocteau's film. Lastly, Cocteau endured severe health problems during the making of *La Belle et la Bête* and thus compared himself to the Beast in his diary.[31] Although there is no proof that Ashman knew of this similarity, reports indicate that Ashman was the one who suggested more focus on the character of the Beast, who, as has been discussed, seemed to carry many connotations of battling AIDS.

Ashman's last project for the studio was *Aladdin*, a film he never lived to see completed (and eventually contained some songs in which Alan Menken collaborated with lyricist Tim Rice). Reports of Ashman's conception of the project link his vision of the tale to the campy appropriation of "Arabian Nights" imagery by various members of the gay community, most particularly 1960s performance artist and avant-garde filmmaker Jack Smith and Italian film director Pier Paolo Pasolini. Long before Smith made the film *Flaming Creatures* (1963) or Pasolini directed his version of *Il Fiore delle Mille e Una Notte* (1974), the "Arabian Nights" cycle of tales had held fascination in gay male culture, describing the "Orient" as an exotic sensual environment that didn't hold to traditional Western morality.[32] English expeditionary Richard Burton in the 1800s, for example, had examined the "Arabian Nights" tales for their erotic content, in which he combined literary analysis with supposed scientific observation of Arabic peoples (including an obsession with penis size and detailed descriptions of homosexual acts).[33] Camping this exotic Neverland much as Smith did in the 1960s is what Ashman seemed to find attractive in the initial discussions for making *Aladdin*.

In fact, characters and situations encouraging a camp reception were a marked (and importantly, widely noticed) development in this new "Golden Period" of Disney animation. Janet Maslin, writing for the *New York Times*, commented that this new period created animation "not only with an eye toward pleasing children but also with an older, savvier audience in mind."[34] In-jokes and sly winks that most children would not catch or understand suddenly started popping up in these fairy-tale musicals. For example, the studio animation department acknowledged modeling Ursula (the villainess in *The Little Mermaid*) on the cult transvestite star Divine.[35] Most (if not all) young children would have had no knowledge of Divine; many adults seemed to make the connection, or at least admired Ursula as "a fabulously campy creation" or a "wonderfully campy villain."[36] Contributing to the increasingly overt camp value of these films, Ashman wrote for each production at least one major show-stopping number that parodied Busby Berkeley extravaganzas. "Under the Sea," in *The Little Mermaid*, contains a fish done up to look like Carmen Miranda, while other undersea creatures samba with abandon. "Be Our Guest," in *Beauty and the Beast*, recreates bathing beauties diving in synchronization into a pool—but with spoons leaping into a tureen. *Aladdin* contains two such numbers: "You've Never Had a Friend Like Me," in which the Genie puts on a Vegas-inspired display (complete with "Applause" sign at the end); and "Prince Ali," in which the over-the-top presentation inspires the Genie to view the sequence as the Macy's Thanksgiving Parade ("Don't they look lovely, June?").

Again, how much of this is due to Ashman needs to be placed in context with others working on the films. For example, Andreas Deja obviously did his share in adding to the camp value of these projects. Ashman himself probably had little say in the model sheet for Ursula. Yet, her campy nature is due at least in part to the words that Ashman gives her to perform. In *The Little Mermaid*, Ashman provided Ursula with a solo number, "Poor Unfortunate Souls."[37] In the number, Ursula uses various methods to convince Ariel the mermaid to sell her soul—from looking penitent and saintlike to shimmying madly in excitement. "In its use of vocalist Pat Carroll's ability to slide up and down the musical register, from shrieks to baritones, 'Poor Unfortunate Souls' is an unmistakable sendup of the campy female impersonation number."[38] Similarly, although Deja must share credit, Ashman not only helped conceive Gaston in *Beauty and the Beast* but emphasizes his campiness through the lyrics of *his* solo number, "Gaston," a hysterical *"male* impersonation" number! As was discussed in chapter 2, the tradition of reading Disney villains as "gay-tinged" reaches much farther back than Ashman's involvement with the studio. Ashman's creation of musical numbers for the villains, though, underlines this position, allowing mainstream audiences and reviewers to positively revel in the campiness of their villainy.

Nowhere is this camp perspective more apparent than in the character of the Genie in *Aladdin*. Just as critics noticed that some aspects of these new Disney animated features were for "savvier" audiences, they wondered "What will children make of a film whose main attraction—the Genie himself—has such obvious parent appeal? They [won't] . . . know precisely what Mr. Williams is evoking."[39] While Robin Williams' impromptu recording sessions contributed mightily to the final character of the Genie, Ashman's songs for the Genie had been written long before Williams was signed, and the character that Ashman creates through his lyrics definitely portrays him as an overblown, larger than life "gay-tinged" figure. The Genie first appears in a huge production number centered around him telling Aladdin, "C'mon whisper what it is you want / You ain't never had a friend like me." Throughout the song, the Genie zips from one metaphor to another in endless enthusiasm, sprinkling his speech with phrases like "true dish!" and a lisping "you big nabob!" Later, as Aladdin enters the palace disguised as "Prince Ali," the Genie promotes him shamelessly by pointing out "That physique! How can I speak? Weak at the knee," and describing how he "got all dolled up and dropped by."

While these examples tend to promote reading the Genie as a "gay male," the character's manic nature often spills beyond this simple category, becoming a truly "queer" figure.[40] While casting Williams makes the Genie ostensibly male, "he" rapidly shifts into a number of caricatures of famous people (William F. Buckley, Groucho Marx, Ethel Merman, Jack Nicholson and Arsenio Hall amongst others) as well as cross-dresses (a flight attendant, a harem girl, a cheerleader) and even becomes different species (a goat, a sheep, a bumblebee). He displays "mucho-macho" male heterosexuality one second as Arnold Schwarzenegger, then a caricature of homosexuality in the next second as a swishy tailor measuring Aladdin for his Prince Ali outfit. Everything is overemphasized (the Hirschfeld-inspired drawings, the hyper-kinetic voice of Williams) and paced lightning fast. The overabundance of transformation flaunts the instability of identity in the viewer's face, hilariously critiquing theories of essentialism in the process. It is all just another costume for the Genie to put on and discard.

Acknowledging the "queerer" nature of the Genie, though, it is much easier to appreciate him (note gender identification) from a gay male viewpoint than, say, a lesbian viewpoint, particularly in his relationship with Aladdin. As mentioned, at one point the Genie transforms into a prissy gay tailor mincing as he advises snippily, "Those rags are much too '3rd-century'—work with me here!" During one emotional high point in the narrative, the Genie tells Aladdin, "I'm getting kind of fond of you too, kid . . . not that I want to go shopping for curtains or anything." The final tearful clinch at the end of the film is not between Aladdin and the princess Jasmine, but between Aladdin and the Genie. The "gay male" aspects of *Aladdin* go much farther than just the presence of the Genie, though. Deja's admitted conception of the villainous Jafar as gay (making his relationship with his male parrot cohort Iago all the more intriguing) is almost in direct juxtaposition to the Genie. Both are tied directly to the hero Aladdin—one trying to help him, one trying to destroy him—and both are constantly concerned with how Aladdin looks.

In fact, the studio itself worked endlessly to create a visually pleasing body and face for Aladdin—a development that would obviously interest more gay male customers than lesbians. Having worked mainly on stories with female leads (Snow White, Cinderella, Sleeping Beauty, Ariel, Belle), Disney's animators were accustomed to creating beautiful (read: fetishized) female figures (large eyes, small waists, pleasing soft curves). Yet, the animation department also had a history of less success in creating visually pleasing male characters. With *Aladdin* then, Disney's animators were faced with creating an objectified male body.[41] Most critics agree that the various princes accompanying Snow White, Cinderella and Sleeping Beauty seem "wooden" and are usually absent from the screen due to their lack of "appeal."[42] In fact, until *Aladdin*, only *Pinocchio* (1940) and *Peter Pan* (1953) had been successful in presenting male figures that came close to the "appeal" of Snow White or her counterparts. (It is interesting that while both are ostensibly male, their masculinity is problematized; the appeal of Pinocchio is more in his wooden puppet form than as the human boy he becomes, and the sexual ambiguity of Pan's persona has been discussed by many.)[43]

Initially conceived as yet another adolescent boy, Glen Keane modeled the first version of Aladdin on Michael J. Fox. Katzenberg was not pleased and demanded that Aladdin go back to the model sheets. By all accounts, Katzenberg wanted Aladdin to be modeled on Tom Cruise; Keane supposedly kept photos of Cruise pinned to his bulletin board because "Jeffrey wanted the hunk side of him present."[44] The final model of Aladdin has a much taller frame with an overemphasized smile and an ever-present (though not overly muscled) chest exposed. Furthermore, Aladdin constantly puts his body on display. As "Prince Ali," Aladdin flexes his biceps, flashes his smile and Ashman has harem girls sigh, "I absolutely love the way he dresses." (The link between Prince Ali and the spectacle of Rudolph Valentino's "sheik" persona is very strong.)

Ashman's involvement in *Aladdin* was cut short by his death, and certain concepts he held for the project ended up dropped or modified by the studio. One major change was the elimination of the character of Aladdin's mother, for whom Ashman had written a song, "Proud of Your Boy," declaring her love for her son no matter how he lives his life.[45] This song of love attempted to tell Aladdin not to be ashamed of himself or want to be someone other than himself. The song's message to homosexuals obviously lies close to the surface. Although Aladdin became a loner in the final version of the film, his self-hatred and desire to become someone else still figures strongly in the narrative. He pretends to be "Prince Ali" in order to find a new life in which he is welcomed and adored by society instead of being labeled a "street rat." Aladdin must learn to accept himself for who he is before the narrative can reach its conventional happy ending.

While Ashman's work predominantly expresses gay male culture, the need for Aladdin to take pride in himself reaches out to all nonstraight individuals. It also ties directly to the last major thematic motif in Ashman's work: fantasizing a world where one can find acceptance. Obviously, this fantasy motif works well with Disney, as mentioned in chapter 2. In *Aladdin*, the Genie manifestly invokes Disney as an escape to fantasy when he mimics the ad campaign for the Disneyland theme park by asking,"Aladdin, you've just won the heart of the princess, what are you gonna do next?" Ashman always made certain to include in each of his scores what he referred to as a "wish song," in which the lead character expresses his or her desire to find a different life or to escape to a new world. What marks Ashman's songs as different from the "wish songs" that already existed in Disney's canon ("Someday My Prince Will Come" from *Snow White and the Seven Dwarfs*, "When You Wish Upon a Star" from *Pinocchio*, "A Dream Is a Wish Your Heart Makes" from *Cinderella*, amongst others) is a desire to specifically escape from the dull, conservative parochial values of the everyday. Ariel wants to get away from her father's restrictions on her life; Belle wants to avoid the societal pressure to marry Gaston. Cynthia Erb notices how "both *Mermaid* and *B and B* . . . deploy the fairy tale musical's bicameral spatial scheme to map a gay dilemma of trying to choose between different worlds—one explicitly associated with family and marriage, the other configured along the lines of fantasy, escape, and forbidden romance."[46] Unlike the earlier "wish songs" in Disney's catalogue that only desire to find happiness in everyday life, Ashman's "wish songs" specifically want to forsake the "normal" world and find happiness somewhere else.

Ashman makes this link (between the dysfunction of "real" families and the escape of Disney fantasy) in a song written by him and Marvin Hamlisch not for Disney but *about* Disney. For a stage musical adaption of the Michael Ritchie film *Smile* (1975), the two wrote a "wish song" entitled "Disneyland." A young girl (much like Ariel and Belle) sings of lonely Sunday nights when she was eleven. With her folks "busy fighting" and her brother already out of the house, she was rescued from her surroundings by turning on the TV set and watching the weekly Disney anthology series. In the chorus, she relives the thrill of watching the show, closing her eyes and wishing hard for a magic carpet to carry her away to Disneyland.

Ashman specifically invokes the appeal of Disney as a method to "get away" from the oppressiveness of the world (encapsulating the attitude that many lesbian and gay men have towards the theme park). In an interview for the PBS series, *In the Life,* Ashman's partner Bill Lauch recalled a dream from Ashman's childhood: "The Mouseketeers from the *Mickey Mouse Club* come to Howard's bedroom window, and they say, 'Howard, come with us. Come be part of our group.' And he would run away with them. He finally did do that—when he was 35." Such a sentiment seemed to be echoed by the predominantly gay male crowd at the *Aladdin* screening described in the Introduction. During the pre-show, many in the audience sang along with the mermaid Ariel as she dreamed of being "part of your world."

Ashman's "wish songs" in *The Little Mermaid* and *Beauty and the Beast* are (respectively) "Part of Your World" and "Belle." Both are sung by characters who feel out of place in the world in which they live. In *The Little Mermaid*, Ariel attempts to vicariously live in the human world by watching them covertly, as well as by collecting various artifacts left in sunken ships. Ariel sings "Part of Your World" amidst this secret collection, opining that (unlike her father) on land "they don't reprimand their daughters" for thinking independently. Belle in her self-titled song longs for "something more than this provincial life," because she wants "so much more than they've got planned." The rest of the town joins in the song, describing her as "strange but special" and commenting that "she doesn't quite fit in." Erb points out that "in 'Belle,' the villagers' lyrics repeat such words as 'strange,' 'distracted,' 'peculiar,' 'a puzzle,' 'different,' and 'funny,' so that eventually this descriptive battery becomes connotative of the way straight people myopically puzzle over the enigmas posed by gay desire."[47]

Both Belle and Ariel in their "wish songs" voice feelings common amongst homosexuals, emotions of separation and longing for acceptance—particularly acceptance of the love they feel. Ariel falls in love with a man, although knowing this is the ultimate taboo in her society. Singing wistfully to him from afar, Ariel seems willing to sacrifice just about anything to live with him, stay beside him and have him smile at her. Soon, the words move from plaintive to determined, as she vows that somehow, someway, "someday I'll be part of your world!" Belle herself finds it "strange and a bit alarming" as she realizes her growing love for the Beast in "Something There," but pleads for Gaston and the villagers to understand her love when they threaten the Beast's life in "The Mob Song." Both films are structured around resolving this unsanctioned love.

It is significant to see how Disney's *The Little Mermaid* changes the original story. Andersen, living in a society that could never accept open same-sex attraction, ends his story tragically, with the death of the mermaid who cannot find comfort in either world. Of course, the Disney studio would never allow such a downbeat ending in its animated films, and Ariel does not die. Still, the acceptance of Ariel into the human world, and her marriage to the Prince with the approval of the undersea kingdom (as personified by her father), also shows an optimism in Ashman's world view—that "just wait and see, someday I'll be part of your world."

In fact, the three animated features that Ashman worked on bear a stamp of reconciliation and acceptance: Ariel is accepted into the human world, Beauty and the Beast reconcile their differences and Aladdin and Princess Jasmine are able to deconstruct the class boundaries that separate them. In all three, Ashman's vision acknowledges the fears and misdirected anger that both sides feel. In *The Little Mermaid* for example, the abuse of human society on the undersea world is repeatedly emphasized (and hilariously conveyed in the musical number "Les Poissons," in which the Prince's chef gleefully beheads and slices various fish). On the other hand, the prejudices and fears of the undersea world (specifically Ariel's father King Triton) are also seen as a hurdle that must be overcome in order for the two worlds to co-exist. Similarly, the townspeople in *Beauty and the Beast* form an angry mob to hunt down the Beast. But the Beast is no lovable victim, and his own fears and resentment carry their burden of the blame for keeping Belle from his side. In *Aladdin*, there is a marked class barrier that keeps street urchin Aladdin from marrying Princess Jasmine, but Aladdin's own self-hatred and self-denial are posited as equally damaging to the potential relationship.

Ashman's work then carries an overriding hope to erase the fear and hatred that each side has for the other. One can quickly translate this message to issues of sexuality in modern Western society. As homosexuality gains more and more public space, the homophobia of certain heterosexual individuals has increased exponentially. This message counsels not to fight irrational fear and hatred with more hatred but with an attempt to ease the fears on both sides. At the end of *The Little Mermaid*, Triton fashions a symbol of the new ties between the two groups by creating a huge rainbow over the shipside wedding (and the rainbow has become a quite potent symbol of community within homosexual culture). It is the optimism that such an outcome is possible that Ashman brings to these three films through his lyrics and his story ideas. Erb notes, "The end result [of Ashman's work] is that the so-called gay subtext actually seems to lie very near the text's surface, so that it is virtually competitive with the meanings that might be construed as 'dominant.'"[48] Placing such easily read "gay-friendly" messages in Disney texts may have been Ashman's own method of reaching across these socially imposed barriers in an attempt to ease the fear and hatred.

A WORLD OF QUEERS? HOMOSEXUALS IN EISNER-ERA DISNEY FILMS

In 1992, the year that *Beauty and the Beast* would become the first animated feature film to be nominated for a Best Picture Oscar, critics noticed a flash of small-budgeted yet stylized independent features made about and by openly gay filmmakers. *The Living End* (1992), directed by Gregg Araki, and *Swoon* (1992), directed by Tom Kalin, heralded a flurry of fiction films by lesbians and gay men. That same year, Jennie Livingston's landmark documentary on the New York drag scene, *Paris Is Burning*, broke through to enjoy national theatrical distribution, encouraging further documentaries with queer subject matter. Critics soon dubbed these films a full-fledged cinema movement: "New Queer Cinema." Noting the profit that these independent films were making (due in part to their low cost of production), major studios began to take interest in making more "gay-themed" films. When Tom Hanks won the Best Picture Oscar in 1994 for playing a gay lawyer with AIDS in *Philadelphia* (1993), a film which took in over $70 million in domestic box office, studios began looking seriously at "Queer Cinema."

Disney, trying to remain competitive with the major studios, also expressed interest. In 1993, Disney acquired a major independent label, Miramax, which had helped distribute a number of major titles during this "Queer Moment," most famously Neil Jordan's Oscar-nominated *The Crying Game* (1992). Maintaining the independence to choose which films it would purchase for distribution, one of Miramax's first releases after Disney's buyout was *Priest* (1994), a film about a Catholic priest coming to terms with his homosexuality.[49] When Lauren Lloyd was recruited to become a film production executive for Hollywood Pictures, she remembers "a Disney exec who carefully pronounced the word 'minority' when pushed to explain her attractiveness to [the] studio."[50] As part of her job, Lloyd was given a discretionary fund that she could use to jump-start projects she considered worthy. Within the year, she had two films in development focusing on lesbian characters: an adaption of Elaine Hollimann's documentary *Chicks in White Satin* and a project called *Story of Her Life*. The studio had also optioned to make a film version of the stage musical *Falsettos*, with a gay male lead character, and financed the making of a short film *Electra Lite*, starring renowned drag diva RuPaul.

Yet, the studio's "flirtation" with openly homosexual subjects initially seemed to falter. *Electra Lite* never made it into theatrical release, and (to this date) the three feature films have died in development. Disney's investment in "New Queer Cinema" seemed stillborn. Certainly, Disney seemed to be wary as to how associated it would become with open discussion of homosexuality. As was mentioned in chapter 3, Disney's reticence in allowing domestic-partner benefits sprung from worries about its "family" image. In 1993, Sweden's version of *The New Mickey Mouse Club* had planned to have the rock group Erasure on one of its programs, but the company decided to drop the act when someone realized that singer Andy Bell was openly gay. In an ironic reversal of what would eventually happen in the United States, newspaper and magazine editorials in the Swedish press criticized this move and there were even calls for boycotts of Disney products.

Still, critiquing the failure to get these projects off the ground ignores that other work coming out of the studio was providing more manifest images of homosexuals. In fact, one of the most overt signs of a new age at the Disney studios was the denotative representation of homosexuality in some of their films. While critics and some audience members were finding it easier and easier to read the gay subtext of Disney's animated musicals, the live-action films coming out of Disney (and their Touchstone and Hollywood Pictures labels) were occasionally providing characters with no subtext at all, characters who were quite simply homosexual.

In the feature that signaled the beginning of the Eisner-Wells-Katzenberg era, *Down and Out in Beverly Hills,* one of the main characters comes out of the closet during the narrative. Max (Evan Richards), the teenage son of David and Barbara Whiteman (Richard Dreyfuss and Bette Midler), is plainly trying to come to terms with his sexual orientation. Max's father catches sight of him in a tutu flouncing around his bedroom, which is decorated with posters of Grace Jones and David Bowie. The father heads to his wife and announces, "I'm very worried about Max, he seems very confused." Throughout the film, Max is obviously trying to tell his parents *something,* but can't say the words so makes a number of experimental videos attempting to express to them what's going on with him. Max finally finds someone he can talk to in Jerry (Nick Nolte), a homeless person the family has adopted. Jerry catches Max putting on lipstick, but in a different reaction than David's to the tutu, Jerry suggests that orange may be a better color for him. Later, as Jerry disrobes unself-consciously in front of Max after a dip in the pool, Max asks Jerry for advice on how to tell his parents. Jerry (and consequently, it seems, the film itself) tells him that he has no problem with "it"—"You gotta be what you gotta be"—and assures Max that his parents are very tolerant people.

Max finally decides to take this advice at the New Year's Eve party that climaxes the film and shows up at the party in an outfit influenced by Culture Club, Adam Ant and the numerous other gender-bending '80s New Wave bands that were popular at the time of the film's release: an earring, orange lipstick, upswept and vaguely punk cut hair, purple eyeshadow and blush, a lime green sheer jacket with wide cuffs and an orange shirt underneath. Accompanying him is his "band," all in similar gender-bending outfits, including an early screen appearance for underground drag diva Alexis Arquette. Max kisses his father on the cheek and tells him "he is who he is" and that he's so glad that Dad accepts him and his friends.

Although the word "homosexuality" is never specifically uttered throughout the film, most viewers seemed to catch what was going on with Max. Keeping with the "saying-it-without-saying-it" attitude of the film, the New York Times described Max as "sexually confused" and Variety obviously thought it was being humorous in saying Evan Richards played "the son who's not sure he wouldn't rather be a daughter."[51] Released in the mid-1980s, just as radical gay rights activism was beginning to reorganize, it's unsurprising to find such tiptoeing around the subject in both the film and in the press. Yet, the references in both reviews to Max's "oddness" indicate an awareness nonetheless. There is evidence that gay males were also paying attention to the film's messages. When Vito Russo updated The Celluloid Closet, he made certain to include mention of the film. Yet, Russo focused not on Max's orientation but on one moment in the film that he considered to be extremely homophobic. When David rescues Jerry from drowning in their backyard pool by giving him mouth-to-mouth resuscitation, David's wife Barbara is aghast, screaming that David will get AIDS from putting "his lips on this man's lips."[52] Russo's critique reflects the anger in gay communities at the time which soon manifested itself in ACT UP. The statement itself is blatantly homophobic and misrepresentative of how AIDS is transmitted. But the film's overall point-of-view seems to critique this type of statement, and the line of dialogue seems to occur mainly to expose the spoiled and unfeeling nature of this rich and sheltered Beverly Hills family. Certainly, the acceptance of Max's orientation takes up more screen time than this one comment, and the film seems to endorse this acceptance.

A later Touchstone comedy, Big Business (1988), also presented obvious representations of homosexuality with the inclusion of a manifestly gay male couple as important supporting characters. Chuck (Daniel Gerroll) and Graham (Edward Herrmann) play executive assistants to Sadie (Bette Midler), co-owner of a major conglomerate. Although some viewers may not initially comprehend the two men as gay, much less a couple, as the storyline progresses it becomes impossible to understand them as anything but homosexual lovers. Chuck and Graham are introduced as Sadie walks through the corporate offices, and Chuck is the only one who seems to be able to match Sadie quip for bitchy quip. Also, both Chuck and Graham have slightly cultured and affected accents. Again, to some audience members, these details could send signals, but others would not read anything into these aspects of the characters' personalities. Throughout the first half of the movie, it becomes clear that the two will function as a comic duo within the narrative. One is never seen without the other. In fact, the two seem to do everything together: lunch, racquetball, dinner as well as corporate dirty work for Sadie. A stronger note of the characters' orientation is revealed when Sadie catches sight of the two of them sharing dinner. They are seated side by side instead of across from each other. As the waiter serves them their food, Graham reacts excitedly by flitting his hands in a move perfected by 1930s "pansy" actors such as Edward Everett Horton and Franklin Pangborn.

Finally, there is no arguing with reading Chuck and Graham as a gay couple when they are shown sharing a hotel suite—as well as the king-size bed in the suite. As part of the farcical machinations of the plot, they invite Roone (Fred Ward), a country bumpkin, to spend the night sleeping on the couch in their suite. As Roone readies for bed by doing pushups wearing only pajama bottoms, Chuck and Graham stand close together and stare agog at him. When he finishes, Roone stands and notices the silk mini-kimono that Chuck is wearing and asks him if he got it "in 'Nam." Chuck smiles somewhat shyly and replies, "No, Fire Island." Even if a viewer does not know of Fire Island's reputation as the summer beach resort for New York City's gay population, Roone's realization, "Don't tell me you two guys are sleeping in the same bed together!" makes the situation plain. (Of course, Roone is too dunderheaded to put one and one together, even after Chuck looks desirously at him and murmurs, "Goodnight.")

Although Chuck and Graham are not above figuring into the ridiculousness of the farce, the film does not seem to single them out for derisive homophobic humor. If anything, the film invites the viewer to look at the farce through their eyes and see the inanity of the world they are forced to work in. For example, after Roone has spent minutes soliloquizing on the rustic charm of his hometown, the film cuts to Chuck and Graham who seem to be suppressing the giggles at Roone's cliched description, cuing the audience to laugh with them at Roone's naivete, to read the soliloquy through the mindset of camp. The presence of such easily read gay characters in these films, like the knowledge of an openly gay artist in other Disney films of this period, seem to "authorize" a gay reading throughout the pictures. The predominantly gay male audience that was present when I saw *Big Business* in its initial release seemed to loudly share a campy enjoyment of the film and not just the presence of Chuck and Graham.

A major aspect of camp value in the film—and in *Down and Out in Beverly Hills*—was the presence of Bette Midler. Disney and Midler almost became synonymous during the late 1980s, as she starred in a long list of films for the studio. Beyond *Down and Out* and *Big Business,* she starred in *Ruthless People, Outrageous Fortune* (1987), *Beaches* (1989), *Hocus Pocus* (1993), provided a voice to one of the characters in the animated feature *Oliver and Company* (1988) and sang over the end credits to *The Hunchback of Notre Dame* (1996). Midler began her career by singing in gay male bathhouses in New York City, an experience that helped her to fashion a camp star persona as "the Divine Miss M." Midler did not relinquish this image as she moved to more mainstream acceptance, thus ensuring the loyalty of her gay fans. Disney did not try to erase this aspect of Midler's image when they used her in their films. In fact, her image perfectly fit into the bright, garish look of the comedies Disney was turning out during this period—a look that also verged on camp.

The "high-concept" farces that Disney produced (mainly under the Touchstone label) during the late 1980s reveled in a highly colorful *nouveau riche* visual design that carried from one film to the next. The pinks and taupes of *Down and Out in Beverly Hills* were followed by the bright primary colors in *Ruthless People,* the colorful comic book murals in the penthouse setting of *Three Men and a Baby* (1987) and the vibrant costumes worn by Midler in *Big Business.* The lively colors stood out usually against a lot of white walls and furniture, and the films invariably employed high-key lighting to create an airy sunny atmosphere. Overall, the visual design of this string of comedies blended well with the farcical narratives to fabricate an almost cartoonish world within a live-action feature. In this setting, Midler's diva antics were not only acceptable but almost demanded.

Although such production design holds much in common with other media texts of the mid-1980s (such as the TV series, *Miami Vice* and *Moonlighting*), the ultimate referent that these films seem to have is the TV series *Dynasty*. In *Down and Out*, when Jerry claims he once dated actress Linda Evans (who played Krystle Carrington), the entire cast is entranced to think that he knows a star from *Dynasty*. *Big Business* features a clip of *Dynasty's* Alexis Carrington (played by Joan Collins) giving a speech to a board of executives, a speech that Bette Midler's character later uses at a stockholder's meeting at the climax of the film. *Dynasty* had a huge gay male following. Gay bars stopped everything to air episodes of the series on Wednesday nights. They watched partly because one of the main characters was gay but mainly because of the "high-diva" antics of villainess Alexis and virtuous Krystle. At least once each season, audiences could look forward to a knock-down, all-out catfight between the two—usually involving torn clothes and getting muddy or sopping wet. Drag queens often looked to the costume design of the show for inspiration (and the wealth of padded shoulders lent itself easily to drag). The costumes added to the overall look of the series: ostentatious, over-the-top, in-your-face wealth that bordered on the absurd.

In picturing the lifestyles of the rich and famous with the same visual design, Touchstone's comedies during the Reagan presidency also evoked a milieu ripe for gay appreciation. Certainly, gay "touches" seemed to fill *Down and Out* beyond Max's inclusion in the storyline. The film lingers over Nick Nolte's bare behind when he strips down. An obviously gay hairdresser undertakes to spruce Jerry up after the family adopts him. Little Richard plays the Whiteman's next door neighbor in full snoopy-diva mode, and enters the film dressed in a leopard print silk mini-robe. The film does provide him with a wife for the final New Year's Eve party, but a wife never mentioned until her appearance and with whom he spends barely any time during the party.

The adoration of the series' divas by many gay men could also find parallels in Touchstone films through Midler. As Sadie in *Big Business*, Midler seems to be specifically channeling Alexis Carrington. She wields power with wicked glee, zinging nasty one-liners and getting sexually aroused by thoughts of corporate mergers. She stalks the hallways in her stiletto heels, barking out orders and shredding employees with biting criticism. "Is this how we dress for the office?," she asks a female employee wearing a black and red print dress, "You look like a blood clot!" Sadie's costume design is itself an ongoing joke in the film. Midler makes her first entrance in the film as the office elevator doors open to reveal her in an absurdly broad-rimmed black hat and power red suit with the requisite '80s padded shoulders. She changes from one outrageously *outré* outfit to another, ending in a tight black skirt and a pink jacket with padded shoulders and big black polka dots!

Dynasty was important in the 1980s more to gay male culture than to lesbian culture, thus again implying that the value of these Touchstone comedies to non-straight audiences was limited to gay men. The inclusion of Lily Tomlin as Midler's co-star in *Big Business* may suggest a possible lesbian audience for the film. (Tomlin's name has figured in rumor mills within lesbian and gay communities for years.) Yet, Tomlin's presence is a slim thread to hang a lesbian reading of the film upon, particularly in the face of much more obvious aspects of the film tied to gay-male culture.

Further, it must be recognized that while Touchstone comedies acknowledged the presence of gay men, their appearance in these films was not always completely accepting. Often, homosexuality functioned as a quick titillating joke in the overall storyline. When Burt Lancaster and Kirk Douglas, as two aging recently released convicts, visit their old neighborhood bar for the first time in years in *Tough Guys* (1987), a few minutes pass until they realize that the bar now caters to gay men. In fact, they don't catch on until one customer asks Kirk to dance and their waiter blows him a kiss from across the room. Kirk and Burt escape as quickly as possible. Similarly, in *Off Beat* (1988), when Judge Reinhold's character unthinkingly follows his best friend into a group shower and hugs him in gratitude, the rest of the men in the locker room watch in amazement. Eventually, Judge realizes what this must look like and hightails it out of the shower. In both cases, the joke is made to distance the male friendships in these two films from being read as homosexual—they're just friends, because look how embarrassed they are over being thought to be gay.

This is definitely the case with the first Touchstone film to make over $100 million in its initial release, *Three Men and a Baby*. Although the narrative deals with three single men living together and raising a child, the film constantly works to quell the homosexual implications. The opening credits sequence parades a line of uncredited actresses through the penthouse apartment that Peter (Tom Selleck), Michael (Steve Guttenberg) and Jack (Ted Danson) share, to underline that these men have girlfriends, *lots* of girlfriends. This type of thing recurs throughout the film, particularly in a Central Park montage where the three men realize that the baby attracts women in droves.

Yet, even as the film protests (almost too much) that this is a heterosexual world, the film revels in the campy visuals common to Touchstone comedies of this era. Their upscale apartment is decorated with brightly colored murals painted by Michael (who is a comic strip artist). The film also continuously engages in farce. During one of these moments, Jack, the biological father of the baby, is dressed in drag. In a somewhat remarkable ending, the final conflict of the baby's mother Sylvia (Nancy Travis) returning to claim her child is solved by having the woman move in with the three bachelors without being romantically involved with any of them, creating a very nontraditional family unit. The "queer" implications of the basic premise were also touched on in the sequel, *Three Men and a Little Lady* (1990), directed by Emile Ardolino. Jack again dresses in drag, this time as Carmen Miranda, and the little girl, now five years old, pointedly asks why none of the men are married, eliciting loud stammers from all three. Ultimately though, the sequel also reasserts heterosexuality, as Peter marries Sylvia at the end of the film, attempting again to quell the "queer" potentiality of the picture.

As the 1980s became the 1990s, these "buddy" relationships became more prevalent at Disney, but often focusing on much younger men than before. Featuring cute "pin-up boys" as the main characters, the films usually provided scenes that required them to take their shirts off. Although probably hoping to attract high-school girls, such casting also caught the attention of a number of gay men as well, an effect that some reviewers seemed to realize—especially since the main emotional attachments in the films were usually between the male characters. Although these films still placed some signifiers to make the lead characters "ostensibly" straight, the attempts were often extremely incidental to the main narrative.

The first in this string of films was *Dead Poets Society* (1989), the first Touchstone picture ever to be nominated for the Best Picture Academy Award and a surprise summer box-office hit. While Robin Williams, as an unconventional English Literature professor at an all-male college preparatory during the 1950s, is the film's ostensible star, most of the story focuses on a group of his students. Amongst these students are roommates Todd Anderson, played by Ethan Hawke, and Neil Perry, played by Robert Sean Leonard, both of whom are dealing with problems of self-worth. Todd is shy and quiet, while Neil is more outgoing (but pressured by his domineering father to follow a strictly laid-out plan for his future adult life). Mr. Keating (Williams) shocks his class when he encourages them to think independently and to follow the proverbial "beat of a different drummer." He demands that his students "look at things in a different way" and "consider not just what the author thinks, consider what you think." Excited by these concepts, Neil soon convinces Todd and his buddies to recreate a secret organization that Keating belonged to when *he* was a student at Welton, the "Dead Poets Society," committed to "sucking the marrow out of life."

As this last quote from Thoreau points out, Keating's choice of texts for teaching his life lessons are filled with implications. The first words he speaks in his first class are "Oh captain, my captain," penned by homosexual poet Walt Whitman. Keating prefers that the students address him in such a fashion, quotes Whitman often, and a portrait of the poet hangs in the front of the classroom. In one of the key scenes of the film, Keating forces the shy Todd to improvise a poem in front of the class based on this portrait. As the camera circles vertiginously around the pair, Keating actually lays hands on Todd, covering his eyes and, like a preacher, wills the poem about "a sweaty toothed madman" out of the boy. Such a focus on Whitman invites comparisons between the poet's recurrent motif of "'frail and endangered male' adolescents, . . . pale and solitary young men" and this film's own preoccupations with male youth.[53]

Certainly, the film's increasing focus on the downward spiral of Neil's life parallels Whitman scholar Byrne R. S. Fone's assertion that "if the death of a beautiful woman was for Poe the most poetic subject, the death of a handsome youth was for Whitman as highly charged."[54] Influenced by Keating, Neil excitedly realizes his calling to be an actor instead of a lawyer, though he knows his father will be dead set against it. Consequently, when Neil lands the role of Puck in a local production of *A Midsummer's Night Dream*, he decides to hide it from his father. Eventually, though, the secret comes out, and, supremely displeased at this seeming act of disrespect, his father demands that Neil quit the play. Neil seeks Mr. Keating out for advice. Teary and shaky, he pleads, "Acting is *everything* to me . . . but, he doesn't know . . . he's planning the rest of my life for me and he's never asked me what I want!" When Keating asks if Neil's ever told his father what the boy has just said, Neil cries as he says, "I *can't*! He'll tell me acting's a whim and I should forget it! He'll tell me to put it out of my mind for my own good!" Thinking that none of Keating's advice will work, Neil trembles as he says, "I'm trapped."

Robert Sean Leonard's performance of this scene makes the conversation seem to be about much more than just whether Neil is going to be an actor or a lawyer. This premonition becomes stronger after he acts in the play anyway and is dragged out after the performance by his father back to the family home. His father demands an explanation and Neil bursts out, "I've got to tell you how I feel!" His father rejoins loudly, "What is it? Is it this 'acting'? Or something else?" The silence after this last question is deadening, and Neil eventually collapses into a chair in futile silence. That night, as his parents sleep, Neil disrobes and ritualistically marches down to his father's den, grabs a revolver out of a desk and kills himself. *Variety*'s review of the film states that "There is no missing the symbolism in the scene where a despondent Neil—naked in his room before an open window on a forbidding, wintry-cold world—dons the crown of brambles from his Shakespeare play."[55] Similarly, Mike Hammond's analysis of the film points out that "*Dead Poets Society* has as its central concern the rite of passage from boyhood to (heterosexual) manhood. Neil fails to make this transition."[56] Like *Down and Out in Beverly Hills*, the word "homosexual" is never uttered in the film—and yet it is nearly impossible to make sense of Neil's suicide without thinking of him as gay.[57]

The success of *Dead Poets Society* was followed by such predominantly male-cast films as *Alive, The Three Musketeers, Newsies, White Fang, Swing Kids, The Jungle Book, Squanto: A Warrior's Tale* and *Tom and Huck*. Ethan Hawke starred in both *Alive* and *White Fang*. *The Three Musketeers* introduced to a number of audience members the cherubic face of Chris O'Donnell, as a D'Artangan in blonde ringlets (and menaced by a Cardinal Richelieu played by Tim Curry, most famous for his role as the transvestite Dr. Frank N. Furter in *The Rocky Horror Picture Show* [1974]). Brandon Lee spent most of the live-action version of *The Jungle Book* wearing little but a loincloth. *Newsies* and *Swing Kids* starred Christian Bale, who had first made a splash as a preteen in Steven Spielberg's *Empire of the Sun*. By 1992, Bale was in his late teens, and this pair of films for Disney contains striking similarities—and not just because both were high-profile box-office failures. Both films fit within the musical genre and focus on very emotionally-charged relationships between Bale's character and another young male.

Variety's review of *Newsies* concretely noticed the lack of female participation in the plotline. While acknowledging that a few women *did* appear in the picture, the reviewer went on to state that "Ann-Margret . . . is shoehorned into the film to provide s[ex] a[ppeal] in a male-dominated story. Only other female role of any substance is Ele Keats' [*sic*] bland tenement girl, who's around so Bale can . . . have someone to clinch at the end."[58] Keats' character (Sara) shows up for a brief moment about half an hour into the film and doesn't return until another hour has gone by. It is only at this second appearance that Bale's character (Cowboy Jack) seems to be vaguely interested. While Sara *is* the one that Jack clinches at the end of the film, her brother David (played by David Moscow) forms the central relationship with Jack in this "male-dominated story." Jack and his buddies work as newspaper hawkers in turn-of-the-century New York City. The picture opens as they wake up in a boarding house—many of them parading about in their underwear or in towels. (*Dead Poets Society* contained a similar bathroom scene but without the singing and dancing.) At the newspaper offices, Jack quickly links up with David (David Moscow) and his little brother, who are new at the job. Sparks fly almost immediately. Jack proposes that he, David and the little brother form a partnership, commenting that David will "get the benefit of observing me at no charge." David quickly rejoins, "If you're so great, what do you need me for?" The rest of the newsboys exchange "oohs" and "ahhs" at every barb. Even with these taunts, the two stick with each other, and soon David has invited Jack to meet his parents and to move in with them.

The relationship between Jack and David forms the core of the film. When the newsies go on strike, the two pair up as leaders—Jack as the charismatic speaker and David as "the man behind the man," who tells him what to say. The major crisis in the film occurs when the evil Pulitzer (Robert Duvall) gets Jack to act as a scab by threatening to set his goons on David and his family. The narrative reaches its emotional peak when Jack has to "break up" with David without explaining that it is for David's safety. The camera lingers on the betrayal in David's eyes, as well as the devastation of Jack afterwards. In fact, the film is fascinated with the images of young men. *Newsies* was directed by choreographer Kenny Ortega, and all of the dance sequences use young men dancing together. In one number, titled "Seize the Day" (the phrase used in the ad campaign for *Dead Poets Society*), the chorus boys roll chest to chest against each other and link arms in solidarity. All the male characters are constantly hugging each other or exchanging deep meaningful glances as they shake hands.

Eventually, some goons of Pulitzer's decide to harass Sara, and David tries to step in. Significantly, Jack doesn't appear on the scene until the goons have forsaken Sara, now cowering in a corner, and are ganging up on David. Jack comes to the rescue, forsaking his role as a scab. David asks him with a sly smile, "What? You couldn't stay away?" Jack answers, "I guess I can't be something I ain't." Guess not. At the conclusion of the film, when the newsies win the strike, David and Jack "swap spit"—albeit by spitting into their hands and shaking warmly. Yet, the cross-cutting between the two as they slowly approach each other through the crowd for this final embrace is reminiscent of many classic Hollywood romantic reunions. As the *Variety* review intimates, Sara shows up at the last second for Jack to give her a big public kiss, as the crowd goes wild. But the happy ending happened for all intents and purposes fifteen seconds before when Jack and David resolved their relationship.

Even though *Newsies* failed spectacularly, the following year saw the release of another Christian Bale musical, *Swing Kids*. This time, the film takes place in prewar Nazi Germany, and Bale's "special" male friend is Robert Sean Leonard, last seen playing the suicidal Neil in *Dead Poets Society*. The historically-based tale, of a group of German teenagers who were devotees of American swing music in defiance of cultural mandates against such "nigger-kike" stuff, focuses specifically on a male-exclusive community. Mainstream media critics did not fail to notice this emphasis on boys. Janet Maslin's review in the *New York Times* points out that the film is "cast with personable, good-looking young actors . . . , [playing] handsome friends who find . . . a shared love for Benny Goodman records," and goes on to note that "'Swing Kids' eventually begins to suggest that any gathering of sensitive adolescent characters can begin to feel like 'Dead Poets Society' after a while."[59] While there are women present at all the dances the characters attend, the story devotes its time almost exclusively to a group of young men, particularly Thomas (Christian Bale) and Peter (Robert Sean Leonard). At school, the female students tell each other that the boys' fondness for American slang is a "secret language" that the girls aren't privileged to know. At the dance that opens the film, Peter and Thomas both dance with women, but, when the song ends, they rush over and hug each other instead of their partners.

Swing culture is described as vaguely underground. Everyone seems to know it exists, but it can't be blatant. Much as gay communities during the '30s and '40s were able to read signals or use code phrases undetected by straight society, these "swing kids" learn how to weave through the restrictions placed upon them. One "swing kid" reads the spectacle of a Nazi bicycling by and whistling a bar from "It Ain't Got a Thing, If It Ain't Got That Swing" as a message that some Hitler Youth are (for lack of a better term) "passing." The parallels between German swing culture and pre-Stonewall era gay life are even more explicit in the dance sequences. Held somewhat secretly in ballrooms across the city, the dances are constantly under pressure of being discovered and broken up. In possibly the most entertaining part of the film, Peter and Thomas do away with female partners and jitterbug with each other. In the midst of this, a whistle blows a warning that Nazis are about to raid the ballroom. Reminiscent of the advance warning alarms in urban gay bars prior to Stonewall, the band quickly changes the music to a polka, and Peter and Thomas find female partners.

Again, the key relationship in the film lies between the two young men in the story. When Peter is forced to join the Hitler Youth, Thomas joins as well. As he explains to Peter, "We can't let them split us apart! Anyway, think about it, it's the perfect cover!" Yet, just as *Newsies* waves Sara through its narrative to possibly mitigate "reading too much" into things, *Swing Kids* also works to deny the homo-erotics of the plot. This time, though, an ubiquitous girlfriend is replaced by the consistent use of the term "pansy" as an epithet. Thomas consistently accuses the Hitler Youth of being "pansies"—once right after the raid that breaks up Thomas and Peter's dance with each other. In contrast, when the young Nazis bash a friend of theirs, one of them comments, "You call *us* pansies—even my girlfriend doesn't wear her hair that long!" (referring to the "swing kid" fashion of longer hair for men). These moments spurred Maslin to warn that "Audiences may also be startled by occasional anti-gay epithets in the dialogue."[60] Being the last sentence of her review, this point is emphasized, even though many Hollywood films regularly spew forth anti-gay rhetoric (as one montage in the film documentary adaption of *The Celluloid Closet* amply shows). Maslin's perceived need to alert viewers indicates an assumption regarding what type of people might be showing up to see the film.

The intensity of Thomas and Peter's relationship is highlighted, just as in *Newsies,* when the two "break up." Thomas becomes "seduced" by Nazi propaganda (the film uses a montage derivative of Leni Reifenstahl's *Olympia* to communicate the hypnotic homoerotic pull the program has on Thomas), while Peter still resists it. Their friendship is consequently torn asunder. The final sign that Thomas has been won over to the Nazis occurs at a cafe where Peter and Thomas both have female dates, but Thomas cannot stop staring in adoration over his shoulder at the Nazi officers behind them. The end of the film climaxes as the two come to blows during a Nazi raid of a swing dance in which Peter is a dance attendee and Thomas is one of the arresting officers. The film seems to view Peter's decision to attend the final swing dance of the story as a political statement—one which is underlined first by a sweaty, intense (and almost laughable) dance solo by Peter on the ballroom floor, and then by the defiant (and *definitely* laughable) final cry of Peter's as he's carted off by the Nazis: "Swing heil!"

This is not the only moment that usually provokes unwanted laughter in viewers. Twice in the film, after "swing kids" have been beaten bloody, they respond mock-heroically by singing "It Ain't Got a Thing If It Ain't Got That Swing," complete with the accompanying "do-wop-do-wop-do-wop." These moments seem to not recognize the inanity of the supposed political resistance and are so deliriously inflated that most viewers cannot help but laugh. After describing one of these scenes, Maslin writes "That can't have been easy to play straight." The main characters are committing suicide and being beaten and arrested for listening to music. Although historically based, the momentous seriousness of the piece seems widely out of proportion to the cause being championed. The only way to begin to justify such bombastic tragedy is by not "playing it straight" and instead reading the film from a homosexual viewpoint.

Reading the casting of "poster boys" in these films through a gay sensibility became manifest once again when the film *Tombstone* (1993) cast Jason Priestly (who became famous on TV's *Beverly Hills 90210*) as "Sister Boy." *New York Times* reviewer Stephen Holden does not hint

around when he describes *Tombstone* as "up-to-date in its political consciousness . . . it even includes one Old West homosexual, a character
nicknamed 'Sister Boy.'"[61] Although a peripheral character in this
retelling of the "Gunfight at OK Corral," Sister Boy is manifestly homosexual. He is introduced when the town gathers to watch a traveling
theatrical troupe. As Priestly enters, wearing a tailored city suit, bowler
and spectacles, one of the cowboys grabs for his behind while shouting,
"Hey, Sister Boy, gimmee some! Gimmee! Gimmee! Gimmee!" Curly
Bill (Powers Boothe), one of the antagonists, stands up and defends Sister Boy, placing his arm around the fellow's shoulder and asking Sister
Boy to sit next to him. An actor named Romulus Fabian (Billy Zane)
comes on stage in tights to recite the "St. Crispin's Day Speech" from
Henry V and Curly Bill immediately states that Fabian is "the prettiest
man I ever saw." After the first close-up of Fabian, to see the man's
beauty, the film cuts to an entranced close-up of Sister Boy saying, "I
think he's wonderful." At the post-theatre celebration, Sister Boy asks
Fabian to sit with him. When it is later revealed that Fabian has been
killed during the feud between the Clantons and the Earps, Sister Boy
gets a teary close-up, as well as a close-up of his hand clasping the dead
Fabian's hand.

While Holden's review minces no words in his description of "Sister Boy," he also hints at how this character's presence colors much of
the homosocial interaction occurring at the center of the film: "[Kevin]
Jarre's dialogue is often anachronistic, combining a campy contemporary edge with a more realistic dialect."[62] Sister Boy is a "friend" of the
Clanton gang, intimating that Curly Bill and others were not above sexual activity with the man, although plainly not considering themselves
as "like him" (at this time in history the insertive "masculine" partner
was not considered homosexual). Johnny Ringo (Michael Biehn) never
specifically associates with Sister Boy, yet he carries the most homoerotic signifiers of those in the Clanton gang. While watching the theatrical troupe's pantomime of the Faust legend, Curly Bill loudly states,
"I'd take the deal and then cross over and drill that old Devil in the ass."
Then, leaning over to Ringo, Curly Bill asks with a leer, "How 'bout
you, Ringo? What would you do?" Looking up at the box seats where
Wyatt Earp (Kurt Russell) and Doc Holliday (Val Kilmer) sit, he replies
"I already did it." Whether "it" refers to making a pact with the Devil
or "drilling someone in the ass" is left for the individual viewer to in-
tuit. Interestingly, directly after the cross-cut between close-ups of

Fabian on the stage and Sister Boy sitting enraptured in the audience, the film presents a similar cross-cut between Ringo transfixed and Earp and Holliday as the figures attracting his gaze.

As portrayed by Kilmer, Doc Holliday is not above affectations in speech and body language that verge on dandyism (calling one fellow "you madcap," for example). As a consequence, the initial meeting between Doc and Ringo is charged with energy that could be easily read as sexual. At the post-theatre celebration, Ringo and Doc Holliday confront each other for the first time just after Sister Boy offers Fabian a seat. The two stare intensely at each other during the following exchange:

RINGO: You must be Doc Holliday.
DOC: *(with a minor cough)* That's the rumor.
RINGO: You retired too?
DOC: Not me. I'm in my prime!
RINGO: *(smiling)* Yeah, you look it.
DOC: You must be Ringo. *(turning to a woman at his side)* Look darlin', Johnny Ringo—the deadliest pistolier since Wild Bill, they say. What do you say, darlin', should I hate him?
WOMAN: You don't even know him.
DOC: No, that's true. But I don't know. There's something about him—something around the eyes. I don't know. He reminds me of . . . me! *(smiling)* No, I'm sure of it. I hate him!

As if this exchange wasn't filled with enough innuendo, the conversation continues as the two speak "their own secret language." Doc tosses off "in vino veritas" after Earp tries to excuse Doc's drunkenness, but is stunned when Ringo answers him in Latin. The two trade barbs in Latin until it becomes obvious that the situation is going to lead to either gunplay or some heated sex (depending on how one is reading the scene) and then friends on both sides intervene. For the rest of the film, Doc and Ringo have a special vendetta against each other that seems to transcend the gang factions, yet is never completely explained. In its immediate juxtaposition to a scene with Sister Boy and Fabian, their initial meeting provides the most vivid example of the "campy edge" Holden seems to be referring to in his review—an edge that brings the homoerotic aspects of the Western genre closer to the surface than most mainstream Westerns have done.

TOUCHSTONE TELEVISION AND TOASTER OVENS: LESBIANISM ON THE AIR

Disney's movement into more manifest representations of homosexuality has mainly focused on male characters. The young "boy toys" that populate films like *Dead Poets Society* and *Swing Kids* certainly are not going to catch much attention from lesbians. Similarly, Bette Midler's homosexual fan base leans heavily towards the male section of the community (although, as stated, the presence of Lily Tomlin in *Big Business* might attract some of the females). Although the films of Howard Ashman celebrate a variety of difference, the musical theatre tradition from which these films consciously borrow is more strongly linked to gay-male culture than to lesbian culture.[63] Some of this emphasis on gay men parallels general trends within the entertainment industry. As mass media present more images of homosexual individuals, gay male characters tend to dominate. The larger ratio of openly gay men to open lesbians in Disney's employee group LEAGUE may also explain the predominance of address to gay men in Disney product. If a larger percentage of the homosexuals working for Disney are male, then it is understandable if reading Disney from a homosexual sensibility privileges a gay-male point of view.

This condition has existed long before the Eisner-Wells-Katzenberg regime. With mostly men working as animators, most of Disney's initial stars were male characters—Mickey Mouse, Donald Duck, Goofy, etc. While female partners existed for these characters, the men were still very much the center of attention, and often Minnie Mouse and Daisy Duck did not even appear. In fact, often the males lived and worked together (*Mickey's Service Station* [1935], *Moving Day* [1936], *Clock Cleaners* [1937], *Lonesome Ghosts* [1938], *Mickey's Trailer* [1938], the "Mickey and the Beanstalk" sequence from *Fun and Fancy Free* [1947]). These teamings, as well as the creation of male duos such as chipmunks Chip and Dale or the mice Jacques and Gus in *Cinderella*, also made (and still makes) a gay-male subject position in Disneyana much easier to find than a lesbian one.

Still, as chapter 2 points out, there are certain texts that lesbians could connect with in Disney's past, even with this accent on male characters (Hayley Mills's dual roles in *The Parent Trap*, "Jet" in *Annette*, the nannies of *Mary Poppins* and *Bedknobs and Broomsticks*, Jodie Foster's character in *Freaky Friday*). Similarly, although the "new" Disney seems to attract the attention of gay men more than lesbians, certain texts do attract a lesbian reading. One of these texts has come to provide the strongest example of overt representation of homosexuality from the company, as well as the strongest example of mainstream attention to and validation of a homosexual reading strategy towards a Disney product.

Touchstone Television's first successful series, running from 1985 to 1992 on NBC, was *The Golden Girls,* a situation comedy about four female senior citizens sharing a home together in Florida. A television equivalent to the work Eisner, Wells and Katzenberg were fashioning with their theatrical features, *The Golden Girls* was filled with risqué dialogue and situations, seeming to announce that the company could produce more than *The Wonderful World of Disney* or *The Mickey Mouse Club.*[64] Mimi White, in a discussion of *The Golden Girls* and other women-centered sitcoms, describes how

> the female characters . . . are firmly established as heterosexual, . . . but at the same time, they validate women's bonding as a form of social stability, a viable and attractive alternative to the traditional family, and even hint at the possibility of lesbian lifestyles—at least as far as possible within dominant ideology.[65]

Alex Doty describes how women-centered series since the 1970s "point toward lesbian readings through double entendres; oblique, displaced, or jokey references to lesbianism; or with 'lesbian episodes.'"[66] Gay men appear with some regularity on the show. A gay houseboy is part of the series pilot, and Blanche's (Rue McClanahan) gay brother appears in two episodes of the show, once with a partner. The series' explicit "lesbian episode" involved Jean (Lois Nettleton), an old friend of Dorothy's (joke partially intended by the author if not the show's creators), coming to visit after the death of her partner Pat. While Dorothy (Beatrice Arthur) and her mother Sofia (Estelle Getty) know Pat was female, they keep this fact from their other two housemates. Rose (Betty White) becomes fast friends with Jean, not realizing that Jean is starting to have "feelings" for her until Dorothy finally spills the beans. The episode ends as Rose and Jean resolve the tension as friends.

As Doty points out, these episodes raise the spectre of homosexuality, only to "contain or deflect . . . the charge of lesbianism . . . the series has accumulated around its regular cast."[67] While the "lesbian episode" of *The Golden Girls* shows Dorothy and Sofia sleeping in bed together and Blanche (Rue McClanahan) feeling jealous that Jean is attracted to Rose instead of her, the episode views these moments as jokes that "laugh off" any consideration of the main characters as lesbian, in effect innoculating them by presenting a "real" lesbian character in comparison. When Rose discovers Jean's sexual orientation, the series is able to create a joke *and* deflect a lesbian taint on the regular cast at the same time:

ROSE: I don't want to shock you, but Jean is—
DOROTHY: I know—Jean is gay.
ROSE: You know already? Well, what about Blanche?
DOROTHY: No, Blanche is not gay.

The series concluded its run with an episode devoted specifically to containing the character most easily read as lesbian. Dorothy, played by husky, aggressive, gravelly-voiced Beatrice Arthur, gets married and moves out of the bungalow for the final episode. By finding a male partner for Dorothy, the series attempts to keep any "lesbian reading" subtextual and marginal to the dominant mode of spectator positioning.

Similar to the covert reading strategies that Doty and others apply to *The Golden Girls*, a number of viewers began appreciating another situation comedy produced by Touchstone Television from a lesbian standpoint when it premiered in 1994. Many gay men and lesbians viewed Ellen Morgan, the main character in the series *Ellen,* as a closeted lesbian character almost from the very first episode. As Robert Dawidoff wrote in the *Los Angeles Times,* "My friends and I always recognized Ellen as in the closet: the way she dressed and interacted, her hilarious ineptitude in trying to meet conventional expectations for a single young woman."[68] Sporting short hair, always wearing slacks or jeans and even owning a book store, Ellen seemed to fit many of the conventions that signify lesbianism in contemporary American culture. Furthermore, her often awkward body language and her manic desire to keep everyone happy, even if that meant refusing to say how she truly felt about a situation, seemed to indicate a woman fearful of expressing herself freely to others—i.e., closeted.

Throughout the first few seasons of the series, Ellen Morgan tried desperately to avoid being pressured into marriage by her mother. When she did date men, the budding relationships always ended horribly and hysterically, as Ellen found something that made the prospective boyfriend unworthy. In one of the more pointed episodes, Ellen Morgan goes out on a date with an outrageously thoughtful and caring man. Although she appreciates his attention to her, the sparks do not fly. Yet, her parents and all of her friends and co-workers think he's wonderful and she can never manipulate the situation to get him alone and break up with him. Throughout the episode, she is constantly "trying to tell him something," but can't get the words out. During the final credits, in what turns out to be a dream sequence, we see her at the wedding altar still protesting, "There's something you've got to know . . ."[69] In another episode, when Ellen Morgan goes for a breast cancer exam, she makes friends with another woman in the doctor's office, played by Janeane Garafolo. The chemistry between the two women, as they support each other through the period waiting for the test results, seems stronger than any attempted relationship that Ellen has forged with a male character.[70]

Part of the reason so many homosexuals understood Ellen Morgan as a lesbian character was that many of them understood actress Ellen DeGeneres as a lesbian. Word of her appearances with female partners at various lesbian dance clubs, coffee shops and restaurants around Los Angeles spread widely throughout the homosexual communities of southern California and many other parts of the country. One of the rumors spread among homosexuals reported that, when the series ended, DeGeneres had planned to "out" her character in the last three episodes. Some tellers even reported that such an idea had been written in as a clause in her contract for the series.[71] DeGeneres' standing in the community was such common knowledge that, by the early summer of 1996, many lesbians and gay men were sporting T-shirts that read "Oh Ellen, Just Come Out!"

Yet, even though this "open secret" was being worn on T-shirts in gay communities, much of the United States still read Ellen Morgan as just another in a long line of kooky sitcom single working girls who "hadn't found the right man yet." After all, Mary Richards in *The Mary Tyler Moore Show* was straight, wasn't she (although Alex Doty has voiced suspicions)?[72] Dawidoff recognized that "millions of nongay viewers appear not to have recognized what made Ellen so endearing and so funny, so angry and self-subverting."[73] In fact, even after the mainstream press began a flurry of reporting that "Ellen Morgan" might be lesbian, an *Entertainment Weekly* poll found that 41 percent of the respondents who had watched the series still considered the character to be straight.[74]

For a period in the series' production, it certainly seemed as if the producers were trying to stress heterosexuality. When the series first premiered on ABC as a "summer replacement," the show (titled at the time *These Friends of Mine*) featured Holly Fulger as Ellen Morgan's best female friend, who, like Ellen, sported short hair and a fashion style and personality that was not conventionally feminine. *TV Guide* found Fulger to be the most refreshing character in the series and lauded her in their pages as the one character who lifted the series out of its image as a "female *Seinfeld*" (referring to the ultra-popular NBC show about single thirty-something friends).[75] Months later, when the series was picked up for the fall season and redubbed *Ellen*, the journal was dismayed to find that Fulger was gone, replaced by the more feminine Paige (Joely Fisher). No one seemed able to explain or analyze exactly why Fulger's character (also named Holly) was eliminated, but a possible explanation might be found by examining the trend in story choices during the ensuing season. After substituting a more "girly" friend for a friend who seemed as potentially lesbian as Ellen herself was, Ellen Morgan jumped into dating a new man almost every week of the 1994–95 season. Just before the season began, DeGeneres co-hosted the Emmy Awards and was convinced to forsake her trademark pants suits and wear a formal dress—a fashion decision trumpeted in the entertainment press.[76] During the hiatus after the 1994-95 season, DeGeneres starred in a feature film for Hollywood Pictures, *Mr. Wrong* (1996), a dark romantic comedy co-starring Bill Pullman as her groom-to-be. Although the film turns Pullman's character into a stalker that DeGeneres' character desperately tries to escape from, the opening of the film goes out of its way to show her desiring the conventional fairy-tale romance and wedding with the man of her dreams.

Possibly the quick failure of the film when it was released in early 1996 had its effect on the TV series, but the 1995–96 season felt noticeably different almost immediately. The previous season ended with a two-part episode in which it seemed that Ellen had finally found "the right guy"—but concluded with the guy flying off to Italy at the end of the second part. In contrast, this new season was noticeably bereft of romantic entanglements for Ellen Morgan. Rather, the show focused on strengthening her relationships with her friends and her parents. One of the new recurrent characters on the show was Peter (Patrick Bristow).

Introduced in one episode of the 1994–95 season, Peter reappeared several times the next season. An overly enthusiastic high-voiced thin man, the show never specifically called him gay, yet his new male "friend," Barrett (Jack Plotnick), was also introduced during the season. Some in the popular press wrote that the series seemed to be adrift during this season, lacking focus and cohesion, and pointed to a slight slip in the ratings as evidence that audiences were no longer sure "what the show was about."[77] Supposedly, one executive remarked that Ellen Morgan should get a puppy as a solution to this lack of focus. While finding that idea preposterous, DeGeneres and the show's producers began discussing an idea that would give the show a definite focus that they humorously labeled as "The Puppy Episode"—and it did not involve a return to heterosexual dating. Instead, it proposed turning the lesbian subtext into the dominant mode of reading the series: rather than proposing a typical "lesbian episode" that would contain and dispel the aura of Ellen Morgan's lesbian tendencies, they began discussing having Ellen Morgan realize that she *is* lesbian.

TV Guide's Sept. 13, 1996 issue previewed the upcoming fall season, announcing almost as an afterthought that talks were going on as to whether or not to have Ellen Morgan be lesbian.[78] Without warning (and according to *TV Guide's* later articles, without understanding the importance of what they had just written), the journal exposed the subtextual reading of the series to the entire nation and indicated that this position may be the "correct" way of watching the show. A geyser of concern, outrage and celebration poured forth from all over the country for the next seven months, as writers and speakers and poll takers weighed in with their views on the possible presentation of the first openly homosexual lead character on American television. Fundamentalist Donald Wildmon of the American Family Association was among the first to call for a boycott of *Ellen's* sponsors and of Disney itself. Typical in his use of understatement, Reverend Fred Phelps announced, "It's a sign we're on the cusp of doom, of Sodom and Gomorrah."[79] Pat Robertson would eventually refer to Ellen DeGeneres as "Ellen DeGenerate."

Although *TV Guide* reported only that such an idea was being discussed, and that nothing had been supposedly decided (a view that the journal maintained until March 1997), from the moment the new season started, "outing" Ellen Morgan seemed a *fait accompli*. Throughout the season, jokes kept appearing that seemed to be laying the groundwork for the ultimate revelation. Peter and Ellen attend a consciousness-raising seminar in one episode and, as one of the exercises, everyone takes turns looking in a mirror and being honest with one's self. Ellen finishes her turn, but continually asks to return to the mirror while hearing Peter's turn, wanting to add what Peter is saying to *her* speech. Peter finally finishes his turn by stating clearly that he is gay and happy with it and then pointedly asks Ellen if she wants the mirror again, to her mortification. A joke such as this in any other series would isolate and dispel any potential "homosexual connotations." (Imagine if this had been a joke in a *Murphy Brown* episode, for example.) Yet, in this instance, the joke only added further credence to the "lesbian rumors," evidenced by the raucous reaction of the studio audience to this moment in the episode. In fact, episodes started making jokes specifically about the brouhaha that the rumors had caused across the country. In one episode's closing credits, Ellen Morgan actually asks her friends if they think the rumors are true about Ellen DeGeneres, with the live audience howling.

Even more amazingly, the mainstream press began pointing out to straight viewers the "inside jokes" within the series, in effect teaching them how to read *Ellen* from a "lesbian sensibility." After revealing the backstage negotiations, *TV Guide* worked to constantly alert viewers to a subtext that wasn't so subtextual anymore. For example:

> The October 2 episode . . . opens with Morgan standing behind a closet door in her new house. She steps out of the closet and says, "Yeah, there's plenty of room, but it's not very comfortable." Later in the episode, when her parents announce their divorce, a distraught Morgan says, "Put yourself in my place. How do you think I feel? What if I said something shocking to you. Like my whole life has been a lie and I'm really . . . left-handed."[80]

By the spring, *TV Guide*'s explanations of these allusions had become so regular that they were turned into a weekly feature titled "*Ellen* Watch"! *TV Guide* was not the only one alerting less-adept viewers to the "clues." Howard Rosenberg in the *Los Angeles Times* pointed out that in the season's opening episode, "there were some . . . hints, including a joke about Ellen wearing boxer shorts (reportedly the underwear of choice for all lesbians) and a gag that seemed to imply that she would never have a conventional family."[81] *Entertainment Tonight* also described the season premiere as being "peppered with subtle-as-a-sledgehammer jokes about her sexuality," such as when Ellen sings "I Feel Pretty" from *West Side Story* in the opening scene, but is startled before saying the word "gay": "I feel witty and pretty and . . . hey!"[82]

The mass media worked overtime to stress that the rumors were that "Ellen Morgan" might be lesbian, attempting to distinguish the character's sexual orientation from the actress portraying her, and initially DeGeneres refused to confirm or refute any of the rumors about her or her character. On a number of talk shows, DeGeneres made jokes about Ellen Morgan's being revealed to be "Lebanese" or that a new male character named "Les Bian" was being introduced. It was not until "The Puppy Episode" had finally been approved by Disney and filmed that DeGeneres finally admitted to a mass audience that she herself was lesbian (in TV interviews with Diane Sawyer on ABC's *PrimeTime Live* and with Oprah Winfrey on her talk show, as well as an interview for *Time*). These later interviews link DeGeneres' struggle with her own identity to that of the character she played. Using an *auteur* viewpoint, *Time* reported that it was DeGeneres' desire to stop Ellen Morgan's dating merry-go-round in the third season, claiming that she "wasn't interested in doing a show that focused on relationships."[83] She also declared, "This has been the most freeing experience because people can't hurt me anymore. I don't have to worry about somebody saying something about me, or a reporter trying to find out information."[84] Consequently, the decision to "out" Ellen Morgan was deeply tied to Ellen DeGeneres' growing desire to live an open life herself.

In March of 1997, the press reported that all signals were go, and that Ellen Morgan would declare herself as a lesbian on an hour-long episode to be aired on April 30th, after meeting an open lesbian played by Laura Dern and recognizing her attraction to the woman. Although bomb-sniffing dogs had to inspect the soundstages where the episode was filmed, and some advertisers decided to pull out of sponsoring the show, the episode encountered little resistance.[85] In fact, the episode itself pulled off its biggest joke by responding to worries that exposure to a lesbian lifestyle would somehow corrupt the population. At the end of the episode, after Ellen has come out, she is introduced to singer Melissa Etheridge by Laura Dern's character. Etheridge has Ellen sign a number of forms before presenting Dern with a toaster oven for "converting" yet another woman.

Even though a *TV Guide* poll reported that over half of those questioned announced they would not watch the episode, and the ABC af-
filiate in Birmingham, Alabama refused to air the episode, 30.6 million
people tuned in on April 30th—more than double the average audience
for the series during the 1996–97 season—and easily ranking first in the
Nielsen ratings for the week. In the last two episodes of the season, as
Ellen came out to her parents and to her boss, ratings went down from
this noticeable spike, but viewership remained higher than it had been
before the coming out, giving an encouraging sign to DeGeneres, the
ABC network and Touchstone Television. Of course, by this point,
Touchstone Television and ABC were connected not just through their
interest in *Ellen*. In 1996, Disney announced its acquisition of the American Broadcasting Company from Cap Cities, thus making Disney dou-
bly involved in delineating Ellen Morgan's sexual orientation. The massive press coverage was consistently intrigued that the Walt Disney
Company would be tied to the development of the first openly gay lead
character on an American television series. Although Disney executives
refused to OK the "outing" of Ellen until they saw a finished script,
there is no indication that Disney created any road blocks once the
show's creative staff decided to pursue the issue, allowing both Ellen
DeGeneres and "Ellen Morgan" to step out of the shadows of "subtextual readings" and into the bright spotlight of denotation.

CONCLUSION: MANIFEST REPRESENTATION
AND SUBVERSIVE POTENTIAL

As *Ellen* and the various other texts made since the late 1980s ably show,
the "gay sensibility" of Disney's product no longer lies submerged and
hidden from mainstream understanding. Whether due to the increased
visibility of lesbians and gay men in American society in general or the
larger presences of openly gay and lesbian employees working for Disney, film and television critics have noted more and more the homosexual spectator position in their reviews. As a consequence, the "typical"
(i.e., straight) viewer has become increasingly aware of the
"lesbian/gay subtext"—until, as in the case of *Ellen*, it overrides the heterosexual spectator position as the dominant reading strategy.

Rightly, Disney's increased manifest representation of homosexuality should be regarded as a momentous event for both the company and

lesbian/gay culture. As Dan Rather points out in his analysis of *Beauty and the Beast*, the millions of people who saw the film not only sympathized with a character who seemed to symbolize a PWA but *identified* with him. Millions of people have also now come to know a lesbian through the character of Ellen Morgan and to see a lesbian as a rounded, complex character instead of a collection of simple stereotypes. While Disney has come under increasing fire from conservative groups battling against the growing acceptance of homosexuality, the company has not backed down from its decisions (although sometimes *making* these decisions takes a while, as LEAGUE's attempts to get domestic-partner benefits and the season-long behind-the-scenes discussion about what to do with Ellen Morgan shows).

The Walt Disney Company should be lauded for these developments, but there are some problems that face lesbian and gay culture as a result of this increased visibility within the company's product—problems that became more apparent when *Ellen* entered its fifth season. In the fall of 1997, DeGeneres told *TV Guide* that "she has returned reluctantly for what she hopes will be the show's last season."[86] While the article did not venture to say this attitude would affect the content of the series, critics and audiences quickly noticed a major shift in the outlook of the show. While ABC entertainment president Jamie Tarses initially downplayed the series' gay themes ("It won't be the lesbian dating show. We're taking baby steps"), *TV Guide* reported that "DeGeneres was proceeding full steam ahead with her own agenda."[87] Most of the cast regulars moved to the margins of the show as Ellen Morgan explored lesbian/gay culture and found a steady girlfriend. Only a few weeks into the season, ABC began posting a warning at the front of many of *Ellen*'s episodes that "some viewers may find certain scenes objectionable." The first of these warnings accompanied Ellen's first on-screen kiss with another woman. Further warnings introduced episodes in which Ellen had to overcome her worries about public displays of affection with her girlfriend, when the two had their first sexual encounter, and a fantasy episode in which Ellen's straight cousin dreams he is a minority in a predominantly homosexual society.

These opening disclaimers and scuttlebutt in the industry indicated that ABC executives were a bit bothered by the direction DeGeneres had taken the series. Referring to Tarses' summer comments, DeGeneres herself said, "When I hear 'baby steps,' . . . it's like they're saying, 'OK, you're gay, and we're tolerating this, but don't show us how you really would be, don't kiss a girl on the lips.'"[88] As DeGeneres pushed the limits of network tolerance by focusing consistently on Morgan's coming to grips with her sexuality, the show's ratings slowly began to slip, further exacerbating ABC's worries. Analysts seemed to think that the show's insistence on addressing lesbian/gay issues was turning off many viewers. Interviews with DeGeneres as the season continued showed a revision of her earlier attitude: now, she wanted the series to be renewed for yet another season. Faced with both low ratings and worrisome content, though, it was not much of a surprise when ABC announced in April that the show would not be renewed. It seemed that Ellen's coming out was an economic asset, but Ellen's *staying* out was a financial liability.

Possibly the final nail in the series' coffin came from reports that even lesbian and gay viewers were critical of *Ellen*'s new focus. In March of 1998, Glenn Lovell wrote in *Variety*, "It's one thing for the critical establishment to carp about 'Ellen's' rigid gay-ness, but when a well-known lesbian activist does it—well, that's news." Lovell had interviewed Chastity Bono, entertainment media director of the Gay and Lesbian Alliance Against Defamation (GLAAD):

> If *Ellen* is going to be picked up for a sixth season by ABC, the creators need to slow down—"take smaller steps" and cart a more moderate path, advises [Bono]. . . . "[*Ellen*] is so gay it's excluding a large part of our society. . . . A lot of the stuff on it is somewhat of an inside joke. It's one thing to have a gay lead character, but it's another when every episode deals with pretty specific gay issues. . . . Originally, she said this wasn't going to be the 'gay Ellen show,' that every episode wasn't going to deal with gay issues. But it pretty much has. And this is something ABC hasn't been happy about."[89]

Word of these statements seemed to fly through the entertainment industry and the southern California homosexual community like wildfire: even a lesbian media advocate was complaining that *Ellen* was too out! GLAAD, which used the series' coming-out episode as a major fundraiser the previous spring, snapped into action to address the article and announced that Bono was not expressing her own attitude towards the show, but was merely repeating theories others had made as to the show's low ratings. The statement continued, "What the article fails to mention is that Ms. Bono and GLAAD strongly believe that the program contains themes that transcend issues of sexual orientation, and are entertaining and appealing to audiences gay and straight."[90]

While the actual quotes by Bono *do* seem to support GLAAD's statement, the furor over Lovell's article may have indicated an awareness that there were indeed many lesbians and gay men who didn't like the new *Ellen*. In a number of different contexts and environments, I encountered lesbians and gay men who had complaints about the show during the 1997–98 season. Some agreed with the opinion that the show had become "too political" and ceased to be funny because of its stridence. These viewers preferred to relax in front of the show; to them, serious discussion belonged somewhere other than on a situation comedy. Yet, others were bothered by Ellen Morgan's openness specifically because understanding her as lesbian was no longer an oppositional reading. They preferred remaining "outlaws," wanting to remain outside of and challenging to the status quo by keeping *Ellen*'s "lesbian sensibility" to themselves.[91]

The latter attitude points to an overarching issue regarding the "more obvious" homosexual readings of Disney discussed in this chapter: if reading from a "lesbian/gay sensibility" is no longer so "underground," it becomes harder and harder to argue that such a subject position is radical or subversive. If the Walt Disney Company is not only aware of the "gay subtext," but—as in the case of *Ellen* or *Tombstone,* for example—actively putting it into the text, a "gay sensibility" is not resisting the work but coming closer to the "ideal subject position." As mainstream society becomes increasingly aware of lesbian and gay culture, there is the attendant danger of this subculture becoming colonized and commodified by mass culture.[92] ABC's desires to keep *Ellen* from becoming the "lesbian dating show" are a perfect expression of corporate interests attempting to control and manage sexual discourse; before Ellen came out, discourse around the series had a freer and wider potential. With no official sanction by the show, certain viewers could interpret Ellen Morgan in a number of ways: as lesbian, as bisexual, as asexual—i.e., as a queer figure.

The previous wealth of possibilities for Ellen Morgan, and the differences in criticism of the series by various homosexual individuals, also points out that "the homosexual community" is not an easily defined and isolated group. The deconstruction of a mythologized unified homosexual community is what has led to the use of the previously derogatory word "queer" in academic and some political circles, thus reinvesting in the term "queer" an inclusiveness of gay men, lesbians, bisexuals, the transgendered—in short, the wide variety of sexualities (and, hopefully, the diverse racial/ethnic and class identities) which are created by the matrices of social discourse. The use of the word "queer" by both theorists and activists tries to keep identity fluid and uncontainable by larger hegemonic concerns.

Increased visibility of overt homosexuals in Disney's employee ranks and in its texts recognizes the existence of homosexuality yet ironically works against the amorphousness of being "queer." With this in mind, one must acknowledge that not all "queer" individuals enjoy Disneyana. In Gregg Araki's *Totally Fucked Up* (1993), which deals with gay, lesbian and bisexual teens, one young man states plainly that he *cannot stand* Bette Midler and is annoyed for feeling that he *has* to like her since he's gay. As was mentioned at the beginning of the discussion of *The Golden Girls* and *Ellen*, Disney lends itself more readily to gay men than to lesbians. And, as reception to the final season of *Ellen* unwittingly pointed out, some "queer" individuals want to retain control of their conceptions of sexuality by remaining out of the hegemonic limelight.

In September of 1997, Ellen DeGeneres won an Emmy for Best Comedy Writing with "The Puppy Episode." In accepting the award, she said, "On behalf of the people—and the teenagers especially—out there who think there is something wrong with them because they're gay: There's nothing wrong with you, and don't let anyone make you ashamed of who you are."[93] As this chapter describes, it became easier to read Disney in the Eisner-Wells-Katzenberg era as saying that there was "nothing wrong" with being homosexual. But it seems increasingly obvious with the cancellation of *Ellen* that the company was actually saying there was "nothing wrong" being a *certain kind* of homosexual— one that served Disney's best interests.

5

You've Never Had a Friend Like Me

Target Marketing Disney to a Gay Community

IN SEPTEMBER OF 1996, when rumors about the lesbian storyline developing on *Ellen* were first reported in the mainstream press, they were met with a certain cynicism by some industry insiders. Some seemed to think that the revelation of these discussions going on at Touchstone Television were purposefully leaked as a means of assessing the public reaction from both audiences and advertisers. "You can't help but think that they're testing the waters, waiting to see if advertisers will balk," an unnamed rival studio executive told *TV Guide.* "The timing is ideal. If the public supports this, they can move ahead with the storyline. If not, they can just shelve their plans and say it was all a rumor."[1] Certainly, divulging that the show's producers were considering having Ellen Morgan come out created instant and widespread publicity for the series, making it one of the most talked about shows of the year. Countless newspaper and magazine articles and columns devoted themselves to the topic, providing publicity that Disney did not have to pay a cent for. Furthermore, only a month before the rumors were reported, Touchstone Television had sold the syndication rights to the Lifetime cable network, and such an enormous awareness of the series had the potential to increase its profitability. While some have theorized that having a signed contract created more security to tackle this volatile subject, it is also quite possible to see how such rumors could provide incentive for viewers to tune in to reruns to find all the "clues" that they might have missed from previous seasons.[2] After all, DeGeneres' manager, Arthur Imparato, told reporters during the period that "If you look hard at the whole series, there are a lot of elements over the years that could be laying the groundwork for that storyline."[3] Consequently, while the brouhaha over whether or not Ellen Morgan was lesbian made the typically divergent homosexual reading the dominant subject position, many also saw it functioning as expert publicity by a company that has often led the industry in marketing.

Disney's reputation in marketing and publicity is well known and somewhat envied within the motion picture industry. With the arrival of Eisner, Wells and Katzenberg, the Walt Disney Company became extremely bold and aggressive in its marketing campaigns for the new Touchstone Pictures films, for the push into television, for the revamped animation department, for the video release of classic Disney films, for the new rides at the theme parks and so on. Eisner was quoted as saying "Once you've got the product, you've got to let people know about it. We are a consumer company and marketing is at the top of the list."[4] Many give credit to Team Disney's enormous advertising push for the rapid turnaround of the company after 1985.[5] Disney's reputation for aggressive marketing has become so well known, even to the general populous, that the studio was able to slyly make fun of itself in the animated feature *Hercules* (1997), where (within the film itself) the hero gets his face and name placed on sneakers, clothing, cups, action figures and the like.

Viewing the surge of discussion about *Ellen* as a marketing strategy points out why advertising and publicity are so vital to analyze when dealing with a "queer" film or television text. The "*Ellen* Watch" feature that developed in *TV Guide*, as well as the numerous other articles that started reading the series with a "lesbian sensibility," reveal how marketing and publicity influences reception. If the press leak was a deliberate maneuver on the company's part, this strategy manifestly discussed the subject of homosexuality at a time when the series itself was still "playing coy." Although *Ellen* itself would not label Ellen Morgan as a lesbian until the final three episodes of the 1996–97 season, the publicity about the show *was* doing the labeling much earlier.

This scenario in which the primary texts may remain somewhat oblique, but the marketing more directly addresses a homosexual subject position, is not unique to Disney. For example, reading Disney's latest animated features from a "queer" viewpoint, or finding a "gay appeal" in the various "boy toy" films may be amusing and enlightening, but such readings are mainly consigned to the realm of connotation rather than denotation. As D. A. Miller notes in his analysis of Alfred Hitchcock's *Rope* (1948), "Defined in contrast to the immediate self-evidence of denotation, connotation will always manifest a certain semiotic insufficiency."[6] Yet, one *can* find that denotation by looking beyond the primary texts themselves (films, TV series, theme parks), and towards the marketing and publicity the studio has created—the press releases, interviews, trailers, TV commercials—seeing *them* as texts in of themselves. Interviews with Jeffrey Katzenberg, as well as studio animators, purposefully indicate that Disney's animated features are made for more than just a "kiddie" market.[7] When joined by press recognition of both the campy villains as well as the openly gay employees working on these features, these interviews begin to address a viewing strategy that once "dared not speak its name." Chon Noriega's survey of journal reviews of "closeted" homosexual films like *Tea and Sympathy* (1956) and *Cat on a Hot Tin Roof* (1958) also sees the importance of the discourse of "nonfilmic events." The contemporary reviews alerted potential ticketbuyers about the homosexual content that was present in the original plays, but had been censored in the films. Noriega writes that "since these 'events' preceded actual film viewing, the censored subject could be reintroduced back into the theatre in the body of the reader/viewer, creating the possibility for authorized 'subtexting.'"[8]

This chapter will examine how Disney marketing works to "authorize subtexting" from lesbian or gay male consumers. While not denying the positive aspects of a major conglomerate acknowledging a homosexual subject position, this chapter will also analyze how such "authorization" poses a challenge to much of the theoretical work done on audience reception. To simply celebrate lesbian/gay readings of Disney as a type of fragmented reception is to ignore how contemporary audience research increasingly capitalizes precisely on this fragmentation in an attempt to control and regulate the reading (*à la* Foucault).[9] After examining the variety of ways in which the Walt Disney Company reaches out to the potential gay market, analysis of specific advertisements and public relations events will theorize how advertising constructs subject positions and toward what ends. By examining how advertising works to "commodify" the subject, this relatively new development by Disney in targeting gay audiences becomes more complex and problematic. Before doing so, though, a short history of Walt's own savvy in cross-promotion and merchandising will display the studio's history of being on the cutting edge of marketing and show how its leadership in the newest developments in advertising research and theory would lead it toward addressing homosexual consumers.

MARKETING THE MOUSE: A SHORT HISTORY
OF DISNEY ADVERTISING AND PUBLICITY

Historians have noted that modern mass production made it necessary to create mass consumption and that this was primarily accomplished through advertising. In the mass production of 1930s Hollywood film-making, Walt Disney learned quickly how to differentiate his shorts from the rest of the pack through the use of merchandise as a form of advertising. Walt's first major contract with a Hollywood distributor was animating Oswald, the Lucky Rabbit. Oswald's success spawned product tie-ins such as a chocolate-coated marshmallow bar, buttons and a stencil set.[10] Charles Mintz, who distributed the cartoons through a contract with Universal Pictures, owned the rights to Oswald, so Disney did not share in the monies received from this merchandising. Yet, when Walt and his brother Roy broke from Mintz and started their own studio with their new character Mickey Mouse, the popularity of the Oswald items (as well as their impact on box-office revenues) was not forgotten.

In January of 1930, Mickey began appearing in his own nationally syndicated comic strip, and, in February, Roy signed a contract with Geo. Borgfeldt and Company, which would license manufacturers (both domestic and foreign) to produce specified Disney character products, import and distribute them and then share the profits with Disney. The enormous success of Mickey Mouse cartoons resulted in a landslide of licensing contracts that helped keep the studio financially afloat. As Walt continually pushed for better "quality" in the cartoons, the budgets often ballooned beyond what most short subjects could expect to make at the box office. Consequently, the company needed the merchandise profits to stay in the black.

Yet, Roy and Walt seemed to initially perceive the relation between the shorts and the merchandise as only flowing one way. The merchandise served to publicize the films, not the other way around.[11] This mindset is evident in the strategy that the studio devised for circumventing their contract with Borgfeldt when the Mickey Mouse stuffed dolls that Borgfeldt was distributing didn't measure up to Walt and Roy's high standards. The studio simply released to the public (through the McCall Company) the pattern of the stuffed doll that *they* approved of and let people make their own dolls. The studio hired Herman "Kay" Kamen to handle the merchandising in 1932. Kamen paid the studio

$50,000 a year and split half the profits from the licensing agreements that Kamen arranged.[12] Unlike the Disney brothers, Kamen saw the reverse potential of the relationship between the films and the merchandise. Just as the merchandise could generate increased revenues at the box office, the films could generate increased revenues at the store counter. Consequently, Kamen energetically licensed Mickey and other Disney characters on watches, handkerchiefs, mugs, trains, underwear, tea sets, books, silverware *ad infinitum*. When Disney realized that millions were being made from licensing and they were only receiving half of the profits, the studio's philosophy changed. In 1948, when Kamen's contract came up for renewal, the studio cut his participation in merchandising to only North and Central America and created a Character Merchandising Division to handle foreign markets. A year later, Kamen died in a plane crash, and the studio assumed total control of merchandising.

At about the same time the studio reevaluated its relationship to merchandising, Disney rapidly expanded into a number of other areas. Disney moved boldly into television when major studios were still wary, seeing the new medium's cross-promotional advantages. The series *Disneyland* (1954–58) won an Emmy its first season for a program that was basically an hour-long advertisement for the new feature *20,000 Leagues Under the Sea* (1954). Disney agreed to produce the program for ABC only when the network agreed to help finance the building of Disneyland, the theme park. Although the series promoted the park relentlessly, the studio did not look on television simply as an advertising medium. Now each division mutually supported the other. The success of "Davy Crockett" on TV, for example, spurred the selling of merchandise, promoted the "Frontierland" section of the new park and was eventually released as a live-action feature, but also spurred further television production by the studio.

Other studios rushed (and are still rushing) to adapt to Disney's strategy of "synergy," creating TV series, licensing characters and investing in theme park attractions that encourage further consumption of studio product. (Even non-film corporations such as Coca-Cola, McDonald's and Marlboro have moved into licensed merchandising.) In the 1960s, after the major film studios had divested themselves of their domestic exhibition branches, various multimedia conglomerates took over most of the studios. The talent agency MCA came from within entertainment and began the acquisition fervor when it acquired Universal as well as Paramount's vault of films for licensing to television and Decca Records. Many came from non-entertainment areas though, such as Gulf + Western's takeover of Paramount or Transamerica's acquisition of United Artists. The effect of these mergers and acquisitions on filmed entertainment was a growing cross-interest. Conglomerates now used the assets of their filmed entertainment to help invigorate other branches (and vice versa). Sony's acquisition of Columbia ensured the production of titles for home video consumption, which also furthered Sony's interest in VCRs, laser discs and TVs. Time, Inc.'s merger with Warner Bros. provided a system in which Time's cable network HBO helped finance Warner films by buying the cable rights, in turn providing product for HBO to broadcast. Other studios have followed Disney's lead in diversifying media outlets by becoming involved in theme parks (i.e., Universal's Studio Tour, Time-Warner's interests in Magic Mountain) and in merchandising (i.e., Warner Bros. Stores). In this way, the iconography of the original films can be sold dozens of times over in different contexts.

Although Disney led this trend in the 1950s, other studios surpassed Disney's "synergetic" abilities during the stagnant years after Walt's death. Eisner, coming from Paramount, and Wells, having worked at Warners, took the corporate lessons they learned and updated Disney's older concepts. Taking advantage of the instant recognition of the Disney name and characters, all aspects of the corporation aggressively sold each other in a hyperefficient model that became the envy of the industry. For example, the popularity of the theatrical feature *Aladdin* was tied to a number of other related areas: miniature action figures of the film's characters; tie-ins with Burger King, which put images of the characters on plastic soft drink cups; the score from the film released on CD, as well as a children's album narrating the story; the release of the feature on home video, and eventually on the Disney Channel; a new show/restaurant in the "Adventureland" section of the theme parks, as well as "Aladdin" parades down Main Street; Little Golden Books' picture book of the story; an animated TV series based on the characters; the selling of original cel work done for the feature; and a CD-ROM based on the film. A more recent example of Disney's continued strategy of synergy between various corporate arms was the acquisition of the American Broadcasting Company in 1996. Almost immediately, a number of the families of different ABC series made pilgrimages to Walt Disney World. *Roseanne, Step by Step* and *Second Noah*

all created "special" episodes that hoped to attract more viewers by
their trips to the park but also effectively worked to advertise the place
as well. ABC's daytime series *All My Children* publicized a "Cinderella"-themed wedding in May of 1996 to increase its audience but
also made explicit reference to the Disney film version, which just happened to have been released on video the month before.

Disney was also one of the first to capitalize on the concept of target audiences, a key development in the eventual attempt to woo the
homosexual customer. In the first half of the century, marketers followed the ideas of many social scientists of the time who conceived of
the population as an undifferentiated "mass." Sociologists from the
Frankfurt School conceived of mass media as a "magic bullet" or "hy-
podermic needle" which was injected into the passive unconscious
minds of the masses.[13] Yet, marketing and public relations firms quickly
realized that if potential buyers passively accepted sponsors' messages,
every advertising campaign would be inordinately successful. After
World War II, target marketing was developed by advertisers as an implicit admission that some potential customers were not "getting the
message" that their clients were communicating. W. R. Smith introduced the idea of "target research" to marketing in 1956, which was defined as a shift from product differentiation (the "attempt to bend demand to the will of supply") to consumer differentiation ("bend[ing]
supply to demand by identifying lucrative segments of the market and
developing products to specifically fit those segments").[14] By moving
from advertising the benefits of the product itself to advertising the benefits of belonging to a certain audience segment which used the product, segmenting moved to increasingly isolate specific groups from this
ill-defined mass, hopefully including those groups which had spending
power but had not been addressed effectively in marketing heretofore.

Disney had already proven the viability of Smith's ideas two years
earlier. With the broadcast of the weekly *Disneyland* series, and especially the daily afternoon episodes of *The Mickey Mouse Club* (1955–58),
the studio helped to create a culture of "children's television" and dominated what became an increasingly lucrative children's market.[15] These
Disney TV shows promoted the theme parks and the new film releases,
as well as a plenitude of tie-in products, by aiming their discourse directly at the child consumer. This trend continues in the present, as the
success of the syndicated "Disney Afternoon" attests. Eisner began his
career in children's programming for ABC and, immediately upon tak-

ing over at Disney, moved to create children's series. The phenomenal response to such syndicated series as *DuckTales* (1986–92) and *Chip n' Dale's Rescue Rangers* (1989–93) proved the company's ability to target and capture the younger consumer.[16]

In the Eisner era, such target research has gone beyond simply breaking up the audience into children and adults. Some ads for the film *Pretty Woman*, for example, were created to sell men on a "woman's" picture, and special ads for *Dead Poets Society* were made to air on David Letterman's late-night talk show, specifically aimed at the person that audience research said watched the program. Since the mid-1980s, the studio has regularly created campaigns for its theatrical releases that feature separate ads written specifically towards a different demographic group. For example, amongst the titles of different ads for the *Aladdin* campaign are "Young Boys/Good vs. Evil," "Kids Imagine," "Young Girls/Jasmine's Dream," "Moms" and "Adult Sneak Preview." Each TV spot attempts to create a reading of *Aladdin* that the studio figures will appeal to the specific group that it is addressing. "Young Boys" emphasizes the action sequences in the film, while "Young Girls" tries to make the film look as if Princess Jasmine is the lead character and Aladdin only a supporting character.[17] Such a strategy is also used now by the company to sell its video releases and to promote theme park attendance, with different commercials for kids, teenagers, young single adults and parents. One of the strongest ad campaigns Disney came up with in the late 1980s focused directly on addressing the heterosexual adult male. In a number of TV spots, various sports celebrities were filmed just after a major victory (an Olympic win, the Super Bowl, the World Series) to announce that now they were "going to Disneyland!"

One of the major strategies developed by the company in its effort to target certain audience segments was the "audience reaction" TV spot. Prior to the 1980s, most of the film industry's ads merely showed individual clips from the feature accompanied by voice-over narration. Occasionally, the studios would also create ads that trumpeted the critic's reviews of the film, much as print ads in newspapers had been doing for decades. Although trying to determine who originated the concept is difficult, Team Disney marketing definitely jumped upon the "audience reaction" idea in the late 1980s. Since marketing research had consistently shown that "word-of-mouth" reaction created the most powerful incentive for individuals to see a film, these TV spots worked to create a *sense* of "word-of-mouth" by cutting together clips of various "everyday" people raving about the film.

Of course, these ads were always carefully orchestrated. Rather than catching people who actually paid to see the film as they left the theatre, people were usually invited to a "special screening" specifically so they could be interviewed after watching the film. Just before the interview, the audience would be handed a sheet listing the type of comments the producers were looking for, with the implication that if someone wanted to make it into the final cut of the ad and be a minor celebrity amongst their friends and family, they had better say these things! Even more importantly, though, the ad companies hired by Disney went to specific sections of the Los Angeles area to invite a certain type of individual to these screenings. This usually meant young, handsome, upscale couples or groups of friends—mainly white, but with a few middle-aged couples and a few non-whites to keep it vaguely diverse. In this manner, the audience reaction ads would tell viewers that if you identified (or, more importantly, *wanted* to identify) with this type of audience, seeing this film was imperative! As the strategy was refined, the company could narrow the target focus even further with these "audience reactions." The aforementioned *Pretty Woman* spot aimed at men was an "audience reaction" ad, with men talking about how "hot" Julia Roberts was in the film.

The increased focus of the company on audience segmentation had to make Disney at least aware of the "gay market," a concept that arose by the early 1980s. Furthermore, at a point when the studio was attempting to get customers by any means necessary, it is unlikely that they would have completely ignored the possibilities of marketing to this segment. As we shall see, there are indications that they did not ignore it. The manipulation at work in such marketing campaigns inevitably creates an ever-shifting struggle between the public and the marketers over who holds the power over meaning.

BE OUR GUESTS: DISNEY MARKETING TO HOMOSEXUAL CONSUMERS

In 1986, eight years after Disneyland unexpectedly had to deal with a horde of openly gay men running rampant through the place, the Walt Disney Company, in conjunction with AIDS organizations in Orange

County, held a benefit at the park to raise funds for AIDS Project Los Angeles (APLA). Not only was the event sponsored directly by the company, but Disney pledged to match the money raised by ticket sales with an equal donation from corporate coffers. The ticket prices for this benefit (and subsequent benefits for the next few years) were higher than normal, thus attracting a "higher-income" crowd, but the success of these benefits started a trend at both Disneyland and Walt Disney World. In the 1990s, the Odyssey Tours travel agency began renting out the park one night a year (usually during the early winter, traditionally a slow period for the park) to hold "Gay Nights" at the park. Although never specifically advertised with such a phrase, the flyers and print ads announced that portions of the proceeds would go to the Aid for AIDS charity, and, judging by the crowds these nights attracted, most people "got the hint." Similarly, a number of organizations worked together to promote such an event at Walt Disney World but without any pretense; they simply announced it as "Gay & Lesbian Day At the Magical Kingdom That Walt Built." Before long, the annual event had become an entire weekend of activities in and around the Disney complex: a day at the Magic Kingdom, a reception and party at Pleasure Island and even a buffet brunch with various Disney characters.

Such benefits and events weren't occurring only at the theme parks at this time. As Joseph Boone recounts, Disney's theatrical film arm worked together with Matt Sterling Productions for a special screening:

> Best known for its extensive video collection of gay male porn, as well as sponsorship of numerous exotic theme parties on the Los Angeles gay club scene, Sterling's company sponsored a "MATT STERLING PRESENTS A GAY NIGHT" at Disney's latest animated family entertainment, *Aladdin*, on December 23, 1992, a special screening serving as an AIDS benefit for the L.A. Project Angel Food.[18]

Many might be surprised to find Disney reaching out to gay audiences. Yet, a number of factors make such a development in the company's business strategy understandable. First, the influx of such openly lesbian and gay employees to the company would obviously have its effect on attempting to attract homosexual customers. Roland Marchand, in his analysis of 1920s and '30s American advertising, noticed that those working in advertising agencies often assumed that their own wants and desires mirrored the rest of the populous, and hence often inadvertently created ads that appealed to their own specific outlook on life.[19] While not necessarily having a "gay agenda" (as paranoid religious conservatives might see it), lesbians or gay men working for Disney marketing might tend to create campaigns that they themselves find appealing (and hence possibly appealing to gay or lesbian customers as well). Also, the close friendship that Jeffrey Katzenberg built with Howard Ashman had a profound effect on the executive according to many who worked at Disney during Ashman's illness, and thus, Katzenberg himself seemed more attuned to gay issues and causes than most Hollywood executives of the time.

Most importantly, when Eisner, Wells and Katzenberg took over the company, they were eager to expand the profit margin to stave off future hostile takeover attempts. While one of the major methods was creating new venues for their product and consolidating control of those venues for maximum profit, the company also worked conscientiously on creating new audiences to consume the product in these new venues. The thoroughness of Disney's audience research had to have made the gay constituency somewhat noticeable to executives, and in such a tight money crunch, reaching out to this already established fan base would be a quick way to generate sales. Such gestures as the APLA benefit at Disneyland in 1986 would not only win brand-name loyalty by some homosexual patrons, but create a new base for the company's synergetic marketing efforts. Once homosexual customers went to see *Aladdin*, for example, and enjoyed all the "subtext" within the film, they would be more likely to buy the soundtrack CD and various tie-in collectibles. Furthermore, adult homosexuals would be more likely than children to move beyond the Burger King or McDonald's "Happy Meal" collectibles and buy the more expensive ceramic replicas of characters, music boxes or original cel artwork from the film.

Of course, companies such as Disney have to proceed carefully when addressing any "gay market," for fear of alienating their larger customer base of traditional heterosexual families. It is thus imperative to find a method of appealing to homosexual customers that will not disturb other consumers. The AIDS benefits previously described exemplify one such method, with the company not specifically championing "gay pride" but raising money for a disease that can strike anyone. Lesbians and gay men could also read this as much needed support for the number of homosexuals with AIDS, but Disney could promote this as larger than the scope of a homosexual audience. When these special nights and weekends were sponsored by various gay-oriented companies, Disney could absolve itself from culpability by claiming that they had just rented the use of the park out to an independent travel agency, and whom that agency brought to the park was none of Disney's responsibility.

Another effective method used to mask marketing to homosexual audiences is the relatively recent concept of "gay window advertising." The term was probably adapted from theorist Judith Williamson's description of conscious "absences" in ads that she labeled "windows." These "windows," according to Williamson, allow readers to "decipher . . . the surface, (and) 'break through' to the 'hidden' meaning. . . . You are invited to slip into it, to enter ITS space, drawn to participate in a 'discovery of meaning.'"[20] Such "windows" were specifically placed by the advertisers to draw the potential consumer into the ad. In 1981, Karen Stabiner reported on advertisers "Tapping the Homosexual Market" for the *New York Times*, noticing what sociologist Laud Humphreys had labeled "gay window advertising."[21] This new marketing approach addressed the gay consumer slyly and without offending the straight consumer (or even letting the straight consumer know that the gay consumer was being addressed). By "breaking through" the ad's surface, a gay consumer could find the "hidden message" aimed at the homosexual reader. As an example, Stabiner's article displays a Times Square ad for Calvin Klein jeans featuring a handsome, bare-chested male model staring seductively out at the viewer. The caption in the article points out another advantage to such a marketing strategy—deniability: "The ad agency denies that this billboard was aimed primarily at homosexuals, adding, 'But you don't want to alienate them.'"[22] In other words, if any straight consumer "caught on," the company could deny any intentions of "gay address."

As the Calvin Klein jeans billboard reveals, "gay window advertising" has become relatively common practice in clothing, cologne and liquor ads since the early 1980s. One could find coded gay messages in such diverse campaigns as: Poco Rabanne's Pour Homme cologne print ads showing a man speaking to his gender-unspecified lover over the phone; Tanqueray Gin's overly cultured fictional spokesperson Mr. Jenkins; as well as the objectified male bodies displayed on Calvin Klein underwear billboards and in Levi's Loose Jeans TV spots. By the late 1980s, an aware viewer of Disney's TV ads could also find these subtle "gay windows." While Disney commonly labels its ads with titles like

"Moms" or "Young Boys," there has never been (to my knowledge) an individual commercial in a campaign labeled "Gay Men/Lesbian Women." But there have been ads that, when watched, do produce a double-take reaction. A perfect example is the TV spot for *Aladdin* entitled "All Genie-B," which was produced for Disney by Craig Murray Productions and New Wave Productions. The spot begins with the narration, "When Aladdin discovered the lamp, he found a genie who gave him everything he wanted—and more than he could handle." In between this narration, the Genie emerges from the lamp to exclaim, "It's good to be *out of there!*" Immediately after the narration finishes, the commercial presents the Genie acting as the "swishy tailor." This is the longest clip in the whole spot, emphasizing the Genie as a "queer figure." Immediately following this clip is a shot of the Genie in the lamp showing Aladdin how to rub the lamp right where his crotch would be, and the next shot shows the Genie transforming into a huge pair of lips, the better to kiss Aladdin with. All through the ad, the song "You've Never Had a Friend Like Me" plays in the background. Indeed. This ad might not be labeled "Gay Men," but it sure reads like it could have been.

Although this particular ad is possibly the strongest example of such "gay window advertising" in Disney's TV spots, one can find an equally strong example in Disney's print ads. During the initial theatrical release of *The Lion King,* Disney took out newspaper ads showing various characters speaking lines from the film that seemed to advise customers to see the film. Two of them stand out from a gay perspective. In one, Scar with a fey smile and a raised pinkie in his claw announces that the film is "to die for!" In another, the meerkat Timon pleads, "What do you want me to do, dress in drag and do the hula?!" The obviousness of this address almost pushes the boundaries of the coded nature of "gay window advertising."[23]

Beyond these instances, a number of other TV spots and trailers also evince "vibes." The trailers for *Tough Guys* and *Off Beat* feature the "gay" moments in the films prominently—the scenes in a gay bar in the former, the hug in the men's shower in the latter. The trailer for *Three Men and a Little Lady* not only shows the little girl asking why her three daddies aren't married and all of them stammering in response, but constantly shows Tom Selleck's character trying to escape the clutches of a sexually aggressive woman. At one point, the woman finds him hiding from her and she asks bluntly what he's doing in the closet! A TV spot for *Big Business,* produced by New Wave Productions, entitled "Man's World," perfectly points out the dual reading positions possible. Although ostensibly showing all the men that are romantically after Bette Midler and Lily Tomlin in the film, the ad features the gay couple, Chuck and Graham, more prominently than any other men—at one point displaying Chuck dropping his shirt and standing bare-chested. The spot also shows a clip of Chuck complaining to Graham, "Look at us! We're standing outside a *ladies' room!*" For a straight viewer, this might play as a joke showing how desperate for female companionship these men are; for a gay viewer, this plays as a joke that they are standing outside the wrong restroom! Similarly, in a TV spot for *Tombstone* promoting all the male stars in the production, there is a shot of Jason Priestly as Sister Boy that did not remain in the final cut of the film. The shot shows Priestly's character lying on a bed as a female prostitute slowly climbs from the foot of the bed towards him. I assume that this shot was chosen in an attempt to make it look like Priestly's character was heterosexual, but, even before seeing the film and realizing who Sister Boy was, I saw the ad and, reading panic and anxiety in Priestly's eyes as the woman crawled up over him, wondered just what was going on in that scene.

As is the point of "gay window advertising," such readings are again based not on denotation but on connotation which, as Miller states, once raised, "tends to light everywhere."[24] As the years have gone on, though, Disney has ventured into more explicit address to gay audiences through marketing, as the advertisements for the special screening of *Aladdin* mentioned above reveal. Joseph Boone points out that "the Disney corporation legitimize[d] its participation in the event . . . [by] being visually linked, on the publicity flyer, with the king of West coast gay porn."[25] On this ad, both the names of Disney and Sterling appear, and a large drawing of Aladdin with a "come-hither" smirk stares straight at the viewer. Another overt appeal to possible gay customers can be found in the number of interviews given by openly homosexual employees of Disney to various gay publications. In journals such as *The Advocate, Out* and *Frontiers,* reporters have done interviews with animator Andreas Deja, Hollywood Pictures executive Lauren Lloyd and animation executive Tom Schumacher. Of course, employees do not need company approval to be interviewed, but these journals do need permission from the Walt Disney Company to publish the film stills that often accompany the articles. Also, not so coincidentally, the interviews are usually published just as one of the studio's films is about to be released to theatres. With the release of *Aladdin*, interviews with Deja appeared in both *The Advocate* and *Frontiers*. In these interviews, Deja "points proudly to . . . examples of gayish humor in *Aladdin*," such as agreeing that "Jafar might be gay."[26] Tom Schumacher's interview with *The Advocate* began by describing the supportive environment at Disney for gay and lesbian employees, "but more exciting to Schumacher . . . is this month's theatrical launch of *The Lion King*."[27] Even with this more direct address, the studio can still keep from disturbing its family market. While these interviews and the Matt Sterling event are more directly geared towards a homosexual subject, all of these are presented in forums far from the eyes of mainstream heterosexual culture. The flyers for the Matt Sterling event were handed out within the gay community, not placed in the *Los Angeles Times*. Interviews with gay employees like Deja and Schumacher or ads for the "Gay Nights" at the theme parks are only in gay newspapers and periodicals—publications that the public at large have neither access to nor (for the most part) knowledge of.

By the 1990s, Disney seemed to be growing gradually more comfortable with speaking openly to a gay market. Three months before Schumacher's interview had appeared in *The Advocate*, the company allowed clips from *The Lion King* to be shown during Barbara Walters' interview with Elton John (who had co-written the songs for the picture). During this interview, John revised the assertion he had made earlier in his career that he was bisexual, now announcing that he was homosexual. Since this interview was broadcast just before or just after the annual Oscar ceremony (depending on the area of the country), millions of people now knew that an open homosexual had worked on a Disney animated feature. Possibly the most famous and overt instance of marketing a Disney film towards a gay audience involved Howard Ashman. As mentioned before, Ashman was posthumously posited by the studio's publicity material for *Beauty and the Beast* as the guiding force of the project. Almost all of the articles written about the film spent much of their time mourning the loss of Ashman, and they all prominently displayed the fact that Ashman was a gay man who had died as a result of the AIDS virus. This coverage was not isolated to the gay press. Stories in *Premiere* magazine, reviews in the *Los Angeles Times*, the *New York Times*, *Variety* and *Newsweek* magazine, all mainstream publications, were part of the phenomenon.[28] With such widespread visibility, it would be impossible *not* to see the place of a gay constitutency in the mass audience that *Beauty and the Beast* was appealing to.

Winning such explicit address from a major studio is quite stunning. Yet, such a celebratory reaction ignores how marketing strategies work to channel the homosexual individual into behavior and consciousness that benefits Disney's profit margin more than the individual. A simple example would be the use of "window advertising," which keeps the gay consumer "in the closet," since the aim of this marketing strategy is to not let the straight consumer know what's going on. By employing this type of marketing, lesbian/gay audiences are told that they are appreciated ($7.50 is $7.50 no matter who shells it out for a ticket), but that they must stay off to one side and not jeopardize Disney's larger public reputation. On a larger scale, reaching out to a gay market exemplifies Mandel's concept of "late capitalism," in which Frederic Jameson sees "a new and historically original penetration and colonization of Nature and the Unconscious."[29] By this, Jameson contends that capitalism now can isolate and commodify time, space and even psychic spaces or definitions of identity. As Bill Short writes: "Many of us who wish to maintain a gay identity, actually buy that identity. . . . We are forced to prove we exist by projecting a gay image or lifestyle."[30] Consequently, when engaged in marketing to homosexuals, the Walt Disney Company—not the audience—attempts to define the identity of the gay community, defining it to suit its own needs.

Stuart Ewen speaks of modern industrial capitalism (and the advertising which supports it) as endowing the mass audience with an "industrial democracy" in which the individual is made to believe that freedom and equality are defined as the ability to consume and acquire, effectively supplanting the desire for actual social reform.[31] A dissatisfied individual is encouraged to create change not through protest and revolt, but through consumption, which only reinforces the established system which made the individual dissatisfied initially. "'Advertising has stimulated more work,' rejoiced the Ayer agency [in the 1920s]. Americans so valued labor-saving devices that they were 'willing to work harder for them.'"[32] For example, in the 1920s, ads celebrated women's suffrage by promoting the liberating feeling of smoking cigarettes. With regard to the call for gay rights, the influx of corporate interest in the gay community encourages lesbians and gay men to show their pride and political commitment by buying a solid gold "AIDS ribbon," a rainbow bumper sticker or a ticket to Disneyland's Gay Night rather than protesting for domestic-partner benefits or national health care.

Much has been said about the "birth" of homosexuality, when the sexual act was no longer seen as an isolated incident, but an indication of a personality or a lifestyle. Most of what has been written has focused on the medical, religious and legal definitions of homosexual identity. It is also important to see how capitalism intersects with science, religion and the law (areas Foucault and others have analyzed) to shape the social discourse on homosexuality and how it attempts to inculcate that discourse into individual psyches who label themselves as gay men or lesbians through advertising. Finding examples of how capitalism attempts to regulate homosexual identity is not hard in the 1990s. In fact, many people were celebrating the early 1990s as "the Gay Moment," in which lesbian and gay male culture seemed to be the "new thing," the "latest fad." Tied into the increased presence of lesbian/gay issues on then presidential candidate Bill Clinton's agenda, and the growth of "New Queer Cinema," was a veritable onslaught of merchandise and cultural artifacts available for purchase to prove that one was either "out and proud" or at least hip and accepting of someone else's "lifestyle." Various gay organizations and businesses suddenly found major corporations willing to underwrite or sponsor community projects. Large conglomerates now took out advertisements in lesbian and gay publications. In 1995, the furniture franchise IKEA released a TV spot in select areas of the United States, showing a gay male couple buying a dining room table. A mainstream fashion trend, eventually labeled "lesbian chic," started hitting the runways as well as fashion magazines like *Elle* and *Mirabella* and eventually places like J. Crew catalogues.[33] Numerous mail-order catalogues emerged specifically aimed at gay consumers. Beyond the earlier established International Male catalogue, there appeared Undergear, Shocking Gray, M2M, Tzabaco, and a wealth of new glossy magazines for lesbians and gay men such as *Out, Genre, Men's Style* and for lesbians *Deneuve*.[34] And in each of these magazines there were (and still are) pages and pages of ads encouraging readers to buy this new onslaught of "gay culture."

Recent recognition by corporate America of the lesbian and gay community can be read as a step forward towards equality, using the power of the dollar to get a voice. But many others have expressed unease and worry over the implications of this "Gay Moment" in marketing. A letter from a "Ms. Beverly Hills" published in the Oct. 19, 1994 issue of the gay 'zine *Planet Homo* angrily announced:

> Pride(TM) is everywhere I look. We've been buying our Pride(TM) by the train load. We wear Pride(TM), we eat Pride(TM), sleep in Pride(TM), we drink Pride(TM), we have all those Pride(TM) festivals. HELLO, HELLOOO . . . CHECK PLEASE! . . . I have a shocking news flash for you darlings: YOU CANNOT BUY, WEAR, EAT OR DRINK PRIDE!!![35]

As early as 1984, Michael Bronski was criticizing this development, claiming that a "gay identity" and a marketed "gay lifestyle" are not necessarily the same thing.[36] While insightfully deconstructing the capitalist discourse of marketing a "gay lifestyle," Bronski's analysis assumes that a "gay identity" is somehow "truer" or "purer" than a marketed "lifestyle." By exposing how identity is created by the economic discourse, Bronski unwittingly helps to naturalize the creation of gay identity by other social discourses. In recognizing the limitations placed upon the definition of homosexuality by advertising, one should point out that gay identity is becoming more obviously constructed, not that it is being constructed for the first time.

The growth of capitalism in Western culture has influenced the identity of homosexuals for over a hundred years, not just in this "Gay Moment." Jeffrey Weeks, in his work on nineteenth-century male prostitutes, states that "perhaps the only people who lived wholly in the [emerging homosexual] subculture were the relatively few 'professionals.'"[37] Whether in Weeks' London or in the Bowery of New York City that George Chauncey describes, communities of male prostitutes were some of the earliest groupings of individuals who consciously based their identity on their same-sex desires.[38] Before this point, evidence seems to show that most of Western society viewed homosexual acts as deviant behavior and not the indication of an entire personality type. The prostitution industry's influence on the beginnings of modern gay identity is apparent. As Weeks describes, "by the 1870's, any sort of homosexual transaction, whether or not money was involved, was described as 'trade.'"[39] Similarly tying sexual desire to "bodies for sale," Gregory Woods points out that "one often hears of gay men whose first images of sexy men—

their earliest masturbatory icons—were the men and boys in the underwear and swimwear sections of mail order catalogues."[40]

John D'Emilio's essay on "Capitalism and Gay Identity" describes a shift in the nineteenth century from a system of household production (in which the family grew its own food, made its own clothes, etc.) to a system of wage labor (in which individuals worked for money to buy food and clothes). "Only when individuals began to make their living through wage labor, instead of as parts of an interdependent family unit, was it possible for homosexual desire to coalesce into a personal identity."[41] As these individuals found each other and started developing a network of friendships, various artifacts—a green carnation, a red tie, certain other accessories of clothing—served to alert "members of the club" to each other's status even if they had never met. In the urban environment of early twentieth-century America, these things were usually purchased rather than handmade.[42] The attempt by many urban homosexual individuals at this time to create an "upper-class" aura by buying "the right things" may have actually had a hand in the appropriation of the word "gay." Many magazine and newspaper ads in the 1920s pointedly depicted the "gay life" of the upper class, and often such a description was used to advertise men's products like Arrow shirts.[43] It is quite possible that this attempt to affect a certain class status furthered the appropriation of the term "gay" as code for "homosexual."[44]

As places for homosexuals to find each other, to feel safe from the hatred of the rest of society, and to form a separate subculture and eventually a political consciousness, bars were (and possibly *are*) the lifeblood of homosexual communities. By the early 1960s, bars such as the Black Cat and the D'Oak Room in San Francisco were focal points for a growing gay activism as owners and customers fought the city and the police to maintain their right to exist.[45] The Stonewall Riots of 1969 were focused around attempts by police to raid and close down the Greenwich Village bar. Bars may have been places for individuals to find others lesbians and gay men, but one had to keep buying rounds in order to stay there. Paris Poirier's documentary *Last Call at Maud's* (1992) shows how important one San Francisco bar was to the lesbian community, but it also shows how many of these women resultingly had to deal with alcoholism.

In the 1970s, lesbians and gay male activists began to discover a new weapon that they could use in the fight for "gay liberation." As part of their protest against a national homophobic campaign led by Anita Bryant, lesbians and gay men across the United States refused to buy Florida orange juice, which used Bryant as its spokesperson. When the boycott succeeded in Bryant's dismissal, lesbians and gay men found that they wielded an economic strength that no one had previously considered. Corporations noticed that strength as well, which led eventually to the "Gay Moment" of the 1990s. Since bars have figured so highly in the history of twentieth-century gay culture, it is only logical that such companies as Seagram, Tanqueray, Cuervo, Miller Beer and Smirnoff led the way by taking ads out in gay publications or sponsoring events in gay communities. In fact, during the height of the "Gay Moment" in 1994, just in time for the twenty-fifth anniversary of the Stonewall Riots, "Pride" beer debuted, offering a way to display with every swig from the bottle that one was a proud (if inebriated) homosexual individual!

In 1993, Owen Frager and Ron Antman, two openly gay men working in advertising and marketing, started their own company devoted to courting the gay consumer. Ron/Owen and Partners, as the new company was named, stated in a promotional video their conviction that "the gay market was easily targeted and would respond to any company that treated it with respect." Soon, they had such companies as Perrier, Calistoga, Simon & Schuster and Hiram Walker as clients. Yet, their approach to these clients points out the limits of recent corporate embrace of the homosexual community. In the video, a narrator assures prospective clients that "you don't need to march in a gay pride parade" to win gay business. As Gregory Woods theorizes, "the lesbian or gay consumer is welcome . . . to the extent that she or he subscribes (literally) to the values of capitalism."[46] This desire by Ron/Owen's potential clients to avoid political activism and merely raid the homosexual's pocketbook fits precisely into Ewen's notion of "industrial democracy" and did not originate with the "Gay Moment." Once the harassment of San Francisco's gay bars abated in the late 1960s, bar owners felt no need to push for further civil rights and requested that activists cultivate a "respectable and established" image that precluded militancy. As Foucault's first volume of The History of Sexuality stresses, the prevailing hegemony is supported by "regulating sex through useful and public discourse."[47] In advertisers' eyes, speaking to a homosexual customer can be considered useful discourse; speaking to a homosexual activist is not.

Disney's relationship with the gay community often mirrors this pattern. Deja, in his studio-sanctioned interviews, makes certain to assert that the work of the homoerotic artist Tom of Finland had no influence on his drawing of *Beauty and the Beast*'s beefy Gaston.[48] In the interviews with Deja conducted just before the release of *Aladdin*, he is questioned about some of the jokes in the film, such as the "Genie-as-prissy-tailor" scene. When told that such humor could easily be read as stereotypical and insensitive towards gays, Deja instead "gives an enthusiastic thumbs-up as a reply."[49] This Disney-positive attitude is shared by Schumacher in his interview when the reporter for *The Advocate* questions him on "defecting to the enemy camp" by hiring renowned homophobe Mel Gibson as a voice for *Pocahontas*.[50] During a season when ABC was running low in the ratings, the Disney-owned network used the coming-out episode of *Ellen* as a way to spike viewership during the May sweeps period. To heighten ratings during this period, the network extended Diane Sawyer's interview with Ellen DeGeneres on *PrimeTime Live* over two nights. During the episode, Disney advertised many of its big summer movies, as well as promoted other ABC shows. Furthermore, within the show itself, Disney found a way to do some "product placement." When Ellen Morgan's therapist (played by Oprah Winfrey) asks her what she's going to do now that she's come out as a lesbian, Ellen parodies Disney's famous ad campaign and announces "I'm going to Disneyland!" Yet, the network refused to allow the Human Rights Campaign (HRC), a homosexual rights organization, to buy time for a public service advertisement during the episode. ABC informed the HRC that the network held "a policy against issue ads."[51] Since ABC has had no trouble in the past airing ads about solving illiteracy, putting "Children First" or curing illegal drug use, this statement seems disingenuous. While ABC and Disney trumpeted the "issue" of Ellen Morgan's lesbianism to boost ratings and profits, political statements were not welcome. Further, the network seemed to be antagonistic towards anyone else making a profit off lesbianism with *Ellen*, since the network not only turned down an ad by the HRC but also one by Olivia Cruises, a vacation company aimed at lesbians. Both organizations eventually bought ad time with local affiliates in certain cities (Atlanta, San Francisco, Los Angeles, Washington, Phoenix, Detroit), but only viewers in these areas saw these TV spots.

Sometimes, "the gay market" is not as cooperative as companies often envision. As capitalism tries to regulate sexual identity, inevitably some rebel against such strictures. In 1995, the lesbian and gay circles of Southern California by and large turned away from the annual "Gay Night" at Disneyland. While not a systemized boycott, word spread throughout the area that Odyssey Tours, who organized the event, was making only token donations of the proceeds to the Aid for AIDS charity—even though the publicity prominently described itself as a charity event. Conceiving of the "Gay Night" as a "con job" on lesbian and gay customers, attendance dropped precipitously. Yet, capitalism learns and adapts to such resistance, creating newer and more nuanced strategies instead of simply admitting defeat. The following year, Odyssey Tours decided not to donate proceeds to any charity and dropped mention of any such charity in their ads for the event. Because many somehow felt that the boycott had worked and made Odyssey more honest, attendance climbed for 1996's Disneyland "Gay Night"—even though now Aid for AIDS was not even getting a token payment. Examples such as these point out that the relationship between homosexuality and capitalism is a constant interplay between autonomy and exploitation, and that gay community and culture have historically been supported by businesses for profit and not for the advancement of homosexual causes.

WHO'S INVITED TO THE BALL: HOMOSEXUAL IDENTITY LIMITS IN DISNEY MARKETING

For the lesbian and gay community or subculture to be recognized as a target group by corporations, it had to display the ability to participate in "industrial democracy." Representation in this theoretical consumer republic rests on the "one dollar, one vote" principle. Some people can cast far more votes than others; those whose income falls below the effective equivalent of "one dollar" in the marketplace are disenfranchised. Unless a group is 1) identifiable, 2) accessible, 3) measurable and 4) profitable, it is not a viable target for marketing.[52] In the past decade, advertisers have begun to see homosexuals as a population group that fits the four requirements: West Hollywood, the Castro district in San Francisco or Greenwich Village in New York City are identifiable gay communities; *The Advocate, Out, Curve* and a wide variety of free "rags" available at bars provide easy accessibility; market analysis such as that done by Walker and Struman Research, Inc. in 1977 and in 1980 of readers of *The*

Advocate provides measurable data of gay and lesbian communities and lifestyles; and a concept of homosexual couples, each with careers but no children to support, provides theoretical profitability.

As Stabiner's research into the beginnings of gay marketing in the early 1980s reveals, though, the boundaries of "the gay market" as defined by corporate interests are very narrow. "Seventy percent of [the 1980 *Advocate* readership survey] . . . were between the ages of 20 and 40, and their annual median income in 1980 was $30,000 . . . 28 percent . . . earned over $40,000 in 1980, while nationally, the number of men earning over $35,000 was only 6.9 percent."[53] Furthermore, she points out that "most people who talk about the 'gay market' make the implicit assumption that it is a male market."[54] The Ron/Owen video presentation of the 1990s updates this conception of the "gay market" but does not challenge its limited definition of gay identity. While asserting that the average homosexual now makes over $50,000 a year, the video shows almost exclusively white men—and nobody over thirty-five years old. It is this small percentage of young, white middle- or upper-middle-class men that marketing research finds identifiable, accessible, measurable and profitable. All those who define themselves as homosexual but do not fit these additional parameters are not considered or addressed (and there is no conception of such "queer" individuals as bisexuals or transgendered persons). The only other development over the past decade is the gradual address of a lesbian consumer, as Danae Clark describes in her article "Commodity Lesbianism."[55] Her analysis of "lesbian chic" and the various ads chosen to accompany her article show that this development only widens the circle of the "gay market" to include young, white monied lesbians. The few women appearing in the Ron/Owen presentation fit this narrow conception of the lesbian consumer.

A number of factors work to keep many homosexual individuals outside of the income bracket discussed in the Ron/Owen presentation. Since women in general are still on average paid less than men for comparable work, lesbians must fight an uphill battle to reach this economic level and have a double set of hurdles before them when in a committed relationship. Since homosexual couples are not allowed to legally wed, they are not able to make use of the economic advantages (joint income tax filing, special tax breaks and incentives) given to people who are married. A more basic problem is the wealth of discrimination that often keeps homosexuals from finding decent employment, or from being able to advance to higher positions within a company. The discussion in chapter 3 of the barriers placed before homosexual employees trying to move into management positions at Disneyland serves as only one example. For lesbians of color, such problems are tripled in the workplace. Since these people do not have that "one dollar," advertisers pass over them and focus on the more lucrative homosexual population.

It is not surprising then, that when Disney targets homosexuals, it seems to be limited to white, middle- or upper-middle-class gay men, the subgroup within the homosexual population with the most disposable income. Those with a lesser ability to consume (lesbians dealing with a gender gap in wages, homosexuals of color) are seldom, if ever, addressed, for they are allegedly not as capable of participating in "industrial democracy." The all-male casts of *Dead Poets Society*, *Newsies* and *Swing Kids* are predominantly, if not exclusively, white. As the analysis of *Aladdin* in chapter 4 describes, the film's conception of Arabia seems influenced by Western homosexual fantasies of "the Orient." Ellen DeGeneres and the character she plays on *Ellen* fit quite perfectly into the upscale fashionable lesbian image that Clark describes. The company's publishing arm, Hyperion, published a lightly comic manual/commentary by Jaffe Cohen, Danny McWilliams and Bob Smith in 1995 called *Growing Up Gay: From Left Out to Coming Out.* The authors labeled themselves "Funny Gay Males," but the picture of proto-queer youth focuses on white middle-class suburbia and ignores any other social experience or racial/ethnic population.[56]

Again, since a large number of the homosexual employees working within the Walt Disney Company fit the "white, middle-class" description themselves, it is not surprising to see such a conception of the homosexual community emerging. As Richard Dyer points out when discussing *auteur* analysis, it is important to be aware of "the authors' material social position in relation to discourse, the access to discourses they have on account of who they are."[57] In her interview for *Time*, DeGeneres said that having people like herself come out would help "show the diversity, so it's not just the extremes. Because unfortunately those are the people who get the most attention on the news. You know, when you see the parades and you see the dykes on bikes or these men dressed as women."[58] Granted, DeGeneres made certain to assert that she didn't "want to judge them . . . the point of what I'm doing is acceptance of everybody's differences," and the interview was in no way controlled by Disney, so this is not necessarily Disney discourse.[59] Yet, Touchstone Television chose to create a situation comedy around De-Generes' "normal" white middle-class persona instead of lesbian comic Lea DeLaria, a butch and burly Italian woman whose fashion sense takes more from urban punk culture than "lesbian chic."

By marketing only to this select group of people within the homosexual community, advertising prizes this subgroup and holds them as representative—an ideal which the lesbian or gay subject is taught to measure him or herself by. Writers such as Mary Ann Doane have discussed how traditionally the female is constructed in economic terms as both consumer of commodities (subject) and as commodity herself (object), that "all consumerism involves the ideal of self-image."[60] In order to "be" a "true" woman, the female consumer is urged to buy cosmetics, clothes, perfume, etc., to transform the body, usually with the fetishized female body presented directly in the ad. Marketing thus works not only to describe and promote the product but to describe and promote a specific type of identity, one which will conform to the needs of modern industrial society—a "commodity self," as Ewen terms it. Yet, when Marchand notes the slippage between the selling of a product and the selling of the "human body itself . . . analogous to a lump of clay to be self-sculpted into a work of art," one can easily expand this concept beyond the female body to images of masculinity, of sexuality, of race, of class, etc.[61] For example, the ideal of a shaved, muscular, washboard-stomached young man with "blow-job" lips has become a standard within gay male culture that gay men are conditioned to aspire to and are taught can be achieved through purchasing gym memberships, tanning beds and plastic surgery (or, conversely, by purchasing an escort).[62] Danae Clark's work gives an excellent account of how "lesbian chic" fashion works to commodify the lesbian as well, idealizing a certain body type and class level. In this way, even ads aimed at white, middle- or upper-middle-class gay male consumers have their effects on those outside the targeted group. By teaching them to admire this target group, these ads also send messages to non-white, working-class queer individuals that they are somehow "less valuable." With this in mind, one can reinterpret the gay subject created by recent Disney product discussed in chapter 4 as supporting Foucault's notion of various subject positions not being repressed but policed.

Of course, it is not necessarily true that such targeting completely and effectively limits definitions of identity. The development of targeting was an acknowledgement of the varying success of creating the desired "commodified" subject position. Even as targeting continually tries to account for various subcultures, the success rate varies. The connection between marketing and individuals is an ongoing power relation, as is the case between individuals and all media systems, as Sandra Ball-Rokeach and others have theorized.[63] The wide reach of the media system to gather, process and disseminate information places it in a dominant position in this relationship, but the degree of dominance varies from moment to moment and is different for each individual. The variety of discourses that work to define and limit self-identity often create contradictions or unintended consequences, exposing the social construction of identity. An African-American lesbian is probably not going to "correctly" respond to ads that attempt to address homosexual consumers as white men. While this new Disney may appeal to a "gay market," it may not necessarily appeal to a "queer market."

Disney has begun to discover this diversity and complexity the hard way. Although their animated features have been extraordinarily successful (*Aladdin* was the first animated feature to make over $200 million domestically, and *The Lion King* has passed it to become, at this date, the sixth most successful film of all time), the studio has encountered protests from various individuals for its stereotypical portrayal of women and race/ethnicity. Women protested the image of Ariel's dependency on men in *The Little Mermaid,* and some found that

> ultimately, the gay subtext of *The Little Mermaid* feels fragmentary and inconsistent, so that it does not necessarily promote progressive meanings . . . [T]he world to which Ariel longs to escape ultimately turns out to be so dull . . . [for] once Ariel's transformation is complete, . . . she enters into a world shaped by the most standard human (read: heterosexual) courtship rituals and eventual marriage.[64]

The studio attempted to respond to these complaints when working on the character Belle in *Beauty and the Beast,* taking care to show her intelligence and independence, although the narrative still focuses on which man she will marry. The protests over *The Little Mermaid* probably had an effect on the studio's hiring a woman (Linda Woolverton) to script *Beauty and the Beast.* The variety of reaction from women when the film was released points out that many of the problems women found in *The Little Mermaid* were not solved. Consequently, while many gay men responded warmly to *Beauty and the Beast*, many lesbians might have had a hard time finding anything they could take from a film in which the female lead's only duty is to choose whether she will marry an egotistical macho jerk or a male behemoth.

Even louder protests have arisen over representations of race in recent Disney animation, revealing their "gay appeal" may only extend to Euro-American homosexuals. Not taking kindly to *Aladdin*'s camp use of their culture and traditions, Arab Americans began to loudly voice their objections to the portrayal of Arabic culture in the cartoon almost immediately upon its theatrical release. Protesting the depiction of Arabs as "cruel, dim-witted sentinels ... thieves and unscrupulous vendors," the American-Arab Anti-Discrimination Committee sought to change portions of the film.[65] One request was to remove a scene which showed "a grotesque Arab, scabbard poised, about to remove Princess Jasmine's hand, simply because she took an apple to feed a starving child."[66] Although this request went unheeded, the Disney studio agreed to another request. In a letter to the *Los Angeles Times*, Jay Goldsworthy and radio personality Casey Kasem requested a change in the lyrics to "Arabian Nights," the song which opens the feature. In the film, the song describes Arabia as "a faraway place ... where they cut off your ear if they don't like your face," concluding that the environment is "barbaric." Goldsworthy and Kasem revealed that lyricist Howard Ashman had written alternate, less offensive, lyrics.[67] The altered lyrics replaced "Where they cut off your ear if they don't like your face" with "Where it's flat and immense and the heat is intense." In this way, the word "barbaric" refers to the landscape rather than the culture. After some discussion, the studio agreed to change the lyrics in time for the film's release on video, announcing the new lyrics would appear in any subsequent re-release of the feature.[68]

The original lyrics of this song were part of Ashman's initial vision of *Aladdin*, which composer Alan Menken described as being in keeping with "Hollywood's treatment of Arabian themes."[69] The description seems to posit Ashman's conception of Aladdin's Arabia as an Arabia in quotes—a parody of Hollywood's typical treatment of the "exotic" Orient. As mentioned in the previous chapter, a recurrent motif in Euro-American gay culture is the setting of "Morocco" as a sexual playland. Yet, although this "camping" of the Orient is used to create a text which challenges received norms about sexuality, it does not necessarily challenge Western received norms about the East. Ella Shohat has argued how colonial discourse speaks even in sexually progressive texts: "Most texts about the 'Empire' . . . are pervaded by White homoeroticism. . . . Exoticising and eroticising the Third World allowed the imperial imaginary to play out its own fantasies of sexual domination."[70] Ashman, it can be argued, is using the imagery of the Orient Shohat has described to imagine a setting capable of allowing a variety of sexual identities, but in doing so replays the colonial imagery thus reinstituting Western domination. Marketing this film to a gay audience then implies a conception that only Western Euro-American men fit the category, and, hence, won't be bothered by the colonialist nature of the representation of Arabia.

This is not to say that the discourse between colonialism and sexuality is solely for consumption by gay culture. Jack Smith's appropriation of the B-grade exotica of Universal's Maria Montez movies displays the popularity of Arab-setting erotica in mainstream Western heterosexual culture as well. The creation of a literature commonly called "Arabian Nights," from which *Aladdin* is taken, is itself a product of colonial discourse, in which the Orient figures as a sexually "Other" place. "Emerging from the oral folkloric tradition central to India, Persia, Iraq, Syria and Egypt . . . Frenchman Antoine Galland created a text, . . . a circular narrative that portrayed an imaginary space of a thousand and one reveries."[71] The fabrication of Scheherezade in Galland's 1704 publication *Les mille et une nuits* portrayed his understanding of Arabic culture as exotic and erotic, via his function as a French emissary in Constantinople. Various European Romantic writers adopted this conception of Arabian society and fleshed it out (so to speak).

If anything, the studio's revision of Ashman's initial concepts tried to play down this hyperstylized view of Arabia. The first draft of the story appears to have overemphasized racial stereotyping to burlesque typical ethnic clichés—including "a big black Genie with an earring" modeled on Fats Waller and Cab Calloway.[72] Disney animation chief Peter Schneider described how executives reacted to Ashman's pitch: "We were nervous because his version was much more Arabian."[73] Although the initial song would remain in the final production, as well as jokes about lying on beds of nails, sword swallowing, snake charming and fire eating, the ethnicity of the project was toned down considerably. The color of the Genie would become a non-ethnic-specific blue, Aladdin and Jasmine's skin color was toned down to shades of tan and there were "a lot of discussions on the arc of the nose."[74]

Of course, one can also read Ashman's initial concept of the project as one of the few instances of someone at the studio attempting to address a non-white homosexual viewer. Certainly, a big black genie with an earring mouthing off some of the dialogue found in the final film would certainly have given strong connotations of a "snap queen" who takes no guff from silly white boys and teaches Aladdin to have pride in himself for who he is instead of trying to be someone else. Seen in this light, Ashman's version might have actually countered some of the notions of the "gay market" that late capitalist conglomerates like Disney have used to define homosexual identity.

Just as the feminist complaints about *The Little Mermaid* may have had a hand in the hiring of Linda Woolverton to script *Beauty and the Beast*, the uproar by Arab Americans over *Aladdin* probably influenced the number of Native Americans involved in the production of *Pocahontas* (1995). Yet, the studio seemed to consider "gay issues" and "race issues" separate aspects still, as was evident by the fact that the various Native American characters were given dignity and complexity while the villainous Governor Ratcliffe was a foppish gay stereotype (wearing pink outfits with ribbons in his hair) with hardly any personality whatsoever. Furthermore, the studio hired Mel Gibson to voice the lead male role of Captain John Smith, an actor often vilified in the gay press for making extremely homophobic remarks to reporters. While trying to placate Native Americans, this film was also driving away many gay customers—as if these were mutually exclusive categories of identity.[75]

The studio might have thought it would avoid the flack it received over *The Little Mermaid* and *Aladdin* when it began work on *The Lion King*, an all-animal cartoon. Similar in strategy to *Pocahontas*, a number of African Americans were hired as voice artists for this story about animals in the African veldt. Yet, the film elicited protests from many groups. Even if Ariel was a problematic character for feminists, at least she was the focus of the narrative. In *The Lion King*, lionesses (not to mention females from other species) are barely present. Many African Americans were also disturbed that the film actively refused to show any existence of human African civilization. The use of actor Robert Guillaume to create a mystic baboon with an Uncle Tom accent and Whoopi Goldberg and Cheech Marin as villainous (and boorish) hyenas who live in what constitutes the veldt's ghetto did not help matters either.

With the songs of Elton John and an ad campaign that included cartoon characters saying that the film was "to die for" or that they would "put on a grass skirt and do the hula" to get customers into the theatre, there seemed to be plenty for gay audiences to enjoy. Contrary to the complaints of nonvisibility by women and African Americans, "gay" animals could be found quite easily in the film—gay *male* animals voiced by *white* actors. The advisor to the lion king is a fussy and pompous bird named Zazu, who seems to be modeled after actor Clifton Webb. Timon and Pumbaa, a meerkat and a warthog that the lion cub protagonist Simba befriends after he is banished from his tribe, can be easily read as a gay male couple. They live happily together, reveling in their marginalization from the rest of jungle society, and look askance at Simba's budding heterosexual romance with a lioness. Voiced by Nathan Lane, who has played a number of gay male roles on stage and screen, Timon has the personality of a New York show queen: all patter and schtick, and ready to burst into a showtune at the drop of a hat. Pumbaa, the slower-witted of the pair, depends on Timon constantly, and the film prominently features his behind. Timon and Pumbaa would eventually star in their own animated TV series within the "Disney Afternoon," where they would actually become even more gay-tinged. As Gael Sweeney discovered in her analysis of the program, the pair often function in episodes as a married couple and act as parents to young children in a number of storylines. Also, the two seem to enjoy dressing up in various types of drag throughout the run of the series.[76]

The most obvious gay figure in the film is the villainous lion Scar, voiced by Jeremy Irons, who archly portrays a physically weak male who makes up for his lack of sheer strength with catty remarks and invidious plotting. Animated by Deja, the character fairly swishes, disdaining the concept of the heterosexual family in his attempt to usurp the throne for himself. When Scar refers to the cub prince Simba as a "hairball," Mufasa (Simba's father and king) warns "That 'hairball' is my son and your future king." Scar dons a mockingly prissy graciousness as he responds snidely, "Oh! I shall practice my curtsy!" Later, when Simba laughs and tells Scar, "You're so weird," the bored villain stares him straight in the eye and intones, "You have *no* idea . . ."

While Disney's villains have routinely veered towards camp (Captain Hook, Cruella de Vil, Ursula, Jafar), the signifiers that seem to ally Scar with homosexuality become disturbing. After the viewer enjoys his dry gay wit in the opening sections of the film, the fey lion sings a musical solo that becomes an animated version of the Nuremberg rallies, with Scar at the podium as hyena henchmen goosestep in perfect cadence before him. The color scheme turns monochromatic during this section, furthering the similarities to the Nuremberg documentary *The Triumph of the Will* (1936). Unlike the other villains, Scar actually kills someone (not even the evil Queen in Disney's *Snow White* [1937] did that), when he throws Mufasa from a cliff into a stampede of wildebeests. His reign over the kingdom seems to directly cause drought, pestilence and the general destruction of the ecosystem. It is only with the restoration of Simba to the throne that the land comes back to life, in a dissolve that makes the change seem miraculously immediate.

Scar's unforgivable sin seems to be his refusal to support the heterosexual patriarchy that Simba and his father represent. This social system is canonized during the film's opening number, "The Circle of Life," which was used in its entirety as a theatrical trailer for the film— drawing in audiences through a ritual performance of heterosexual male privilege. While Scar actively defies the social order celebrated in this number, the other gay figures help the young "straight" lion and are not seen as monsters mainly because they view him as the rightful ruler of the land. Zazu, Timon and Pumbaa all aide Simba in his quest to reestablish his claim to the throne, endorsing his "divine right." This would fit directly into how the corporations that target "the gay consumer" would like to define homosexual individuals as a market but not as a political social group.[77] By buying into the society, "the gay consumer" effectively supports the hegemonic order, much as Simba's gay friends aid his return to power. The power of the film's endorsement of heterosexual patriarchy on audience members was made clear when the *Timon and Pumbaa* TV series began airing. Since Simba did not appear in the show, Timon and Pumbaa's "gayness" became all the more obvious and was not used to endorse the "natural order" of heterosexual dominance. Some Internet fans of the original film voiced outrage because the series seemed to be reveling in gay camp, countering the philosophies they found valuable in *The Lion King*.[78]

Not all homosexual individuals willingly bought into the messages that *The Lion King* seemed to be sending. While some were entertained by Timon and Pumbaa, and identified with the "father issues" that

Simba had to work through after being cast out by his community, others noticed the "lasting impression" of Scar (to coin a phrase). Writing for the gay periodical *Christopher Street,* John E. Harris noted how:

> On a deep level, *The Lion King* dramatizes the danger of single "affected" males to any society, implying that they have the power to destroy an entire civilization. This is, of course, the message that Pat Robertson and Pat Buchanan routinely sign-off on in order to scapegoat homosexuals for such heterosexual problems as abortion, single mothers, and the high divorce rate.[79]

Harris also noted in his review the possible racist implications of the hyenas, an aspect that Todd Hayward analyzed in great detail for an article in the West Hollywood gay 'zine *Planet Homo.* Unlike the film, which conceives of race, gender and sexuality as mutually exclusive concepts, Hayward links the negative racial and gender connotations with issues of sexuality: "Disney's moral hierarchy has implications which are damaging for all of us who lie outside the 'mainstream.'"[80] Hayward's analysis explicitly displays how "queer" activism and theory counters concepts of "the gay consumer" with the recognition that not all homosexuals are white upscale men with the money or the inclination to support Disney's product.

> Readers may be asking themselves, "But if you substitute Disney's simplicity with relativity, and if you make good characters physically indistinguishable from bad characters, or if you do away with all *The Lion King*'s polarizations of good and evil, then everyone in the theatre has to come to his or her own conclusions about the film's content." To objections of this nature, I respond with a resounding, "*Good!*" Films that set up neat systems of good and evil— do's and don'ts—are part of the pervasive simplemindedness that posits heterosexuality and queerdom as irreconcilable opposites which cannot co-exist respectfully.[81]

By arguing against easily understood narratives based on "black-and-white" concepts of good and evil, Hayward's challenge to Disney and the entire Hollywood film industry proves that sometimes being a "queer subject" places one outside "the gay market."

CONCLUSION

Disney's acknowledgement of the lesbian/gay audience that exists for its product can neither be dismissed lightly nor cynically criticized. Such a development is one of the many steps necessary for further social acceptance in American society of homosexuality (and other non-straight sexualities). It is precisely developments like these that worry conservative political and religious forces that try to keep homosexuality stigmatized. Yet, while giving credit where it is due to the Walt Disney Company, one must not be blinded from seeing what else is going on. As Disney and its advertising seem to encourage homosexual viewers to "do" gay readings of their product, such advertising also regulates how that reading is supposed to be done and who is authorized to do it, turning a subversive strategy into a potential for more profit.

As some of the responses from lesbians and gay men in this chapter show, though, such target marketing is not completely effective. The ongoing power struggles between the media industry and audiences is just that—*ongoing*. While the media may consistently have the upper hand, audiences have in the past and will continue at times to play David to the entertainment industry's Goliath. The positions are continually in flux. Just as this work has provided a corrective to the sometimes overly optimistic pronouncement of some reception studies, this doesn't mean that the audience is yet again trapped into passive acceptance of the marketing strategies that have been developed. Just as various groups found ways to negotiate and resist the "preferred" subject positions that Disney created in the past, there is no doubt that it will happen again—and that the studio will try once again to bend that resistance to its own gain.

Epilogue

"The Circle of Life"

Most of Disney's animated features end with some version of the words "And They All Lived Happily Ever After." Yet, "The Circle of Life," the song that opens *The Lion King,* describes life as a constant movement between "despair and hope." On a more theoretical level, relationships and balances of power continue to shift back and forth in an unending pattern, as various discourses impact upon individuals or groups of individuals, and they in turn react, adapt or resist. Nowhere is this more evident than in the interactions between the Walt Disney Company and social discourse on homosexuality in the past few years. Since 1994, there have been marked changes both in the company's management and in popular opinion towards the company. Now, certain sections of heterosexual society no longer implicitly trust Disney's traditional "wholesome" image and have actually begun to demonize the corporation and its output.

In early 1994, Frank Wells died in a helicopter crash during a ski vacation. In August of that year, Jeffrey Katzenberg and the Walt Disney Company parted ways, leaving Michael Eisner to reign over the empire that the three had rebuilt over the past decade. At the time, many felt this would effect the close of one more era in Disney's history and the start of another. Since Katzenberg held a firm commitment to lesbian/gay issues, some employees worried that his departure would end the more open and accepting atmosphere at the studio and that the company would backtrack from its increasingly overt ties to lesbian/gay culture and consumers. Certain early signs seemed to indicate this possibility. Two film projects dealing with homosexual themes were in development when Katzenberg left: an adaption of the stage musical *Falsettos* and a fictional reworking of the documentary film *Chicks in White Satin*. Both these projects were dropped after Katzenberg moved on.

Disney had reason enough to justify a scaling back. In the summer of 1994, just before Katzenberg's departure, some fundamentalist Christian groups became aware of the "lesbian/gay weekend" at Walt Disney World and mounted a media campaign against the event. While protesters did not appear in front of the park's gates, David Caton, director of the American Family Association, told reporters that they had sent "non-confrontational observers" possibly in an attempt to intimidate some patrons, as well as to take notes on how Disney itself dealt with the "homosexual element." While the park did place signs in front of ticket booths informing uninformed heterosexual customers of the gay and lesbian group attending the park that day, spokespeople for the company made certain to reiterate that such an event was not sponsored by Walt Disney World. Still, the park did receive some complaints from customers who had not known that the event was going to take place, and Caton contended that Disney was giving tacit approval "by allowing organizers, including a group called Digital Queers, to hand out literature on Disney World grounds."[1]

With glimmers of controversy finally appearing on the horizon, it would have been understandable if Disney had pulled in its wagons. Yet, such thinking had held the company back in the 1970s, and Team Disney had brought the corporation out of the economic ashes by aggressively pursuing markets and projects even when stockholders and board members complained that such strategies tarnished the Disney name. Instead, in October 1994, the American Family Association's "non-confrontational observers" would read in newspapers that the Walt Disney Company had extended employee benefits to domestic partners of lesbian and gay male employees. The decision sparked the letter from Florida legislators that opened chapter 1. In it, they announced, "We strongly disapprove of your inclusion and endorsement of a lifestyle that is unhealthy, unnatural and unworthy of special treatment."[2] The Florida Baptist Convention passed a resolution in November of 1994 expressing "our high degree of disappointment" with Disney's move and asked that Florida's Southern Baptists "prayerfully reconsider their continued purchase and support of Disney products."[3] While not directly calling for a boycott, the American Family Association's leader Donald Wildmon interpreted it as such and urged that the national Southern Baptist Convention vote to join the movement when it convened in the summer. Although 1995's convention did not take up the war cry, the battle lines had been drawn, and a number of conservative groups now began to eye Disney warily. Alarmed by Disney's "anti-family, anti-Christian drift," Reverend Wiley S. Drake of the First Southern Baptist Church in Buena Park, California, weekly faxed letters to Eisner and was infuriated when they were ignored. A report from the Baptists' Christian Life Commission complained that the company "not only ignored our concerns but flagrantly furthered this moral digression in its product and policies."[4]

Ironically, Disney's next animated feature was a version of Victor Hugo's *The Hunchback of Notre Dame* (1996), in which the villain Frollo is described as a man who "longed to purge the world of vice and sin," but significantly "saw corruption ev'rywhere except within." He looks upon the hunchback Quasimodo as an "unholy demon." Locking him up in the bell tower of Notre Dame, Frollo teaches Quasimodo to feel ashamed of his "wretchedness." While Quasimodo is not expressly a homosexual character, his "abnormal" status, which forces him to remain "closeted," certainly resonates with queerness—particularly when he climbs the balustrades and parapets of the cathedral while singing about his desire to live at least one day "Out There." In the opening number, "The Bells of Notre Dame," the picture explicitly compares the queerness of Quasimodo to the righteousness of Frollo, asking "Who is the monster and who is the man?"

Quasimodo's "one day out there" is Disney's first specific rendition of the medieval Carnivale or, as the number "Topsy Turvy Day" describes it, "the day we mock the prig and shock the priest." The film's narrative specifically pivots on which behavior is more Christian: punishing those who fall outside the accepted norms, or welcoming and celebrating the diversity of humankind. Whereas the former is plainly represented by Frollo, the latter is represented by Quasimodo and the gypsy girl Esmerelda, who bond over their shared status as "outcasts" (she for her ethnicity, he for his physical appearance). When in the cathedral, Esmerelda offers a song to God, "God Help the Outcasts," and ponders "I thought we *all* were the children of God" while the more respectable parishioners pray for wealth, fame and glory. Similarly, while Quasimodo views Esmerelda as akin to "Heaven's Light," Frollo views the woman as "Hellfire."

Frollo is not a simple stereotype of hatred and persecution though, and, in the stunning number "Hellfire," Frollo is seen castigating himself for having the same feelings that he finds heinous in others. In the song, he plainly states his burning passion for Esmerelda, one of the most open displays of sexual desire within a Disney animated feature. What makes this number even more remarkable is that Frollo's hatred for Esmerelda is shown to stem from the fear of his own feelings. Instead of taking responsibility and learning to accept his emotions, Frollo feels he is "turning to sin" and feels he must punish the girl. "It's not my fault, it's not my blame," he cries out, "It's the gypsy girl, the witch, who sent this flame!" Frollo's inculcation of certain fervent religious attitudes about sexuality has led him to consider his own desires as horrid. His shame so overwhelms him that, rather than accepting his emotions, he denies culpability and blames others.

While Frollo's simultaneous lust for/loathing of Esmerelda is quite plainly heterosexual, his behavior mirrors conclusions from studies about homophobia. Research seems to support Gregory M. Herek's contention that homophobia tends to spring from "unconscious conflicts about one's own sexuality or gender identity" and that these feelings are then "attributed to lesbians and gay men through a process of projection." Herek continues, "such a strategy permits people to externalize their conflicts and to control their own unacceptable urges by rejecting lesbians and gay men (who symbolize those urges) without consciously recognizing the urges as their own."[5] Frollo's grim determination to punish Esmerelda stems from his attempt to deny that even he himself has "urges" that fall outside the rigid parameters of social acceptance.

Somehow, the "family-values" groups and Christian conservatives did not protest *Hunchback*'s manifest critique of religious zealotry aimed at demonizing social outcasts. But that didn't mean that they weren't searching through the Disney catalogue looking for proof that Disney was promoting some sort of "gay agenda." Protesters pointed out that the Disney-owned Miramax distributed the British film *Priest* in 1995, which deals with a Catholic priest's coming out. Similarly, they noted that Disney owned Hyperion Press which had published *Growing Up Gay*. Just as Touchstone Pictures was releasing the film *Powder* in late 1995, word spread that the director, Victor Salva, had once served time for engaging in sexual activity with a minor. With this information, many found new resonances in the film, which sympathetically focused on the specialness of a literally closeted teenage male (having been shut up in a cellar his entire childhood).

This "homosexual" reading spread not so much within the lesbian/gay community but within various conservative and fundamentalist communities. This remarkable development vastly changes the terms of the relationship between homosexuals, Disney and the larger society. Whereas certain lesbians and gay men in the past appreciated Disney differently than did the larger society (particularly those who were arrayed against their existence), now both sides were beginning to read Disney texts in similar fashions. By the mid-1990s, a battle for meaning over Disney increasingly ceased to exist. Homosexuals and Christian fundamentalists both agreed that "something queer was going on." The difference initially seemed to be only that one group was happy about it and the other was horrified. Yet, in closely examining "gay readings" by conservative protest groups, subtle and important distinctions in reading strategies emerge. *Priest* and *Growing Up Gay* were explicitly and avowedly concerned with homosexuality and could not be read in any other fashion. The announcement of Victor Salva's arrest record also created clear-cut overt evidence of homosexuality for conservative groups. The entire *Ellen* controversy in 1996 and 1997 became another example of open homosexual representation that protestors could easily target.

These were not the only instances of "scandalous" readings of Disney; some went much more deeply into the texts. Rumors of subliminal sexual messages found in videotapes of Disney's recent animated features began circulating. While these rumors weren't specifically homosexual in nature, such accusations imagined Disney as a hotbed of vice and lewdness—an image that would obviously intersect with arguments that the company was trying to foster a "gay agenda." Some saw a turret on the undersea castle sketched on the video box for *The Little Mermaid* as an erect penis. Others claimed they could see the word "sex" spelled out in a dust cloud in one scene from *The Lion King*. Still others swore they could hear someone whispering "All good teenagers, take off your clothes" on the soundtrack of the videos for *Aladdin*. In the laser disc of *Who Framed Roger Rabbit?*, someone noticed that one could freeze-frame on a certain section of the film which showed that voluptuous Jessica Rabbit wasn't wearing any panties beneath her dress.

Again, it would seem that these close (*really* close) textual analyses are very similar to the lesbian/gay or "queer" readings discussed throughout this book—finding messages or meanings that might resonate for a sexually marginalized group. Closer examination of these readings reveals crucial differences between those protesting Disney and "queer" individuals, differences that were highlighted by a clever hoax perpetrated on the Internet in December of 1995. Just as the rumors of subliminal messages spread through various newsgroups, web pages and chat rooms, a mass e-mailing—claiming to be authored by Donald Wildmon—informed readers of the "obscene pornography disguised as 'family entertainment'" hiding within Disney's current release *Toy Story*:

> The main characters, "Woody"—note sexual reference—and "Buzz"—note drug reference—are owned by a child in a single-parent household in which the father is noticeably absent. "Woody" and "Buzz" have equally disturbing toy friends, including a sex-obsessed talking potato, a sex-obsessed Bo Beep doll who cannot keep her hands (or lips) off "Woody," and an Etch-a-Sketch whose "knobs" must be "adjusted" to produce results.[6]

As Karl Cohen's research bears out, the announcement was a fake. The American Family Association publicly denied authoring the letter or calling for a boycott of the film. In analyzing the statement, the AFA pointed out various errors in the memo:

> First, it gives the wrong website address for the AFA. It mentions an article about *Toy Story* in the December issue of the *AFA Journal*, but there was no December issue and the November/December combined issue did not discuss *Toy Story*. . . . In fact, the AFA has said positive things about the feature. The July 1996 *AFA Journal* has an article about people going to good films at the box office, and it lists *Toy Story* as one of several films that "brought a broad audience of moral Americans back to local theaters."[7]

Clearly, someone had observed the sex-phobic readings of Disney by Wildmon's organization and other groups and expertly parodied the subliminal messages they were finding.

Many who read the original statement did not question its authenticity. A number of gay-rights groups quickly jumped on the memo as "an example of the irrational backlash against Disney" after its decision to grant domestic-partner benefits.[8] The basically wholesale acceptance of the announcement's authorship makes it instructive, for obviously the anonymous author understood how conservative groups were reading Disney. The easiest thing to note, and the main source of humor in the statement, is its overt obsession with sex. All of the "authentic" subliminal readings are specifically focused on messages about sex—not sexual orientations, lesbian/gay cultures, etc., but sex. They do not point to, say, men wearing earrings or a comment about some female character going to Michigan this summer. Rather, they look for references to sexualized areas of the body or sex acts (and, in the case of *The Lion King*, the word "sex" itself). Since the readings are done by individuals who stand outside of non-straight subcultures, their ignorance leads them to focus specifically on sex itself. Ironically, in their attempts to find evidence of the company's new licentiousness, these individuals seem to be as obsessed with sex as those they are purportedly condemning!

These subliminal readings point out how the protestors are able to conceive of sexuality—as separate and easily marked off. Yet, as I've argued throughout, a *number* of discourses work to define sexual identity, and a conception of sexuality based solely on concrete sexual acts ignores the wealth of other factors involved. Fundamentalists seem to think that the hidden meaning in *The Little Mermaid* with which non-straight individuals might find resonance is the penis-turret; fundamentalists do not seem aware that non-straights could appreciate the implications of an outsider finding happiness with a forbidden love. Similarly, these protestors seem unaware of the camp value of Disney in lesbian/gay culture. Conservative readings would rather focus on what we do than on how we feel. The protests over *Priest, Powder* and *Growing Up Gay* also factor here. While the texts or, in the case of *Powder*, the publicity surrounding the text, are obviously more overt than the supposed subliminal messages, their explicitness similarly allows conservative protest groups to mark a clear line between the approved and the disapproved.

What protestors seem to not acknowledge—and probably do not want to acknowledge—are those readings of Disney that blur the boundaries of sexual identities. While going out of their way to convince people that the word "sex" has been secretly airbrushed into the night sky of *The Lion King*, there is no awareness that Timon and Pumbaa could be read as a gay couple. While swearing that someone on *Aladdin*'s soundtrack is trying to covertly urge young viewers to strip naked, there is no comment on the gender-bending of the Genie or his gay-tinged jokes, much less the deep emotional bond between the Genie and Aladdin. Am I, in response, claiming that the Genie and Aladdin are somewhere engaging in homosexual acts and that the protestors just haven't caught on yet? Nothing of the sort. Rather, I am pointing out that, while the protestors are looking for clear-cut black-and-white moments (either overtly or subliminally), most non-straight individuals seem drawn to a more fluid idea of sexuality in Disney. Conservatives seem to work under the assumption that, unless two buddies are seen kissing and groping each other in a Disney text, the two *must be* heterosexual. In contrast, non-straight consumers of Disney are less strict: Aladdin and the Genie may not be explicit gay lovers, but who's to say where intense heterosexual male bonding ends and homosexual affection begins? This fluidity is precisely what is meant in the recent appropriation of the term "queer," and precisely what conservative groups want to keep at bay through the rigid demarcation of categories.

Whatever the similarities and differences in how fundamentalists and non-straights were reading Disney, there was no question that both sides ended up sharing the same weapons for battle: dollars and cents. On June 18, 1997, less than two months after Ellen DeGeneres and her character Ellen Morgan came out, the Southern Baptist Convention in Dallas voted that its 15.7 million followers (the largest Protestant denomination in the country) should "refrain from patronizing the Disney Co. and any of its related entities."[9] Lisa Kinney brought the convention to a standing ovation by vowing that the resolution "will affirm to the world that we love Jesus more than our entertainment."[10]

Although the measure passed at the convention, many Southern Baptists not at the convention disagreed with the boycott. Bryan Chloe, a youth director at a Los Angeles church, declared that he "would be very surprised if the kids at church are not allowed to have any Disney products, wear their T-shirts, watch Disney videos and go to Disneyland during summer vacation."[11] In fact, when asked about rumblings of a boycott back in 1996, Ralph Reed, then executive director of the Christian Coalition, told the *Los Angeles Times*, "I'm taking my kids to Disneyland."[12]

As the above quotes point out, the discourse of late capitalism affects conservative Christians just as strongly as it addresses homosexuals. Even those who voted for the measure seemed aware that the boycott would be impossible, due to both the extensiveness of Disney's holdings by 1997 and the commercial strength that Disney still holds over family pocketbooks.[13] This is no more apparent than when boycott supporter Marie Caulkins was interviewed by the *Los Angeles Times* just as the vote was being taken in Dallas. Caulkins stated, "I'm pleased they took a stand and sent a message. I have boycotted Disney's movies," while standing at a Disney Store in Northridge, California to buy a video copy of *Sleeping Beauty*.[14] Caulkins explained "I support the things I like," not recognizing that the Walt Disney Company still profits whether she's buying a video of a film made during Walt's lifetime or of a film made during Eisner's tenure. Even the American Family Association, which had encouraged the Southern Baptist Convention to take up the boycott, seemed to not notice this contradiction, as evidenced by its approval of Disney's *Toy Story*. As if to stress the economic bottom line that has made the company more "gay-friendly," Disney's stock actually went up 87 cents after the announcement of the boycott.

The boycotters were cheered by the cancellation of *Ellen*, and the 1998 announcement by Odyssey Adventures that its annual "Gay Night" at Disneyland had been canceled might also have seemed a sign of changing attitudes at the studio. On the other hand, the release of the animated feature *Mulan* in 1998 seemed to revel in confounding gender conventions, as it told the legend of a young Chinese woman who disguised herself as a man to fight in a medieval war. The Walt Disney Company has officially refused to alter either its EEO policy or its domestic-partner benefits plan. In November of 1997, Michael Eisner said in a *60 Minutes* interview that the boycott "hasn't had a financial effect." The following April, Eisner was on *Today* to promote the opening of Walt Disney World's new Animal Kingdom and asserted that Disney's profits "have been going up substantially."

Criticism of the boycott often pointed out the seeming lack of Christian understanding by the Southern Baptists. "By criticizing Disney for extending health benefits to same-sex partners," wrote one man in a letter to *USA Today*, "the Southern Baptists are promoting a value that is hardly Christian—intolerance."[15] Another wrote, "Baptists say such [domestic-partner] coverage encourages 'immoral' gay relationships, but denying benefits wouldn't result in fewer gay couples. The only result would be more American citizens without access to health-care protection. I see no morality in that."[16] As pointed as these criticisms may be, evidence supports the view taken by Ann G. Sjoredsma, editorial columnist for *The Virginian-Pilot*, who wrote that Disney's morality had nothing to do with the company's actions: "It has no interest in gay lifestyles, much less gay rights. . . . Disney doesn't give a Mighty Duck about anything but the almighty buck."[17]

With this in mind, it may seem ironic that, by and large, the gay and lesbian community (and its supporters) were encouraged to take action against the boycott using precisely the same weapon—the pocketbook. In a number of instances, non-straight individuals were told to *spend* in order to show their support for Disney. In 1998, Operation Rescue (ostensibly an anti-abortion group) planned to protest outside Walt Disney World during that summer's annual Lesbian/Gay Weekend at the park. During the same period, the American Family Association announced plans to picket Disney Stores around the country. In response to this, a counter-event was organized under the title "Stand Our Ground." Alana Hommel, the organizer of the project, explained that, "On June 6 our participants will be making purchases in the Disney Stores using $2.00 bills or by writing SOG on checks or credit slips." In the same announcement, she declared that "Our goal is to prove to corporate America that a boycott by the Religious Right can be overcome."[18]

Consequently, early June showed concerted efforts by many individuals consuming their way to freedom and equality. At the Disney World complex, estimated thousands of non-straight people arrived throughout the weekend. In order to fully participate in the Lesbian/Gay Weekend, one had to book through a specific travel arranger and pay for certain special events and a red T-shirt proclaiming participation in the event. One participant reported in the gay 'zine *4Front*, "Unofficially, Mannequins [one of several nightclubs at Pleasure Island] is gay every Thursday, although on this particular Thursday, I can't imagine how things could have been any more official. . . . [Another] party . . . at Disney/MGM, featured a huge dance floor, replete with go-go boys, in front of the Mann's Chinese replica."[19]

Meanwhile, Alana Hommel reported that "Disney Stores in every state had Stand Our Ground participants. There were participants from every state and many countries overseas. . . . Almost every Disney Store in the country received $2.00 bills, payments marked SOG, or supportive phone calls. Some stores had one or two supporters while others were overwhelmed." In her press release, Hommel further sees the success of the action on the estimated amount spent by "Stand Our Ground" supporters: "From those that reported dollar amounts spent, the average was $150."[20] Even the author of the article on the Lesbian/Gay Weekend continually returns to the economic base of the event. In describing the Operation Rescue protests, the reporter mentions an unsuccessful proposal to chart a private airplane to circle the park with a banner reading "Jesus saves." He then jokes that "maybe he has a coupon"![21]

Such tactics as the Lesbian/Gay Weekend at Disney World and the "Stand Our Ground" action at the Disney Stores may help to stem the tide of the Southern Baptists' boycott. With that in mind, such events have their purpose. Yet, as I have discussed in the second half of this book, such actions implicitly acquiesce to capitalist discourse and its preferred regulation of how sexualities are conceived and defined. The weekends at Disney World, for example, are specifically labeled "Lesbian/Gay," thus narrowing the diversity of non-straight identities and desires. Granted, the businesses involved in the event (travel agencies, hotels, etc.) most likely wanted a quick easy name for the event—and "Lesbian/Gay/Bi/Transgender/Queer Weekend" just wouldn't fit onto a T-shirt. Yet, this excuse only underlines the point that the marketing of the event determined a less inclusive title. "Stand Our Ground" seems like a textbook example of minority groups being encouraged to consume rather than engage in overt political action. In a reworking of the Reagan era trickle-down theory, rights for homosexuals (and other non-straight individuals) will be furthered if Disney stays economically flush—so one should conceivably buy a knick-knack at a Disney Store instead of working to ban employment discrimination against non-straights or to get hate crime legislation passed. In other words, the latest skirmish over Disney has not radically altered the terms of the relationship between Disney and lesbian/gay culture. By seeing economic support as political action, homosexual consumers seem to literally "buy into" a capitalist conception of being "gay" or "lesbian."

Seemingly in reaction to restrictions placed on individuals by the strict categories of "gay" and "lesbian," the late 1990s have seen the rise of the term "post-gay." According to James Collard, who became editor-in-chief of *Out* in 1998, the term was "coined by gay British journalist and activist Paul Burston in 1994."[22] Journalist Jonathan Van Meter seems to have brought the concept to the United States in an article for *Esquire*, titled "The Post-Gay Man."[23] So far, "post-gay" seems to mean slightly different things to different people. Some see the term as a critique of the marketing of "gayness," and that being "post-gay" means moving beyond the white, middle-class, young buffed male image promoted by gay target marketing (as described in chapter 5).[24] Others seem to use the term to critique radical gay activism. Collard writes that "Post-gay is . . . a critique of gay politics . . . by gay people, for gay people. . . . There's a pressure to conform within gay-activist politics, one that ultimately weakens its fighting strength by excluding the many gay people who no longer see their lives solely in terms of struggle."[25] Under this definition, "post-gay" is a critique not of capitalist discourse's regulation of homosexual identity but of *activist* discourse's regulation.

Because of the amorphous meaning of the term, it potentially speaks to both radical progressive thinkers and to Log Cabin Republicans alike. Elise Harris notes that the concept "draws me, a lefty dyke, into the same orbit as, say, an apolitical guy who feels there's nothing to fight for merely to justify the sad fact that he's never fought for anything but a Prada sweater at a Barneys warehouse sale."[26] In answer to its critique (whether of capitalism or of activism), "post-gay" advocates propose a shift away from an emphasis on sexual identity and suggest that one's sexual orientation is only a part of one's identity, and possibly not the most important part. Labeling one's self as "gay" is seen as limiting and confining, and "post-gay" individuals want to move on (whether they are dykes with boyfriends or homosexual men living a quiet life in the suburbs).

"Post-gay" takes a number of concepts from the early '90s use of the term "queer"—looking at sexuality in its diversity and fluidity. Van Meter even seems to equate the two terms. At the end of his *Esquire* article, he writes of his admiration of basketball star and cross-dresser Dennis Rodman. While plainly holding up Rodman as a model of "the Post-Gay Man," the last sentence of the article refers to Rodman as "queer," i.e., outside of the rigid parameters of either "heterosexual" or "homosexual."[27] In acknowledging that non-straight individuals negotiate their sexual identity in concert with their racial/ethnic, gender and class identities, "post-gay" further draws connections with "queer theory."

Yet, "post-gay" diverges from "queer" in its often apolitical attitude. Succinctly, Elise Harris writes that "Post-gay is less a movement than a mood." As the above quote from Collard mentions, many "post-gay" adherents feel that the struggle for acceptance and equality is over for them. The idea of "post-gay" for them means an end to political protest, because the battle has been won. Thinking that non-straight sexualities have won general acceptance seems willfully blind when the U.S. Congress has passed a "Defense of Marriage" Act, designed to disallow same-sex marriages, signed by a President who is supposedly "gay-friendly"; when full page ads in major U.S. newspapers announce that being homosexual is a disease that can be cured; and when the Southern Baptists are boycotting Disney for extending domestic-partner benefits. Harris points out that "Post-gay critics are loath to admit our fairly abject political position. . . . Yes, many of us are bored of being angry and having to react to homophobia. But being exhausted doesn't make it go away."[28] Similarly, Michelangelo Signorile advises that "As long as the religious Right is breathing down our necks, we don't have the luxury of being post-gay."[29]

Whereas "queer" acknowledged the diversity of sexual desire in order to bond individuals together against a shared oppression, "post-gay" seems to acknowledge the diversity only to propose that there is "no" oppression. The previous pages have conscientiously critiqued the limitations of contemporary concepts of "gay" and "lesbian." But announcing that suddenly one is "post-gay" is a simplistic solution to a complex and heavily imbricated problem. Even if homosexual individuals were able to somehow fully divest themselves from the discourses about sexuality that surround them (a highly unlikely possibility), those discourses would still control and regulate the conceptions of the rest of Western society. You may consider yourself "post-gay"; the gang with the baseball bats coming after you probably will not. Hate crimes against lesbian, gay, bisexual and transgender people increased nationally by 2 percent in 1997. In high schools and colleges, violence against gays and lesbian youth increased 34 percent, according to the National Coalition of Anti-Violence Programs. A 1998 University of Washington study wrote that one in ten community college students admitted to committing hate crimes against homosexuals.[30]

Underlining that a "post-gay" society is yet to exist is the tragic death of Matthew Shepard. A twenty-one-year-old University of Wyoming student, Shepard was savagely beaten with a pistol butt after being robbed, tied to a fence outside of Laramie and left to die (which he did a few days after being found by a bicyclist who at first thought Shepard was a scarecrow). The father of one of the men charged with the murder said "his son told him he committed the crime because he was embarrassed when Shepard flirted with him in front of his friends."[31] "Queer" acknowledges the violence and discrimination practiced against any and all non-straight individuals; "post-gay" seems to ignore that such hatred is still prevalent.

Reading Disney through a queer perspective similarly acknowledges the various factors involved in regulating and controlling societal conceptions of sexuality. In surveying the annual Lesbian/Gay Weekend at Walt Disney World, for example, queer theory analyzes how economic concerns attempt to place constraints on how sexual identity is expressed. Yet, queer theory also creates a space to notice the wealth and diversity of sexual desires—and to see how numerous and interlacing discourses often fail to fully manage and encircle how people feel in their day-to-day lives. As Judith Butler points out, the overlap, contradictions and complications of these multiple discourses create spaces for individuals to find loopholes in the hegemonic conceptions of sexual identity. Further, de Certeau and his adherents point out that concrete material individuals do not always fully accept the rules and regulations handed down to them from official institutions.

Consequently, while a queer theorist (such as myself) can critique the capitalist imperative underlying the Lesbian/Gay Weekend at Disney World, a queer theorist can also acknowledge that those attending the weekend may (and probably do) span a wide range of sexual identities—a range far beyond the limits established by the official marketing of the event. One account of 1998's Weekend describes, "Most Gay Days participants wear red T-shirts as a means of identifying each other . . . and when all of that red found its way to Main Street to view the Magical Moments Parade, we were an overwhelming force. From any vantage point, a sea of red was the view and it was thrilling."[32] Although labeled as a "Lesbian/Gay" event, who's to say what blend of identities were wearing those red T-shirts, cheering the pre-parade appearances by Cruella DeVil, TweedleDee and TweedleDum, and Suzy and Perla, the two girl mice from *Cinderella*, who came out holding hands? Although paying to participate, the gay men, lesbians, bisexuals, transgendered people and the many other queer individuals who were standing there on Disney World's Main Street (or marching in the parade as Cast Members) had gathered together to share a communal experience, using Disney to celebrate their lives. The crowd may not have been "resisting" the reading strategy those at Disney had intended for them (to use Stuart Hall's term). Yet, the estimated thousands that were in the Magic Kingdom that day used this corporate space as an opportunity to make connections and bond together in a shared expression of their existence in the face of a still vibrant hatred and oppression. While not being expressly political, that swath of red that encircled Main Street effectively announced to all in attendance, "We're here, we're queer . . . get used to it!"

Notes

NOTES TO THE INTRODUCTION

1. "Cheers n' Jeers," *TV Guide* 38:28 (July 14, 1990): 31.

2. Joseph Boone, "Rubbing Aladdin's Lamp," *Negotiating Lesbian and Gay Subjects,* Monica Dorenkamp and Richard Henke, eds. (New York: Routledge, 1995), 148. While my attendance was at a regular screening, Boone refers to a special screening benefiting Los Angeles' AIDS charity, Project Angel Food.

3. B. Ruby Rich, "What's a Good Gay Film?" *Out* 60 (Nov. 1998): 58.

4. Wayne Koestenbaum, *The Queen's Throat: Opera, Homosexuality and the Mystery of Desire* (New York: Poseidon Press, 1993), 12.

5. Taken from the "alt.disney.criticism" Internet newsgroup in April of 1997, under the heading "DISNEY: A Homo-Show from Top to Bottom."

6. Francis J. Haefner, Sr., "Southern Baptists Are Right in Their Disney Stand," *Lancaster Sunday News,* unknown date or page (ca. Sept. 1997).

7. John Dart, "Southern Baptist Delegates OK Disney Boycott," *Los Angeles Times* (June 19, 1997): A1.

8. Eddie Shapiro, "Gayety in the Magic Kingdom: Even the Wrath of Pat Couldn't Stop the Fun," *4Front Magazine* 3:24 (Aug. 19, 1998): 13.

9. In 1993, when Congress began debating the "Gays-in-the-Military" issue, the Springs of Life Ministry from Lancaster, California, created a video attempting to show the wretched and diseased lives of homosexuals that was then sent out to every single congressperson in order to convince them not to allow homosexuals to enter the armed forces. The video's title: "The Gay Agenda."

10. In 1933, Magnus Hirschfeld's Institute for Sex Research had its research collection destroyed by the Nazis in its first major organized book burning. In 1954, the Kinsey Institute for Sex Research lost most of its funding after it published results that 37 percent of the American men surveyed had engaged in at least one homosexual act (See Alfred Kinsey, et al., *Sexual Behavior in the Human Male* [Philadelphia: W. B. Saunders, 1948]). In 1982, scholars traveling to Canada for an international gay history conference had to misrepresent the purpose of their visit to the country for fear of being refused entrance.

11. Ernest Mandel, *Late Capitalism,* trans. Joris De Bres (London: Verso,

1978); Frederic Jameson, "Postmodernism, or the Cultural Logic of Late Capitalism," *New Left Review* 146 (July/August 1984): 53–92.

12. John D'Emilio, "Capitalism and Gay Identity," *Powers of Desire: The Politics of Sexuality*, Ann Snitow, Christine Stansell and Sharon Thompson, eds. (New York: Monthly Review Press, 1983), 100–113, and Michael Bronski, *Culture Clash: The Making of Gay Sensibility* (Boston: South End Press, 1984) stand as some of the earlier attempts to analyze how economics affect notions of homosexuality and "gay culture." More recently, authors such as Michelangelo Signorile, *Life Outside* (New York: HarperCollins, 1997) have begun to analyze and criticize the influence of capitalism on gay and lesbian identity.

13. During World War II, for example, psychologists were able to convince the U.S. Armed Forces that homosexuality was not a criminal problem but a medical one. Allan Berube, *Coming Out Under Fire: The History of Gay Men and Women in World War II* (New York: Plume, 1991) provides an in-depth account of the examinations and attempted "cures" given to homosexual American soldiers during World War II.

More recently, scientists have been surveying the brain and DNA in order possibly to link certain brain centers or chromosomes that marked an individual as having the propensity to become homosexual. Articles in the popular press reporting these developments include: Natalie Angier, "Male Homosexuality May Be Linked to a Gene," *New York Times* (July 18, 1993): E2; Thomas H. Maugh II, "Study Strongly Links Genetics, Homosexuality," *Los Angeles Times* (July 16, 1993): A1; Chandler Burr, "Genes vs. Hormones," *New York Times* (Aug. 2, 1993): A15; and Curt Suplee, "Study Provides New Evidence of 'Gay Gene,'" *Washington Post* (Oct. 31, 1995): A1.

14. On July 13, 1998, a number of conservative groups and fundamentalist Christian ministries started taking out full page ads in major newspapers such as the *New York Times*, the *Washington Post* and the *San Francisco Examiner* touting that with help from groups such as Exodus International, homosexuals could be cured of their sexual orientation. See John Leland and Mark Miller, "Can Gays 'Convert'?" *Newsweek* 132:7 (Aug. 17, 1998): 47–50.

15. George Chauncey, Jr., *Gay New York* (New York: Basic Books, 1994).

16. Lillian Faderman, *Odd Girls and Twilight Lovers: A History of Lesbian Life in Twentieth-Century America* (New York: Penguin, 1992).

17. Michel Foucault, *The History of Sexuality, Vol. 1, An Introduction*, trans. Robert Hurley (New York: Vintage Books, 1990), 101.

18. Ibid., 159.

19. Ibid., 106–107.

20. Alexander Doty, *Making Things Perfectly Queer: Interpreting Mass Culture* (Minneapolis: University of Minnesota Press, 1993), xv. Lisa Duggan, "Making It Perfectly Queer," *Socialist Review* (Apr. 1992): 11–31, provides a good

survey of the development of the term "queer" as it is used by activists and theorists in the late 1980s and 1990s.

21. Michel de Certeau, *The Practice of Everyday Life*, trans. Steven Rendall (Berkeley: University of California Press, 1984); John Fiske, *Understanding Popular Culture* (Boston: Unwin Hyman, 1989); Henry Jenkins, *Textual Poachers: Television Fans and Participatory Culture* (New York: Routledge, 1992).

22. It must be noted here that, by melding Foucault's notions of power and social discourse with economic analysis, I venture into slightly choppy theoretical waters. Foucault consistently and definitively distinguishes his ideas from Marxist and para-Marxist perspectives—particularly over the notion of power being localised within "the State." "Nothing in society will be changed," Foucault answered in an interview that asked about his opinion on Marxist thought, "if the mechanisms of power that function outside, below and alongside the State apparatuses, on a much more minute scale and everyday level are not also changed." ("Body/Power," *Power/Knowledge: Selected Interviews and Other Writings, 1972–1977*, trans. Colin Gordon et al., Colin Gordon, ed. [Brighton: Harvester Press, 1980], 60.) Foucault's work often focuses on the variety of "specialized" discourses not specifically controlled by the State in the definition and control of sexuality. My work on Disney's relationship with homosexual culture examines mass media discourse as one of the discourses Foucault describes as existing "alongside" the State in creating conceptions of sexuality and the body.

How Foucault and Marx may oppose or compliment each other are intriguing and important questions—but ones that go beyond the scope of this project (and assuredly require an entire book of their own). For the present discussion, I follow much more heavily a Foucauldian theoretical framework, but envision and employ a concept of an "economic discourse" that is not anymore aligned with "the State" than any of the other discourses that Foucault deconstructs (such as medical or legal discourse). I do not see the "economic discourse" as somehow more important or superceding other discourses—but believe that it must not be ignored either, especially when dealing with an organization focused on production, marketing and sales.

NOTES TO CHAPTER I

1. Reps. Bob Brooks, Randy Ball, Jerry Burroughs, Marvin Couch, Jim Fuller, Stephen Wise, Carlos Lacasa, Ken Pruitt, Bob Starks, John Trasher, Mike Fassano, Mark Flanagan, Buddy Johnson and Sens. John Grant and Everett Kelly, "An Open Letter to Michael Eisner and the Walt Disney Board," reprinted in *A League of Their Own* 23 (Nov. 1995): 6. All the Florida lawmakers who signed (except Democrat Sen. Kelly) are Republican.

2. For example, in the introduction to their anthology, *From Mouse to Mermaid: The Politics of Film, Gender, and Culture* (Bloomington: Indiana University Press, 1995), Elizabeth Bell, Lynda Haas and Laura Sells describe how "even our own students . . . are extremely resistant to critique of Disney film . . . complain[ing], 'You're reading too much into this film!' and 'You can't say that about Walt Disney!'" (4).

3. Foucault, *History of Sexuality,* 86.

4. Ibid., 107.

5. Ibid.

6. Judith Butler, *Gender Trouble: Feminism and the Subversion of Identity* (New York: Routledge, 1990), 131. In this quote, Butler is discussing the theories of "the body" posited by Mary Douglas, *Purity and Danger* (London: Routledge and Kegan Paul, 1969).

7. Chauncey, *Gay New York,* similarly points out the importance of understanding "normal" society's conceptions in order to more fully appreciate any "subculture": "The relationship between the gay subculture and the dominant culture was neither static nor passive: they did not merely coexist but constantly created and re-created themselves in relation to each other in a dynamic, interactive, and contested process" (25).

8. Russell Merritt, *Walt in Wonderland: The Silent Films of Walt Disney* (Baltimore: Johns Hopkins University Press, 1993), 18, 20.

9. Ibid., 18.

10. Mikhail Bakhtin, *Rabelais and His World,* trans. Helene Iswolski (Bloomington: Indiana University Press, 1968). Amongst those who have adapted Bakhtin's work, the most notable is John Fiske, in such works as *Television Culture* (London: Methuen, 1987) and *Understanding Popular Culture* (Boston: Unwin Hyman, 1989).

11. Merritt, 25. The notion of "the cow" as sidekick applies at least to the bovine's most important appearance in *The Mechanical Cow.*

12. Ibid., 87.

13. Quoted in Leonard Maltin, *Of Mice and Magic: A History of American Animated Cartoons* (New York: Plume, 1987), 98.

14. Merritt, 74.

15. Donald Crafton, *Before Mickey: The Animated Film (1898–1928)* (Chicago: University of Chicago Press, 1993), 294.

16. Ibid., 292.

17. *Poor Papa* was eventually released after the Oswald character had been established through other cartoons.

18. Merritt points out that "if there is a simple thread or theme in these [silent] years, it is an economic one—Disney's determination to become a successful independent entrepreneur, beholden to no one" (15).

19. Ollie Johnston and Frank Thomas, *The Disney Villain* (New York: Hyperion, 1993), 39.

20. Amongst the early Mickeys that were reworked Oswalds were *Mickey's Nightmare* (1932) (from *Poor Papa*), *The Karnival Kid* and *When the Cat's Away*.

21. Quoted in Russell Merritt and Karen Merritt, "Mythic Mouse," *Griffithiana* 34 (Dec. 1988): 58–71.

22. Richard Schickel, *The Disney Version* (New York: Simon and Schuster, 1968), 105.

23. Ibid., 106.

24. Henry James Forman, *Our Movie-Made Children* (New York: Macmillan Co., 1933), 51.

25. For example, one of the researchers, Dr. Edgar Dale, stated, "It is apparent that children will rarely secure from the films goals of the types that have animated men like Jenner, Lister, Pasteur, Jesus, Socrates, Grenfell, Edison, Moguchi and Lincoln" (47–48). Such comments occur regularly throughout the study. Among the faulty research methods was "emphasiz[ing] that participants were not expected to strain toward an exaggerated attention or an especial alertness" before testing viewer's memories of films—not seeming to notice how such an instruction itself alters the viewing of a film. Research on how films affected children's sleep was collated through the invention of a device called a "hypnograph" that counted periods of restlessness in a child's sleep (somehow equating all moments of restlessness with the deleterious effects of cinema on the subject). The device was used on children kept at the Ohio Bureau of Juvenile Research, a halfway house for problem children or orphans about to be adopted. Again, researchers seemed not to notice how this cross-section might fail to ideally replicate the social experience of most children. As a side note, it is amazing to me that in the introduction to this work, which actively warns against the "wrong" subject matter being shown to young minds, Forman includes in a list of films that he finds laudable, the German lesbian film *Maedchen in Uniform* (32). My only guess is that Forman could not even conceive of female-female sexual acts and consequently did not see anything "immoral" in the film!

26. Quoted in Maltin, 37.

27. Karl F. Cohen, *Forbidden Animation: Censored Cartoons and Blacklisted Animators in America* (Jefferson, NC: McFarland and Company, Inc., 1997), 24, discusses how the popular press used this anecdote repeatedly during this period.

28. "Regulated Rodent," *Time* (Feb. 16, 1931): 21.

29. Quoted in Maltin, 37.

30. Johnston and Thomas, 35.

31. For some reason, Minnie at the piano became a leitmotif during this

period, as if this were all she could do. She appears this way in *The Birthday Party, Mickey Cuts Up, Mickey's Orphans* (1931), *Mickey's Revue* (1932), and *The Whoopee Party* (1932).

32. Robert Sklar, "The Making of Cultural Myths: Walt Disney and Frank Capra," *Movie-Made America: A Cultural History of American Movies* (New York: Random House, 1975), 201.

33. Harry M. Benshoff, "Heigh-Ho, Heigh-Ho, Is Disney High or Low? From Silly Cartoons to Postmodern Politics," *Animation Journal* 1:1 (Fall 1992): 67.

34. Sklar, 61.

35. Ibid., 65.

36. Benshoff, "Heigh-Ho," marks this development as well.

37. Norman M. Klein, *Seven Minutes: The Life and Death of the American Animated Cartoon* (New York: Verso, 1993), also discusses this previous conception of animation: "To paraphrase Resnais, if we ask how far back the castle is in *Felix in Fairyland*, the answer might be: about five feet from the bottom, along the surface of the screen" (5).

38. John Canemaker, *Treasures of Disney Animation Art* (New York: Abbeville Press, 1982), 15.

39. Although I am describing silent animation conventions, it would be easy to apply this analysis of the body in animation to certain sound cartoons as well. Chuck Jones' Wile E. Coyote, and the title character in *Who Framed Roger Rabbit?* (1988), serve as examples.

40. Walt, and subsequent historians working for Disney, would describe the years from 1927–1931 as an era of primitivism. Ollie Johnston and Frank Thomas, two of the top animators at Disney throughout its history, state in *Disney Animation: The Illusion of Life* that while "the early Mickeys displayed great vitality . . . they had never achieved the quality of life in individual drawings" (8). Regarding the character of Mickey during this period, they comment that "Mickey Mouse lacked . . . consistency in his first pictures. He was often just any character. . . . His reactions to the problems facing him were whatever made the funniest gag for that situation in the story" (35). Johnston and Thomas argue that the animation during this period was primitive and inferior because figures were too "stiff," that there was no sense of volume or weight, much less what would eventually become known as "total animation," a process in which the whole body is in motion rather than, for example, the one hand that is waving. In describing early animation this way, Johnston and Thomas privilege the style that Disney's animators would later develop and do not acknowledge that most animation during the silent and early sound era was not only *drawn* differently but *conceived of* differently. Consequently, to judge a previous style through the eyes of a later conception is to see only its deficiencies and none of its merits.

41. This was also the first year the Academy included a category for Best Animated Short Subject—probably in response to the sustained success of Disney's studio. (Walt had been given a special Oscar the year before for creating Mickey Mouse.) Disney would win the category every year throughout the rest of the 1930s.

42. The Multiplane process placed animation cels and various levels of background scenery on superimposed glass panes, so that a three-dimensional composition appeared in front of the vertically positioned camera. In simulating a live-action camera pan, figures in the background would be shifted less than figures in the foreground, heightening the illusion of depth. The process worked well, but was very time consuming and hence, pushed the budgets of projects up enormously. The studio stopped using the Multiplane process after the production of *Bambi* (1942).

43. This is not to say that the processes themselves inherently pushed towards this direction but that this was the main way in which the Disney studio conceived of using them—to create a more "real" world.

44. Richard Neupert, "Painting a Plausible World: Disney's Color Prototypes," *Disney Discourse: Producing the Magic Kingdom,* Eric Smoodin, ed. (New York: Routledge, 1994), 106–117, makes a similar argument about color being used in a greater attempt at realism.

45. Donald Mosley, *Disney's World* (New York: Stein and Day, 1985), 144. The italics are Mosley's.

46. Giannalberto Bendazzi, *Cartoons: One Hundred Years of Cinema Animation,* trans. Anna Taraboletti-Segre (Bloomington: Indiana University Press, 1994), 65.

47. Walt Disney, from a 1935 studio memo, quoted in John Canemaker, 18.

48. Johnston and Thomas, *Disney Animation,* 9.

49. Schickel, 148.

50. Maltin, 42. The italics are his.

51. Schickel, 117.

52. Quoted in Schickel, 115.

53. For articles in popular news magazines, see "Portrait: Walt Disney," *Newsweek* (Oct. 7, 1933): 48; "Profound Mouse," *Time* (May 15, 1933): 37. Art and literary journals: "On the Screen: Three Little Pigs," *Literary Digest* (Oct. 14, 1933): 45–46; C. A. Lejeune, "Disney-Time: Not-So-Silly Symphonies," *Theatre Arts* (Feb. 1934): 84. Film fan magazines: Sara Hamilton, "The True Story of Mickey Mouse," *Movie Mirror* (Dec. 1931): 100–101; Walt Disney, "Mickey Mouse is Five Years Old," *Film Pictorial* (Sept. 30, 1933): 5; "He's Mickey Mouse's Voice and Master," *Movie Classic* (Nov. 1933): 30, 74–75; Richard H. Syring, "One of the Greats," Silver Screen (Nov. 1932): 46–47. "High-class" periodicals: Gilbert Seldes, "Mickey-Mouse Maker," *The New Yorker* (Dec. 19, 1931): 23–25; Walt Disney, "The Cartoon's Contribution to Children," *Overland*

Monthly (0ct. 1933): 138; Arthur Mann, "Mickey Mouse's Financial Career," *Harpers' Magazine* (May 1934): 714–721. Business and political journals: "Disney and Others," *The New Republic* 71:914 (June 8, 1932): 101–103; Claude Bragdon, "Mickey Mouse and What He Means," *Scribners' Magazine* 96:1 (July 1934): 40–43; "The Big Bad Wolf and Why It May Never Huff Nor Puff at Walt Disney's Door," *Fortune* 10:5 (Nov. 1934): 146–157. Women's and family magazines: Harry Carr, "The Only Unpaid Movie Star," *The American Magazine* 11:3 (Mar. 1931): 55–57; Henry Pringle, "Mickey Mouse's Father," *McCall's Magazine* (Aug. 1932): 7; "*Parents' Magazine* Medal to Walt Disney," *Parents' Magazine* 9:1 (Jan. 1934): 17; Alva Johnson, "Mickey Mouse," *Woman's Home Companion* (July 1934): 12–13.

54. J. B. Kaufman, "Good Mouse-keeping: Family-Oriented Publicity in Disney's Golden Age," *Animation Journal* 3:2 (Spring 1995): 78–85, lists all of the "Disney pages," pointing out that often the released short would have no correspondence to the description in the magazine. As Disney began releasing features in the late 1930s, the "Disney page" promoted these as well. *Good Housekeeping* ran "Disney pages" until 1945.

55. Gregory A. Waller, "Mickey, Walt, and Film Criticism from *Steamboat Willie* to *Bambi*," in *The American Animated Cartoon: A Critical Anthology*, Gerald Peary and Danny Peary, eds. (New York: E. P. Dutton, 1980), 53.

56. Disney, "The Cartoons Contribution to Children," 138.

57. Ibid..

58. Ibid.

59. "*Parents' Magazine* Medal to Walt Disney," 17.

60. David Frederick McCord, "Is Walt Disney a Menace to Our Children?" *Photoplay* 45:5 (Apr. 1934): 30–31, 92, 103.

61. Dr. Walter Bera Wolfe, as quoted in McCord, 130. Accompanying McCord's piece in *Photoplay* is a small article entitled "Dr. Brill Analyzes Walt Disney's Masterpieces," (92) in which a similar conclusion is reached.

62. "Profound Mouse," 37.

63. Seldes, 23.

64. L. H. Robbins, "Mickey Mouse the Economist," *New York Times Magazine* (Mar. 10, 1935): 22.

65. "The Cartoons Contribution to Children," 138. These words are not ascribed to Disney himself, but are part of an anonymously written preface to the article.

66. Seldes, 23–24.

67. "Man and Mouse," *Time* (Dec. 27. 1937): 21.

68. The quote is from "Profound Mouse," 28 and the full text reads: "His wife, Lillian Marie Bounds, a Hollywood girl who has never had anything to do with the cinema . . . "Compare this with the *New Yorker*'s version in Seldes' 1931 article: "He is married to Lillian Marie Bounds, who he met in Hollywood,

where she was probably unique, as she had nothing to do with pictures" (23). Disregarding the factual omission that Walt met Lillian when she was working at his studio as an "ink-and-paint girl," the almost verbatim repetition belies the press release handed out by the studio.

69. Seldes, 24.

70. "Man and Mouse," 21.

71. "The Big Bad Wolf and Why It May Never Huff Nor Puff at Walt Disney's Door," 146.

72. "Family Movie Guide," *Parents' Magazine* 9:1 (Jan. 1934): 30. This warning accompanied each "movie guide" in every issue.

73. Dr. Edgar Dale, "Helping Youth Choose Better Movies," *Parents' Magazine* 9:4 (Apr. 1934): 26–27, 71–73; Fred Eastman, "How to Choose Movies for Your Children," *Parents' Magazine* 9:3 (Mar. 1934): 18–19, 67–68; and Marguerite Benson, "Will the Code Bring Better Movies?" *Parents' Magazine* 9:6 (June 1934): 26, 66–67. Dr. Edgar Dale was part of the research team whose work for the Payne Fund project served as the basis of *Our Movie-Made Children*.

74. Janet Flanner, "Boom Shot of Hollywood," *Harpers' Bazaar* (Nov. 1, 1936): 183.

75. Maureen Furniss, "Animation and Color Key: The Career of Phyllis Craig," *Animation Journal* 5:1 (Fall 1996): 58–70.

76. Mosley, 165.

77. Bob Thomas, *Walt Disney: An American Original* (New York: Simon and Schuster, 1976). Thomas' work is the only authorized biography of Disney, and certain facts—such as the adoption of Walt's second daughter—were obscured at the request of the family. So, for Thomas to include such an anecdote in such a laundered work gives it a certain credence.

78. Mosley, 165–166.

79. Ibid., 166.

80. Ibid., 167. Although the animator who tells this anecdote is never named, the detail about "whether your shorts fit or not" leads to the speculation that the source is animator Ward Kimball, who in a different section of Mosley's book, describes how he was informed to buy a better-fitting pair of volleyball shorts because the female employees were enjoying a little too much how his pants kept falling down when he played volleyball during lunch. See Mosley, 165.

81. Eric Smoodin analyzes how a number of popular journals reported (or, in some cases, did not report) the 1941 strike in his chapter, "The Popular Press Views Cartoons: Shaping Public Opinion While Creating Walt Disney," in *Animating Culture: Hollywood Cartoons from the Sound Era* (New Brunswick: Rutgers University Press, 1993).

82. The picture reference is to a photo accompanying a *Business Week* article from Feb. 10, 1945, and represented in Smoodin, 126.

83. *The Reluctant Dragon* (1941) was also made at the studio during this period, but is not conventionally listed as part of the "Golden Age." Presaging the "package" films that would emerge from the studio from 1942–49, the film is a tour of the studio led by Robert Benchley, stopping to present a few pieces of animation in the process such as "Baby Weems" and "The Reluctant Dragon." Although "Baby Weems" is shown mostly as a storyboard, it does create a type of experimental animation which is quite unique for Disney at the time. The set piece that gives the film its title though is done quite in the richly detailed style of Disney during this period. *The Reluctant Dragon* was released during the strike, and its blatant promotionalism of the studio was in stark contrast to the picketers standing outside the studio and in front of some theatres. *The Reluctant Dragon* will be discussed further in chapter 2.

84. It was outdone in 1939 by *Gone With the Wind.*

85. R. D. Feild, *The Art of Walt Disney* (New York: Macmillan, 1942), 197.

86. Douglas Gomery, "Disney's Business History: A Reinterpretation," *Disney Discourse: Producing the Magic Kingdom,* Eric Smoodin, ed. (New York: Routledge, 1994), says explicitly that "World War II saved Disney" (74). Smoodin in *Animating Culture* also analyzes the relationship between the federal government and Disney in "Disney Diplomacy: The Links between Culture, Commerce, and Government Policy," as does biographer Mosley, 195–196, and Disney animator Jack Kinney in his reminiscences *Walt Disney and Assorted Other Characters: An Unauthorized Account of the Early Years at Disney's* (New York: Harmony Books, 1988), 138.

87. Gomery, 74.

88. Richard Shale, *Donald Duck Joins Up: The Walt Disney Studio During World War II* (Ann Arbor: UMI Research Press, 1982), 16.

89. Shale, 22–23, discusses correspondence between the Disney studio and the U.S. Navy about making a series of aircraft and warship identification films.

90. Gomery, 74.

91. Kinney, 138.

92. Smoodin, 147.

93. Shale, 26.

94. Ibid., 19.

95. The films in which the above topics are covered are *Dental Health* (1945), *Ward Care for Psychotic Patients* (1944) and *A Few Quick Facts* #7 (1944).

96. Lisa Cartwright and Brian Goldfarb, "Cultural Contagion: On Disney's Health Education Film for Latin America," *Disney Discourse: Producing the Magic Kingdom,* Eric Smoodin, ed. (New York: Routledge, 1994), 170. Quote from "A Survey Conducted for the CIAA by the Walt Disney Studio on the Subject of Literacy," Rockefeller Archives Center, Washington, D.C., Series, RG 4, Box 7, Motion Picture Division Folder.

97. Shale, 56.

98. Cartwright and Goldfarb, 170.

99. Ibid., 175.

100. Ibid., 177.

101. Janice Delaney et. al., *The Curse: A Cultural History of Menstruation* (New York: E. P. Dutton, 1976), 95–96. The quote misidentifies the sponsor as Kimberly-Clark instead of International Cellucotton.

102. Karl Cohen, "The Importance of the FBI's 'Walt Disney File' to Animation Scholars," *Animation Journal* 3:2 (Spring 1995), 76 (Footnote 11). The quote is from a memo dated Jan. 25, 1961.

103. *"The Three Caballeros," Time* (Feb. 19, 1945): 92.

104. "Mr. Disney's Caballeros," *The Saturday Review* (Feb. 24, 1945): 24.

105. Smoodin, 112. The ad referenced occurred in *The Saturday Review* (Feb. 24, 1945): 23.

106. An example of such a photo is included in the photo inset for Marc Eliot, *Walt Disney: Hollywood's Dark Prince* (New York: Birch Lane Press, 1993), between 104–105.

107. Letter from Joseph I. Breen to Spencer Olin at the Walt Disney Studios, dated Mar. 7, 1946.

108. *"Make Mine Music," Time* (May 6, 1946): 101.

109. Preston Blair recounts this anecdote in Maltin, 293.

110. Ollie Johnston and Frank Thomas state this when discussing the film in *The Disney Villain*, 97–102.

111. Even then, after critics had become aware of Disney's potential for lasciviousness in the 1940s, John Mason Brown of *The Saturday Review* ("Recessional," [June 3, 1950]: 30) would unfavorably compare Disney's Cinderella to Al Capp's voluptuous Daisy Mae in the comic strip *Lil' Abner.*

112. Donald Crafton, "Walt Disney's *Peter Pan:* Woman Trouble on the Island," *Storytelling in Animation: The Art of the Animated Image*, Vol. 2, John Canemaker, ed. (Los Angeles: American Film Institute, 1988), 123–146.

113. Richard Shale's research (112) indicates that, although the Educational Division continued to exist, no records of specific films produced exclusively for the 16 mm market can be found until 1964.

114. Shale, 112.

115. Derek Bouse, "True Life Fantasies: Storytelling Traditions in Animated Features and Wildlife Films," *Animation Journal* 3:2, (Spring 1995): 36.

116. Ibid., 20.

117. Ibid., 31.

118. The Production Code Administration files, held at the Academy of Motion Picture Arts and Sciences Library, often contain within the file for each film reviews from various publications. In the file for *The Vanishing Prairie*, every mention of the calf birth in the reviews was underlined with a red pen.

119. "Thousands of Crockett Fans Cheer Bowl's Disney Night, " *Los Angeles Times* (July 15, 1955): B1.

120. It is interesting to watch this exhibit in the present day, as the edited speech does not refer to the importance of the union or the rights of minorities, but addresses as its main topic "internal subversion," obviously referring to Walt's personal involvement in ferreting out American Communist sympathizers. Walt's testimony to the House on Un-American Activities Committee can be found in "The Testimony of Walter E. Disney Before the House Committee on Un-American Activities," *The American Animated Cartoon: A Critical Anthology*, Gerald Peary and Danny Peary, eds. (New York: E.P. Dutton, 1980), 92–98.

121. Max Rafferty, "The Greatest Pedagogue of All," *Los Angeles Times* (Apr. 19, 1965): B5.

122. The studio's preoccupation during Walt's life with controlling the body might have also influenced the very popular legend that Walt's body was cryogenically frozen until a cure for cancer could be found.

NOTES TO CHAPTER 2

1. Vito Russo, *The Celluloid Closet: Homosexuality in the Movies* (New York: Harper and Row, 1987), 48.

2. Chauncey, 16–20, recounts the development of the term "gay" in homosexual culture of at least one urban environment.

3. Personal interview with Allan Berube, Minneapolis, MN (April 1994).

4. "Box-Car Bertha," as told to Dr. Ben L. Reitman, *Sister of the Road: An Autobiography* (1937; reprint, New York: Harper and Row, 1975), 65–67. Quoted in Faderman, 106.

5. If Porter was using the term "Mickey Mouse" to refer to homosexuality, it seems to have been coded enough to be included in the official lyrics, for Porter also wrote a complete alternate lyric that stressed the bawdy nature of considering one side of romantic duo "the top" and the other "the bottom." Amongst the lines are "You're the breasts of Venus, you're King Kong's penis, you're self-abuse" and "I'm a eunuch who has just gone through an op." See Robert Kimball, ed., *The Complete Lyrics of Cole Porter* (New York: Knopf, 1983), 120–121.

6. A possible modern allusion to using "Mickey Mouse" as a signifier of homosexuality can be found in the Hong Kong film *The Killer* (1989), directed by John Woo. In the film, the highly charged chemistry between the two main male characters (a hired assassin and a police detective) is accented by their nicknaming each other "Mickey Mouse" and "Donald Duck."

7. Michel de Certeau, *The Practice of Everyday Life*, trans. Steven Rendall (Berkeley: University of California Press, 1984), 174.

8. Stuart Hall, "Encoding/Decoding," *Culture, Media, Language*. Stuart

Hall, Dorothy Hobson, Andrew Lowe and Paul Willis, eds. (London: Unwin Hyman Ltd., 1980), 128–138.

9. Henry Jenkins, *Textual Poachers: Television Fans and Participatory Culture* (New York: Routledge, 1992), 23.

10. Doty, xii.

11. Jenkins, *Textual Poachers*, 26. The quote is from de Certeau, 175.

12. de Certeau, 174.

13. Jenkins, *Textual Poachers*, 45.

14. Although Jenkins does not explicitly tackle this issue within his discussions of media fandom, he does discuss the appearance of "slash" literature and art (focusing on homosexual liaisons between male characters on favorite TV series) in fan culture in *Textual Poachers*. In "Out of the Closet and Into the Universe: Queers and *Star Trek*," in *Science Fiction Audiences: Watching Dr. Who and Star Trek,* John Tulloch and Henry Jenkins, eds. (New York: Routledge, 1995), 237–265, Jenkins specifically examines how queer viewers of the various *Star Trek* TV series have lobbied to have a gay or lesbian character introduced into this future universe.

15. Jack Babuscio, "Camp and the Gay Sensibility," *Gays and Film,* Richard Dyer, ed. (London: British Film Institute, 1977), 40.

16. This is one of the main tenets of Chauncey's study of New York City homosexual cultures. See in particular chapters 2–4.

17. Lillian Faderman discusses these "intense friendships" in chapter 1 of *Odd Girls and Twilight Lovers.* See especially 31–34.

18. Richard deCordova, "The Mickey in Macy's Window: Childhood, Consumerism, and Disney Animation," *Disney Discourse: Producing the Magic Kingdom,* Eric Smoodin, ed. (New York: Routledge, 1994), 207.

19. For example, "Disney-Time: Not-So-Silly Symphonies," *Theatre Arts.*

20. Thomas M. Pryor, "The Screen Grab-Bag," *New York Times* (Nov. 10, 1940): Sec. 9, 5.

21. E. M. Forster, "Mickey and Minnie," *Spectator* (Jan. 19, 1934): 81.

22. According to photos of Sergei mugging with Walt and a cutout of Mickey, Sergei was at the Disney studio in October of 1930.

23. Forster, 81.

24. E. M. Forster, "Story of a Panic," *Collected Tales* (New York: Knopf, 1952), 8–9. Cited in Klein, 35.

25. E. M. Forster, *Aspects of the Novel* (New York: Harcourt, Brace and Co., 1927), 162.

26. Ibid., 160.

27. *Webster's New Collegiate Dictionary* (Springfield: G. and C. Merriam Co., 1979), 719.

28. Sylvia Cole and Abraham H. Lass, *The Facts On File Dictionary of 20th Century Allusions* (New York: Facts On File, 1991), 179.

29. Peter Blake, "The Lessons of the Parks," in Christopher Finch, *The Art of Walt Disney* (New York: Harry N. Abrams, Inc., 1973), 425–429.

30. Sergei Eisenstein, "Film Form: New Problems," *Film Form*, trans. Jay Leyda (New York: Harcourt, Brace, Jovanovich, 1949), 144–145.

31. Sergei Eisenstein, *Eisenstein on Disney*, Jay Leyda, ed., trans. Alan Upchurch. (London: Methuen, 1988), 10.

32. A more rigorous examination of how Eisenstein's interest in the "ecstasy" of Disney's "plasmaticness" coincides with his interest in theories of collision can be found in Anne Nesbit, "Inanimations: *Snow White* and *Ivan the Terrible*," *Film Quarterly* 50:4 (Summer 1997): 20–31.

33. Eisenstein, *Eisenstein on Disney*, 21.

34. For a history of Cohl's work, see Donald Crafton, Emile Cohl, *Caricature and Film* (Princeton: Princeton University Press, 1996), and Crafton, *Before Mickey*, 59–88.

35. Eisenstein, *Eisenstein on Disney*, 10.

36. Amongst these critics are Richard Schickel, and Arthur Asa Berger, "Of Mice and Men: An Introduction to Mouseology or, Anal Eroticism and Disney," *Journal of Homosexuality* (1991): 155–165.

37. Examples of this type of criticism can be found in Frances Clarke Sayers, "Why a Librarian Deplores Some of the Works of Walt Disney," *The National Observer* (Feb. 14, 1966): 24; "The Magic Kingdom," *Time* (Apr. 15, 1966): 84; and Jill P. May, "Butchering Children's Literature," *Film Library Quarterly* 11:1–2 (1978): 55–62.

38. Bruno Bettelheim, *The Uses of Enchantment: The Meaning and Importance of Fairy Tales* (New York: Penguin, 1976), 24.

39. Ibid., 24.

40. Michael Bronski, *Culture Clash: The Making of a Gay Sensibility* (Boston: South End Press, 1984), 41.

41. Ronald Bayer, *Homosexuality and American Psychiatry: The Politics of Diagnosis* (New York: Basic Books, 1981), 23.

42. Karl Menninger, "Introduction" to the authorized American edition of *Great Britain Committee on Homosexual Offenses and Prostitution, The Wolfenden Report* (New York: Stein and Day, 1963), 7. Ironically, the British report works to repudiate many of the era's commonly held notions of homosexuality as a "deviancy," yet the added introduction for the United States edition counters these findings.

43. Bayer, 20.

44. Charles Socarides, *Beyond Sexual Freedom* (New York: Quadrangle Books, 1975), 11.

45. Bettelheim, 12.

46. Ibid., 6.

47. Cassandra Amesley, "How to Watch *Star Trek,*" *Cultural Studies* 3:3 (Oct. 1989): 334.

48. Bronski, 54–55.

49. J. M. Barrie, *Peter Pan; or The Boy Who Would Not Grow Up* (New York: Charles Scribner's Sons, 1956), 94.

50. Susan Sontag, "Notes on 'Camp,'" *Against Interpretation and Other Essays* (New York: Doubleday, 1966), 277.

51. Sontag, 280.

52. Babuscio, 44. The anthology *The Politics and Poetics of Camp,* Moe Meier, ed. (New York: Routledge, 1994) also strongly emphasizes the importance of acknowledging homosexual culture when discussing camp.

53. Alan Cholodenko, "Introduction," *The Illusion of Life: Essays on Animation* (Sydney: Power Publications, 1991), 15–16.

54. Eve Kosofsky Sedgwick, *The Epistemology of the Closet* (Berkeley: University of California Press, 1990), 1.

55. Butler, *Gender Trouble.*

56. Maltin, 56.

57. Johnston and Thomas, *Disney Animation,* 36.

58. Laura Mulvey's article, "Visual Pleasure and Narrative Cinema," *Film Theory and Criticism,* Gerald Mast and Marshall Cohen, eds. (Oxford: Oxford University Press, 1985), 803–816, describes how classic Hollywood cinema constantly recreates a viewing subject that is engendered male, with the female as a fetishized object, presented with enormous "appeal" to the heterosexual male gaze.

59. Grim Natwick, quoted in Maltin, 56.

60. This is not to intimate that Disney is exclusive in this regard. Most U.S. animation studios which attempt "realistic" animation recreate the same scenario described here.

61. Other works that are appreciated from a camp viewpoint specifically because the texts don't seem to realize how absurd they are would include Maria Montez' "Arabian Nights" films for Universal in the 1940s, the TV series *The Brady Bunch* and the film *Showgirls* (1996).

62. Frank Browning, *The Culture of Desire: Paradox and Perversity in Gay Lives Today* (New York: Vintage Books, 1993), 72–73.

63. Mary Ann Doane, "Film and the Masquerade: Theorizing the Female Spectator," *Screen* 23:3–4 (Sept./Oct. 1982): 74–87.

64. Judith Butler, "Imitation and Gender Insubordination," *Inside/Out: Lesbian Theories, Gay Theories,* Diana Fuss, ed. (New York: Routledge, 1991), 21, 28.

65. Jon Adams, "Critiquing the Cartoon Caricature: Disney, Drag and the Proliferation and Commodification of Queer Negativity." Paper presented at

Society for Cinema Studies Conference, Dallas, 1996. Reference to Leonard Maltin, *The Disney Films* (New York: Crown Publishers, Inc., 1973), 183.

66. Harry M. Benshoff, *Monsters in the Closet: Homosexuality and the Horror Film* (Manchester: Manchester University Press, 1997), while looking at the horror genre specifically, also notes how the monsters or villains in traditional horror films are figured often as "queer" outcasts who somehow threaten the security of the normalized heterosexual couple.

67. Russo, 75.

68. Such a representation of pirates can be linked back to the social structure of pirate life, where male-only crews unable to dock at established ports of call often turned to each other (and to those males kidnapped during raids) for sexual favors and sometimes formed emotional ties. For further comment on this topic, see B. R. Burg, *Sodomy and the Pirate Tradition: English Sea Rovers in the Seventeenth-Century Caribbean* (New York: New York University Press, 1984).

69. The common association of cultured British male characters with homosexuality in popular culture is analyzed in Robert Dickinson, "Anglo Agonistes: English Masculinities in British and American Film," diss., University of Southern California, 1996. Although not referring specifically to *The Jungle Book*, George Sanders' place in this tradition is discussed on 89–90. Discussion of Jeremy Irons playing the villainous fey lion in *The Lion King* is analyzed on 176–178.

70. Discussion of the racial makeup of the orangutan, voiced by jazz great Louis Prima, is outside the scope of this book's topic. Yet, the blatant racial stereotyping of this character does not seem to have bothered African Americans who were effective in keeping *Song of the South* (1947) out of rerelease (and video release).

71. Henry Jenkins, "'Going Bonkers!'" 190.

72. Ibid.

73. Ibid.

74. Armistead Maupin, *28 Barbary Lane: The Tales of the City Omnibus, Vol. 1* (New York: HarperCollins, 1990), 393.

75. In 1997, the Gay Men's Chorus of Los Angeles performed the title song from the film in one of their concerts. As a prelude to the concert, the chorus was shown clips from the movie—to the delighted howls of all who were present. My thanks to Richard Dupler and David Cobb for bringing this gay reading to my attention.

76. Taylor Harrison's paper on the "Annette" serial, "How Will I Know My Love? Annette Funicello and the Screening of Transgression," presented at the Console-ing Passions Conference, University of Madison at Wisconsin, 1996, discussed precisely her shock and recognition of the implications of Jet when rewatching the serial on the Disney Channel.

77. Posted to "rec.arts.tv.soaps.abc" newsgroup by Ashley Lambert-

Maberley on Apr. 4, 1996. The newsgroup is focused on TV soap operas, and the subject was raised on its own within the group.

78. Posted to "rec.arts.tv.soaps.abc" newsgroup by Rob Hartmann on Apr. 4, 1996. My knowledge of this poster's sexuality is based upon personal correspondence.

79. Chris Cuomo, "Spinsters in Sensible Shoes: *Mary Poppins* and *Bedknobs and Broomsticks*," *From Mouse to Mermaid: The Politics of Film, Gender, and Culture*, Elizabeth Bell, Lynda Haas and Laura Sells, eds. (Bloomington: Indiana University Press, 1995), 212–223.

80. Cuomo, 222.

81. Ibid., 221–222.

NOTES TO CHAPTER 3

1. Quoted in Martin Duberman, *Stonewall* (New York: Dutton, 1993), 208.

2. Eric Marcus, *Making History: The Struggle for Gay and Lesbian Equal Rights (1945–1990)—An Oral History* (New York: HarperCollins, 1992), 171–172; and John D'Emilio, *Making Trouble: Essays on Gay History, Politics and the University* (New York: Routledge, 1992).

3. Duberman describes the collapse of the coalition quite vividly in the last section of his book, particularly in recounting the experiences of the drag queen Sylvia, 235–239.

4. Quoted in Signorile, *Life Outside*, 53, who makes the same argument as I make here. Signorile points out that one of the most popular gay male clubs in New York City during this period, the Mineshaft, enforced a dress code of conventional masculinity (jeans, boots, etc.) that effectively kept out transgendered persons or effeminate males.

5. Browning, 41.

6. Quoted in Signorile, *Queer in America: Sex, the Media, and the Closets of Power* (New York: Doubleday, 1993), 316. Although people outside the Shrine Auditorium, where the Awards were held, did protest, the invasion of the proceedings never materialized.

7. Quoted in Ryan Murphy, "Out of the Closet, Onto the Screen," *Out* 17 (Nov. 1994): 141–142.

8. Signorile, *Queer in America*, 319–320.

9. Quoted from a personal interview with Marc Eliot in Eliot's *Walt Disney: Hollywood's Dark Prince*, 138.

10. This anecdote was relayed to me by Walt Disney Company assistant archivist Robert Tieman. It has been impossible to verify this in some form of official writing. The list of actors and actresses is compiled from mainly from the interviews done by Boze Hadleigh published in such works as *Conversations With My Elders* (New York: St. Martin's Press, 1986), *Hollywood Lesbians* (New

York: Barricade Books, 1994) and *Hollywood Gays* (New York: Barricade Books, 1996).

11. Stephen D. Moore, "Disney Downfall, or Whatever Happened to Tommy Kirk," *Frontiers* 13:13 (Nov. 4, 1994): 68.

12. Ibid., 70.

13. Ibid., 68–70, suggests this reading. It is impossible to verify exactly how the studio dealt with Tommy Kirk's last days at the studio, for all records relating to Tommy Kirk during this period have mysteriously disappeared from the Walt Disney Archives according to Walt Disney Company assistant archivist Robert Tieman. In contrast to the hushed-up homosexual "scandal," the press played up Kirk's arrest the following year for smoking marijuana at a Hollywood party with headlines such as "Former Disney Child Star Arrested for Pot."

14. Moore, 70.

15. Ibid.

16. Ron Grover, *The Disney Touch: How a Daring Management Team Revived an Entertainment Empire* (Homewood: Business One Irwin, 1991), 12; the phrase is also mentioned in Joe Flower, *Prince of the Magic Kingdom: Michael Eisner and the Re-Making of Disney* (New York: John Wiley and Sons, 1991), 53. Douglas Gomery's article, "Disney's Business History: A Reinterpretation," in *Disney Discourse*, 78, acknowledges that "All sought to 'do what the founders might have done.'"

17. Flower, 58.

18. Ibid., 96.

19. Grover, 190, describes that the company negotiated to invest only $2.5 million on the park, agreeing to receiving only 10 percent of admissions, 5 percent of food and merchandise sales, and 10 percent of corporate sponsorship agreements. Mitsuhiro Yoshimoto's "Images of Empire: Tokyo Disneyland and Japanese Cultural Imperialism," *Disney Discourse: Producing the Magic Kingdom,* Eric Smoodin, ed. (New York: Routledge, 1994), 181–199, while not explicitly commenting on this business arrangement, analyzes Tokyo Disneyland not as American culture colonizing Japan, but with Japan as the imperial power, importing exotica from the areas under its control.

20. Flower, 188.

21. Ibid., 96. Flower states that this quote was in a magazine interview but does not mention the source, and the quote contains no citation.

22. A number of sources describe the following few months in the company's history. The most thorough of these is John Taylor, *Storming the Magic Kingdom* (New York: Knopf, 1987). Flower and Grover also cover this material.

23. *New York Magazine* (Mar. 10, 1986): 42, quoted in Grover, 100. This same anecdote is also related in Flower, 200.

24. These box-office figures are from Grover, 101.

25. Steven Gaines, "Will the Mouse Come Out?" *Buzz* 6:4 (May 1995): 68, makes the same point.

26. Personal interview with Thomas Pasatieri, Los Angeles, CA (June 30, 1996). Amongst the projects Pasatieri has worked on are *The Little Mermaid* (1989) and *Dick Tracy* (1990).

27. Gaines, 68.

28. *Out* 17 (Nov. 1994) devoted thirty-four pages to three different articles and a photo spread dealing with gays and lesbians in the entertainment industry. Hollywood Pictures debuted as a third filmmaking subsidiary within the Walt Disney Company in 1990.

29. Personal interview with Jeff Kurti, Burbank, CA (July 31, 1994).

30. Quoted in Stephen D. Moore, "A LEAGUE of Their Own: Dragging Disney into the Gay '90's," *Frontiers* 13:13 (Nov. 4, 1994): 60.

31. Moore, "A LEAGUE of Their Own," 60.

32. Personal interview with Jeff Kurti.

33. Personal interview with Garrett Hicks, Burbank, CA (May 25, 1994).

34. Ibid.

35. Personal interview with Tina Shafer, Burbank, CA (Aug. 12, 1994).

36. Moore, "A LEAGUE Of Their Own," 60.

37. Quoted in Mark Stuart Gill, "Never Say Never-Never Land," *Out* 52 (Mar. 1998):113.

38. LEAGUE's "The ABCs of Domestic Partner Benefits" (April 1994) explicitly handles the question, "Should domestic partner benefits cover same-sex partnerships only or also include opposite-sex partnerships?" on 2–3. Although granting that "the Company retains the choice of recognizing same-sex and/or opposite-sex couples in their Domestic Partner definition," they also conclude with a quote from Catherine Iannuzzo and Alexandra Pinck's analysis "Benefits for the Domestic Partners of Gay and Lesbian Employees at Lotus Development Corporation" (paper for the Simmons College Graduate School of Management, November 1991): "Choosing not to be married is not the same thing as not being able to marry."

39. Janice Radway's "Ethnography Among Elites: Comparing Discourses of Power," *Journal of Communication Inquiry* 13:2 (Summer 1989), makes similar remarks, pointing out that "ethnography is produced by the collision of two social worlds, the previously erased home-world of the writing ethnographer, and that distant world in the field inhabited and made meaningful by the group the ethnographer wishes to understand" (3).

40. James D. Woods and Jay H. Lucas, *The Corporate Closet: The Professional Lives of Gay Men in America* (New York: The Free Press, 1993), examine this strategy of homosexuals separating "work" from "personal life" in chapter 5, entitled "Maintaining Boundaries."

41. This was expressed to me by the female and African-American

LEAGUE members that I interviewed and is also expressed in Woods and Lucas, 211–212, 256.

42. Also, taking into account the predominance of white men working within the entertainment industry, it is not inconceivable that the proportion of male to female employees or white to non-white employees at Disney approximates the number of female or non-white employees that show up at LEAGUE meetings.

43. Personal interview with Garrett Hicks.

44. Amongst the other employee groups are LEAGUE MGM/UA, EAGLE (Universal/MCA) and Gay Men and Lesbians of Time/Warner. As of this writing, Universal/MCA, Paramount, MGM/UA, Columbia/TriStar/Sony, Time/Warner and Disney all grant domestic partner benefits, with 20th Century-Fox the only remaining studio holding out.

45. In Jane Keunz, "Working the Rat," *Inside the Mouse: Work and Play at Disney World* (Durham: Duke University Press, 1995), 153–155, there is a good description of the social and corporate environment that faces homosexual employees at Florida's Walt Disney World.

46. Personal interview with Garrett Hicks.

47. Reps. Bob Brooks, et al., "An Open Letter to Michael Eisner and the Walt Disney Board."

48. Quoted in Grover, 58.

49. Flower, 188.

50. All the comments by "Kent" are from a personal interview with the author, Burbank, CA (Sept. 12, 1994).

51. Personal interview with Garth Steever. Long Beach, CA (July 8, 1994).

52. Ibid.

53. David Koenig, *Mouse Tales: A Behind-the-Ears Look at Disneyland* (Irvine: Bonaventure Press, 1994), 212.

54. Personal interview with the author, name withheld by request.

55. Disneyland decided to tone down the jocular presentation of rape presented in the Pirates of the Caribbean ride in 1996 by altering the scenes to intimate that the pirates were after the food the women were carrying. Certain customers complained about the change, claiming that chasing women was what pirates did historically. None of these complainers seemed to want the historical accuracy to include pirates' chasing after young boys as well.

56. "The 'Disney Look,'" published by the Walt Disney Company (1987), 3.

57. Ibid., 6. Looking at the pictures that accompany the brochure, it is evident that the bias is not only, or even predominantly, against homosexuals. A strong sense of ageism is apparent in those chosen to embody the "Disney Look," and there is a strong emphasis on white European-descent faces. Also, there are no photos of overweight or physically challenged people.

58. Eddie Shapiro, "Gayety in the Magic Kingdom," 12–13. The lesbian/

gay appeal of "Ellen's Energy Adventure" in the EPCOT Center's "Universe of Energy" exhibit is also described in Gill, 74, 113.

59. Keunz, 153.

60. Personal interview with Sue Schiebler, Los Angeles, CA (May 31, 1994).

61. Keunz, 154.

62. Keunz, 154–155 (and endnote 36, 241).

63. Quoted in Keunz, 154.

64. Personal interview with Garth Steever.

65. Personal interview with Sue Schiebler.

66. Quoted in Keunz, 153.

67. Personal interview with Sue Schiebler.

68. Koenig, 209.

69. Personal interview with the author, name withheld by request.

70. Koenig, 134.

71. Koenig, 134.

72. Personal interview with the author, name withheld by request.

73. Personal interview with Sue Schiebler.

74. Personal interview with the author, name withheld by request.

75. George Herold, quoted in Koenig, 72.

76. Koenig provides a decent recounting of the history of this strike, and the fallout in workplace relations after the strike ended (68–77).

77. Quoted in Koenig, 76.

78. Personal interview with Sue Schiebler.

NOTES TO CHAPTER 4

1. Charles Isherwood, "Cel Division," *The Advocate* (Dec. 1, 1992): 84–85, contains an interview with openly gay animator Andreas Deja; B. Ruby Rich, "Lauren Lloyd: Disney's Crossover Achiever," *Out* 17 (Nov. 1994): 81, details how film executive Lloyd's lesbianism affects not only her choice of projects to put in development, but how it helped get her hired by the company; Bruce Handy, "He Called Me Ellen DeGenerate," *Time* (Apr. 14, 1997): 50, is an interview with Ellen DeGeneres in which she explains her decision to make the character she played in the Disney-produced sitcom *Ellen* a lesbian. All of these individuals will be discussed at length within this chapter. Additionally, some employees working for the parks have spoken in confidence to me of parts of various attractions that express gay pride—but done covertly, and those interviewed did not want these details revealed for fear that the company would find out and eliminate these elements of the attractions.

2. The history of mainstreaming "camp" is too large a topic to go into detail here, but certain events point to "camp" moving out beyond the homosexual subculture: Susan Sontag's popular essay on the topic, the growth of the

midnight movie circuit (particularly *The Rocky Horror Picture Show* [1975] in the late '70s), the movement in many areas of popular culture into postmodern pastiche and the recent "lounge" music trend.

3. Dan Rather, "The AIDS Metaphor in *Beauty and the Beast*," *Los Angeles Times Calendar* (Mar. 22, 1992): 42.

4. Cynthia Erb, "Another World or the World of an Other?: The Space of Romance in Recent Versions of 'Beauty and the Beast,'" *Cinema Journal* 34:4 (Summer 1995): 67.

5. Benshoff, *Monsters in the Closet*, 3.

6. Rather, 42.

7. Rather's sources are correct to an extent—the project of creating an animated version of the popular fairy tale had been in discussion even during Walt's life. But, the project lay dormant until Ashman revived it, and quotes from collaborator Alan Menken indicate that Ashman was fully aware of his condition long before he revealed it to anyone at Disney. Exactly how much AIDS colored Ashman's take on the tale is still up for discussion.

8. François Truffaut, "A Certain Tendency of the French Cinema," *Movies and Methods, Vol. 1*, Bill Nichols, ed. (Berkeley: University of California Press, 1976), 224–236.

9. Andrew Sarris, *The American Cinema: Directors and Directions, 1929–1968* (New York: Dutton, 1968).

10. Bill Nichols, *Movies and Methods, Vol. 1* (Berkeley: University of California Press, 1976), 221.

11. Richard Dyer, "Believing in Fairies: The Author and the Homosexual," *Inside/Out: Lesbian Theories, Gay Theories*, Diana Fuss, ed., 185–201, makes a similar initial assessment of the status of *auteur* studies.

12. Butler, "Imitation and Gender Subordination," 21, 28. Although Butler is writing specifically about gender and sexuality, her discussion of performance applies equally to issues of race according to social constructionist theories. The italics are mine.

13. Others have noticed that such concepts simultaneously withhold the mantle of "authorship" from women, homosexuals and non-Caucasian individuals just at the moment when there are more opportunities for these groups to have access to methods of production and mass distribution. Amongst those who have lamented this double-edge are Patricia Waugh, *Feminine Fictions: Revisiting the Postmodern* (New York: Routledge, 1989), 6; and Jeffrey Weeks, *Sexuality and Its Discontents* (London: Routledge, 1985), 200.

14. Dyer, 187.

15. Ibid., 188.

16. Isherwood, 85.

17. Deja reportedly modeled Jafar after not only Conrad Veidt in *Thief of*

Baghdad, but (in a delightfully nasty comment by Deja) Nancy Reagan! (Janet Maslin, Review of *Aladdin, New York Times* [Nov. 11, 1992]: C15).

18. The most famous equivalent to Deja's hypermasculine characters is Chernobog, the demon in the "Night on Bald Mountain" sequence from *Fantasia* (1940). The only other comparable figure would be Brom Bones in the "Sleepy Hollow" section of *The Adventures of Ichabod and Mr. Toad* (1949)—not a memorable character in Disney's filmography.

19. Isherwood, 85. Ironically, Jeffrey Katzenberg initially wanted Deja to base his design of Gaston on Tom Cruise, a quite popular star in American gay male culture who *would* come to influence the design of another Disney animated character in future years.

20. Erb, 64.

21. The lyrics of the song, written by Ashman, also help create this simultaneous worship/ridicule of the male body. As the women in the inn delight that he's "burly" and "brawny," Gaston himself declares he has "biceps to spare" and boasts that "Ev'ry last inch of me's covered with hair!" Ashman's contribution to the character of Gaston, and to "gay readings" of Disney during this period, will be analyzed more thoroughly in the next section of this chapter.

22. Some feminist critics have found Disney's version of *Beauty and the Beast* to have progressive elements: Marina Warner, "Beauty and the Beasts," *Sight and Sound* 2:6 (Oct. 1992): 6–11; Harriett Hawkins, "Maidens and Monsters in Modern Popular Culture: *The Silence of the Lambs* and *Beauty and the Beast*," *Textual Practice* 7:2 (Summer 1993): 258–266. Others have responded negatively to its representation of women: Kathi Maio, "Mr. Right Is a Beast: Disney's Dangerous Fantasy," *Visions Magazine* 7 (Summer 1992): 44–45; Elizabeth Dodson Gray, "Beauty and the Beast: A Parable for Our Time," *Women Respond to the Men's Movement: A Feminist Collection*, Kay Leigh Hagan, ed. (San Francisco: Pandora, 1992), 159–168; Susan Jeffords, "The Curse of Masculinity: Disney's Beauty and the Beast," *From Mouse to Mermaid: The Politics of Film, Gender and Culture*, Elizabeth Bell, Lynda Haas and Laura Sells, eds. (Bloomington: Indiana University Press, 1995), 161–172.

23. Clemente and Musker's work on *The Great Mouse Detective* also presages the resurgence of the campy "gay-tinged" villain in Disney's animated features, with the outrageous Ratigan voiced with exceptional verve by Vincent Price. Price's camp villain persona is expertly analyzed in Benshoff, *Monsters in the Closet*, 208–219.

24. David Ansen, et al., "Just the Way Walt Made 'Em," *Newsweek* (Nov. 18, 1991): 74–80; David J. Fox, "Looking at 'Beauty' as Tribute to Lyricist Who Gave 'Beast His Soul,'" *Los Angeles Times* (Nov. 15, 1991): F1, 17; Janet Maslin, Review of *Beauty and the Beast, New York Times* (Nov. 13, 1991): C17; Review of *Beauty and the Beast, Variety* (Nov. 11, 1991): 53.

25. Erb, 59.

26. Mimi Avens, "Aladdin Sane," *Premiere* 6:4 (Dec. 1992): 67.

27. Oscar Wilde, "The Fisherman and His Soul," *Complete Fairy Tales of Oscar Wilde* (New York: Penguin, 1990), 129–179.

28. Erb, 70, footnote 35.

29. Ibid., 54.

30. Ibid., 60.

31. Jean Cocteau, *Beauty and the Beast: Diary of a Film,* trans. Ronald Duncan (New York: Dover, 1972), 67.

32. Joseph Boone's article, "Rubbing Aladdin's Lamp," analyzes the homoerotic orientalism in Pasolini's work; Michael Moon's "Flaming Closets," *Out in Culture: Gay, Lesbian, and Queer Essays on Popular Culture,* Corey K. Creekmur and Alexander Doty, eds. (Durham: Duke University Press, 1995), 282–306, examines the orientalism in Jack Smith's avant-garde gay film and theatrical work.

33. Richard Burton's sexuality has come under question in the late twentieth century, and two films explicitly use him as a quasi-homosexual figure: *Mountains of the Moon* (1990), directed by Bob Rafelson, about his relationship with John Hanning Speke, and *Zero Patience* (1994), directed by John Grierson, positing a fictional relationship between Burton and the infamous Canadian "Patient Zero" who supposedly brought AIDS to North America (first described in Randy Shilts, *And the Band Played On: Politics, People and the AIDS Epidemic* [New York: St. Martin's Press, 1987]).

34. Maslin, Review of *Beauty and the Beast,* C17.

35. For example, "Those Faces! Those Voices . . . ," *People* 32:24 (Dec. 11, 1989): 125; Elizabeth Brevitz, "A Little Attitude," *Premiere* 3:4 (Dec. 1989): 135; and Michael Wilmington, "'Little Mermaid' Makes Big Splash," *Los Angeles Times* (Nov. 15, 1989): F10.

36. Janet Maslin, "Cinderella of the Sea," *New York Times* (Nov. 15, 1989): C17; Review of *The Little Mermaid, Variety* (Nov. 8, 1989): 32.

37. The only precedent to this number is "Cruella de Vil" in *101 Dalmatians,* which drips with camp potential, but is sung not by Cruella herself but by the lead human male, Roger, who is making fun of her without Cruella's knowledge.

38. Erb, 62. Interestingly, although many "queer" readers view Ursula as a drag queen, this number also supports a lesbian viewpoint. Pat Carroll's place in lesbian culture (having played Gertrude Stein in a one-woman stage show) takes on importance in this number as she attempts to seduce a young woman to the "dark side." (My thanks to Sue Schiebler for pointing this out!)

39. Janet Maslin, Review of *Aladdin,* C15.

40. Although there are indications that Ashman's original conception of the Genie was eventually modified, his seeming conception of the Genie as

"queer" definitely remained in the final version. These modifications will be discussed in chapter 5.

41. The spectacle of the male body has become a recently noticed phenomenon—but not just recently produced. Sticking to cinema history (the history of the male nude in art would take us back much farther), Miriam Hansen's "Pleasure, Ambivalence, Identification: Valentino and Female Spectatorship," *Star Texts: Image and Performance in Film and Television,* Jeremy G. Butler, ed. (Detroit: Wayne State University Press, 1991), 266–297, has analyzed the silent cinema star Rudolph Valentino as an object "to-be-looked-at," as has Steven Cohen's analysis of the image of William Holden in "Masquerading as the American Male in the Fifties: *Picnic,* William Holden and the Spectacle of Masculinity in Hollywood Film," *Camera Obscura* 25–26 (1991): 43–72. Hansen describes that the presence of a male body as spectacle announces a variety of subject positions, not exclusively engendered heterosexual and patriarchal. Although Laura Mulvey describes female spectatorship as "transvestitism"—taking on masculine subjectivity—the notion of "cross-dressing" in itself complicates the notion of essentializing subject positions.

42. Finch, 198.

43. For example, Donald Crafton, "Walt Disney's *Peter Pan:* Women Trouble on the Island," speaks of the "tradition of having him played by a girl or young woman" in stage productions (125).

44. Avens, 70.

45. *The Entertainment Weekly Guide to the Greatest Movies Ever Made* (New York: Warner Books, 1994), 203.

46. Erb, 61.

47. Erb, 63. Erb focuses on the film specifically as an expression of a gay male viewpoint. While I obviously share her assessment, at times—as I am pointing out in this example—Ashman's gay-male outlook can find common ground with other non-straight identities.

48. Erb, 63.

49. Disney's one stipulation in its agreement with Miramax was that Miramax could not distribute any film that had received an NC-17 rating. Consequently, when Harvey Weinstein, the president of Miramax, bought the distribution rights for the NC-17-rated *Kids* (1995), he formed a new label to release the film outside of Disney.

50. Rich, "Lauren Lloyd," 81.

51. Review of *Down and Out in Beverly Hills, Variety* (Jan. 15, 1986): 23.

52. Russo, 256. Although Russo does mention that director Paul Mazursky is "usually very sensitive," he discusses only this line of dialogue and nothing about the character of Max.

53. Byrne R. S. Fone, *Masculine Landscapes: Walt Whitman and the Homoerotic Text* (Carbondale: Southern Illinois University Press, 1992), 46. The quote within

the quote is taken from Caroll Smith-Rosenberg, *Disorderly Conduct: Visions of Gender in Victorian America* (New York: Oxford University Press, 1985), 91.

54. Fone, 45.

55. Review of *Dead Poets Society, Variety* (May 31, 1989): 26.

56. Mike Hammond, "The Historical and the Hysterical: Melodrama, War and Masculinity in *Dead Poets Society,*" *You Tarzan: Masculinity, Movies and Men,* Pat Kirkham and Janet Thumin, eds., (New York: St. Martin's Press, 1993), 63.

57. After the suicide, the film cuts directly to Todd in his dorm room, being awakened by the other students who tell him of Neil's death. Todd's reaction is stunned shock as he walks out into the snowy grounds of Welton, kneels and vomits. When his friends rush to his side, he breaks free and runs chaotically while keening loudly until the end of the scene. Because reading Todd as a homosexual character is more "subtextual" than Neil, not all viewers would necessarily read a relationship between Todd and Neil, but clues can be found readily. The two have no female interests in the film, and, when one of their friends brings girls to a Dead Poets meeting, both seem somewhat annoyed. In fact, both Todd and Neil seem to eventually accept the presence of women in this previously all-male space when the film shows the two glancing at each other and smiling as if to indulge their friend. Certainly, Todd and Neil form the key friendship in the film if nothing else. When Todd receives a "desk set" from his parents in the mail for his birthday (which is what they gave him *last* year as well), it is Neil who comforts him and cheers him up with the idea of tossing the gift off the roof of the dorm. Lastly, Neil's death seems to push Todd out of his shyness, to realize that silent acceptance of what others want of him will only kill him. When Keating is fired from Welton, Todd pays final tribute to him by standing on his desk and saluting "Oh captain, my captain!" While Welton's dean attempts to quell the action, most of the rest of the class follows suit, and the final shot of the film is of a courageous Todd—provocatively shot through the legs of another student.

58. Joseph McBride, Review of *Newsies, Variety* (Apr. 6, 1992): 166.

59. Janet Maslin, Review of *Swing Kids, New York Times* (Mar. 5, 1993): C8.

60. Ibid.

61. Stephen Holden, Review of *Tombstone, New York Times* (Dec. 24, 1993): C6.

62. Ibid.

63. This is not to say that lesbian culture has no place for theatre or the musical genre. A number of female performers have become iconic figures in lesbian culture—for example, Pat Carroll, who voiced Ursula in *The Little Mermaid.* And listening to a lesbian chorus sing "Kiss the Girl" from *The Little Mermaid* shows that they can appropriate this "new" Disney as well as lesbians who had "Mickey Mouse parties" in the 1930s did.

64. Amusingly, the series carried over the bright colors and *nouveau riche*

visual design that dominated the comedies released by Touchstone Pictures into Disney's television production as well!

65. Mimi White, "Ideological Analysis and Television," *Channels of Discourse*, Robert Allen, ed. (Chapel Hill: University of North Carolina Press, 1987), 162.

66. Doty, 43.

67. Ibid.

68. Robert Dawidoff, "Gays Saw Between the Lines of 'Ellen'; Now for an Open Act 2," *Los Angeles Times* (Apr. 18, 1997): B9.

69. The storyline of this episode seems to have directly inspired Ellen DeGeneres' first starring role in a theatrical feature film—*Mr. Wrong* (1996), distributed by Disney's Hollywood Pictures.

70. According to some reports, the sparks that were generated in this episode were pointed out when DeGeneres and her allies argued that Morgan should "come out of the closet."

71. Whether or not such rumors have any validity in fact is hard to know although, as it turned out, the final three episodes of the 1996–97 season did end having Ellen Morgan come out and, about a month after the season finale, reports surfaced that DeGeneres had expressed a desire to end the show then and there.

72. Doty, 48–51, discusses lesbian subtexts in *The Mary Tyler Moore Show* (1970–77).

73. Dawidoff, B9.

74. Reported in A. J. Jacobs, "Out?" *Entertainment Weekly* (Oct. 4, 1996): 20.

75. Jefferson Graham, "Ellen Happy with Women at Helm," *USA Weekend* (Dec. 19, 1995): D3; and Bruce Fretts, "This Week," *Entertainment Weekly* (Oct. 25, 1996): 102.

76. In fact, the same issue of *TV Guide* (42:35, Aug. 27, 1994) that mentions the possibility of DeGeneres's wearing a dress for the Emmys (5) also contains an item bemoaning the loss of Holly Fulger from the series (6).

77. This attitude by critics towards the show is discussed by Ron Becker in "Bringing Ellen Out of the Closet," paper presented at Console-ing Passions, Concordia University, Montreal, 1997. Becker's paper does a wonderful job describing the number of economic factors that might have helped explain the support for allowing Ellen Morgan to be lesbian.

78. "Returning Favorites," *TV Guide* 44:37 (Sept. 13, 1996): 46.

79. Quoted in A. J. Jacobs, 25.

80. Daniel Howard Cerone, "*Ellen* May Be Telling Even Though Not Asked," *TV Guide* 44:39 (Sept. 28, 1996): 59–60.

81. Howard Rosenberg, "The Outing of 'Ellen'? It's Got Me Hooked," *Los Angeles Times* (Sept. 30, 1996): F1.

82. A. J. Jacobs, 20.

83. Handy, 48.

84. Ibid.

85. The companies that decided to withdraw their sponsorship of the show included Wendy's Restaurants, Chrysler, General Motors, JC Penney and Johnson & Johnson.

86. Hilary de Vries, "Ellen DeGeneres: Out and About," *TV Guide* (Oct. 11, 1998): 22.

87. Ibid., 24.

88. Ibid.

89. Glenn Lovell, "'Ellen' Too Gay, Bono Chastises," *Daily Variety* (Mar. 9, 1998): 87.

90. "Chastity on 'Ellen' Misleading," NewsPlanet Staff internet posting on "Planet Out" webpage, www.planetout.com/pno/newsplanet/article.html, March 10, 1998.

91. The concept of the homosexual as a "sexual outlaw" was popularized by John Rechy, who purportedly was one of those who was unhappy about Ellen Morgan declaring her lesbian status. The weekend after the "coming-out" episode aired, the Console-ing Passions television conference was held in Montreal, and, in a panel/discussion about *Ellen,* a sizable number of those present preferred it when they could read Ellen Morgan as a lesbian, but most heterosexual viewers could not.

92. Walter Benjamin, *Illuminations* (New York: Shocken Books, 1969) was among the first to warn against this usurption of popular culture by mass culture. Many others have also studied and theorized this development in Western society, such as Frederic Jameson, "Reification and Utopia in Mass Culture," *Social Text* 1:1 (1979): 134–138; William Fox, "Folklore and Fakelore: Some Sociological Considerations," *Journal of the Folklore Institute,* 17:2–3 (May/December 1980): 249–256; George Lipsitz, *Time Passages: Collective Memory and American Popular Culture* (Minneapolis: University of Minnesota Press, 1990).

93. Quoted in de Vries, 22.

NOTES TO CHAPTER 5

1. Cerone, 59.

2. Cerone's article in *TV Guide* suggests this analysis, which is also mentioned by Ron Becker, "Bringing Ellen Out of the Closet."

3. Cerone, 60.

4. Quoted in Pamela Ellis-Simons, "Hi Ho, Hi Ho; It's Off to Work He Goes as Michael Eisner Puts the Magic Back into the Walt Disney Co.," *Marketing & Media Decisions* (Sept. 1986), 52.

5. For example, Joe Flower refers often in his work about the Eisner era to the emphasis on Disney marketing, including describing how "In the first nine

months after he [Eisner] took charge, the company issued 40 press releases—more than one a week" (163), the decision to market the theme parks by hiring the advertising firm Young and Rubicam (186) and Katzenberg's aggressive push to publicize their film output (199–203).

6. D. A. Miller "Anal *Rope*," *Inside/Out: Lesbian Theories, Gay Theories*, Diana Fuss, ed. (New York: Routledge, 1991), 123–124.

7. For example, interview with John Musker and Ron Clemente, directors of *The Little Mermaid, Aladdin* and *Hercules*, University of Southern California (Nov. 19, 1992), USC Cinema Library; and Marcy Magiera, "'Mermaid' Aims to Reel in Adults," *Advertising Age* 60:45 (Oct. 16, 1989): 38.

8. Chon Noriega, "'SOMETHING'S MISSING HERE!' Homosexuality and Film Reviews during the Production Code Era, 1934–1962," *Cinema Journal* 30:1 (Fall 1990): 35.

9. Others who have pointed out this complication have included: Jody Berland, "Angels Dancing: Cultural Technologies and the Production of Space," *Cultural Studies*, Cary Nelson, Paula A. Treichler, Larry Grossberg, eds. (New York: Routledge, 1992): 38–51; Stephen Kline, *Out of the Garden: Children's Culture in the Age of TV Marketing* (London: Verso, 1993); and Cary Nelson, Paula A. Treichler and Larry Grossberg, "Cultural Studies: An Introduction," *Cultural Studies*, 1–22.

10. Cecil Munsey, *Disneyana: Walt Disney Collectibles* (New York: Hawthorn Books, 1974), 1. Unless otherwise noted, all other data from the Walt Disney era of the studio on merchandising is from this text.

11. According to collector/author Cecil Munsey, "At first his [Walt's] thoughts ran along the lines that such merchandise would provide valuable publicity for his characters and therefore make his films very popular. . . . Not only would character merchandise increase the popularity of their films but it would bring in additional revenue to the film which, in turn, would allow them to make better films" (32).

12. Mosley, 152. Munsey's research does not provide as much detail of the financial relationship as Mosley's does.

13. Harold D. Lasswell, *Propaganda Technique in the World War* (New York: Knopf, 1927) provides a good overview of the "magic bullet" theory that was promulgated at the time.

14. James E. Grunig, "Publics, Audiences and Market Segments: Segmentation Principles for Campaigns," *Information Campaigns: Balancing Social Values and Social Change*, Charles T. Salmon, ed. (Newbury Park: Sage Publications, 1989), 201.

15. Amongst those who have analyzed *Mickey Mouse Club* and marketing towards children have been Kline, 166–167; and Lynn Spigel, "Seducing the Innocent: Childhood and Television in Postwar America," *Ruthless Criticism: New Perspectives in U.S. Communications History*, William S. Solomon and

Robert W. McChesney, eds. (Minneapolis: University of Minnesota Press, 1993), 280–281.

16. An analysis of the company's specific marketing strategies towards children with the "Disney Afternoon" can be found in Pamela C. O'Brien, "Everybody's Busy Bringing You a Disney Afternoon: The Creation of a Consumption Community," paper presented at the Seventh Annual Society of Animation Studies Conference, University of North Carolina at Greensboro, 1995.

17. Kline's work on TV marketing towards children also discusses how commercials for children are often bifurcated into specific gender reception.

18. My thanks to Joseph A. Boone for relating the *Aladdin* event to me, which is further detailed in the introduction to his essay "Rubbing Aladdin's Lamp," complete with a reproduction of an advertisement for the event on page 149.

19. Roland Marchand, *Advertising the American Dream* (Berkeley: University of California Press, 1985), xxi.

20. Judith Williamson, *Decoding Advertisements: Ideology and Meaning in Advertising* (New York: Marion Boyars, 1979), 77.

21. Karen Stabiner, "Tapping the Homosexual Market," *New York Times Magazine* (May 2, 1982): 80.

22. Ibid., 76.

23. Calvin Klein has also pushed up against the limits of coding with its 1996 underwear campaign. Featuring models that looked just under the "age of consent," the TV spots were a pastiche of low-budget "nudie loops." Although the campaign also featured female models, the ads mainly showed young men recreating scenes from the super-8 films sold by the Athletic Models Guild in the 1950s and 1960s that were targeted at homosexual men. Apparently, a number of straight viewers caught what was going on, and recognition of the appropriation of pornographic *mise-en-scène* led to talk of legal action against the company for a few months.

24. Miller, 125.

25. Boone, 149.

26. Steve Warren, "Deja View," *Frontiers* 11:20 (Jan. 29, 1992): 48. Isherwood, 85.

27. Tom Provenzano, "The Lion in Summer," *The Advocate* (June 28, 1994): 66.

28. Ansen, et al.; Fox; Janet Maslin, Review of *Beauty and the Beast*; Review of *Beauty and the Beast, Variety*.

29. Frederic Jameson, "Postmodernism, or the Cultural Logic of Late Capitalism," *New Left Review* 146 (July/August 1984): 78.

30. Bill Short, "Queers, Beers and Shopping," *Gay Times* 170 (Nov. 1992): 20.

31. Stuart Ewen, *Captains of Consciousness: Advertising and the Social Roots of Consumer Culture* (New York: McGraw-Hill, 1976).

32. Marchand, 162.

33. This trend in "lesbian chic" was the basis for Danae Clark's influential article, "Commodity Lesbianism," *Camera Obscura* 25–26 (Jan./May 1991): 181–201.

34. Actress Catherine Deneuve eventually brought suit against this journal, and it subsequently changed its name to *Curve.*

35. Ms. Beverly Hills, "Beat Reporter?" *Planet Homo* 71 (Oct. 19, 1994): 6.

36. Bronski.

37. Jeffrey Weeks, "Inverts, Perverts and Mary-Annes: Male Prostitution and the Regulation of Homosexuality in England in the 19th and Early 20th Centuries," *Hidden from History: Reclaiming the Gay and Lesbian Past,* Martin Duberman, Martha Vicinus and George Chauncey Jr., eds. (New York: Meridian, 1990), 202.

38. Chauncey, chapter 1.

39. Weeks, "Inverts," 202.

40. Gregory Woods, "We're Here, We're Queer and We're Not Going Catalogue Shopping," *A Queer Romance: Lesbians, Gay Men and Popular Culture,* Paul Burston and Colin Richardson, eds. (New York: Routledge, 1995), 155. Historical research seems to point out that "gay" had already been appropriated to refer to prostitution in general by the beginning of the twentieth century ("the gay life"), yet the above analysis may help explain the shift in the use of the term to mean specifically "homosexuality."

41. John D'Emilio, "Capitalism and Gay Identity," *Powers of Desire: The Politics of Sexuality,* Ann Snitow, Christine Stansell and Sharon Thompson, eds. (New York: Monthly Review Press, 1983), 105.

42. Jennie Livingston's *Paris Is Burning* points out the social importance of a store-bought item over handmade wardrobe in the New York drag scene of the 1980s—as individuals either stole clothes, or stole labels to sew into their handmade clothes.

43. An example of an Arrow shirt ad doing just this can be found in Marchand, 201. Marchand, 196, describes "the gay life" of the upper classes in 1920s ads. Harry Benshoff describes the overtly gay male appeal of *Esquire* magazine in the early 1930s, and the ads contained within its issues, in *Monsters in the Closet,* 34.

44. George Chauncey points out that "gay" at the turn-of-the-century was often a connotation of prostitution ("the gay life"). While this obviously predates magazine ads of the 1920s, associating homosexuality with "sex-for-hire" further reinforces by point of capitalism's influence on homosexual identity.

45. John D'Emilio, *Sexual Politics, Sexual Communities: The Making of a Homosexual Minority in the United States, 1940–1970* (Chicago: University of Chicago Press, 1983). Chapter 10 contains information on the battles waged by San Francisco's gay bar owners to stay in business.

46. Woods, 160.

47. Foucault, *History of Sexuality*, 25.

48. Isherwood, 85.

49. Warren, 49.

50. Provenzano, 67.

51. "Rights Group Buys Air Time on 'Ellen,'" *New York Times* (Mar. 20, 1997): C6.

52. Roberta Astroff, "Commodifying Cultures: Latino Ad Specialists as Cultural Brokers," Paper presented at the Seventh International Conference on Culture and Communication, Philadelphia, 1989.

53. Stabiner, 36.

54. Ibid., 74.

55. Clark.

56. Jaffe Cohen, Danny McWilliams and Bob Smith, *Growing Up Gay: From Left Out to Coming Out* (New York: Hyperion, 1995).

57. Dyer, 188.

58. Handy, 50.

59. Ibid.

60. Mary Ann Doane, "The Economy of Desire: The Commodity Form in/of the Cinema," *QRFV* 11:1 (1989): 30; Judith Williamson and Roland Marchand also analyze how advertising constructs women as commodities.

61. Marchand, 138.

62. The marketing of this specific body image to the gay community is also noted by Michelangelo Signorile, *Life Outside.*

63. For a lucid account of Media Systems Dependency Theory, see Melvin L. DeFleur and Sandra Ball-Rokeach, *Theories of Mass Communication* (New York: D. McKay Co., 1975), 297–327.

64. Erb, 62.

65. Jack G. Sheehan, "Arab Caricatures Deface Disney's *Aladdin*," *Los Angeles Times* (Dec. 21, 1992): F5.

66. Ibid.

67. Casey Kasem and Jay Goldsworthy, "No Magic in *Aladdin*'s Offensive Lyrics," *Los Angeles Times* (Apr. 19, 1993): F3.

68. David J. Fox, "Disney Will Alter Song in Aladdin," *Los Angeles Times* (July 10, 1993): F1.

69. Avens, 67.

70. Ella Shohat, "Gender and Culture of Empire: Toward a Feminist Ethnography of the Cinema," *QRFV* 13:1–3 (1991): 75, 69.

71. Rana Kabbani, *Europe's Myths of Orient* (Bloomington: Indiana University Press, 1986), 23–24.

72. Avens, 67.

73. Ibid.

74. Avens, 70. Aladdin's skin tone is browner than Jasmine's, which could be construed as an indication of their class status (his poverty, her royalty), yet Jasmine's eyes are more slanted or "Orientalized," which might have been done to accent the "exotic" appeal of the Middle Eastern woman in Western society.

75. A number of people have written on the variant expressions of sexuality that existed within various Native American tribal cultures with terms such as the "berdache," the "koskalaka" or the "two-spirited person." See Paula Gunn Allen, "Lesbians in American Indian Cultures," *Hidden from History: Reclaiming the Gay and Lesbian Past,* Martin Duberman, Martha Vincinus and George Chauncey, Jr., eds. (New York: Meridian, 1990), 106–117; Harriet Whitehead, "The Bow and the Burden Strap: A New Look at Institutionalized Homosexuality in Native North America," *The Lesbian and Gay Studies Reader,* Henry Abelove, Michele Aina Barale and David M. Halperin, eds. (New York: Routledge, 1993), 498–527; Sue-Ellen Jacobs, Wesley Thomas and Sabine Lang, eds., *Two-Spirit People: Native American Gender Identity, Sexuality and Spirituality* (Urbana: University of Illinois Press, 1997).

76. Gael Sweeney, "'What Do You Want Me to Do, Dress in Drag and Do the Hula?': Pumbaa and Timon's Alternative Life Style Dilemma in Disney's The Lion King," paper presented at the Seventh Annual Society of Animation Studies Conference, University of North Carolina at Greensboro, 1995.

77. D'Emilio, "Capitalism and Gay Identity," 102.

78. Sweeney, in her paper, describes the range of resistance to the TV series by many of the film's fans on the Internet.

79. John E. Harris, "Stereotyping for Fun and Profit," *Christopher Street* (Sept. 1994): 4.

80. Todd Hayward, "The Lyin' King," *Planet Homo* 69 (Sept. 21, 1994): 16–17.

81. Hayward, 17.

NOTES TO THE EPILOGUE

1. "Gay Day at Disney World Goes Off Without Incident, Park Aide Reports," *Los Angeles Times* (June 5, 1994): A21; Mike Clary and James Bates, "Moral Crusading: Conservative Christians Shun Disney Over Gay-Partner Policy," *Los Angeles Times* (Dec. 25, 1995): A4.

2. Rep. Bob Brooks, et al., "An Open Letter to Michael Eisner and the Walt Disney Board," 6.

3. Clary and Bates, A4.

4. Dart, A19.

5. Gregory M. Herek, "Beyond Homophobia: A Social Psychological Perspective on attitudes Toward Lesbians and Gay Men," *Bashers, Baiters and*

Bigots: Homophobia in American Society, John P. DeCecco, ed. (New York: Harrington Park Press, 1985), 10.

6. "The Religious Right on *Toy Story,*" *A LEAGUE of Our Own* 24 (Jan./Feb. 1996): 2.

7. Cohen, *Forbidden Animation,* 115–116.

8. The quote is from an introduction before the full quotation of the memo in "The Religious Right on *Toy Story,*" 2.

9. Dart, A1.

10. Ibid., A19.

11. Ibid.

12. Ibid.

13. In addition to its film production arms (Walt Disney Pictures, Touchstone Pictures, Hollywood Pictures, Miramax), and the various branches specifically using the Disney name (the theme parks, the Disney stores, Walt Disney Records, the Disney Channel cable network), by 1997, the company had expanded into a variety of areas (holding interests in ESPN and E! cable networks, sports teams such as the Anaheim Ducks, some city newspapers and the entire ABC television network). An article in the Southern Baptists' own *Baptist Press* reported that a poll conducted by the University of North Carolina, in conjunction with the *Atlanta Journal* and *Atlanta Constitution,* found that only about 30 percent of Southern Baptists surveyed were likely to participate in the economic action against Disney. The poll suggested that 75 percent of non-Southerners and 72 percent of Southerners were unlikely to participate in the boycott. Dwayne Hastings, "Eisner: Boycotters a Splinter Group with Nazi Leanings," (Apr. 22, 1998).

14. James Bates and Marla Dickerson, "Disney's Strategy Takes Calls for Protest in Stride," *Los Angeles Times* (June 20, 1997): A17.

15. David Verbraska, "Southern Baptists 'Misplace' Outrage," *USA Today* (June 18, 1997).

16. John A. Nelson, "Disney Wrong Target," *USA Today* (June 18, 1997).

17. Quoted in Gill, 72. The "Mighty Duck" phrase refers to the Disney-owned pro hockey team, the Anaheim Mighty Ducks—named after the successful Disney live-action feature *The Mighty Ducks* (1992) about a Little League hockey team.

18. Alana Hommel, "Disney Support." (Email sent ca. May 1998).

19. Shapiro, 13.

20. Alana Hommel, "Stand Our Ground" (Email sent ca. June 1998).

21. Shapiro, 13.

22. James Collard, "Leaving the Gay Ghetto," *Newsweek* 132: 7 (Aug. 17, 1998): 53.

23. Jonathan Van Meter, "The Post-Gay Man," *Esquire* 126:5 (Nov. 1996): 88–89, 132–134.

24. Elise Harris analyzes this aspect of the term in "Going Post-al," *Out* 58 (Sept. 1998): 82–87, 184.

25. Collard, 53.

26. Harris, 82.

27. Van Meter, 134.

28. Harris, 86.

29. Michelangelo Signorile, "641,086 and Counting," *Out* 58 (Sept. 1998): 188.

30. Eleaine Herscher, "Wyoming Death Echoes Rising Anti-Gay Attacks," *San Francisco Chronicle* (Oct. 13, 1998): A7.

31. Herscher, A7.

32. Shapiro, 14.

Bibliography

Adams, Jon. "Critiquing the Cartoon Caricature: Disney, Drag and the Proliferation and Commodification of Queer Negativity." Paper presented at Society for Cinema Studies Conference, Dallas, 1996.

Allen, Jeanne. "The Film Viewer as Consumer," *Quarterly Review of Film Studies* 5:4 (Fall 1980): 481–499.

Allen, Paula Gunn. "Lesbians in American Indian Cultures," *Hidden from History: Reclaiming the Gay and Lesbian Past,* Martin Duberman, Martha Vincinus and George Chauncey, Jr., eds. (New York: Meridian, 1990), 106–117.

Amesley, Cassandra. "How to Watch *Star Trek,*" *Cultural Studies* 3:3 (Oct. 1989): 323–339.

Angier, Natalie. "Male Homosexuality May Be Linked to a Gene," *New York Times* (July 18, 1993): E2.

Ansen, David, et al. "Just the Way Walt Made 'Em," *Newsweek* (Nov. 18, 1991): 74–80.

Astroff, Roberta. "Commodifying Cultures: Latino Ad Specialists as Cultural Brokers." Paper presented at the Seventh International Conference on Culture and Communication, Philadelphia, 1989.

Avens, Mimi. "Aladdin Sane," *Premiere* 6:4 (Dec. 1992): 64–72.

Babuscio, Jack. "Camp and the Gay Sensibility," *Gays and Film,* Richard Dyer, ed. (London: British Film Institute, 1977), 40–57.

Bakhtin, Mikhail. *Rabelais and His World,* trans. Helene Iswolski. (Bloomington: Indiana University Press, 1968).

Balio, Tino, ed. *Hollywood in the Age of Television.* (Boston: Unwin Hyman, 1980).

Barrie, J. M. *Peter Pan; or The Boy Who Would Not Grow Up.* (New York: Charles Scribner's Sons, 1956).

Bates, James, and Marla Dickerson. "Disney's Strategy Takes Calls for Protest in Stride," *Los Angeles Times* (June 20, 1997): A1, A17.

Bayer, Ronald. *Homosexuality and American Psychiatry: The Politics of Diagnosis.* (New York: Basic Books, 1981).

Becker, Ron. "Bringing Ellen Out of the Closet." Paper presented at Console-ing Passions Conference, Concordia University, Montreal, 1997.

Bell, Elizabeth, Lynda Haas and Laura Sells, "Introduction: Walt's in the Movies," *From Mouse to Mermaid: The Politics of Film, Gender, and Culture.* (Bloomington: Indiana University Press, 1995), 1–17.

Bendazzi, Giannalberto. *Cartoons: One Hundred Years of Cinema Animation,* trans. Anna Taraboletti-Segre. (Bloomington: Indiana University Press, 1994).

Benjamin, Walter. *Illuminations.* (New York: Shocken Books, 1969).

Benshoff, Harry M. "Heigh-Ho, Heigh-Ho, Is Disney High or Low? From Silly Cartoons to Postmodern Politics," *Animation Journal* 1:1 (Fall 1992): 62–85.

———. *Monsters in the Closet: Homosexuality and the Horror Film.* (Manchester: Manchester University Press, 1997).

Benson, Marguerite. "Will the Code Bring Better Movies?" *Parents' Magazine* 9:6 (June 1934): 26, 66–67.

Berger, Arthur Asa. "Of Mice and Men: An Introduction to Mouseology or, Anal Eroticism and Disney," *Journal of Homosexuality* (1991): 155–165.

Berland, Jody. "Angels Dancing: Cultural Technologies and the Production of Space," *Cultural Studies,* Cary Nelson, Paula A. Treichler and Larry Grossberg, eds. (New York: Routledge, 1992), 38–51.

Berube, Allan. *Coming Out Under Fire: The History of Gay Men and Women in World War II.* (New York: Plume, 1991).

———. Interview by author, Minneapolis, MN, Apr. 1994.

Bettelheim, Bruno. *The Uses of Enchantment: The Meaning and Importance of Fairy Tales.* (New York: Penguin, 1976).

"The Big Bad Wolf and Why It May Never Huff Nor Puff at Walt Disney's Door," *Fortune* 10:5 (Nov. 1934): 146–157.

Blake, Peter. "The Lessons of the Parks," *The Art of Walt Disney,* Christopher Finch, ed. (New York: Harry N. Abrams, Inc., 1973), 423–449.

Boddy, William. "The Studios Move into Prime Time: Hollywood and the Television Industry in the 1950s," *Cinema Journal* 24:5 (Summer 1985): 23–37.

Bogart, Leo, ed. *Current Controversies in Marketing Research.* (Chicago: Markham, 1969).

———. *Strategy in Advertising: Matching Media and Messages to Markets and Motivation.* (Chicago: Crain Books, 1984).

Boone, Joseph A. "Rubbing Aladdin's Lamp," *Negotiating Lesbian and Gay Subjects,* Monica Dorenkamp and Richard Henke, eds. (New York: Routledge, 1995), 147–177.

Bordwell, David, Janet Staiger and Kristin Thompson, *The Classical Hollywood Cinema: Film Style and the Mode of Production to 1960.* (New York: Columbia University Press, 1985).

Bouse, Derek. "True Life Fantasies: Storytelling Traditions in Animated Features and Wildlife Films," *Animation Journal* 3:2 (Spring 1995): 19–39.

"Box-Car Bertha," *Sister of the Road: An Autobiography,* as told to Dr. Ben L. Reitman. (New York: Harper and Row, 1975).

Bragdon, Claude. "Mickey Mouse and What He Means," *Scribners' Magazine* 96:1 (July 1934): 40–43.

Breen, Joseph I. Letter to Spencer Olin at the Walt Disney Studios (Mar. 7, 1946).

Brevitz, Elizabeth. "A Little Attitude," *Premiere* 3:4 (Dec. 1989): 134–136.

Bronski, Michael. *Culture Clash: The Making of Gay Sensibility.* (Boston: South End Press, 1984).

Brooks, Rep. Bob, et al. "An Open Letter to Michael Eisner and the Walt Disney Board," *A League of Their Own* 23 (Nov. 1995): 6.

Brown, John Mason. "Recessional," *The Saturday Review* (June 3, 1950): 30.

Browning, Frank. *The Culture of Desire: Paradox and Perversity in Gay Lives Today.* (New York: Vintage Books, 1993).

Burg, B. R. *Sodomy and the Pirate Tradition: English Sea Rovers in the Seventeenth-Century Caribbean.* (New York: New York University Press, 1984).

Burr, Chandler. "Genes vs. Hormones," *New York Times* (Aug. 2, 1993): A15.

Butler, Judith. *Gender Trouble: Feminism and the Subversion of Identity.* (New York: Routledge, 1990).

———. "Imitation and Gender Insubordination," *Inside/Out: Lesbian Theories, Gay Theories,* Diana Fuss, ed. (New York: Routledge, 1991), 13–31.

Canemaker, John. *Treasures of Disney Animation Art.* (New York: Abbeville Press, 1982).

Carmen, Ira. *Movies, Censorship and the Law.* (Ann Arbor: University of Michigan Press, 1967).

Carr, Harry. "The Only Unpaid Movie Star," *The American Magazine* 11:3 (Mar. 1931): 55–57.

Cartwright, Lisa, and Brian Goldfarb. "Cultural Contagion: On Disney's Health Education Film for Latin America," *Disney Discourse: Producing the Magic Kingdom,* Eric Smoodin, ed. (New York: Routledge, 1994), 169–180.

Cerone, Daniel Howard. "*Ellen* May Be Telling Even Though Not Asked," *TV Guide* 44:39 (Sept. 28, 1996): 59–60.

"Chastity on 'Ellen' Misleading." NewsPlanet staff internet posting. "Planet Out" Webpage. www.planetout.com/pno/newsplanet/article.html. Mar. 10, 1998.

Chauncey, George, Jr. *Gay New York.* (New York: Basic Books, 1994).

"Cheers n' Jeers," *TV Guide* 38:28 (July 14, 1990): 31.

Cholodenko, Alan. "Introduction," *The Illusion of Life: Essays on Animation.* (Sydney: Power Publications, 1991), 9–36.

Clark, Danae. "Consumer Lesbianism," *Camera Obscura* 25–26 (Jan./May 1991): 181–201.

Clary, Mike, and James Bates. "Moral Crusading: Conservative Christians Shun Disney Over Gay-Partner Policy," *Los Angeles Times* (Dec. 25, 1995): A4.

Cocteau, Jean. *Beauty and the Beast: Diary of a Film,* trans. Ronald Duncan. (New York: Dover, 1972).

Cohen, Ed. "Who Are 'We'? Gay 'Identity' as Political (E)motion," *Inside/Out: Lesbian Theories, Gay Theories*, Diana Fuss, ed. (New York: Routledge, 1991), 71–92.

Cohen, Jaffe, Danny McWilliams and Bob Smith. *Growing Up Gay: From Left Out to Coming Out.* (New York: Hyperion, 1995).

Cohen, Karl F. *Forbidden Animation: Censored Cartoons and Blacklisted Animators in America* (Jefferson, NC: McFarland and Company, Inc., 1997).

———. "The Importance of the FBI's 'Walt Disney File' to Animation Scholars," *Animation Journal* 3:2 (Spring 1995): 67–77.

Cohen, Steven. "Masquerading as the American Male in the Fifties: *Picnic*, William Holden and the Spectacle of Masculinity in Hollywood Film," *Camera Obscura* 25–26 (1991): 43–72.

Cole, Sylvia, and Abraham H. Lass. *The Facts On File Dictionary of 20th Century Allusions.* (New York: Facts On File, 1991).

Collard, James. "Leaving the Gay Ghetto," *Newsweek* 132: 7 (Aug. 17, 1998): 53.

Crafton, Donald. *Before Mickey: The Animated Film (1898–1928).* (Chicago: University of Chicago Press, 1993).

———. Emile Cohl, *Caricature and Film.* (Princeton: Princeton University Press, 1996).

———. "Walt Disney's *Peter Pan:* Woman Trouble on the Island," *Storytelling in Animation: The Art of the Animated Image,* Vol. 2, John Canemaker, ed. (Los Angeles: American Film Institute, 1988), 123–146.

Cuomo, Chris. "Spinsters in Sensible Shoes: *Mary Poppins* and *Bedknobs and Broomsticks*," *From Mouse to Mermaid: The Politics of Film, Gender, and Culture,* Elizabeth Bell, Lynda Haas and Laura Sells, eds. (Bloomington: Indiana University Press, 1995), 212–223.

Dale, Dr. Edgar. "Helping Youth Choose Better Movies," *Parents' Magazine* 9:4 (Apr. 1934): 26–27, 71–73.

Dart, John. "Southern Baptist Delegates OK Disney Boycott," *Los Angeles Times* (June 19, 1997): A1, A18–19.

Dawidoff, Robert. "Gays Saw Between the Lines of 'Ellen'; Now for an Open Act 2," *Los Angeles Times* (Apr. 18, 1997): B9.

de Certeau, Michel. *The Practice of Everyday Life,* trans. Steven Rendall. (Berkeley: University of California Press, 1984).

deCordova, Richard. "The Mickey in Macy's Window: Childhood, Consumerism, and Disney Animation," *Disney Discourse: Producing the Magic Kingdom,* Eric Smoodin, ed. (New York: Routledge, 1994), 203–213.

DeFleur, Melvin, and Sandra Ball-Rokeach. *Theories of Mass Communication.* (New York: D. McKay Co., 1975).

D'Emilio, John. "Capitalism and Gay Identity," *Powers of Desire: The Politics of Sexuality,* Ann Snitow, Christine Stansell and Sharon Thompson, eds. (New York: Monthly Review Press, 1983), 100–113.

———. *Making Trouble: Essays on Gay History, Politics and the University.* (New York: Routledge, 1992).

———. *Sexual Politics, Sexual Communities: The Making of a Homosexual Minority in the United States (1940–1970).* (Chicago: University of Chicago Press, 1983).

Delaney, Janice, et al. *The Curse: A Cultural History of Menstruation.* (New York: E. P. Dutton, 1976).

de Vries, Hilary. "Ellen DeGeneres: Out and About," *TV Guide* (Oct. 11, 1998): 20–27.

Dickinson, Robert. "Anglo Agonistes: English Masculinities in British and American Film." Diss., University of Southern California, 1996.

"DISNEY: A Homo-Show from Top to Bottom." Posting to alt.disney.criticism newsgroup. Apr. 1997.

"Disney and Others," *The New Republic* 71:914 (June 8, 1932): 101–103.

"The 'Disney Look.'" (The Walt Disney Company, 1987).

Disney, Walt. "The Cartoon's Contribution to Children," *Overland Monthly* (Oct. 1933): 138.

———. "Mickey Mouse Is Five Years Old," *Film Pictorial* (Sept. 30, 1933): 5.

Doane, Mary Ann. "The Economy of Desire: The Commodity Form in/of the Cinema," *QRFV* 11:1 (1989): 23–33.

———. "Film and the Masquerade: Theorizing the Female Spectator," *Screen* 23:3–4 (Sept./Oct. 1982): 74–87.

Donahue, Suzanne Mary. *American Film Distribution: The Changing Marketplace.* (Ann Arbor: University of Michigan Press, 1987).

Dorfman, Ariel, and Armand Mattelart. *How to Read Donald Duck: Imperial Ideology in the Disney Comic.* (New York: International General, 1975).

Doty, Alexander. *Making Things Perfectly Queer: Interpreting Mass Culture.* (Minneapolis: University of Minnesota Press, 1993).

Douglas, Mary. *Purity and Danger.* (London: Routledge and Kegan Paul, 1969).

Duberman, Martin. *Stonewall.* (New York: Dutton, 1993).

Duberman, Martin, Martha Vicinus and George Chauncey, Jr., eds. *Hidden from History: Reclaiming the Gay and Lesbian Past.* (New York: Meridian, 1990).

Duggan, Lisa. "Making It Perfectly Queer," *Socialist Review* (Apr. 1992): 11–31.

Dyer, Richard. "Believing in Fairies: The Author and the Homosexual," *Inside/Out: Lesbian Theories, Gay Theories,* Diana Fuss, ed. (New York: Routledge, 1991), 185–201.

Eastman, Fred. "How to Choose Movies for Your Children," *Parents' Magazine* 9:3 (Mar. 1934): 18–19, 67–68.

Eckert, Charles. "The Carole Lombard in Macy's Window," *Quarterly Review of Film Studies* 3:1 (Winter 1978): 1–21.

Eisenstein, Sergei. *Eisenstein on Disney,* trans. Alan Upchurch, Jay Leyda, ed. (London: Methuen, 1988).

Eisenstein, Sergei. "Film Form: New Problems," *Film Form*, trans. Jay Leyda. (New York: Harcourt, Brace, Jovanovich, 1949), 122–149.

Eliot, Marc. *Walt Disney: Hollywood's Dark Prince.* (New York: Birch Lane Press, 1993).

Ellis-Simons, Pamela. "Hi Ho, Hi Ho; It's Off to Work He Goes as Michael Eisner Puts the Magic Back into the Walt Disney Co.," *Marketing & Media Decisions* (Sept. 1986), 52.

The Entertainment Weekly Guide to the Greatest Movies Ever Made. (New York: Warner Books, 1994).

Erb, Cynthia. "Another World or the World of an Other?: The Space of Romance in Recent Versions of 'Beauty and the Beast,'" *Cinema Journal* 34:4 (Summer 1995): 50–70.

Ewen, Stuart. *Captains of Consciousness: Advertising and the Social Roots of Consumer Culture.* (New York: McGraw-Hill, 1976).

Ewen, Stuart, and Elizabeth Ewen. *Channels of Desire: Mass Images and the Shaping of American Consciousness.* (New York: McGraw-Hill, 1982).

Faderman, Lillian. *Odd Girls and Twilight Lovers: A History of Lesbian Life in Twentieth-Century America.* (New York: Penguin, 1992).

"Family Movie Guide," *Parents' Magazine* 9:1 (Jan. 1934): 30.

Feild, R. D. *The Art of Walt Disney.* (New York: Macmillan, 1942).

Fiske, John. *Television Culture.* (London: Methuen, 1987).

———. *Understanding Popular Culture.* (Boston: Unwin Hyman, 1989).

Flanner, Janet. "Boom Shot of Hollywood," *Harpers' Bazaar* (Nov. 1, 1936): 106–107, 183–184.

Flower, Joe. *The Prince of the Magic Kingdom: Michael Eisner and the Re-Making of Disney.* (New York: John Wiley and Sons, Inc., 1981).

Fone, Byrne R. S. *Masculine Landscapes: Walt Whitman and the Homoerotic Text.* (Carbondale: Southern Illinois University Press, 1992).

Forman, Henry James. *Our Movie-Made Children.* (New York: Macmillan Co., 1933).

Forster, E. M. *Aspects of the Novel.* (New York: Harcourt, Brace and Co., 1927).

———. "Mickey and Minnie," *Spectator* (Jan. 19, 1934): 81–82.

———. "Story of a Panic," *The Collected Tales of E. M. Forster.* (New York: Knopf, 1952), 8–9.

Foucault, Michel. "Body/Power," *Power/Knowledge: Selected Interviews and Other Writings, 1972–1977,* trans. Colin Gordon et al., Colin Gordon, ed. (Brighton: Harvester Press, 1980), 55–62.

———. *The History of Sexuality, Vol. 1, An Introduction,* trans. Robert Hurley. (New York: Vintage Books, 1990).

Fox, David J. "Disney Will Alter Song in Aladdin," *Los Angeles Times* (July 10, 1993): F1, F4.

————. "Looking at 'Beauty' as Tribute to Lyricist Who Gave 'Beast His Soul,'" *Los Angeles Times* (Nov. 15, 1991): F1, 17.

Fox, William. "Folklore and Fakelore: Some Sociological Considerations," *Journal of the Folklore Institute* 17:2–3 (May/Dec. 1980): 249–256.

Fretts, Bruce. "This Week," *Entertainment Weekly* (Oct. 25, 1996): 102.

Furniss, Maureen. "Animation and Color Key: The Career of Phyllis Craig," *Animation Journal* 5:1 (Fall 1996): 58–70.

Fuss, Diana, ed. "Inside/Out," *Inside/Out: Lesbian Theories, Gay Theories* (New York: Routledge, 1991), 1–10.

Gaines, Jane. "The Queen Christina Tie-Ups: Convergence of Show Screen and Screen," *QRFV* 11:1 (1989): 35–60.

————. *Contested Culture.* (Chapel Hill: Univeristy of North Carolina Press, 1991).

Gaines, Steven. "Will the Mouse Come Out?" *Buzz* 6:4 (May 1995): 64–69.

"Gay Day at Disney World Goes Off Without Incident, Park Aide Reports," *Los Angeles Times* (June 5, 1994): A21.

Gill, Mark Stuart. "Never Say Never-Never Land," *Out* 52 (Mar. 1998): 70–74, 113.

Gomery, Douglas. "Disney's Business History: A Reinterpretation," *Disney Discourse: Producing the Magic Kingdom,* Eric Smoodin, ed. (New York: Routledge, 1994), 71–86.

Graham, Jefferson. "Ellen Happy with Women at Helm," *USA Weekend* (Dec. 19, 1995): D3.

Gray, Elizabeth Dodson. *"Beauty and the Beast:* A Parable for Our Time," *Women Respond to the Men's Movement: A Feminist Collection,* Kay Leigh Hagan, ed. (San Francisco: Pandora, 1992), 159–168.

Grover, Ron. *The Disney Touch: How a Daring Management Team Revived an Entertainment Empire.* (Homewood: Business One Irwin, 1991).

Grunig, James E. "Publics, Audiences and Market Segments: Segmentation Principles for Campaigns," in *Information Campaigns: Balancing Social Values and Social Change,* Charles T. Salmon, ed. (Newbury Park: Sage Publications, 1989), 199–228.

Hadleigh, Boze. *Conversations With My Elders.* (New York: St. Martin's Press, 1986).

————. *Hollywood Gays.* (New York: Barricade Books, 1996).

————. *Hollywood Lesbians.* (New York: Barricade Books, 1994).

Haefner, Francis J., Sr. "Southern Baptists Are Right in Their Disney Stand," *Lancaster Sunday News,* unknown date or page (ca. Sept. 1997).

Hall, Stuart. "Culture, the Media and the 'Ideological Effect,'" *Mass Communication and Society,* James Curran, et al., eds., (London: E. Arnold, 1977), 324–346.

Hall, Stuart. "Encoding/Decoding," *Culture, Media, Language.* Stuart Hall, Dorothy Hobson, Andrew Lowe and Paul Willis, eds. (London: Unwin Hyman Ltd., 1980), 128–138.

Halperin, David M., John J. Winkler and Froma I. Zeitlin. "Introduction," *Before Sexuality: The Construction of Erotic Experience in the Ancient Greek World.* (Princeton: Princeton University Press, 1990), 3–20.

Hamilton, Sara. "The True Story of Mickey Mouse," *Movie Mirror* (Dec. 1931): 100–101.

Hammond, Mike. "The Historical and the Hysterical: Melodrama, War and Masculinity in *Dead Poets Society,*" *You Tarzan: Masculinity, Movies and Men,* Pat Kirkham and Janet Thumin, eds. (New York: St. Martin's Press, 1993), 52–64.

Handel, Leo A. *Hollywood Looks at Its Audience.* (Urbana: University of Illinois Press, 1950).

Handy, Bruce. "He Called Me Ellen DeGenerate," *Time* (Apr. 14, 1997): 50.

Hansen, Miriam. "Pleasure, Ambivalence, Identification: Valentino and Female Spectatorship," *Star Texts: Image and Performance in Film and Television,* Jeremy G. Butler, ed. (Detroit: Wayne State University Press, 1991), 266–297.

Haralovich, Mary Beth. "Advertising Heterosexuality," *Screen,* 23:2 (July/Aug. 1982): 50–60.

———. "Mandates of Good Taste: The Self-Regulation of Film Advertising in the Thirties," *Wide Angle* 6:2 (1984): 50–57.

Harris, Elise. "Going Post-al," *Out* 58 (Sept. 1998): 82–87, 184.

Harris, John E. "Stereotyping for Fun and Profit," *Christopher Street* (Sept. 1994): 4.

Harrison, Taylor. "How Will I Know My Love? Annette Funicello and the Screening of Transgression." Paper presented at the Console-ing Passions Conference, University of Madison at Wisconsin, 1996.

Hartman, Rob. Posting to rec.arts.tv.soaps.abc newsgroup. Apr. 4, 1996.

Hastings, Dwayne. "Eisner: Boycotters a Splinter Group with Nazi Leanings," *Baptist Press* (Apr. 22, 1998).

Haug, Wolfgang Fritz. *Critique of Commodity Aesthetics: Appearance, Sexuality and Advertising in Capitalist Society,* trans. Robert Bock. (Cambridge, MA: Polity Press, 1986).

Hawkins, Harriett. "Maidens and Monsters in Modern Popular Culture: *The Silence of the Lambs* and *Beauty and the Beast,*" *Textual Practice* 7:2 (Summer 1993): 258–266.

Hayward, Todd. "The Lyin' King," *Planet Homo* 69 (Sept. 21, 1994): 16–17.

Herek, Gregory M. "Beyond Homophobia: A Social Psychological Perspective on Attitudes Toward Lesbians and Gay Men," *Bashers, Baiters and Bigots: Homophobia in American Society,* John P. DeCecco, ed. (New York: Harrington Park Press, 1985), 1–21.

Herscher, Eleaine. "Wyoming Death Echoes Rising Anti-Gay Attacks," *San Francisco Chronicle* (Oct. 13, 1998): A7.

"He's Mickey Mouse's Voice and Master," *Movie Classic* (Nov. 1933): 30, 74–75.

Hicks, Garrett. Interview by author, Burbank, CA, May 25, 1994.

Hills, Ms. Beverly. "Beat Reporter?" *Planet Homo* 71 (Oct. 19, 1994): 6.

Hilmes, Michele, *Hollywood and Broadcasting: From Radio to Cable.* (Urbana: University of Illinois Press, 1990).

Holden, Stephen. Review of *Tombstone, New York Times* (Dec. 24, 1993): C6.

Holmlund, Christine. "When Is a Lesbian Not a Lesbian: The Lesbian Continuum and the Mainstream Femme Film," *Camera Obscura* 25–26 (Jan./May 1991): 145–180.

Hommel, Alana. "Disney Support." Email sent to author, ca. May 1998.

———. "Stand Our Ground." Email sent to author, ca. June 1998.

Iannuzzo, Catherine, and Alexandra Pinck. "Benefits for the Domestic Partners of Gay and Lesbian Employees at Lotus Development Corporation." MS, Simmons College Graduate School of Management (Nov. 1991).

Isherwood, Charles. "Cel Division," *The Advocate* (Dec. 1, 1992): 84–85.

Jacobs, A. J. "Out?" *Entertainment Weekly* (Oct. 4, 1996): 18–25.

Jacobs, Sue-Ellen, Wesley Thomas and Sabine Lang, eds. *Two-Spirit People: Native American Gender Identity, Sexuality and Spirituality.* (Urbana: University of Illinois Press, 1997).

Jameson, Frederic. "Postmodernism, or the Cultural Logic of Late Capitalism," *New Left Review* 146 (July/Aug. 1984): 53–92.

———. "Reification and Utopia in Mass Culture," *Social Text* 1:1 (1979): 134–138.

Jeffords, Susan. "The Curse of Masculinity: Disney's *Beauty and the Beast*," *From Mouse to Mermaid: The Politics of Film, Gender and Culture,* Elizabeth Bell, Lynda Haas and Laura Sells, eds. (Bloomington: Indiana University Press, 1995), 161–172.

Jenkins, Henry. "'Going Bonkers!' Children, Play and Pee-Wee," *Camera Obscura* 17 (May 1988): 169–193.

———. "Out of the Closet and Into the Universe: Queers and *Star Trek*," *Science Fiction Audiences: Watching Dr. Who and Star Trek,* John Tulloch and Henry Jenkins, eds. (New York: Routledge, 1995), 237–265.

———. *Textual Poachers: Television Fans and Participatory Culture.* (New York: Routledge, 1992).

Johnson, Alva. "Mickey Mouse," *Woman's Home Companion* (July 1934): 12–13.

Johnston, Ollie, and Frank Thomas. *Disney Animation: The Illusion of Life.* (New York: Abbeville Press, 1984).

———. *The Disney Villain.* (New York: Hyperion, 1993).

Kabbani, Rana. *Europe's Myths of Orient.* (Bloomington: Indiana University Press, 1986).

Kasem, Casey, and Jay Goldsworthy. "No Magic in Aladdin's Offensive Lyrics," *Los Angeles Times* (Apr. 19, 1993): F3.

Kaufman, J. B. "Good Mouse-keeping: Family-Oriented Publicity in Disney's Golden Age," *Animation Journal* 3:2 (Spring 1995): 78–85.

"Kent." Interview by author, Burbank, CA, Sept. 12, 1994.

Keunz, Jane. "Working at the Rat," *Inside the Mouse: Work and Play at Disney World.* (Durham: Duke University Press, 1995), 110–162.

Kimball, Robert, ed. *The Complete Lyrics of Cole Porter.* (New York: Knopf, 1983).

Kindem, Gorham, ed. *The American Movie Industry: The Business of Motion Pictures.* (Carbondale: Southern Illinois University Press, 1982).

Kinney, Jack. *Walt Disney and Assorted Other Characters: An Unauthorized Account of the Early Years at Disney's.* (New York: Harmony Books, 1988).

Kinsey, Alfred, et al. *Sexual Behavior in the Human Male.* (Philadelphia: W. B. Saunders, 1948).

Klein, Norman M. *Seven Minutes: The Life and Death of the American Animated Cartoon.* (New York: Verso, 1993).

Kline, Stephen. *Out of the Garden: Toys and Children's Culture in the Age of TV Marketing.* (London: Verso, 1993).

Koenig, David. *Mouse Tales: A Behind-the-Ears Look at Disneyland.* (Irvine: Bonaventure Press, 1994).

Koestenbaum, Wayne. *The Queen's Throat: Opera, Homosexuality and the Mystery of Desire.* (New York: Poseidon Press, 1993).

Kurti, Jeff. Interview by author, Burbank, CA, July 31, 1994.

Lambert-Maberly, Ashley. Posting to rec.arts.tv.soaps.abc newsgroup. Apr. 4, 1996.

Lasswell, Harold D. *Propaganda Technique in the World War.* (New York: Knopf, 1927).

Leff, Leonard J., and Jerold L. Simmons, *The Dame in the Kimono.* (New York: Grove Weidenfeld, 1990).

Lejeune, C. A. "Disney-Time: Not-So-Silly Symphonies," *Theatre Arts* (Feb. 1934): 84.

Leland, John, and Mark Miller. "Can Gays 'Convert'?" *Newsweek* 132:7 (Aug. 17, 1998): 47–50.

LEsbian And Gay United Employees. "The ABCs of Domestic Partner Benefits," (Apr. 1994).

Levy, Emanuel. Review of *Tombstone, Variety* (Jan. 3, 1994): 53.

Lipsitz, George. *Time Passages: Collective Memory and American Popular Culture.* (Minneapolis: University of Minnesota Press, 1990).

Lovell, Glenn. "'Ellen' Too Gay, Bono Chastises," *Daily Variety* (Mar. 9, 1998): 87.

"The Magic Kingdom," *Time* (Apr. 15, 1966): 84.

Magiera, Marcy. "'Mermaid' Aims to Reel in Adults," *Advertising Age* 60:45 (Oct. 16, 1989): 38.

Maio, Kathi. "Mr. Right Is a Beast: Disney's Dangerous Fantasy," *Visions Magazine* 7 (Summer 1992): 44–45.

"Make Mine Music," *Time* (May 6, 1946): 101.

Maltin, Leonard. *Of Mice and Magic: A History of American Animated Cartoons.* (New York: Plume, 1987).

———. *The Disney Films.* (New York: Crown Books, 1984).

Mandel, Ernest. *Late Capitalism,* trans. Joris De Bres. (London: Verso, 1978).

"Man and Mouse," *Time* (Dec. 27. 1937): 21.

Mann, Arthur. "Mickey Mouse's Financial Career," *Harpers' Magazine* (May 1934): 714–721.

Marchand, Roland. *Advertising the American Dream.* (Berkeley: University of California Press, 1985).

Marcus, Eric. *Making History: The Struggle for Gay and Lesbian Equal Rights (1945–1990)—An Oral History.* (New York: HarperCollins, 1992).

Marcus, George, and Michael Fischer. *Anthropology as Cultural Critique.* (Chicago: University of Chicago Press, 1986).

Martin, Biddy. "Lesbian Identity and Autobiographical Difference(s)," *The Lesbian and Gay Studies Reader,* Henry Abelove, Michele Aina Barale and David M. Halperin, eds. (New York: Routledge, 1993), 274–293.

Maslin, Janet. "Cinderella of the Sea," *New York Times* (Nov. 15, 1989): C17.

———. Review of *Swing Kids, New York Times* (Mar. 5, 1993): C8.

———. Review of *Aladdin, New York Times* (Nov. 8, 1992): C15.

———. Review of *Beauty and the Beast, New York Times* (Nov. 13, 1991): C17.

Maugh, Thomas H., II. "Study Strongly Links Genetics, Homosexuality," *Los Angeles Times* (July 16, 1993): A1.

Maupin, Armistead. *28 Barbary Lane: The Tales of the City Omnibus,* Vol. 1. (New York: HarperCollins, 1990).

May, Jill P. "Butchering Children's Literature," *Film Library Quarterly* 11:1–2 (1978): 55–62.

McBride, Joseph. Review of *Newsies, Variety* (Apr. 6, 1992): 166.

McCord, David Frederick. "Is Walt Disney a Menace to Our Children?" *Photoplay* 45:5 (Apr. 1934): 30–31, 92, 103.

Meier, Moe, ed. *The Politics and Poetics of Camp.* (New York: Routledge, 1994).

Menninger, Karl. "Introduction" in the authorized American edition of Great Britain Committee on Homosexual Offenses and Prostitution, *The Wolfenden Report.* (New York: Stein and Day, 1963), 5–7.

Merritt, Russell, and Karen Merritt. "Mythic Mouse," *Griffithiana* 34 (Dec. 1988), 58–71.

Merritt, Russell. *Walt in Wonderland: The Silent Films of Walt Disney.* (Baltimore: Johns Hopkins University Press, 1993).

Meyer, Richard. "Rock Hudson's Body," *Inside/Out: Lesbian Theories, Gay Theories,* Diana Fuss, ed. (New York: Routledge, 1991), 259–288.

Miller, D. A. "Anal *Rope*," *Inside/Out: Lesbian Theories, Gay Theories,* Diana Fuss, ed. (New York: Routledge, 1991), 119–141.

Monaco, James. *American Film Now: The People, the Power, the Money, the Movies.* (New York: Oxford University Press, 1979).

Moon, Michael. "Flaming Closets," *Out in Culture: Gay, Lesbian, and Queer Essays on Popular Culture,* Corey K. Creekmur and Alexander Doty, eds. (Durham: Duke University Press, 1995), 282–306.

Moore, Stephen D. "Disney Downfall, or Whatever Happened to Tommy Kirk," *Frontiers* 13:13 (Nov. 4, 1994): 68–70.

———. "A LEAGUE of Their Own: Dragging Disney into the Gay '90's," *Frontiers* 13:13 (Nov. 4, 1994): 58–64.

Mosley, Leonard. *Disney's World.* (New York: Stein and Day, 1985).

"Mr. Disney's Caballeros," *The Saturday Review* (Feb. 24, 1945): 24.

Mulvey, Laura. "Visual Pleasure and Narrative Cinema," *Film Theory and Criticism,* Gerald Mast and Marshall Cohen, eds. (Oxford: Oxford University Press, 1985), 803–816.

Munsey, Cecil. *Disneyana: Walt Disney Collectibles.* (New York: Hawthorn Books, 1974).

Murphy, Ryan. "Out of the Closet, Onto the Screen," *Out* 17 (Nov. 1994): 78–80, 92–94, 138–143.

Musker, John, and Ron Clemente. Interview at University of Southern California (USC Cinema Library), Nov. 19, 1992.

Nelson, Cary, Paula A. Treichler and Larry Grossberg, "Cultural Studies: An Introduction," *Cultural Studies.* (New York: Routledge, 1992), 1–22.

Nelson, John A. "Disney Wrong Target," *USA Today* (June 18, 1997).

Nesbit, Anne. "Inanimations: *Snow White* and *Ivan the Terrible,*" *Film Quarterly* 50:4 (Summer 1997): 20–31.

Neupert, Richard. "Painting a Plausible World: Disney's Color Prototypes," *Disney Discourse: Producing the Magic Kingdom,* Eric Smoodin, ed. (New York: Routledge, 1994), 106–117.

Nichols, Bill. *Movies and Methods,* Vol. 1. (Berkeley: University of California Press, 1976).

Noriega, Chon. "SOMETHING'S MISSING HERE! Homosexuality and Film Reviews during the Production Code Era, 1934–1962," *Cinema Journal* 30:1 (Fall 1990): 20–41.

O'Brien, Pamela C. "Everybody's Busy Bringing You a Disney Afternoon: The Creation of a Consumption Community." Paper presented at the Seventh Annual Society of Animation Studies Conference, University of North Carolina at Greensboro, 1995.

"On the Screen: Three Little Pigs," *Literary Digest* (Oct. 14, 1933): 45–46.

Palmer, William J. *The Films of the Seventies: A Social History.* (Metuchen, NJ: Scarecrow Press, 1987).

"*Parents' Magazine* Medal to Walt Disney," *Parents' Magazine* 9:1 (Jan. 1934): 17.

Pasatieri, Thomas. Interview by author, Los Angeles, CA, June 30, 1996.

Petersen, Paul. *Walt, Mickey and Me* (New York: Dell, 1977).

"Portrait: Walt Disney," *Newsweek* (Oct. 7, 1933): 48.

Potts, Mark, and Peter Behr. *The Leading Edge: CEOs Who Turned Their Companies Around.* (New York: McGraw-Hill, 1987).

Pringle, Henry. "Mickey Mouse's Father," *McCall's Magazine* (Aug. 1932): 7.

"Profound Mouse," *Time* (May 15, 1933): 37.

Provenzano, Tom. "The Lion in Summer," *The Advocate* (June 28, 1994): 64–70.

Pryor, Thomas M. "The Screen Grab-Bag," *New York Times* (Nov. 10, 1940): Sec. 9, 5.

Radway, Janice. "Ethnography Among Elites: Comparing Discourses of Power," *Journal of Communication Inquiry* 13:2 (Summer 1989): 3–11.

Rafferty, Max. "The Greatest Pedagogue of All," *Los Angeles Times* (Apr. 19, 1965): B5.

Rather, Dan. "The AIDS Metaphor in *Beauty and the Beast*," *Los Angeles Times Calendar* (Mar. 22, 1992): 42.

"Regulated Rodent," *Time* (Feb. 16, 1931): 21.

"The Religious Right on *Toy Story*," *A LEAGUE of Our Own* 24 (Jan./Feb. 1996): 2.

"Returning Favorites," *TV Guide* 44:37 (Sept. 13, 1996): 46.

Review of *Beauty and the Beast, Variety* (Nov. 11, 1991): 53.

Review of *Dead Poets Society, Variety* (May 31, 1989): 26.

Review of *Down and Out in Beverly Hills, Variety* (Jan. 15, 1986): 23.

Review of *The Little Mermaid, Variety* (Nov. 8, 1989): 32.

Rich, Adrienne. "Compulsory Heterosexuality and Lesbian Existence," *The Lesbian and Gay Studies Reader,* Henry Abelove, Michele Aina Barale and David M. Halperin, eds. (New York: Routledge, 1993), 227–254.

Rich, B. Ruby. "Lauren Lloyd: Disney's Crossover Achiever," *Out* 17 (Nov. 1994): 81.

———. "What's a Good Gay Film?" *Out* 60 (Nov. 1998): 56–58.

"Rights Group Buys Air Time on 'Ellen,'" *New York Times* (Mar. 20, 1997): C6.

Robbins, L. H. "Mickey Mouse the Economist," *New York Times Magazine* (Mar. 10, 1935): 22–23.

Rosenberg, Howard. "The Outing of 'Ellen'? It's Got Me Hooked," *Los Angeles Times* (Sept. 30, 1996): F1.

Rovin, Jeff. *Of Mice and Mickey: The Complete Guide to the Mickey Mouse Club.* (New York: Manor Books, 1975).

Russo, Vito. *The Celluloid Closet: Homosexuality in the Movies.* (New York: Harper and Row, 1987).

Sarris, Andrew. *The American Cinema: Directors and Directions, 1929–1968.* (New York: Dutton, 1968).

Sayers, Frances Clarke. "Why a Librarian Deplores Some of the Works of Walt Disney," *The National Observer* (Feb. 14, 1966): 24.

Schickel, Richard. *The Disney Version.* (New York: Simon and Schuster, 1968).

Schiebler, Sue. Interview by author, Los Angeles, CA, May 31, 1994.

Schudson, Michael. *Advertising, the Uneasy Persuasion.* (New York: Basic Books, 1984).

Sedgwick, Eve Kosofsky. *Between Men: English Literature and Male Homosocial Desire.* (New York: Columbia University Press, 1985).

———. *The Epistemology of the Closet.* (Berkeley: University of California Press, 1990).

Seldes, Gilbert. "Mickey-Mouse Maker," *The New Yorker* (Dec. 19, 1931): 23–25.

Shafer, Tina. Interview by author, Burbank, CA, Aug. 12, 1994.

Shale, Richard. *Donald Duck Joins Up: The Walt Disney Studio During WWII.* (Ann Arbor: UMI Research Press, 1982).

Shapiro, Eddie. "Gayety in the Magic Kingdom: Even the Wrath of Pat Couldn't Stop the Fun," *4Front Magazine* 3:24 (Aug. 19, 1998): 12–14.

Sheehan, Jack G. "Arab Caricatures Deface Disney's Aladdin," *Los Angeles Times* (Dec. 21, 1992): F5.

Shilts, Randy. *And the Band Played On: Politics, People and the AIDS Epidemic.* (New York: St. Martin's Press, 1987).

Shohat, Ella. "Gender and Culture of Empire: Toward a Feminist Ethnography of the Cinema," *QRFV* 13:1–3 (1991): 45–84.

Short, Bill. "Queers, Beers and Shopping," *Gay Times* 170 (Nov. 1992): 18–20.

Signorile, Michelangelo. *Life Outside.* (New York: HarperCollins, 1997).

———. *Queer in America: Sex, the Media, and the Closets of Power.* (New York: Doubleday, 1993).

———. "641,086 and Counting," *Out* 58 (Sept. 1998): 72–74, 188.

Sklar, Robert. "The Making of Cultural Myths: Walt Disney and Frank Capra," *Movie-Made America: A Cultural History of American Movies.* (New York: Random House, 1975), 195–213.

Smith-Rosenberg, Caroll. *Disorderly Conduct: Visions of Gender in Victorian America.* (New York: Oxford University Press, 1985).

Smoodin, Eric. *Animating Culture: Hollywood Cartoons from the Sound Era.* (New Brunswick: Rutgers University Press, 1993).

Socarides, Charles. *Beyond Sexual Freedom.* (New York: Quadrangle Books, 1975).

Sontag, Susan. "Notes on 'Camp,'" *Against Interpretation and Other Essays.* (New York: Doubleday, 1966), 275–292.

Spigel, Lynn. "Seducing the Innocent: Childhood and Television in Postwar America," *Ruthless Criticism: New Perspectives in U.S. Communications History,* William S. Solomon and Robert W. McChesney, eds. (Minneapolis: University of Minnesota Press, 1993), 280–281.

Stabiner, Karen. "Tapping the Homosexual Market," *New York Times Magazine* (May 2, 1982): 34–36, 74–85.

Staiger, Janet. "Announcing Wares, Winning Patrons, Voicing Ideals: Thinking About the History and Theory of Film Advertising," *Cinema Journal* 29:3 (Spring 1990): 3–31.

Steever, Garth. Interview by author, Long Beach, CA, July 8, 1994.

Suplee, Curt. "Study Provides New Evidence of 'Gay Gene,'" *Washington Post* (Oct. 31, 1995): A1.

Sweeney, Gael. "'What Do You Want Me to Do, Dress in Drag and Do the Hula?': Pumbaa and Timon's Alternative Life Style Dilemma in Disney's *The Lion King*." Paper presented at the Seventh Annual Society of Animation Studies Conference, University of North Carolina at Greensboro, 1995.

Syring, Richard H. "One of the Greats," *Silver Screen* (Nov. 1932): 46–47.

Taylor, John. *Storming the Magic Kingdom.* (New York: Knopf, 1987).

Terry, Jennifer. "Theorizing Deviant Historiography," *differences* 3:2 (Summer 1991): 55–74.

"The Testimony of Walter E. Disney Before the House Committee on Un-American Activities," *The American Animated Cartoon: A Critical Anthology,* Gerald Peary and Danny Peary, eds. (New York: E. P. Dutton, 1980), 92–98.

Thomas, Bob. *Walt Disney: An American Original.* (New York: Simon and Schuster, 1976).

"Those Faces! Those Voices . . . ," *People* 32:24 (Dec. 11, 1989): 125.

"Thousands of Crockett Fans Cheer Bowl's Disney Night," *Los Angeles Times* (July 15, 1955): B1.

"The Three Caballeros," *Time* (Feb. 19, 1945): 92.

Truffaut, François. "A Certain Tendency of the French Cinema," *Movies and Methods, Vol. 1,* Bill Nichols, ed. (Berkeley: University of California Press, 1976), 224–236.

TV Guide 42:35 (Aug. 27, 1994).

Van Meter, Jonathan. "The Post-Gay Man," *Esquire* 126:5 (Nov. 1996): 88–89, 132–134.

Verbraska, David. "Southern Baptists 'Misplace' Outrage," *USA Today* (June 18, 1997).

Waller, Gregory A. "Mickey, Walt, and Film Criticism from *Steamboat Willie* to *Bambi*," *The American Animated Cartoon: A Critical Anthology,* Gerald Peary and Danny Peary, eds. (New York: E. P. Dutton, 1980), 46–57.

Warner, Marina. "Beauty and the Beasts," *Sight and Sound* 2:6 (Oct. 1992): 6–11.

Warren, Steve. "Deja View," *Frontiers* 11:20 (Jan. 29, 1992): 48–49.

Wasco, Janet. *Movies and Money: Financing the American Film Industry.* (Norwood, NJ: Ablex Publishing, 1982).

Waugh, Patricia. *Feminine Fictions: Revisiting the Postmodern.* (New York: Routledge, 1989).

Webster's New Collegiate Dictionary. (Springfield: G. and C. Merriam Co., 1979).

Weeks, Jeffrey. "Inverts, Perverts and Mary-Annes: Male Prostitution and the Regulation of Homosexuality in England in the 19th and Early 20th Centuries," *Hidden from History: Reclaiming the Gay and Lesbian Past,* Martin Duberman, Martha Vicinus and George Chauncey Jr., eds. (New York: Meridian, 1990), 195–211.

———. *Sexuality and Its Discontents.* (London: Routledge and Kegan Paul, 1985).

White, Mimi. "Ideological Analysis and Television," *Channels of Discourse,* Robert Allen, ed. (Chapel Hill: University of North Carolina Press, 1987), 134–171.

Whitehead, Harriet. "The Bow and the Burden Strap: A New Look at Institutionalized Homosexuality in Native North America," *The Lesbian and Gay Studies Reader,* Henry Abelove, Michele Aina Barale and David M. Halperin, eds. (New York: Routledge, 1993), 498–527.

Wilde, Oscar. "The Fisherman and His Soul," *Complete Fairy Tales of Oscar Wilde.* (New York: Penguin, 1990), 129–179.

Williams, Raymond. *Problems in Materialism and Culture.* (London: Verso, 1980).

Williamson, Judith. *Decoding Advertisements: Ideology and Meaning in Advertising.* (New York: Marion Boyars, 1979).

Wilmington, Michael. "'Little Mermaid' Makes Big Splash," *Los Angeles Times* (Nov. 15, 1989): F10.

Wood, Robin. *Hollywood from Vietnam to Reagan.* (New York: Columbia University Press, 1986).

Woods, Gregory. "We're Here, We're Queer and We're Not Going Catalogue Shopping," *A Queer Romance: Lesbians, Gay Men and Popular Culture,* Paul Burston and Colin Richardson, eds. (New York: Routledge, 1995), 147–163.

Woods, James D., and Jay H. Lucas. *The Corporate Closet: The Professional Lives of Gay Men in America.* (New York: The Free Press, 1993).

Yoshimoto, Mitsuhiro. "Images of Empire: Tokyo Disneyland and Japanese Cultural Imperialism," *Disney Discourse: Producing the Magic Kingdom,* Eric Smoodin, ed. (New York: Routledge, 1994), 181–199.

Index

About the Author

SEAN GRIFFIN received his doctorate in Critical Studies from the School of Cinema-Television at the University of Southern California in 1998, and is currently teaching film and television courses at Florida Atlantic University. In-between his graduate studies, he worked at New Wave Productions, which produced television advertisements for Disney's theatrical features. Beyond his interest in Disney and animation, he has also written on television soap operas, the internet and media fan culture and the film musical genre. He lives happily ever after with his partner, Harry Benshoff.